HAVANA MODERN

EDITED BY RUBÉN GALLO

Havana Modern: Critical Readings
in Cuban Architecture

First edition, 2023
ISBN 978-607-8880-11-9

Ámsterdam 163 A
Colonia Hipódromo, 06100
Mexico City
arquine.com

Editor
Rubén Gallo

Director
Miquel Adrià

Editorial Managers
Brenda Soto Suárez
Guillermo S. Arsuaga

Copy Editing
Lorna Scott Fox

Design
José Luis Lugo

Prepress
A. Andrés Monroy

This publication is made possible in part by the Barr Ferree Foundation Fund for Publications, Department of Art and Archaeology, Princeton University.

Havana Modern: Critical Readings in Cuban Architecture was printed and bound in March 2023 by Artron Art Printing Ltd. in China. It was printed on 128 g Chinese OJI Art paper and set in typefaces of the Alternate Gothic and Labernia families. The print run was 1,000 copies.

HAVANA MODERN

CRITICAL READINGS IN CUBAN ARCHITECTURE

EDITED BY RUBÉN GALLO

CONTENTS

HAVANA: MODERNISM AND REVOLUTION

Rubén Gallo

Both pages:
Los Carpinteros, *Downtown Series* (2003).
Wood, variable dimensions.
Courtesy of Daros Latinamerica Collection, Zurich.

The idea for this volume came out of a graduate seminar on Havana's Modern Architecture I co-taught with Beatriz Colomina at Princeton's School of Architecture in 2017. We had a lively and diverse group of students—a mix of Cubans and non-Cubans, architects and humanists, Latin-Americanists, and Europeanists—which included some of the authors featured in this book: Guillermo S. Arsuaga, Darja Filippova, Iván L. Munuera, and Bart-Jan Polman. As part of our research, we spent a week in Havana, where Terence Gower and Mark Wigley joined us for a series of visits that took us to the American and Russian embassies, the National Art Schools, the Girón (or Experimental) building, the Coppelia ice-cream parlor and the Radiocentro complex.

Roberto Gottardi, the only one of the Art School's architects who stayed in Cuba, met us for a long lunch at the Habana Libre's Polynesian restaurant—a relic of 1950s modernist design—and we spent several hours discussing the history and politics of Cuban architecture. He was frail but alert, and spoke with his characteristic good will and sense of irony: he recounted his life after construction of the Art Schools was stopped in 1965; about his ideological disagreements with government bureaucrats and hardliners like critic Roberto Segre and architect Antonio Quintana; about his displeasure at Norman Forster's recent proposal to complete Vittorio Garatti's unfinished ballet school: "that would be like a painter finishing someone else's landscape," he fumed.

Our conversation made me realize that Cuban architecture was a field ripe for new critical and theoretical interventions. Things were changing quickly in Cuba: since Barack Obama's 2015 decision to re-open the United States Embassy, not a week went by without a visit by a delegation of trustees from museums in Europe and the United States. Everyone wanted to see Havana, and the architecture built in the 1950s and 1960s was one of the main draws. After decades of neglect, the Art Schools risked being overrun, though this menace did not last long: the hordes of travelers stopped abruptly after Donald Trump tightened restrictions against Cuba following his election in 2017.

After our return home, we continued the conversations about the island's architecture and its relationship to twentieth-century culture and history in the seminar. Eventually those discussions grew into the chapters included in this volume, covering projects built over a period of forty years: from Miguel Domínguez's 1947 Radiocentro, to Alexandr Rochegov's 1987 Soviet (now Russian) embassy. The authors discuss International Style projects built by foreign architects in the 1950s—Harrison and Abramovitz's US Embassy, Richard Neutra's De Schulthess House—, wildly experimental buildings sponsored by the Revolution in its early years—the Art Schools, Coppelia—as well as later, quasi-brutalist constructions like Antonio Quintana's Edificio Experimental and Rochegov's Soviet Embassy.

Before giving an outline of the chapters and the issues they address, it would be important to consider how this volume fits into the historiography of Cuban architecture.

SHIFTING HISTORIOGRAPHIES

The historiography of Cuban architecture in the past sixty years can be divided into three moments. The first moment, defined by political and ideological discussions, lasted from the first months of the Revolution until the 1990s. The question—"what is Revolutionary Architecture?"—dominated virtually all publications. The answer had the power to make or break an architect's career: those who were judged to be unrevolutionary could see their projects canceled and their names blacklisted. Some, like Ricardo Porro and Vittorio Garatti—the architects of the National Art Schools—were eventually driven to exile.

In those turbulent decades, the question "what is Revolutionary architecture?" was, more than an invitation to critical speculation, a call to judgment that sought to separate projects and architects who were in from those who were out. It was a question that had a programmatic intent—it looked to the future and sought to outline the direction that state-driven construction would take in the years ahead—, and that rhymed with Fidel Castro's famous pronouncement to the country's intellectuals: "Within the Revolution, everything; against the Revolution, nothing."[1] Architectural projects that ventured beyond the strict parameters established by the state—austere aesthetics, cost-effective production and prefabrication—were denounced as anti-revolutionary, as happened with the Arts Schools: after critics questioned the project's compatibility with revolutionary ideology, construction stopped abruptly in 1965, leaving the buildings unfinished and the three architects—Vittorio Garatti, Roberto Gottardi, and Ricardo Porro—tainted as bourgeois individualists who, by privileging formal experimentation and sensuality, demonstrated they were out of tune with the Revolution's needs.[2]

Cuba's most influential architecture critic during this period was Roberto Segre, an Argentinean who rapidly rose to become one of the most powerful figures in the island's cultural bureaucracy. In a series of books published over three decades, Segre praised a few architects—notably Antonio Quintana—as revolutionary figures, while rejecting many others—including the architects of the Art Schools—as bourgeois individualists. His ideas shaped the official doctrine of the Ministry of Construction and determined the type of projects that were sponsored by the Revolutionary government.[3]

A shift inaugurating the second moment in architectural historiography came after the fall of the Berlin Wall and the collapse of the Soviet Union, events that sparked a new interest in Cuba and its architecture and attracted critics from outside the island. By then, the Cuban Revolution could be seen as an event belonging to the past, strangely frozen in time and surviving as a socialist relic. From the vantage point of a post-Cold War world, everything that had been built in Cuba since 1959 could be considered revolutionary architecture. Ironically, the very projects that Segre had decried as unrevolutionary—especially the Art Schools—were now heralded as the most original creations of the Cuban experiment (and conversely, as Mark Wigley shows in Chapter Eight, the projects which Segre touted as great achievements of Revolutionary architecture, like the Edificio Experimental, were now forgotten). The release of John Loomis's *Revolution of Forms: Cuba's Forgotten Art Schools* in 1999 triggered a wave of scholarly interest in this unfinished project that led to the publication of dozens of articles, scholarly books, memoirs, documentary films, and even an opera.[4]

Segre's prescriptive focus—oriented towards the architecture that should be built in the future—gave way to an interpretative turn that

1 Fidel Castro, *Palabras a los intelectuales* (Montevideo: Comité de Intelectuales y Artistas de Apoyo a la Revolución Cubana, 1961).

2 See, for instance, the criticism by Roberto Segre in *Diez años de arquitectura revolucionaria* (Havana: Cuadernos de la Revista Unión, 1970), p. 86.

3 In addition to *Diez años*, other books written by Roberto Segre on Cuban architecture include: *Cuba: l'architettura della rivoluzione* (Padova: Marsilio Editori, 1970); *La vivienda en Cuba: república y* revolución (Havana: Universidad de La Habana, 1979); *Arquitectura y urbanismo de la Revolución cubana* (Havana: Editorial Pueblo y Educación, 1989); *Arquitectura y urbanismo: Cuba y América Latina desde el siglo XXI*, ed. Eliana Cárdenas (Havana: Editorial Arte y Cultura, 2013).

4 John Loomis, *Revolution of Forms: Cuba's Forgotten Art Schools* (New York: Princeton Architectural Press, 1999); Alma Guillermoprieto, *Dancing with Cuba: A Memoir of the Revolution* (New York: Pantheon Books, 2004); Benjamin Murray and Alysha Nahmias, dirs. *Unfinished Spaces* (2011); Charles Koppelman and Roberto Varela, *Cubanacán: A Revolution of Forms* (2015).

sought new ways of analyzing the past. Architectural criticism had finally broken free of the ideological strait jacket, and it could now venture in new directions, engaging with larger issues and theoretical questions.

One tendency that emerged in writings on Cuban architecture during the 1990s was a new emphasis on architectural history: after decades of ideological discussions, a new generation of scholars devoted considerable effort to establishing the historical record. Seeking to correct the many imprecisions concerning dates, authors, and materials that had marred earlier publications, these figures worked on establishing a detailed chronology of Cuba's modern architecture, gathering photographic documentation and bibliographic information, and rectifying errors in dates and attribution. Eduardo Luis Rodríguez was one of the pioneering figures in this trend, and his efforts resulted in publications such as *La Habana: Arquitectura del siglo XX* (1998), and *The Havana Guide: Modern Architecture 1925-1965* (2000). Perhaps the most comprehensive history of Cuban architecture and urbanism in the twentieth century resulting from this historical turn is Francisco Gómez Díaz's *De Forestier a Sert: Ciudad y Arquitectura en La Habana, 1925-1960* (2008).[5]

A third shift came in the 2000s, when scholars of Cuban architecture shifted away from a strict focus on the island's architecture to adopt a larger, comparative perspective that examined how local projects related to larger questions and debates that emerged elsewhere in Latin America. The Museum of Modern Art's 2015 exhibition and accompanying catalog *Latin America in Construction: Architecture 1955-1980*, edited by Barry Bergdoll, Carlos Eduardo Comas, Jorge Francisco Liernur, and Patricio del Real, highlights the connections between Cuban projects and those built in Mexico, Brazil, and other parts of Latin America. This expanded frame of reference is an important correction to a tradition of architectural criticism that had been marked by extreme insularity: most authors discussed Cuban architecture as if it existed in a vacuum, thus neglecting the exchanges among the island's architects and their colleagues in the rest of the world.[6]

Another model for thinking about Cuban architecture was proposed by Víctor Deupí and Jean-François Lejeune in their recent volume *Cuban Modernism* (2021). For years, critics assumed that architectural modernism came to an abrupt end with the Revolution, and was followed by a Soviet-inspired emphasis on prefabrication that some called "socialist realism."[7] Deupí and Lejeune reject the notion of a radical break by demonstrating that several modern architects who had been in private practice in the 1950s—most notably Mario Girona and Antonio Quintana—stayed in Cuba after the Revolution and continued to build, though their practices shifted from hotels and condominiums to schools, hospitals, and housing blocks. The cases of

5 Eduardo Luis Rodríguez's publications include: *La Habana: Arquitectura del siglo XX* (Barcelona: Blume, 1998); *The Havana Guide: Modern Architecture 1925-1965* (New York: Princeton Architectural Press, 2000). See also Francisco Gómez Díaz's *De Forestier a Sert: Ciudad y Arquitectura en La Habana, 1925-1960* (Madrid: Abada Editores, 2008)

6 Barry Bergdoll, et al., *Latin America in Construction: Architecture 1955-1980* (New York: Museum of Modern Art, 2015).

7 Roberto Segre, "Encrucijadas de la arquitectura en Cuba: Realismo mágico, realismo socialista y realismo crítico," *Tres décadas de reflexiones sobre el hábitat latinoamericano* (Bogotá: Universidad Nacional de Colombia, 2005), pp. 319.

Quintana, Girona, and others demonstrate that there is some continuity between modernism and the architecture of the Cuban Revolution.

Other, recent studies examine Cuban architecture from a cultural studies perspective, highlighting the connection between architecture, history, and politics. Timothy Hyde's *Constitutional Modernism: Architecture and Civil Society in Cuba, 1933-1959* (2012) and Joseph R. Hartman's *Dictator's Dreamscape: How Architecture and Vision Built Machado's Cuba and Invented Modern Havana* (2019) analyze the major building and urbanistic projects launched by the Machado and Batista regimes, emphasizing the links between architecture and events that include the authoritarian turn of the Machado presidency in the late 1920s, the 1933 military coup d'état, and the rise of Batista as the leading political force.

In the past decade, the rise of digital technologies has opened the debate, in and outside of the island, to enthusiasts who have set up blogs devoted to Cuban architecture. One of the most notable is www.arquitecturacuba.com, maintained by an anonymous but indefatigable reader of historical journals. There are also several websites published by young architects who have found ways to run small practices in Cuba: Martirena's Infraestudio, Albor Arquitectos, and the Grupo de Estudios Cubanos de Arquitectura.[8]

Lastly, there has also been a recent wave of interest in Cuban architecture by visual artists who have used their work—photography, film, installations—to explore the formal aspects of some of the most striking projects built before and after the Revolution. The last chapter in this volume includes a selection of these creative readings of built spaces: Coop Himmelb(l)au's 1994 sketch of Havana's underground water system; Carlos Garaicoa's 2003 installation *Letter to the Censors*, featuring photos and models of Havana's movie palaces; and Marco Castillo and Los Carpinteros' playful refashioning of the Russian Embassy and other iconic structures of the Havana skyline (see pp. 6-7). Since 2000, the artist collective formed by Lisa Schmidt-Colinet, Alexander Schmoeger, and Florian Zeyfang, has used film, installation, and architectural interventions to investigate the Cuban Revolution's forgotten projects, from Garatti's pavilion for the 1967 Expo in Montreal to the André Voisin Institute near Güines.[9]

Following the paths opened by these recent developments, the authors in this volume propose new directions for thinking about Cuban architecture. Among the theoretical and critical concepts developed by these authors, four stand out: a discussion of revolutionary temporalities, a consideration of the change of function that affected hundreds of buildings after 1959, an analysis of how architecture became entangled in the revolutionary gender politics, and an evaluation of how the discursive spaces of architecture shifted over time.

8 See the websites: www.infraestudio.com; www.alborarquitectos.com; www.facebook.com/gecacuba/ See also the articles published on Cuban architecture by Belmont Freeman in Places Journal, www.placesjournal.org

9 Two exhibitions devoted to art projects engaging with architecture were: *Arquitectura joven cubana*, presented at the Centro de Desarrollo de la Artes Visuales in 1990, and *La utopía paralela: ciudades soñadas en Cuba, 1980-1993*, curated by Iván de la Nuez for Es Baluard in Palma de Mallorca in 2021.

REVOLUTIONARY TEMPORALITIES

All revolutions since 1789—from the French to the Mexican—aimed to rebuild their capital to reflect the new regime's values. Cuba is the notable exception: the Revolution launched an ambitious building program and constructed hundreds of schools, hospitals, and housing projects, but these were mostly in the countryside and left the central districts of Havana virtually untouched. The idea was to correct a historical injustice: for centuries, the island's wealth had been concentrated in Havana: urbanistic and architectural projects had all centered on the capital—90% of the island's architects were based in Havana[10]—while the countryside languished, impoverished and undeveloped: 66% of rural dwellings were precarious constructions with palm roofs and dirt floors.[11] After 1959, developing rural areas by creating the infrastructure for education and health care emerged as one of the new government's priorities: "a rejection of the previous conception of the architect isolated in his urban ivory tower," as Segre wrote.[12]

The effect on Havana was uncanny: for six decades virtually nothing was built in the central districts, making the capital appear as if it were frozen in time. The effects of this time-freeze are especially apparent in the city's modern constructions. By 1959, Havana had become a vitrine for modernism: in just seven years, starting with the passage of a 1952 law allowing the construction of condominiums, dozens of modernist towers rose in the Vedado district. One was the American Embassy, designed by Harrison and Abramovitz in 1953; others were hotels, casinos, residential complexes, and mixed-use buildings that housed apartments, professional offices, as well as shops, bars, and restaurants on the street level. Cuban architects—Antonio Quintana, Nicolás Arroyo, Gabriela Menéndez, and Mario Girona, among others—collaborated with American colleagues—Welton Becket and Igor Polevitzky—on these projects.

When Jean-Paul Sartre visited Cuba in 1960 to write a chronicle of the Revolution in its first year, he was surprised to find himself surrounded by American-style skyscrapers. The tallest tower was a mere 25 stories, but Sartre saw the city as a miniature New York.[13] When Mikhail Kalatozov and his Soviet crew arrived to make a film three years later, they experienced a similar fascination and spent hours shooting the city's modernist towers, deploying bird's-eye views and oblique angles. The resulting scenes in *I am Cuba* read like a love-letter to the International Style—a message that did not sit well with Soviet or Cuban cultural commissaries and which led in part to the film's failure. In Cuba, Sartre and Kalatozov got a glimpse of both modernism and the future.[14]

After six decades, the modernist city is still there, virtually intact, but it is now experienced as a remnant from the past. Nowhere else

10 Segre, *Diez años*, p. 47.

11 Ibid., p. 51.

12 Ibid., p. 174.

13 Jean-Paul Sartre, "Ouragan sur le sucre," *Les Temps Modernes* 649 (April-June 2008): 5-220. On skyscrapers see pp. 6-7. An English version of the book was published as *Sartre on Cuba* (New York: Ballantine Books, 1961).

14 Mikhail Kalatozov, *I am Cuba* (1964).

in the world can a visitor wander through the streets of a city of the 1950s, where steel-and-glass towers stand undisturbed by later constructions. In the rest of the world, modernist buildings were left to fight for their survival in the concrete jungle, sandwiched between the new constructions of the 1960s and 1970s, obstructed by freeways and exchanges, and dwarfed by postmodernist skyscrapers of the 1980s and 1990s. None of this took place in Havana, where the modern towers of the 1950s continue to rule, unchallenged, over a city that has not altered its scale for sixty years.

In Havana, modernism has survived as a relic. And not only the glass towers: much of the city operates as if the clock had stopped in 1959. Residents traverse the city in 1950s Chevrolets, Buicks, and Oldsmobiles, now converted into collective taxis; vehicles circulate with the same ease they did sixty years ago: the number of cars on the island has remained almost unchanged, and traffic jams are unknown. Most of the cabarets that operated before the Revolution, including the celebrated Tropicana, are still open, though they are now state owned, and they continue to offer shows featuring music and dance numbers. The vast movie houses of the 1950s are still there, and, unlike in other parts of the world, they have not been divided or turned into multiplexes: one can still watch a film, sitting with a thousand moviegoers, in a vast theater.

Like socialism, modernism was predicated on the promise of a utopian future. In Havana, that promised future is now experienced as a relic of the past. But only for visitors: Cubans do not inhabit their city as a vestige from the past but rather, as a present that has remained unchanged since 1959. For them the modernist city, like Freud's unconscious, is timeless: it lives in a time that does not know the past or the future, a seemingly eternal present that, because of its unchanging nature, appears to be outside of time.

Nowhere in the world is modern architecture so present and so alive—along with its promises, its vision of the future, its conception of the world and of the human—as it is in Havana.

FLUCTUATING FUNCTIONS

The Cuban Revolution inherited dozens of constructions designed in the 1940s and 1950s for purely capitalist use: luxury hotels, casinos, resorts, private clubs, and golf courses. In other countries, these might have been destroyed as symbols of an *ancien régime*, but in Cuba resources were tight—especially after the imposition of the US embargo in 1960—and all buildings from the past were preserved, though most underwent a radical change in their function.

The most famous example is the Cubanacán Country Club, developed in the 1950s as the island's most exclusive association.

In 1960 Fidel Castro visited the golf course and decided it should be transformed into the world's most important art schools, offering a revolutionary education to students from around the globe. The Art Schools were only one example of the many sites that changed function after 1959. Buildings that once housed Woolworth's and Ten Cent stores survive to this day, transformed into state-run stores selling canned goods and other food products: in some, the former milk bars now dispense rum to patrons sitting on fixed bar stools that have not budged since the fifties. The Havana Hilton, renamed Habana Libre after its expropriation in 1960, evolved from a luxury hotel catering to American tourists to a dormitory for Fidel Castro's rebel army. Segre also mentions "barracks transformed into schools; private clubs refashioned into social circles for the people; the bourgeoisie's mansions turned into dormitories for students."[15]

15 Segre, *Diez años*, p. 80.

Radio and television stations ceased operating as commercial ventures—immensely profitable thanks to advertising revenue—to become official organs of state-sponsored information. Likewise, cinemas became sites for disseminating the films produced by the newly created ICAIC, designed to broadcast revolutionary culture. These changes were less visible than the transformations of the golf course or the Hilton, but they were no less radical since they reflected a transformation of the social function of mass media.

Two of the chapters included in this volume focus on projects built in the 1940s and 1950s that underwent a radical change of function after 1959: Andrés Jaque writes about Radiocentro, focusing on the role played by broadcasting and mass media in Revolution, and Miguel Caballero analyzes the Art Schools that were erected on the grounds of the former golf course, emphasizing how despite major social changes, one aspect of Cuban life that remain unchanged in the 1960s was a rather conservative understanding of gender and sexuality. Ironically, the one project included in this volume that could be considered the most antithetical to the values of the Revolution—the Neutra house commissioned by a Swiss banker as a luxury residence—did not undergo a change of function: after leaving Cuba in 1959, De Schulthess sold the house to the Swiss government, and it has since served as the official residence of that country's ambassador, who continues to use the spaces in exactly the same way Neutra planned them.

GENDER TROUBLE

The Cuban Revolution launched a new understanding of gender which celebrated the guerrillero as an ideal of masculinity. In his writings, Che Guevara called for a "new man" attuned to socialism, and soldiers of the rebel army promoted with tremendous success the look associated with this new masculinity: unkempt hair, long beards and military uniforms.[16] Within the government, a complex machinery was set up to enforce this revolutionary manliness by stamping out dissenting gender expressions: by the mid 60s, urban gay men—along with other "anti-social elements"—were deported to rural work camps, where they were to be reeducated through manual labor into a conforming masculinity. In recent years there has been much attention devoted to this episode, but very little has been written about how architecture became entangled in this idealization of revolutionary masculinities.[17]

One fascinating example is the case of the National Art Schools, which came to be associated with homosexuality by the regime—one of the many factors that contributed to its fall from revolutionary grace in the mid 1960s. Porro recalls how revolutionary officials argued that the schools, by teaching disciplines such as dance, were breeding grounds for homosexuality.[18]

Contrary to the regime's interpretation, the Art Schools were built to fulfil a heterosexual fantasy. All three architects who worked on the project were heterosexual. Porro, who was the only one who managed to complete his buildings, described his School of Visual Arts as a tribute to the female body: the cupulas were shaped like pointy breasts, complete with plaster nipples; there were curves everywhere, and one of the patios featured a stone fountain shaped like a vagina.[19]

When Castro visited the site in 1965, he was shocked at Porro's architectural eroticism. Castro was famously puritanical—he did not drink, did not dance, and had little time for love or sex in his life—, and this playful homage to the female body, while heterosexual to the core, did not sit well with the regime's masculine ideal of the bearded guerilla. Segre was similarly opposed to sensuality, which he associated with pre-Revolutionary Afro-Cuban traditions and "idleness."[20] In a paradoxical twist, Porro's male heterosexual celebration of the female body came to be associated with homosexuality.

Allen Ginsberg, who spent three months in Cuba in 1965, recalls the homosexual panic sparked by the Art Schools. At one point, he writes, "the whole Dramatic Arts School was shut down" and the students sent to re-education camps. "Boys sent to the country to cut sugar, girls sent home," he jotted in his diary.[21] The association of the Art Schools with homosexuality was still in place in 1970, when Alma Guillermoprieto spent a year teaching dance there: she recalls the principal lamenting that he was not trained to direct a place full of *patos* and queers.[22]

A year after the UMAP camps were opened, the Cuban Revolution inaugurated one of its only architectural projects in central Havana: the Coppelia Ice-Cream Parlor designed by Mario Girona, across the street from the former Havana Hilton in the Vedado neighborhood. Like Porro's Art Schools, Coppelia privileged round shapes and sinuous paths, organic forms integrated into the lush tropical

16 Ernesto "Che" Guevara, *El hombre nuevo* (Buenos Aires, Editorial del Noroeste, 1973).

17 On the UMAPS, see Lilian Guerra, *Visions of Power in Cuba: Revolution, Redemption and Resistance, 1959-1971* (Chapel Hill: University of North Carolina, 2012), pp. 227ff.

18 Guillermoprieto, *Dancing with Cuba*, pp. 134-5.

19 María Elena Martín Zequeira, "Arquitectura: Hallar el marco poético. Entrevista con Ricardo Porro," *Revolución y cultura* 5 (1996): 44-51.

20 Segre, *Diez años*, p. 88.

21 Allen Ginsberg, *Iron Curtain Journals, January-May 1965*, ed. Michael Schumacher (Minneapolis: University of Minnesota Press, 2016), p. 135

22 Guillermoprieto, *Dancing with Cuba*, pp. 270-1.

vegetation that framed the project. The parlor, built as a state-run purveyor of subsidized ice cream—a socialist alternative to pre-revolutionary American milk bars—was an instant success, and it quickly became one of the most popular spots in Havana. Every day, thousands of Cubans frequent Coppelia, where they can sit for hours in the tropical gardens, enjoying an ice-cream for less than a penny.

Coppelia quickly became a preferred gathering spot for the city's gay men. As long as certain codes were observed, they could patronize the parlor, sit together, cruise each other and even flirt with allegedly heterosexual men. *Fresa y chocolate* (1993), the last film directed by Tomás Gutiérrez Alea, celebrated Coppelia's importance as a discrete site for gay sociability, an island of freedom in a sea of intolerance and a hunting ground for gay men intent on seducing heterosexual machos. Following the logic analyzed by Lacan in his "Seminar on the Purloined Letter," gay men discovered that the best way to conceal their desire was by placing it in the open, at the center of the most crowded, visible, and popular spot in central Havana. In Gutiérrez Alea's film, Coppelia becomes the stage for a seduction that debunks the ideal of revolutionary masculinity: using language alone, Diego manages to seduce David, who until then had identified as a strict heterosexual, card-carrying communist, and decidedly un-modernist subject.[23]

Though Coppelia became the country's most famous gay cruising spot, it seems like only homosexuals were in the know. Unlike the Art Schools, the ice-cream parlor never fell from revolutionary favor, and it was never accused by government officials of favoring or promoting homosexuality. Dancing and art making, it appears, threatened revolutionary masculinities more than eating sorbet.

Some buildings, like the Country Club Golf course, changed use by official decree. Others, like Coppelia, spontaneously acquired a new, covert function: it was the city's gay men, following a grassroots and organic impulse, that transformed the ice-cream parlor into a cruising spot that was at once secret and public, hidden from view yet located in the center of heterosexual crowds.

ARCHITECTURE'S DISCURSIVE SPACES

As we can see in projects like the Art Schools and Coppelia, the Cuban Revolution radically transformed what we can call, following Rosalind E. Krauss's discussion of photography, architecture's discursive spaces.[24] Before 1959, the practice of architecture was firmly inscribed in the island's capitalist logic: architects worked mostly for private clients, which included both companies and individuals, as we can see in Richard Neutra's De Schulthess House and Mies van der Rohe's unbuilt Bacardí office building: two projects funded by proceeds from lucrative Cuban businesses—a bank and a liquor company—,

23 Tomás Gutiérrez Alea, dir. *Fresa y chocolate* (1993).

24 See Rosalind E. Krauss, "Photography's Discursive Spaces," *The Originality of the Avant-Garde and Other Modernist Myths* (Cambridge: MIT Press, 1985), pp. 131-150.

and designed to promote business interests: De Schulthess planned to entertain the bank's clients in his residence, and expanding the company was the *raison d'être* for Bacardí's new headquarters. De Schulthess and Bacardí officials understood that the prestige of modern architecture could be exploited to maximize profits for their employers. As Deupí and Lejeune have written, Bacardí "used architecture to reinforce the corporate identity that it was striving to build on the American model."[25] Segre pointed to Mies's projects as an example of how "all the technological potential of our epoch is consumed in advertising slogans or formal experiments."[26]

Modern architecture thrived in the 1950s, and it became an extremely lucrative affair for local architects, especially for those who were close to power: in the last years of his rule, Batista launched an ambitious public works campaign that include the construction of a vast new government center in what is now the Plaza of the Revolution (most of the buildings which now house the Cuban ministries were in fact designed and built under Batista). The case of Nicolás Arroyo illustrates the entanglement of modern architecture, private capital, and government commissions: Arroyo designed or co-designed some of the most important constructions of the decade —the National Theater, the Ciudad Deportiva sports complex, and the Habana Hilton among others. Some of these were commissioned by the government, other by private clients. In the process, he became extremely wealthy and moved to the Country Club. While running a private practice, he occupied key positions in the Batista administration: first as Minister of Public Works and then, just on the eve of the Revolution, as Cuban Ambassador to the United States.

Such closeness to wealth and power explains why, after Castro's victorious entry into Havana, modern architects were among the first to leave the country. Virtually all the architects who had built the steel-and-glass towers in Vedado—with the notable exceptions of Mario Girona and Antonio Quintana—went into exile and most of them never set foot in Cuba again, though most continued their architectural practices abroad, as Deupí and LeJeune have documented in *Cuban Modernism*.

From the first days of the Revolution, the discursive spaces of architecture changed: there were no more private clients and no more private commissions. The state became the only client, and all new construction had to satisfy the country's urgent needs: schools, hospitals, and housing blocks. Architects became civil servants and their only compensation was now a fixed monthly salary (along with the other perks, from cars to housing, that revolutionary officials could receive).

These new conditions were not attractive to established architects, used to collecting a percentage of the total cost of the project, but they were ideal for a new generation of young men in their

25 Deupí and Lejeune, *Cuban Modernism*, p. 190.

26 Segre, *Diez años*, p. 18.

twenties—led by Garatti, Gottardi, and Porro—who appreciated the creative freedom that came with designing and building for the Revolution. Gottardi recalls that working on the Art Schools was an architect's dream: he would draw at night, deliver the plan to the foremen in the morning, and inspect the built portions by evening. There was no need to submit the plans for approval or even inform the Ministry of Construction.[27]

This radical re-orientation of architectural practice and the ensuing shift away from capital might explain why architects from around the world remained cool to the Cuban Revolution. In the early sixties, writers, artists, and filmmakers from around the world flocked to Havana to see the Revolution in action: the list of visitors includes Jean-Paul Sartre, Hans-Magnus Enzensberger, Ernest Hemingway, Graham Greene, Agnès Varda, Allen Ginsberg, Mario Vargas Llosa, Gabriel García Márquez... but not a single notable architect.

Even when Havana hosted the 1963 Union of International Architects Congress, the most illustrious invitees—among them Le Corbusier, Buckminster Fuller, and Oscar Niemeyer—excused themselves (Le Corbusier sent a message to Cuban architects, urging them to: "Regarder, voir, observer, discerner, inventer, créer"; Niemeyer had agreed to attend, to serve on the jury, and to award one of the prizes in person, but canceled at the last minute).[28] Could it be that architects feared that, under the provisions of the US embargo, a trip to Cuba might imperil their future projects? Was it because the Cuban organizers could not afford high speaking fees? Or perhaps because the Cuban Revolution, after its withdrawal from market economies, was not attractive to practitioners that depended on vast amounts of capital to build their projects? It remains a mystery why Niemeyer, who over the years befriended Fidel Castro and often expressed support for Cuba, never made the trip in these early years.[29] One possible answer is that the real architectural revolution was happening elsewhere in Latin America: when Castro marched into Havana in 1959, the world's architects were focused on Brasilia, an unprecedented and monumental project, the most radical experiment in modern architecture, which was to be inaugurated a year later. Brasilia overshadowed Cuba: the modest projects launched by the Cuban Revolution could not compete with the monumental dimension of the new South American planned city. In the world of architecture, the real revolution was happening in Brazil.

Writers, artists, and intellectuals were fascinated by post-Revolutionary Cuba, but modern architects preferred the pre-Revolution era: the list of figures who worked on Cuban projects in the fifties is impressive—Josef Albers, Franco Albini, Welton Becket, Walter Gropius, Philip Johnson, Richard Neutra, Jose Luis Sert, Mies van der Rohe—but no modernist set foot in Cuba after 1959.

27 See the comments by Garatti, Gottardi and Porro in Benjamin Murray and Alysha Nahmias, dirs. *Unfinished Spaces* (2011).

28 Cuban architect Fernando Salinas conveyed the invitation to Le Corbusier in person during a visit to his Paris office in 1963. Le Corbusier declined but made a drawing which he asked Salinas to give to the Cuban architects. See Carlos Véjar Pérez-Rubio, ed. *Y el perro ladra y la luna enfría. Fernando Salinas: Diseño, ambiente y esperanza* (Mexico City: Universidad Autónoma Metropolitana, 1994), p. 103. See letter from Le Corbusier to Cuban Architects, 4 September 1963. Reproduced in www.arquitecturacuba.com/2008/09/le-corbusier-y-cuba-i.html

29 "Entrevista: Oscar Niemeyer, arquiteto," *Viagem*, 13 March. 2007. https://viagem.estadao.com.br/noticias/geral,entrevista-oscar-niemeyer-arquiteto,20070313p14178

Only after the collapse of the Soviet Union did architects return to Cuba. In 1994, a group of architects invited by Peter Noever—Coop Himmelb(l)au, Morphosis/Thom Mayne, Eric Owen Moss, Carme Pinós, Lebbeus Woods, and C. P. P. N.—traveled to Havana and imagined architectural projects for a city that had been deeply scarred by the Cold War, the American embargo, and an unprecedented economic crisis stemming from the end of Soviet aid. In a text reproduced in this volume, Coop Himmelb(l)au argued that architects from around the world should try to learn from Havana, a modern metropolis that, despite its myriad problems, offers a model of how a city should work: "we came to see Havana," Wolf Prix writes, "as the fulfillment of every urban planner's dream—the city as a public space."[30]

Architects' fascination with Cuba peaked following Barack Obama's 2014 reestablishment of diplomatic relations: Frank Gehry made the trip in 2015; Norman Foster proposed a project to complete Garatti's unfinished ballet school; and some years earlier, Niemeyer, regretting his missed encounter with the Cuban Revolution, sent a sketch for a monument celebrating Cuban resistance to the US Embargo (the project was built at the entrance to the Universidad de Ciencias Informáticas in 2008).

On the island, the role of the architect has remained frozen in time, like Havana's architecture. In 2011—three years after assuming the presidency—Raúl Castro introduced a series of economic reforms that legalized small-scale capitalist ventures. Cubans were no longer required to work for the state and, for the first time since 1968, small private businesses were allowed: it was now possible to run a restaurant, rent rooms to tourists, sell food on the streets and drive passengers around town. But several professions, deemed essential to society, were excluded from private practice: doctors, schoolteachers, professors, and scientists could only work for the government, and the same restriction applied to architects and engineers.[31]

A decade after these economic reforms were introduced, this nascent capitalism is not mixing well with old-school socialism. In this new economic landscape, entrepreneurs make a good living while most Cubans, who still work for the state, earn low wages that can barely cover bare necessities. Waiters and bartenders often earn more money than doctors, who survive on less than $100 a month; high-school students have little incentive to study science or engineering when they can skip college, set up a small shop selling films or video games, and earn more than the average scientist. Like all government employees, architects must scrape by with low salaries, while those serving drinks in nightclubs often make hundreds or thousands of dollars a month.

30 Peter Noever, ed. *The Havana Project: Architecture Again* (Vienna: MAK, 1994), pp. 97-98.

31 See Carmelo Mesa-Lago and Jorge Pérez-López, *Cuba under Raúl Castro: Assessing the Reforms* (Boulder: Lynne Rienner Publishers, 2013); Carmelo Mesa-Lago et al. *Voices of change in Cuba from the Non-state Sector* (Pittsburgh: University of Pittsburgh Press, 2018).

Architects have found ways to navigate this complex system. The country's most prestigious architecture school is now at the CUJAE—housed in one of the Revolution's most accomplished architectural projects—but, paradoxically, many of the students withdraw from their studies just before completing their degrees to avoid working for the government. Instead, they set up architectural practices that are disguised as interior designers, renovation consultants or contractors, where they can make a good living working for private clients, mostly entrepreneurs or exiled Cubans. Fernando Martirena, a young architect who runs a small studio practice in Havana, recently explained that the only state-issued license category that he could apply for was that of "decorator for parties and festivities."[32] Not without humor, he summarized the current situation as follows: "an independent architect in Cuba works in an indeterminate legal terrain, with an inefficient infrastructure and kept alive by commissions without a contract. No one can accuse him of anything since technically he does not exist."[33]

In one of the strangest twists in the story of architecture after the Revolution, many young architects are now renovating houses and apartments that have sat untouched for almost six decades: the very ruins that fascinate tourists and foreign architects alike. But most materials—from floor tiles to bathroom fixtures—can only be bought in the grey market: most are stolen from the construction sites of hotels and resorts by workers and resold in an underground market. The practice of architecture now has much in common with prostitution, foreign-currency exchange, gambling, and other activities that, while technically illegal, are openly tolerated on the island: "a-legal operations," as Martirena calls them.[34]

In the past sixty years, the figure of the architect in Cuba has evolved from a hyper-capitalist entrepreneur, to a civil servant, and finally to an unlicensed but tolerated *cuentapropista* operating in the realm of a-legality that encompasses much of the island's market ventures.

THE CHAPTERS

In the chapters that follow, the authors propose a series of new readings of the most iconic buildings of Cuban modernism: they analyze architecture in the context of an expanded field and explore how built projects relate to the historical, cultural, and political events that framed their construction and later use.

The book opens with three projects that illustrate how modern architecture was inextricably linked to consumer capitalism in 1950s Cuba. Terence Gower discusses Harrison and Abramovitz's United States Embassy (1953), Sylvia Lavin examines Richard Neutra's

32 "Fernando Martirena: Contemporary Cuban Architecture is Alegal and Almost Non-Existent," Interview with Fabián Dejtiar, November 19, 2020. https://www.archdaily.com/951496/fernando-martirena-contemporary-cuban-architecture-is-alegal-and-almost-non-existent.

33 Fernando Martirena, "De qué hablamos cuando hablamos de arquitectura cubana," *Rialta*, 23 September 2020. https://rialta.org/arquitectura-contemporanea-cubana/ My Translation.

34 Ibid.

residence for Alfred De Schulthess (1955), and Bart-Jan Polman analyzes Mies van der Rohe's unbuilt office building for Bacardí (designed between 1956-59).

The purpose of these three projects was to promote capitalist expansion in different ways. One of the principal roles of the US Embassy during this time was to facilitate and safeguard American investments on the island, which grew exponentially in the decades following independence. By the 1950s, a new embassy building was needed to accommodate the hundreds of diplomats and local employees working on American interests. Neutra was brought to Cuba by a Swiss banker who was the ultimate hyper-capitalist: he made money with money, investing the profits of wealthy Cubans and earning commissions in the process. Officials at Bacardí, one of the most successful Cuban transnationals, had long understood that modern architecture was the best medium to promote the company: in 1930 they commissioned two Cuban architects—Esteban Rodríguez and Rafael Fernández—to construct an art-deco building to house the company's Havana headquarters, and in 1956 they chose Mies to design their Santiago offices.

Jane C. Loeffler has shown how the State Department promoted modern architecture as the preferred style for embassy buildings, since it communicated the values of American democracy: transparency, openness and freedom of movement.[35] 1950s Havana was living under a dictatorship: glass towers and houses came to symbolize not democracy but the free-frow of capital and the unrestricted trade between Cuba and the rest of the world. Transparent surfaces contrasted with the opacity that shrouded the origins of much of the wealth that fueled the Cuban economic boom during the Batista regime.

35 Jane C. Loeffler, *The Architecture of Diplomacy: Building America's Embassies* (New York: Princeton Architectural Press, 1998).

In Chapter Three, Andrés Jaque writes about a fourth project that placed modernism at the service of consumerism: the Radiocentro complex—consisting of radio and television stations, a cinema, and a series of bars, restaurants, and offices—designed by Miguel Domínguez in 1947. Jaque shows how this temple to what Theodor Adorno called, in the same year, "the culture industry," was briefly hijacked in 1957 by rebel students who sought to put broadcasting at the service of Revolution. The story of this site since 1959 is one of the most fascinating tales involving the change of social function of a building: selling advertising gave way to broadcasting the Cuban Revolution.

The history of Radiocentro shows how the architecture of the Cuban Revolution encompasses much more than what was built after 1959. The Revolution re-purposed more than it constructed, and the story of its architecture is also the tale of how hundreds of buildings erected for consumerist ends were reconfigured to work in a new socialist context.

In Chapters Five and Six, Miguel Caballero and Iván L. Munuera write about two projects built in the 1960s that found themselves entangled in the heated debate about the production of revolutionary masculinities. The National Art Schools and the Coppelia ice-cream parlor were both celebrated internationally as early examples of revolutionary architecture. But by 1965 the Cuban government briefly closed the Art Schools after these were denounced as breeding grounds for homosexuality. Coppelia, in contrast, thrived as an underground cruising area for gay men, who for decades met, unnoticed, in plain daylight, on the parlor's grounds. Something similar happened with the theater at Radiocentro: The Yara—as the Warner cinema was rebaptized—became a favorite haunt for *tiradores*, exhibitionist masturbators who went to the movies with an auto-erotic intent.[36]

The Art Schools, Coppelia, and Radiocentro were carefully planned to fulfill specific social functions. Havana's residents spontaneously found new erotic uses for these spaces: this erotic refashioning as an instrument of resistance is one of the least studied chapters in the history of the Cuban Revolution, and one that Reinaldo Arenas recounts in his novel *Before Night Falls*, where he shows that, even at the height of anti-homosexual repression, gay men found ways to turn public spaces into havens for sexual fulfillment.[37]

In Chapter Seven, Guillermo S. Arsuaga discusses the history of the pavilion sent by Cuba to the 1967 International Expo in Montreal. Much has been written about Cuba's efforts to export its Revolution to other parts of the world, from Bolivia to Angola, but this was the only attempt to export revolutionary architecture. Paradoxically, the pavilion's main author was Vittorio Garatti, one of the architects who, after working on the Art Schools, had been labelled anti-revolutionary by the regime's cultural commissars. At a world's fair where every country showcased its technological advances, Garatti's pavilion promoted a curious blend of film, press clippings, and cocktail drinks, but what most captured the visitor's imagination was the architecture of the pavilion itself: angular and futuristic, machine-like and hedonistic.

The Revolution put an end to the International Style towers that came to dominate 1950s architecture, but—unlike countries like Mexico or Russia—did not establish a clearly recognizable revolutionary style. In the early sixties, it appeared as if organic forms—as in the Art Schools—and circular structures—as in Coppelia—would set the tone for future architecture, but this morphology all but disappeared by the late 1960s.

Several architectural projects built after 1959 featured an aesthetic that was heavy, massive, and projected a sense of solidity and strength. Mark Wigley and Darja Filippova examine two experiments in what might be termed tropical brutalism: the Experimental (or Girón) building

36 See Marilyn Solaya, dir. *Mírame mi amor* (2002).

37 Reinaldo Arenas, *Before Night Falls*, trans. Dolores Koch (New York: Viking, 1993).

on the Malecón and the Soviet (now Russian) embassy in Miramar. In contrast to the playful eroticism of the Art Schools or Coppelia, these towers make it known that there was no more play: they are grave and serious, stoic and massive, architectures of the new masculinity that proved to be so elusive in the first years of the Revolution.

As Wigley shows, the Girón became the most published building in architectural accounts of the Cuban Revolution, and it appeared invariably in all the books and articles Segre devoted to revolutionary architecture.

Filippova examines one of the least researched buildings in Havana: the Soviet Embassy, a vast project completed in 1987 by Alexandr Rochegov. This extraordinary complex—which includes offices, reception rooms, apartment buildings, schools, and a gym—has never been included in surveys of Cuban architecture and it is seldomly discussed in accounts of Soviet modernism. Even monographs on Rochegov tend to omit it. As Marco Castillo recalls in the discussion of his sculptures based on the Embassy, it is a building no one seems to want to own, as if it were a national or even multi-national embarrassment.

By including this Soviet complex as the last chapter in a selection of Cuban modernism, this book asks a provocative question: what happens if we think of the Russian Embassy not only as an example of Cuban architecture, but perhaps even as the last project of the Cuban Revolution? Thinking of this pseudo-brutalist tower as the bookend to an architectural adventure that began in 1959 allows us to tell a new kind of story, one that bypasses many of the received ideas and critical impasses that have marred the historiography of this period: modernist glass towers debunked by brutalist bunkers.

Modern Havana closes with a selection of four artists' projects that revisit Havana's modern architecture. The artist collective Los Carpinteros investigated the constructivist structure of the Russian Embassy and paid homage to a building that every Cuban loves to hate. *Embajada rusa* transforms the embassy into a chest of drawers, a playful project that would potentially allow the average Cuban to have a replica of the building in his home, where it could find a useful, everyday function, storing the Soviet garments that most Cubans wore in the 1970s and 1980s.

In a series of films, installations, and publications, the Austro-German artists' collective formed by Lisa Schmidt-Colinet, Alexander Schmoeger, and Florian Zeyfang have investigated the most utopian projects of the Cuban Revolution: the 1963 Pabellón Cuba on La Rampa, the 1967 Pavilion for Montreal Expo, and the 1965 André Voisin Technological Institute.

When contemplating the decayed state of architecture in Cuba—modernist and otherwise—, visitors tend to adopt one of two

38 For a literary take on this debate, see Antonio José Ponte, "Un arte de hacer ruinas," *Un arte de hacer ruinas y otros cuentos*, ed. Esther Whitfield (Mexico City: Fondo de Cultura Económica, 2005).

positions: either a romantic fascination with ruins, taken as evidence that Cuba has remained outside of capitalist time, or a sense of outrage at the island's ruined buildings, read as signs of a political and social failure.[38] Schmidt-Colinet, Schmoeger, and Zeyfang found a way out of this binarism by bringing to the front the utopian nature of many architectural projects that are now decayed.

One of the most moving examples is the film *Institute Above Ground* (2015), which tells the story of the André Voisin Institute. Completed in 1965—the year in which work on the Art Schools stopped—, this was one of the most utopian projects of the period: a technical college, designed to train the agronomists of the future and to revolutionize Cuban agriculture, named after a French agronomist who authored the first plans for revolutionary food production. The building itself embodies the dreams and ideals of the Revolution: nestled amid rice paddies and elevated from the ground on pilotis, these classrooms and dormitories created idyllic spaces for studying agriculture in nature.

But then came a series of catastrophic failures: by the time the three artists visited in 2014, all they found was a collection of ruins. Broken windows, missing doors and leaky roofs make the classrooms unusable; the school has been abandoned by students and teachers alike. Walkways had collapsed and the Institute read like the scene of a post-apocalyptic nightmare.

It would be easy to take the sorry state of the André Voisin Institute as evidence of the Revolution's catastrophic failure, but *Institute Above Ground* resists such an easy conclusion. Instead, it shows both the utopian promises and harsh realities, dreams and disillusionments, possibilities and frustrations. One does not cancel the other: both are present in the project.

Schmidt-Colinet, Schmoeger, and Zeyfang are artists who came of age in Austria and West Germany, countries that bordered the former German Democratic Republic. Perhaps it was this proximity to a failed socialist state that led them to think of Cuba in a manner that is both empathetic and critical, attentive to promises and aware of the failures. They understand that utopias can only exist in the promise of a distant future, and nothing can be more disheartening that looking back, from the vantage-point of the present, on what was once a utopian possibility. All utopias are indissociable from failure, but focusing exclusively on failure can blind us to their real achievements: the poetry, energy, intensity that animated the promise of a better future.

Carlos Garaicoa adopts a similar strategy: his photographs of ruined cinemas around Havana seem to present a sad coda to a city that once housed close to a hundred pleasure palaces. But the photos of ruins are shown together with an oversize model of the Payret, one of Havana's largest and most luxurious cinemas, a true palace of film. The installation is an homage to a utopian space that for decades allowed moviegoers to escape the harsh reality of everyday life so that they could spend an hour or two dreaming, traveling in their imagination. The Payret, too, is now ruined, but it lives again in Garaoicoa's model, where it emerges as a fully functional miniature.

CODA: AMID THE ART SCHOOL RUINS

Visitors to Cuba tend to equate ruins with failure, but, as the case of the Art Schools demonstrates, sometimes ruined buildings can fulfill their function. Readers of Cuban history can be left with the impression that the Art Schools project was a catastrophic failure, but in fact the Instituto Superior de Arte—as the school is now called—has been fully functional for six decades: the unfinished spaces and decayed buildings were put to use from day one, and in this time the institution has formed thousands of Cuba's leading singers, musicians, dramaturgs and theater directors, dancers and visual artists—including those featured in this book.

When former students recall their years at the Art Schools, they remember a utopian period, roaming free around the grounds—in the evening, after professors and administrators left, the former Country Club became a vast playground—, throwing pool parties, staging exhibitions, performances, and even raves in Garatti's unfinished ballet school. The music school might be the most decrepit structure in the complex, but music students choose to practice their instruments there, nestled by monumental *jaguey* trees, rather than in the plush interiors of the practice rooms set up in the former club house. Though the architecture is in ruins, the Schools continue to fulfill the dream that inspired their creation: to train generations of Cuban and foreign artists.

The Art Schools have been rightly considered the most emblematic project of the Cuban Revolution. Their synthesis of utopian promise, ruined materiality, and improvised functionality are emblematic of the fate of post-revolutionary Cuban architecture.

I began this introduction by evoking our meeting with Roberto Gottardi at the Polynesian restaurant. Gottardi did not live to see the publication of this book—he died in August 2017—, but much of what he taught us that day inspired the pages that follow: we have tried to think of Cuba's architecture with the same sense of play, irony, humor, and distrust for orthodoxies that Roberto embodied, and which animated his projects. *Havana Modern* is, among other things, a tribute to Gottardi, one of the most original architects of the twentieth century, marginalized for decades, but now returned to his central place in the history of Cuban architecture.

HAVANA CASE STUDY: THE AMERICAN EMBASSY

Terence Gower

Havana Case Study is a research and exhibition project that I started in 2010 with a Guggenheim Fellowship to study the United States government's post-WW2 embassy building program. This is the second in an ongoing series of projects that use US embassy complexes as case studies on American international relations. But more importantly, these studies show how buildings are used—by both the US and the host countries where these embassies were built—to represent the progressive aspirations of the United States, and conversely, to represent perceived American injustices abroad.

The first project in the series studied the 1960 US embassy in Baghdad, designed by José Luis Sert. In 2007 the US built a new embassy in Baghdad (four years after the American invasion of Iraq), the largest, most expensive, and most fortified embassy in the world. The two embassies project contrasting American worldviews, from post-WW2 optimism to post-9/11 entrenchment, and in this way act as bookends to a narrative of diplomatic disintegration.

Above:
US embassy, Havana, 1953.
Max Abramovitz Papers. Avery Architectural and Fine Arts Library. Columbia University, New York. Photo: Alex Langley.

Opposite page:
Preliminary rendering for US embassy, Havana, 1950.
Max Abramovitz Papers. Avery Architectural and Fine Arts Library. Columbia University, New York.

The 1953 US embassy in Havana was never replaced, and thus stands as a rare example of a building that has had its meaning repeatedly reassigned since its conception. Conceived in the late 1940s as one of the first projects in a State Department program to build modern buildings representing a new era of post-war openness, dialogue, and progress, after 1961 the building acquired a new function as a convenient propaganda tool for the new revolutionary government of Cuba, who held it up as a symbol of American imperialism.

My exhibition project hinges on a single feature of the embassy building: a sculptural balcony that projects off the blank sea façade of the embassy's five-story tower. This balcony, perhaps the most elegant and expressive element of the building's design, was specifically requested by an outgoing ambassador. It has the placement and unmistakable appearance of an imperial tribune—it was criticized by the State Department itself as "Mussolini-type"—but has remained in place, overlooking the countless protests organized against the US by the Cuban government. I have used the balcony's form as the template for a series of sculptures.

Balcony (2016) is a full-scale outline of the US ambassador's balcony—that symbol of limbo caused by diplomatic stalemate and its accompanying political and economic fallout. The sculpture is in five parts, true to the embassy balcony's five original modules. The balcony is rendered in rebar, one of the few building materials available under the embargo, and as with many of my sculptural works, it is left to the viewer to decide if we are looking at an object under construction, ready to be hoisted triumphantly into place, or a rusting artifact, recently crashed to the ground.

The first thing that strikes a foreign visitor to post-Revolution Havana is the effect of the US-led embargo on Cuban material culture. The most famous examples are the cars from the 1940s and 50s that give off the sense of time having stopped. New construction has slowed to a few government projects and some recent international collaborations in poorly designed luxury housing and hotels. According to friends involved in construction on the island, these few building sites, using imported materials, are the source of what little construction material is in circulation in the country. Rebar—a steel bar used to reinforce concrete, still produced in Cuba—is the material most in evidence, and it is put to impressive use: furniture, fences, security grilles, car parts, even fairground rides. A series of five smaller metal rod sculptures titled *Modules* (2016) incorporate panels of woven rattan.

The second element at the center of the *Havana Case Study* installation is a large display of documentation laid out as if we are in 1958 and revolutionary troops have yet to march into Havana to declare a new form of government. Period photographs, plans,

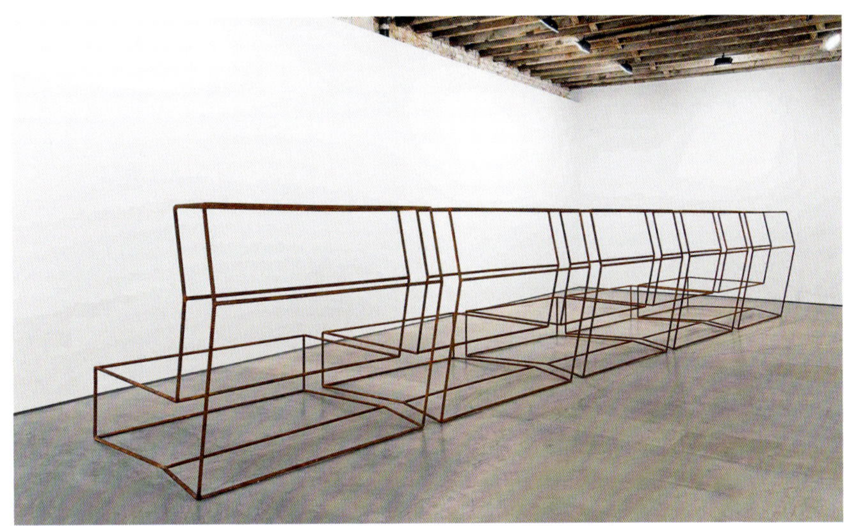

Terence Gower.
Havana Case Study: Balcony, 2016.
Simon Preston Gallery, New York.
Photo: Bill Orcutt.

architectural models, and publications are displayed in vitrines modeled on those used in the 1953 exhibition *Architecture for the State Department* at the Museum of Modern Art in New York—the first public presentation of the new embassy construction program. This presentation takes us back to the last years of Batista's regime, a time of new zoning and new investment models that had a huge impact on Vedado, the neighborhood where the US had just built its new diplomatic headquarters. A subtle reference is made to these financing schemes, notorious for linking American organized crime with the Cuban leadership. This document display is nearly buried under another layer of documentation made up of newspapers, photographs, and printouts that show how the building was used by both the Cuban and US governments in a public relations battle that began in early 1961, when the State Department severed diplomatic relations with Cuba and sent home its embassy staff.

The layering of documents in the vitrines provides the template for a series of collages titled *Political Services*. The title is taken from an interview with the embassy's architect, Max Abramovitz, in a discussion of his long career straddling US military and government contracts on the one hand, and work for private clients on the other. The collages are based on carefully cropped details from the table display.

This essay gives an overview of the research behind *Havana Case Study*, including detailed references to some of the published and archival sources that have had particular relevance to the project.

THE FBO

What style of architecture best represents a country? This is the question that every government must ask itself when planning a

Terence Gower.
Havana Case Study: Political Services, 2016.
Simon Preston Gallery, New York.
Photo: Bill Orcutt.

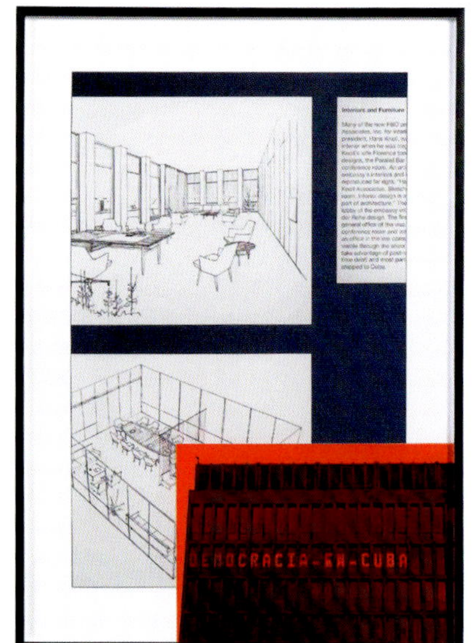

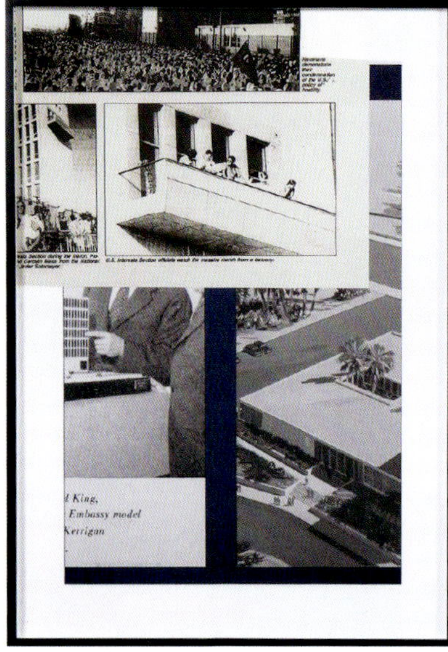

new diplomatic post. In the case of the US, the answer was naturally the building typology that was at the heart of the country's early expansion and success: the plantation house. The formal vocabulary of this architecture, sometimes assembled into near copies of the White House, with a brief flirtation with "Jeffersonian" styles under President Roosevelt in the 1930s, was the model for US diplomatic architecture until the late 1940s. But already in the 1930s, the representational aptness of the plantation house started to be questioned due to its association with the institution of slavery.

In 1946, the State Department created a new office called Foreign Buildings Operations (FBO) and appointed a design board headed by Ralph Walker. The new building directive, calling for architecture that represents "the US as an open, dynamic and cooperative modern country" was a radical departure from earlier directives that stressed expressions of tradition, democracy, and "dignity" (a word that comes up a lot in criticism of post-war embassy buildings). The new focus was on modern architecture, and the FBO board was soon in touch with the leading contemporary architects of the day. Modern architecture was a building philosophy developed in the early 20th century that began with the rejection of the academicism and historicism of Beaux-Arts practice, to propose a new approach where the final form of a building is arrived at through the satisfaction of a set of technical and functional criteria. In Beaux-Arts practice, meaning was established by designing buildings that represented their function—a bank looked like a bank, a school like a school—and a codified aesthetic system of orders and composition determined the façade details. Modern buildings were not designed to represent or symbolize their functions. Instead, when they could be told apart, they directly expressed their functions through their form—a theatre is recognizable by the form of the auditorium and fly-tower, a school by its blocks of classrooms, a factory by its workshops and chimneys.

But very quickly, modern architecture started to represent beyond its function. In my previous research on the pre-WW2 "Bauhaus Style" architecture of Tel Aviv, I found a utilitarian building form, modern architecture, that also very quickly came to stand for the new, progressive *society* under construction on Palestine's Mediterranean coast in the 1930s. The architecture of the new apartment houses and municipal buildings of Tel Aviv was both a tool of expansion and progress and a "style" that represented the aspirations of a new society. In the same way, a building form that could stand for an "open, dynamic, and cooperative modern country"—as stated in the State Department post-war design directive—could only be modern architecture. To me, the most compelling part of the directive was its call for transparency and an architecture that would represent free speech and the free flow of ideas. Post-war building technology and the new representational and practicable style of "modernism" could satisfy this desire functionally and symbolically at the same time, with floor-to-ceiling glazing used as extensively as possible. This factor is also what piqued my interest in the post-war embassy construction program. Having visited US embassies designed or upgraded in recent decades, I recognized how the early design ideal described above stands in opposition to the current norm, in which embassies have become little more than glorified bunkers whose forms are determined by blast-walls and setbacks.

After my general research on the FBO (the basis for pieces such as *Cause & Effect?*, 2012) I decided to narrow my focus to embassy buildings with complicated diplomatic histories, and to study the role that their architecture itself has played in those histories. As mentioned above, the first installation that came out of this research was *Baghdad Case Study*. The story of the Baghdad embassy complex—one of Sert's largely unknown masterpieces—starts with all the best diplomatic intentions on the part of the State Department, but quickly devolves into a narrative of ideological conflict. Sert's project is interesting as a manifestation of dialogue through design, the result of the FBO program funding architects' travel and research into the host culture's building traditions. The roof form of Sert's ambassador's residence, reminiscent of multi-dome spanning systems of the bazaar as well as of decorative Islamic woodwork, expressed this cultural dialogue most clearly. As the focal point of my installation, I created a scale reproduction of the thin-shell concrete roof form, translated into a virtuoso work of marquetry in fragrant cedar wood. Baghdad is of course rich territory for this kind of investigation, being the site of a (neo-Conservative) ideology-fueled invasion and occupation by the US in 2003. Thus the country that commissioned Sert's masterpiece of enlightened, diplomatic design in 1960 somehow devolved into the sponsor of the "super-bunker" embassy that opened in Baghdad's Green Zone in 2007.

The firm Harrison Abramovitz, with Max Abramovitz in charge of design, was awarded the first two embassy commissions after the FBO was formed in 1946. In addition to his private practice with Wallace Harrison, Abramovitz had continued working as an official government and military architect, a position he first took up in the Second World War. His many international military design contracts, combined with the firm's coordination of the United Nations headquarters in New York, made Abramovitz a logical candidate for the new Rio de Janeiro and Havana embassy buildings. Interestingly, his next major commission following the embassies was also in the public sector: the "invisible" new CIA headquarters in Langley, Virginia.

These embassies were the State Department's first forays into modernism, and they seemingly took for granted that Abramovitz, with his international experience, could design for a tropical climate. The Rio embassy functioned well, though briefly, as Brasilia was soon under construction as the new capital, requiring a new US embassy building. The Havana embassy design was much lauded in the press, but faced a number of functional problems, described in detail by a State Department inspector soon after the building was opened.

CONSTRUCTION

An early birds-eye view watercolor rendering of the new US embassy shows the building's strong geometric massing made up of a vertical slab spanning the two legs of an irregular "A," lying flat to form a horizontal slab. These two forms in turn represent the two principal functions of the building: the vertical slab houses the diplomatic offices, requiring more privacy, and the horizontal slab houses the visa and cultural functions of the embassy, open to the public. The gridded façade is also an expression of the building's structure: these thick mullions are in fact perimeter columns supporting a full-span floor slab at each level.

There was a clever funding structure built into the FBO's construction project, conceived by its director Frederick Larkin: the post-war projects were designed to be mostly funded and supplied through foreign credit swaps, the repayment of wartime debt to the US. This meant a minimal requisition of funds from Congress and little congressional oversight, allowing much more operational and design freedom. But it also meant that the many components of each building were imported from a large number of different indebted nations. In Havana, the marble cladding came from Italy, the structural steel from Belgium, all interior partitions from England, and the furniture from France, with the air conditioning system and aluminum window frames imported from the US. Unfortunately, the last two items on this list posed problems when the building opened.

The building is distinguished on both principal façades by the stone-clad structural grid mentioned above. This system of perimeter structural support (the same system used in the World Trade Center towers in New York) left the floor slabs column-free. But a miscalculation of the ratio of glazing to solid structural framing led to a greenhouse effect inside the building—standing under tropical sun all day—that couldn't be overcome by the air conditioning system. The tower slab of the building was oriented north–south, with the east façade exposed to the morning sun, and the west to the afternoon sun. But the central air conditioning had just a single control for the whole

PROGRESS PREVIEW

A new landmark on Havana's gulf front will be the gleaming travertine-and-glass tower of the seven-story office building now under construction for the United States Embassy to Cuba. The site is between the fashionable Paseo del Malecon and apartment-lined Calzada Street, with a public park just across from the east, or entrance, front. The new building will be visible from the sea and from a two-mile stretch of the Malecon.

Harrison & Abramovitz, New York, architects for the Department of State, Foreign Buildings Operations (Fredrick Larkin, Chief Architect and L. W. King, Jr.), designed the building to accommodate United States Consular business in the one-story portion, with entrance on Calzada Street, and Embassy affairs in the five stories and penthouse of the tower over the main entrance. The building is placed on a raised terrace, for protection from sea water that may rise during storms. Patios introduce greenery and vistas within the building.

The building will be completely air conditioned. During winter months, however, the air-conditioning machinery, housed in the south half of the penthouse, will be turned off and the building will be cooled by ocean breezes and protected from sun heat by heat-resistant glass used for the east and west walls. Sash will be operable. The reinforced concrete structure will be faced with creamy Roman travertine, with local materials used for interiors. The 12"

embassy office building

On the Malecon, famed boulevard of Havana bordering the Gulf of Mexico, a seven-story office building for the United States Embassy to Cuba is under construction. Harrison & Abramovitz, Architects, New York, expect it to be completed early in 1952. *Rendering: Robert Schwartz*

October 19

"Progress Preview: Embassy Office Building," *Progressive Architecture* (October 1951): 15-16.

building, meaning half the staff was either too hot or too cold for half of each day. The system, discreetly housed behind the top-floor conference room, was gradually upgraded, then replaced entirely in the 1990s, entailing the addition of a full new mechanical floor on top of the building. The new system completely altered the original lines of the building and closed in the elegant top-floor peristyle.

Coordinating the assembly of so many parts imported from different sources was an enormous task, and unfortunately the aluminum windows, as originally designed, didn't quite fit, leaving gaps open to Havana's tropical downpours. Improvements were gradually made to both the windows and air conditioning, but a third element of the design that had been heavily criticized by

P/a

PROGRESS PREVIEW

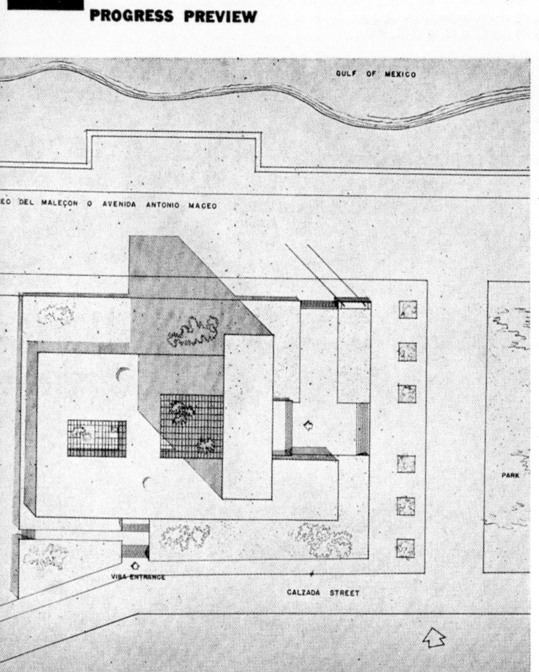

slabs spanning the 40′ width of the tower will be carried by 10″ by 24″ piers, 5′ oc. Ceiling lighting will be recessed in the slabs on the center-line of the piers.

Approaching the new building along the Malecon or through the park to the east, to be developed by the Cuban Government as an extension of the existing park near the Hotel Nacional, the patio just behind the tower will be an alluring background to the entrance lobby. As one passes through the building, this patio will afford a glimpse of the Gulf of Mexico, across the Malecon. In the heart of the Consular portion of the building, a second patio will be faced by a lounge, visa offices, and general work space.

Orientation of the tower was dictated by the prevailing ocean breezes, to which the east and west windows will be opened when the air-conditioning system is off, and by the view along the Malecon, in both directions. The architects expect the building to be completed in 1952.

Windows, of solar heat-resisting glass, will be operable, for cleaning and for use in the months when the air conditioning will be off. No fins, louvres, overhangs, or other sun control devices were thought necessary.

gressive Architecture

State Department inspectors was never addressed: the balcony off the ambassador's office. Here is the report from the State Department inspector:

> Purely from an aesthetic standpoint it is unfortunate that the "Mussolini-type balcony" was permitted to deface the North façade of the building. It completely destroys the lines and architectural simplicity of the building which is its charm. This is particularly unfortunate since the balcony serves no useful purpose and in all probability will never be used. It is understood that FBO seriously objected to the addition of this architectural monstrosity but was overruled. The balcony was demanded by a former Ambassador.[1]

1 A two-day search (with the assistance of archive staff) for the papers of the FBO at the National Archives in Maryland finally turned up a single document, a *Request for Authority to Dispose of Records*, specifying the procedure for *Correspondence with Posts—FBO Central File*: "Destroy when 14 years old." But an exhaustive search through all State Department correspondence with foreign posts from 1945 through 1953 turned up a number of Havana embassy treasures, including the inspector's report cited here. Security at this point in the Cold War referred almost exclusively to anti-espionage measures (this is before a wave of violent attacks on US foreign properties began in the early 1960s), and a State Department security report from this time deals almost exclusively with the protection of information generated by the embassy, down to details like keeping the door to the switchboard operator's room closed. In the wake of the Guy Burgess and Anthony Blunt spying revelations, homosexuality suddenly became an added security risk, so the denouncement of a flamboyant Cuban office boy as an "*afeminado*" by a visiting contractor occasioned a surprising flurry of correspondence between the Cuban embassy, still in its rented quarters in Habana Vieja, and the State Department in Washington, DC.

Jane Loeffler, the authority on post-war embassy design, has also hinted that there were concerns within the State Department that the balcony posed a security risk for pinpointing the whereabouts of the ambassador.[2]

2 Loeffler's book *The Architecture of Diplomacy* (Princeton Architectural Press, New York, 1998), is the standard reference for anyone interested in US embassy design. My interview with Loeffler at her Washington, DC home was the starting point for my research.

The inspector's report accurately evokes the idea of the balcony as a tribune, installed at an impressive height from which the ambassador may address the Cuban masses, gathered meekly along the seawall. Masses did eventually assemble below the balcony, but for the very opposite reason, as is made clear by press photographs of huge anti-US demonstrations organized by the Cuban government over the ensuing decades. Despite the early complaints of the State Department, the ambassador's balcony remained in place, like an abstract symbol of the state of limbo that has characterized the material culture of post-revolutionary Cuba.

Sea façade with ambassador's balcony, US embassy, Havana, 1953.
Max Abramovitz Papers. Avery Architectural and Fine Arts Library. Columbia University, New York. Photo: Alex Langley.

The continued existence of the balcony can suggest several things. Does it represent the defeat of the American imperialist dream, recently upstaged by Fidel Castro's work of ideological guerrilla urbanism, the Plaza of Anti-Imperialism? Or does the balcony's persistence suggest the mere suspension of this dream—where the potential exists for the "Mussolini" balcony to regain its original function: as the pulpit from which Cuba's future American rulers will once again address their subjects. Or perhaps there was no imperialist intention to begin with, and that outgoing ambassador just wanted a little perch on which to escape the office, drink a cup of excellent Cuban coffee and gaze lazily out to sea, towards Florida.

Another characteristic of the new embassy program was an emphasis on transparency. The FBO in the 1950s believed embassy buildings should have an air of openness and permeability. Glass façades were held to represent both honesty—nothing to hide—and accessibility, with the embassy's many cultural functions clearly on display. The Havana embassy, as it was originally designed, was remarkably transparent (on the public, ground floor), with a main lobby furnished with Barcelona chairs visible through floor-to-ceiling glass windows and doors, and an interior courtyard visible beyond the lobby, through a second glass wall. Because of all this glass, a visitor could peer all the way into the heart of the building as they entered, before moving on to the public library, auditorium, gallery, or offices. This directive for transparency sounds utopian compared to the new design directives issued in the early 1980s and the modifications that followed. Following the 1990s renovation at the Havana embassy, a visitor to the diplomatic offices now encounters a security kiosk with metal detector set into a 10-foot fence, followed by a heavy gate, then steps up to the outer glass façade (replaced with 1-inch blast-proof glass). A second security booth in the lobby is set into a solid concrete wall that now completely blocks the view into the interior courtyard.

Night view of façade, US embassy, Havana, 1953.
Max Abramovitz Papers. Avery Architectural and Fine Arts Library. Columbia University, New York. Photo: Alex Langley.

Left:
Foreign Building Operations director Leland King pointing out model of new US embassy, Havana to deputy director Kerrigan in Washington office. Early 1950s. Published in *Architectural Forum* (March 1953).

Right:
Vertical consular block over horizontal visa block, US embassy, Havana, 1953.
Max Abramovitz Papers. Avery Architectural and Fine Arts Library. Columbia University, New York. Photo: Alex Langley.

URBAN CONTEXT

In 1949 the State Department bought a parcel of land on the recently extended Malecón (seawall) of the Vedado neighborhood of Havana. El Vedado received its name in the 17th century as a zone where habitation, agriculture, and woodcutting were forbidden (*vedado*) in order to leave a dense forest, strategically planted with spiny plants, as a natural defense against pirates entering the city from the west. By the 19th century, the area was dotted with country villas, and by the 1940s it was a densely settled and fashionable residential neighborhood. New zoning laws and building technology introduced in the 1950s were responsible for a flurry of high-rise and hotel construction in the area, including the Edificio FOCSA, declared the second-largest poured-concrete building in the world when it was completed in 1956.

Vedado is also located halfway between the downtown financial and government sector—where the embassy had been renting space—and the traditional diplomatic neighborhoods further west, where the ambassador's 1930s residence stands. President Batista made it a priority to develop the hotel and casino trade in the area. The most notorious product of this collaboration between private foreign investors and government was the Riviera Hotel and Casino, backed by the American gangster Meyer Lansky. This was also the era of the new Havana Master Plan, José Luis Sert's unexecuted redesign of the city center, including a new business core running through the historical center, a new island for leisure activities, and an enormous new presidential compound across from the old city. If it had been built, Batista's presidential palace would have been visible from the US ambassador's new office.

RECEPTION

In the first week of June 1953, the embassy staff moved into their new building on the Malecón. In the following weeks, the State Department sent an employee to Cuba to prepare an inspection report on the new embassy. This report gives a detailed list of problems relating to the air conditioning and aluminum window mullions, mentioned above. But equally interesting are the aesthetic judgements made on the new building and its furnishings. In addition to the criticism of the famous "Mussolini" balcony, the report included a scathing critique of the "modernistic" furnishings provided by Knoll: "The new furniture purchased in France especially for the new building is lacking in aesthetic beauty, efficient usefulness and dignity of appearance which is normally expected in American Embassies."

Although Knoll is an American company, the FBO encouraged them to fabricate the pieces for the embassy in France, in order

Glass-walled main lobby with Knoll furniture. "U.S. Embassy Office Building: Havana, Cuba," *Progressive Architecture* (February 1955): 109.

Hans Knoll rendering for ambassador's office. "U.S. Architecture Abroad," *Architectural Forum* (March 1953): 105.

Ambassador's office, US embassy, Havana, 1953.
State Department Collection.
US National Archives.

p/a interior design data

embassy rooms

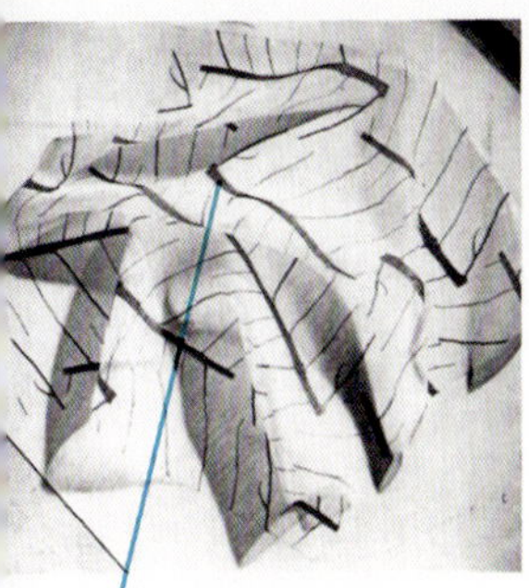

gauze divider on overhead track

space	conference lounge
location	U. S. Embassy Office Building, Havana, Cuba
architects	Harrison & Abramovitz*
furnishings	Knoll Associates, Inc.

*For U. S. Department of State, Foreign Buildings Operations

data

furnishings and fabrics

All Furniture: Knoll Associates, Inc., 575 Madison Ave., New York, N.Y.

Gauze Room Divider: #K80/2/ pure silk, black and white print/ Knoll Textiles, Inc., 575 Madison Ave., New York, N.Y.

Upholstery Fabrics: #575 **Sofa/** #K500/8, cotton, linen, jute, wool, and rayon/ persimmon; **#96 Chair/** #K540 Scotch linen plaid/ black and white; **#44 Chairs/** #K510/14 Avisco/ black and white/ Knoll Textiles, Inc.

walls, ceiling, flooring

Walls: travertine marble/ off-white.

Ceiling: acoustic units applied to slab/ white.

Flooring: carpeting/ off-white/ Cuba.

black-and-white Scotch linen

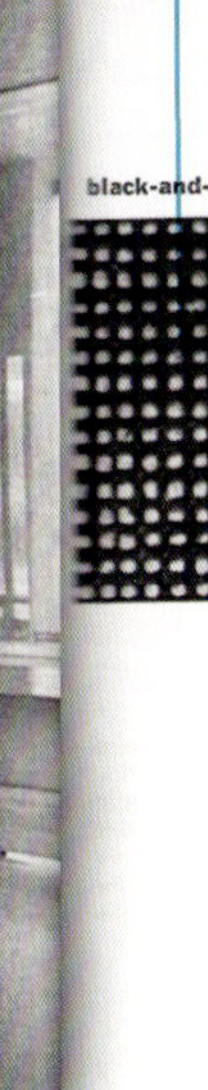

Since the penthouse area atop the Embassy is used both for small conferences and for social purposes, the furniture was selected for flexibility of arrangement as well as for ample seating. Color planning stresses white as foil for the naturally brilliant Cuban spectrum. Ceiling is painted white, floor is covered in white carpeting. For accent, upholstery fabrics are in clear values of blue-green, yellow, and persimmon. Light-blue, translucent silk draperies act as sun screens as well as color areas. Predominant wood is walnut. Black-and-white fabrics, in bold checks and tweed mixtures, repeat the black of oxidized steel furniture frames. *Photos (penthouse): J. Alex Langley*

sofa with drawer unit—single base

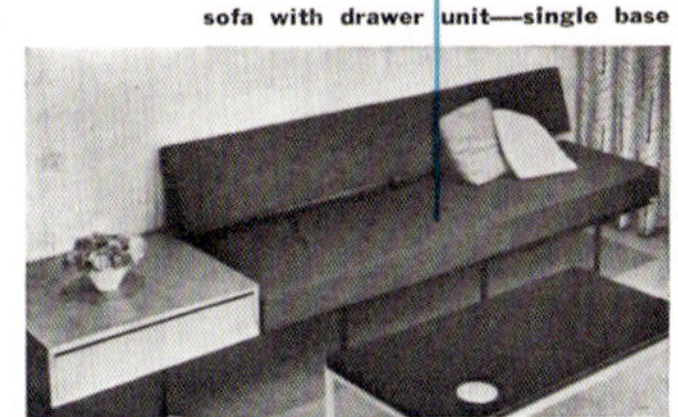

February 1955 137

Louise Sloane, "Embassy Rooms," *Progressive Architecture* (February 1955): 131.

to take advantage of the foreign credit swap system used for most of the construction materials in the embassy. Knoll was (and still is) the furniture company preferred by many architects, due to the fact that they commission furniture plans from the best international designers. The exquisite renderings supplied by Knoll for each of their interior design projects show how well their furniture integrates with the modern architecture of their clients. Nevertheless, in the early 1950s a member of Congress—unable to fathom that the highly suspicious secret understanding between designer and provider was based on the quality and beauty of their products—raised the specter of a "racket" between FBO architects and Knoll, as if there might be kickbacks involved. As with the modern architecture of the new embassy construction program, the underlying conflict here was between two symbolic ideals: how should this young, progressive country (represented by modern architecture and furniture) express itself according to the traditional protocol of diplomacy? Here are the inspector's notes on the beautiful Florence Knoll desk and chair in the ambassador's office (the rest of the furnishings were more traditional, carried over from the old embassy office): "The Ambassador's office is excellent, well designed and furnished in quiet, dignified taste except for the desk and a settee. The desk appears crude, entirely out of harmony with the rest of the room and without the dignity properly expected in the office of a senior representative of the United States Government."

In contrast to the criticism coming from the State Department and Congress, the new Havana embassy was well received by the contemporary architectural community and press.[3] Trade journalists gave the building very positive reviews, highlighting aspects such as the clean separation of functions into distinct vertical and horizontal volumes, the column-free interiors, and technical details like the building's deep-water cooling system. The two interior "tropical" patios were celebrated as a nod to a local building form, but the State Department didn't recognize the hygienic advantage of the extra light and fresh air and immediately roofed over the patio in the visa section. The US embassy's main façade was also used as the backdrop for a 1954 Hudson automobile advertisement, a display of cutting-edge architectural modernity as a backdrop to the very latest in automotive technology. And finally, in 1953, New York's Museum of Modern Art featured the new Havana embassy prominently in its exhibition *Architecture for the State Department*.

AFTER THE CUBAN REVOLUTION

In 1960, it became evident from statements by Cuba's new leaders that the revolutionary government was rapidly reorganizing itself

3 *Progressive Architecture* featured an early progress report in October, 1951, and a six-page feature in February, 1955. In March 1953, *Architectural Forum* included extensive coverage of the new embassy in its *US Architecture Abroad* survey, including a photograph of FBO director Leland King with a model of the building. *Architectural Record* published a short article in April, 1955, including details of the embassy tower's peripheral column load system.

4 Although President Carter managed to engineer a moderate diplomatic opening to Cuba with the establishment of the US Special Interests Section in 1977, two years later, facing pressure from Congress and as a concession to his famously hawkish National Security Advisor, Carter signed a much stricter directive on Cuban "containment," Presidential Directive 52. This is typical of how the relationship between the US and Cuba since the Revolution has been beholden to internal politics in each country. Fidel Castro may have been willing to negotiate with the US for the removal of the embargo at many points in the last 55 years. But he also needed to appease the more hawkish members of his government by acting tough—this is one of the ways the Castro brothers have remained in power. In addition to internal power dynamics, until the late 1980s, Cuban foreign policy had to answer to the USSR. Meanwhile, in the US, starting in the early 1960s, political election campaigns have traditionally featured a good dose of anti-Castro saber-rattling, a display for the benefit of the Cuba lobby, considered gatekeepers to the Florida vote. For this reason, seemingly progressive US presidents have signed some of the most draconian laws against Cuba. Bill Clinton also attempted an opening to Cuba during his presidency, but ended up signing the Helms-Burton law—perhaps the most destructive component of the embargo—under pressure from the Florida Cuba lobby after exile planes were shot down for violating Cuban airspace. The best account of the constant, labyrinthine negotiations between the US and Cuba, and a prime reference for my project, is William LeoGrande and Peter Kornbluh's *Back Channel to Cuba* (Chapel Hill: University of North Carolina Press, 2014).

in accordance with communist doctrine and American property-holders and companies were going to have their assets seized. The US and Cuba severed diplomatic relations on January 3, 1961, and the embassy staff was recalled to the US. Photojournalists documented the US flag and seal being taken down and stored, as well as trucks piled high with the possessions of American employees as they prepare to leave the island by ferry to Florida. A small maintenance staff was left in place to safeguard the building, which entered a peculiar state of limbo. It did not regain its diplomatic function until President Carter opened the US Special Interests Section on September 1st, 1977.[4]

Closing of the US embassy. Havana, January 1961. Photo: Mario Rizzo.

The simple functional meaning of the building, along with the progressive ideas the architects were trying to express in its design, were soon buried by a number of new associations the building acquired after the Cuban Revolution. The building and its surrounding urban sites were the platform for an incredibly inventive media battle that started in the 1960s and climaxed during the US interventions in the Middle East during the 2000s.

Ever since the US broke ties with Cuba in 1961, the Cuban government has used the former US embassy building as a destination for carefully choreographed mass protests. A young Cuban filmmaker described the organization of these events to me: soon after the 1980 Mariel boatlift crisis, his entire school was given the afternoon off, bussed to an assembly point on the Malecón, and formed into a vast column of marchers who filed past the former US embassy, to be collected further down the Malecón and bussed back to school. These marches were photographed by the official press from the air and from neighboring buildings, to appear on the cover of the following day's journals with headlines such as "*¡Que vibra la patria entera!*" (The whole country vibrates!) or "*¡Y la marcha fue!*" (And the protest happened!) These are spectacles performed for the camera in the tradition of the "mass ornaments" of 20th-century dictatorships, yet the main actor in each performance was always the same building, the former US embassy. Indeed, this building, forever the target of a demonstration, was so often the subject of Cuban photojournalists that we are offered a clear document of its life during the years it was out of commission. For example, an image of a 1980 anti-blockade protest that I photographed at the Museum of the Revolution in Havana shows workers on hanging platforms, recladding the façade.

Each time a new confrontation with the US has occurred, a new protest has been organized, and after the restaffing of the former embassy as the US Special Interests Section in 1977, official news photographs sometimes show employees enjoying the view of the spectacle from the former ambassador's fifth floor balcony. One of the grandest protests on the Malecón, for the return of Elián González in April 2000, coincided with the opening of the José Martí Anti-Imperialist Tribune, a stage built directly across from the embassy building. This work of protest urbanism eventually incorporated a large audience area defined by a row of arching gantries, a forest of flagpoles, and—perfectly on axis with and at the extreme tip of the whole complex—a bronze statue of José Martí. Martí cradles an infant in one arm and points accusingly at the embassy building with the other. The residents of Havana, with their sophisticated sense of irony, insist he is saying, "*La salida es por allá*" (the exit is that way).

The year 2000 marked the beginning of a colorful public relations battle between the US and Cuba, with the embassy building as its focal point. The Anti-Imperialist Tribune was refined and added to during George W. Bush's time in office, and at the moment of the US invasion of Iraq, a series of temporary billboards were erected across the street, blocking the view of the sea from the lower floors of the embassy building. The first was a caricature of Bush with "*Asesino*" (Murderer) scrawled across it, soon to be joined by blow-ups of Abu Ghraib torture victims and a two-meter-high swastika. The billboards formed a cyclorama of American atrocities, arranged around some optimum viewpoint inside the embassy building.

On January 16, 2006, the US Special Interests Section, under orders from the Bush administration, finally retaliated in kind, switching on a huge electronic billboard that occupied the windows of the entire fifth floor. In this way, the structural grid of the façade acquired a new function, operating like a huge sheet of gridded paper on which appeared the US government's messages. The practice

5 The official line of the US government, since pulling out of Cuba in 1961, is that they will not negotiate unless the Cuban government make certain changes to their internal and international policy—hold free elections, renounce interventionism, and, most explicitly during the Cold War, stop practicing and preaching communism. These US-imposed preconditions to dialogue have been normalized and have come to seem acceptable to Americans over the last 50 years. Yet it's difficult to imagine Russia insisting the US change its internal political system and foreign policy as a precondition for Richard Nixon's visits in 1972. Mikhail Gorbachev set the record straight during a visit to Cuba in the late 1980s—implicating both the Soviet Union and the US—when he stated, "We have no right to dictate to Fidel Castro how he should manage the affairs of his country."

A protest marches by the United States Interests Section. Havana, May 1980. Photo: Museum of the Revolution, Havana.

Electronic billboard at the United States Interests Section. Havana, 2005. Photo: *The Daily Mail.*

of attempting to turn Cubans against their rulers by broadcasting American propaganda has been a well-funded strategy of the US government since the early 1980s, with the launch of Radio Martí (and later Televisión Martí). In the same vein, the new electronic billboard displayed a steady stream of messages directed at the residents of Havana, visible from anywhere on the Malecón as far as Habana Vieja. The messages were quotes from American comedians, human rights activists, and pro-democracy supporters (one news photograph shows the simple phrase DEMOCRACIA EN CUBA).[5]

The efficacy and legality of Radio and Televisión Martí has been debated since its inception, especially in light of the rumors of corruption in management and the half-billion-dollar price tag of the service. By contrast, the electronic billboard was turned off after just three-and-a-half years, followed by this deadpan statement from State Department spokesman Ian Kelly: "We believe that the billboard was really not effective as a means of delivering information to the Cuban people."[6]

Kelly continued, "It was evident that the Cuban people weren't even able to read the billboard because of some obstructions that were put in front of it." He was referring to the Cuban response to the electronic billboard, the Mountain of Flags. Rumored to be erected under direct order from Fidel Castro, this consists of over 100 flagpoles, originally flying black flags printed with a single white star (said to represent victims of CIA-backed terrorism in Cuba).[7] A February 2006 inscription at the base of the flagpoles reads:

> This mount of flags serves as a response from the people of Cuba to the clumsy arrogance of the US government: 138 Cuban flags will wave with dignity in front of the eyes of the empire, to remind it, starting today,

6 "Obama turns off pro-democracy new ticker on U.S. building in Havana to improve relations with Cuban government," *Daily Mail Reporter*, July 28, 2009, https://www.dailymail.co.uk/news/article-1202687

7 Which brings up the relationship between the State Department and the Central Intelligence Agency. According to William Langewiesche in his article "The Mega-Bunker of Baghdad" (*Vanity Fair*, October 29, 2007), "U.S. Embassies are not pristine diplomatic oases, but full-blown governmental hives, heavy with CIA operatives, and representative of a country that however much it is admired is also despised." The activities of the CIA abroad were often in direct opposition to the diplomatic aims of the State Department. In Cuba, the CIA has caused untold havoc with a well-documented campaign of state-sponsored terrorism—hotel and airplane bombings, crop destruction, and so on—often countering the State Department's efforts at diplomacy. Until the Vietnam War, the largest CIA office in the world was in Miami. Each time diplomatic negotiations—always carried out in secret—between the two countries bore fruit in the form of concessions from Cuba, the CIA interpreted this as a sign of weakness, and by extension, as evidence that their covert campaign of attacks and intimidation was sapping the enemy's strength. To the directors at the CIA, this was proof of effectiveness and a sign to step up their campaign. The Castro brothers have been obliged to wait for a US president who could put an end to this State-CIA feedback loop, and it was amazingly the *eleventh* president to hold power since the Cuban Revolution, Barack Obama, who finally attempted to put an end to this cycle.

> of every year that the Cuban people have struggled, since our founding fathers gave the cry for independence in 1868. Like then, before the bright shadow of this great mount of flags, we continue fighting as free men and women.

After President Obama took office and the electronic billboard was dismantled, the black flags gradually disappeared. On important national holidays, workers appeared on the plaza to hoist 138 Cuban flags. A diplomat at the embassy told me that, soon after John Kerry's visit in 2015, he went out to the plaza to raise the embassy's American flag. He arrived just as a government worker began the task of once again attaching Cuban flags to each pole. The worker stared in disbelief when he suggested alternating Cuban and American flags, at which point it dawned on the diplomat that the orders really were coming from the very top and this was likely one of Fidel's personal projects.

This is the semantic journey Max Abramovitz's building has travelled since 1950, when it was conceived in the spirit of American post-war idealism. But that new idealism was quickly eroded by the realities of the Cold War, which contributed their own set of associations. The meaning of this building, with its simple horizontal and vertical slabs, underwent another transformation in the Cuban collective imagination as barriers to diplomacy were slowly but systematically removed under the administrations of Barack Obama and Raúl Castro.

Since Donald Trump's election in November, 2016, the fate of Obama's Cuba project looks impossible to predict. During his presidential campaign Trump vowed to "cancel" all the initiatives of the outgoing president, which would supposedly reset US–Cuba relations to Cold War levels. The death of Fidel Castro provoked a short, childishly gleeful statement from the president-elect, followed by a series of threats that sounded like voices from the past. Here was the old mantra, going back decades, that any dialogue with Cuba must be predicated on changes in internal Cuban policy. This mantra, repeated by each incoming president, was finally broken when Obama rolled out his experiment in person-to-person contact in 2014. Diplomats I spoke to at the US embassy in early 2017 had been confident that Hilary Clinton would be elected, leading to a major increase in embassy staff—Cuba has been gradually increasing its quota for US diplomats, but a Republican-controlled Congress has steadfastly refused to add more US posts—and the probable design of a new embassy building. That prediction was a product of a political paradigm that now feels as remote as some faraway galaxy.

Thus every day brings a change of course and new uncertainty. And reports from contacts and journalists in Cuba indicate that events there may be mirroring those in the US: There are rumors of increased activity among the military and secret police, actions that appear to be in opposition to the recent political and economic opening. I am hearing reports of censorship, militarization, and restrictions on commercial activity, as well as more stories of emigration to the US despite a tightened visa system.

Those visas are of course granted in the US embassy building, which will take on a new set of associations in the new political reality of the coming years. A friend in Havana is a trained nurse who is now working in the booming tourism sector, cleaning the apartments of American tourists for what I have calculated to be about a twenty-fold increase in pay. Although the money is welcome, this is not the career she had pictured for herself. She feels her options in Cuba are limited to this kind of work if she wants to simply rise above subsistence level. She has decided to use her money to emigrate to the US and spends hours in the line outside the embassy, returning repeatedly to provide more documentation. She complains bitterly and despairingly about the heartlessness of the officers in the visa section, viewing them as representatives of a cold, forbidding, northern culture. Yet she has come to believe such a visa is her only hope for a better future.

These private dramas are played out every day in the US embassy. They mirror the aspirations and failures of the building itself, caught in a political drama that has continually reset its meaning over its 64 years of existence. The Cuban political succession programmed for 2018, and the volatility of the current US administration, indicate that the building's function and signification will continue to fluctuate well into the future.

EPILOGUE: MARCH 1, 2022

Each time I have presented *Havana Case Study* in a public context, I have been asked for my opinion on the "Havana Syndrome" controversy: a series of alleged "sonic attacks" that affected US diplomatic staff in Havana starting in 2016, either at the embassy or in their living quarters. Similar attacks have now been reported by hundreds of US State Department and military employees around the world. My response was usually: At best, mass hysteria; at worst, some outdated Cold War KGB (or CIA) device.

In late January 2022, the CIA issued a preliminary report on the attacks in which a senior official concluded "we don't see a global campaign by a foreign actor." The response to this report was swift and angry by members of Congress who have used the purported attacks to justify continuing sanctions against Cuba. The timing of the first "attacks" followed on the heels of President Obama's

Mountain of Flags. Havana, 2006.
Photo: Francis Alÿs.

rapprochement with Cuba. They also marked the beginning of Donald Trump's expansion of the Cuban embargo. 2016 to 2020 have been some of the harshest years for Cuba since the beginning of the 20th century, caused by the Trump administration's anti-Cuba policies, the dithering of the post-Castro government, and the Covid-19 pandemic. Sadly, President Biden doesn't seem to be ready to pay the political costs of ending the embargo.

The US embassy building took a beating from Hurricane Irma in September 2017, with some seafront façade panels still awaiting replacement. Then the building's environs saw another transformation, the latest (and last?) in the US–Cuba volley of symbolic interventions described in my essay. The *Mountain of Flags* has now disappeared and a new monument has been raised in its place. Announced on the website of the Empresa de Construcción y Mantenimiento (ECOM), this massive concrete structure was immediately condemned in articles in the anti-regime press. It has been criticized as a colossal waste of concrete in a country where one third of the housing stock is considered unsound.

The new monument represents a Cuban flag hung vertically, with its triangle uppermost and stripes hanging down. The flag has been expanded into three dimensions so that the triangle with its star becomes a sloping roof held up by three columns (standing in for the flag's blue stripes). The structure stands before the US embassy, the visual resolution point of the Tribune of Anti-Imperialism (now popularly known as the *protestódromo*). Here the symbolism becomes complicated: A viewer standing in front of the monument can see the vertical windows and mullions of the US embassy façade through

Installation of new sculpture at the Anti-imperialist Tribune. Havana, 2021. Photo: EFE / Yander Zamora.

the open slots that stand for the white stripes of the flag. In this way Max Abramovitz's 1953 façade grid, custom designed as a symbol of the US presence in Cuba, provides the geometry that completes the composition of this massive new flag. Is one symbol *imposed* on the other? Or is one symbol *bleeding through* the other? In either case, the symbolism of the embassy and its modern architecture is enriched by the sculpture's careful placement.

PSYCHES AND SPECIFICATIONS: RICHARD NEUTRA IN HAVANA

Sylvia Lavin

Richard Neutra (with Raúl Álvarez), De Schulthess House, view from garden, from W. Boesiger, ed. ***Richard Neutra, 1950-60, Buildings and Projects*** (Zurich: Girsberger, 1959), p. 53.

Opposite page:
Richard Neutra (with Raúl Álvarez), De Schulthess House, view of entry with spider legs, from W. Boesiger, ed. ***Richard Neutra, 1950-60, Buildings and Projects*** (Zurich: Girsberger, 1959), p. 55.

Richard Neutra claimed he decided to be an architect in 1898, when he was eight years old, while taking his first underground ride in the just-completed Wiener Stadtbahn.[1] This cunningly and retroactively crafted origin story brought together all the tropes that Neutra eventually wove into his qualifications as an architect: an urbane appreciation for the sophistication of modern engineering, a masterful capacity to convert the underbelly of modern experience into a means of self-realization, and a preternatural ability to move through the rapidly expanding world with ease. During the more than 50 years he spent practicing architecture, Neutra emphasized different aspects of this expertise matrix so that he would always be ideally matched with the exigencies of specific commissions and shifts in the general circumstances shaping his profession. While sometimes adopting the role of impartial technical expert and other times presenting as the empathic, psychologizing therapist, he typically moved smoothly between these antithetical poles that, during the post-war period, he

1 The definitive architectural biography of Neutra remains Thomas Hines, *Richard Neutra and the Search for Modern Architecture* (New York: Oxford University Press, 1982).

Richard Neutra, *Amerika: die Stilbildung des neuen Baues in den Vereinigten Staaten* (Vienna: A Schroll, 1930). Cover design by El Lissitkzy.

increasingly associated with distinct geographies. That is, until he found himself in Havana and discovered that he had misplaced his travel diary somewhere along the Malécon. Neutra went to Cuba to construct a house designed to celebrate multiple forms of mastery, but, agitated by the loss of this record of his own becoming, he left Havana unsettled by the discovery of incommensurability between the very elements out of which he had made himself an architect.

Like many modern architects, Neutra wrote books to verify credentials that could migrate across international borders and satisfy distinct professional standards. His *Wie Baut Amerika?* and *Amerika*, both from early in his career, established a command of US building practices as key to developing his reputation as an Americanized architect.[2] Travelling along a path well-known to other Austrians, from Vienna to New York and then across the United States, via Chicago, to California, Neutra spent his time on the road documenting innovations in architectural engineering and construction methods.[3] The resulting publications were widely read both in Europe and in the United States and helped him secure the commission for the

2 See Richard Joseph Neutra and Dione Neutra, *Wie Baut Amerika?* (Stuttgart: J. Hoffmann, 1927) and his *Amerika, Die Stilbildung Des Neuen Bauens In Den Vereinigten Staaten* (Vienna: A. Schroll, 1930).

3 As is well known, many artists, musicians, and writers from the avant-garde circles of Vienna found their way to Los Angeles. In relation to architects, see E. McCoy, *Vienna to Los Angeles: Two Journeys* (Santa Monica, CA: Arts & Architecture Press, 1979).

4 For H. R. Hitchcock and Philip Johnson's discussion of Neutra's work in the context of what they called the International Style, borrowing the term used by art historians to describe the movements of Gothic builders, see the exhibition catalog *Modern Architecture: International Exhibition: New York, Feb. 10 to March 23, 1932, Museum of Modern Art* (New York: The Museum, 1932), pp. 157.

5 There is a growing literature on Neutra's work outside the United States, particularly in Latin America but also in Europe, Pakistan and elsewhere. See, for example, Brett Tippey, "Richard Neutra in Spain: Consumerism, Competition, and U.S. Air Force Housing," *Journal of the Society of Architectural Historians*, vol. 80, no. 1 (2021): 48-67, as well as Tippey's "Richard Neutra's Search for the Southland: California, Latin America and Spain," *Architectural History* 59 (2016): 311-352. See also Catherine R. Ettinger and Richard Joseph Neutra, *Richard Neutra y América Latina: Una mirada desde el Sur* (Guadalajara, Mexico: Arquitónica, 2018). Neutra is also included in the contemporary literatures on modernism in Latin America more broadly, including Miguel Ángel Roca, *The Architecture of Latin America* (London: Academy Editions, 1995); Luis E. Carranza, Fernando Luiz Lara, and Jorge Francisco Liernur, *Modern Architecture in Latin America: Art, Technology, and Utopia* (Austin: University of Texas Press, 2014) and Barry Bergdoll, Carlos Eduardo Comas, Jorge Francisco Liernur, and Patricio Del Real, *Latin America in Construction: Architecture 1955-1980* (New York: Museum of Modern Art, 2015).

Lovell Health House, the first all-steel frame residential structure, and earn inclusion in the Museum of Modern Art's *Modern Architecture: International Exhibition* of 1932.[4] The Lovell House was merely the first in a series of "firsts," and Neutra eventually became known as the architect who had not only constructed the first all-steel frame house, but was the first to use gunite and shotcrete for domestic architecture; to use radiating floor and wall heating for small buildings, prefab footings, plywood for both structure and exterior skin, and shop-fabricated sheet metal, both as bearing wall construction and roofing. *Wie Baut Amerika?* and *Amerika* were early steps in a process that transformed Neutra from an Austrian Jew into an American specialist.

Over the course of WWII, Neutra's reputation as a technical expert in American know-how launched him on a new series of journeys, this time sponsored by the US arm of CIAM, of which he became President in 1944, and by the US State Department.[5] He traveled to Singapore, Pakistan, South Africa and Nigeria in Asia and Africa, and to the Dominican Republic, Puerto Rico, Ecuador, Peru, Bolivia, Argentina, Uruguay, Brazil, Venezuela and Cuba in the Americas—all trips taken under more or less official governmental auspices. Neutra's movement mapped an emerging geography, not of MoMA's Western European Internationalism but of what in 1952 Alfred Sauvy dubbed the Third World.[6] To demonstrate that his technical expertise, originally developed for well-to-do clients in Southern California, could equally serve to expand the US sphere of influence across this Third World, Neutra published another book documenting construction methods. Unlike *Wie Baut Amerika*'s focus on new materials and complex construction methods, Neutra's emphasis in *Architecture of Social Concern in Regions of Mild Climate* was on the standardization of simple building components and their assembly.[7] Addressed to what his Brazilian publishers described as a community "for which techniques of contemporary construction [are] needed in the widened world stage," Neutra suggested ways of using architecture to spread "technological civilization" and conduct a "guerilla warfare against backwardness."[8] Using his work on US settlements in Guam and Puerto Rico as models, *Architecture of Social Concern* provided detailed descriptions of the prefabricated components, architectural equipment and programmatic elements that would be required for this civilizing mission. Especially important were Neutra's publication of technical drawings that demonstrated how the design of outdoor space and roof systems managing air and water flow could temper the lethargy- and disease-producing environments that curtail the development of what he understood to be a rigorous modern society.[9] The *Architecture of Social Concern*

6 On the complex history of this term, see B.R. Tomlinson, "What was the Third World," *Journal of Contemporary History*, 2 (2003): 307-321; Leslie Wolf-Phillips, "Why 'Third World'? Origin, Definition and Usage," *Third World Quarterly* 9, 4 (1987): 1311-1327.

7 Neutra's *Architecture of Social Concern in Regions of Mild Climate* (São Paulo: G. Todtmann, 1948) was the first in a large number of publications that indicated a broadening of his focus to include wider geographies and climates. See Richard Neutra, *Life and Human Habitat* (Stuttgart: Alexander Koch, 1957); Richard Neutra, *Realismo biológico: Un nuevo renacimiento en la arquitectura* (Buenos Aires: Nueva Visión, 1958). See also Neutra's "Projects of Puerto Rico: Hospitals, Health Centers, and Schools," in *Architecture d'Aujourd'hui*, vol. 16, no. 5 (May 1946): 71-77. In *Architecture of Social Concern* Neutra explicitly promotes the idea that the "migrant architect offering expertise" to developing nations was only one in an array of "experts" and consultants that would be necessary to serve US interests both internationally and domestically.

8 See the preface to *Architecture of Social Concern*, p. 7, and Neutra's discussion of development in Latin America, pp. 37, 39.

9 According to Neutra, his schemes could mitigate just about everything, from the spread of tuberculosis to illiteracy and boredom, and, could also remedy an insufficient appetite for consumption. For Neutra, cooling is itself a civilizing function. Neutra's interest in the interaction between climate and social systems is addressed in José Tavares Correia de Lira, "From Mild Climate's Architecture to Third World Planning: Richard Neutra in Latin America," in *Proceedings of the 14th International Planning History Conference: Controversies, Contrasts and Challenges*, 1-15, Istanbul, 2010, and Daniel A. Barber, *Modern Architecture and Climate: Design before Air Conditioning* (Princeton: Princeton University Press, 2020); also Barber's "The Form and Climate Research Group, or Scales of Architectural History," in *Climates: Architecture and the Planetary Imaginary*, James Graham, ed. (New York: Columbia Books on Architecture and the City, 2016), pp. 303-317. See also Neutra's "Projects of Puerto Rico: Hospitals, Health Centers, and Schools" in *Architecture d'Aujourd'hui*, vol. 16, no. 5 (May 1946): 71-77.

in Regions of Mild Climate was, in effect, a "gift" of epistemic aid, an offering of specifications detailing how to deploy architecture to convert the bodies of agrarian populations into modern subjects.[10]

If Neutra presented his capacity to spread technological civilization across the Third World as an asset to the US State Department, he was also attentive to the rise of resistance to technological determinism within the so-called First World that began to emerge at mid-century. To address this concern, Neutra published *Survival Through Design* in 1954, in which he pivoted his claim to architectural expertise away from the hard science of engineering and toward the softer science of psychology.[11] Already in 1949 he had appeared on the cover of an issue of *Time* magazine containing an article on the general state of architecture that expressed concern, not for rural populations in Latin America or other "warm climate" regions, but rather for the growing middle class in the US. According to *Time* magazine, Americans increasingly lived in mass-produced housing—identical spaces that put Americans at risk of becoming more and more standardized themselves.[12] New kinds of architect, with expertise in the "warm overtones of home," were necessary to invigorate psyches made cold and undifferentiated by technocratic culture.[13] Regulating behavior through the use of standardized and standardizing architecture was a goal appropriate to the antipodes, so implied *Time* magazine, but civilized society demanded individualized

10 He neatly summed up his "aid package" as follows: "with the worldwide spread of a technological and industrial civilization goes a cosmopolitan migration of experts and contemporary technical leaders to areas which have not yet had the opportunity and experience to produce all the needed, indigenous, professional leadership of their own. Such an influx and influence of outsiders temporarily transplanted into soil foreign to them, may regularly pose a psychological problem. The newcomers must have not only technical qualifications; they need themselves the emotional ability of sympathetic assimilation or else they will fail to be the carriers of cultural goods which can readily be assimilated." See *Architecture of Social Concern*, p. 118.

11 See Richard Neutra, *Survival Through Design* (New York: Oxford University Press, 1954).

12 See "New Shells," *Time Magazine*, August 15, 1949. 58-66. See also, for example, the Dean of Harvard's GSD Joseph Hudnut's critique of what he called the "cloudburst" of identical houses that promised middle-class consumers happiness in his "The Post-Modern House," *Architectural Record* 97, no. 5 (May 1, 1945): 70. For more on Hudnut's essay, see my *Architecture Itself and Other Postmodernization Effects* (Montreal: Canadian Centre for Architecture; Leipzig: Spector Books, 2020), p. 69.

13 The simultaneous anti-fascism and anti-communism of these concerns was implicit in this rhetoric.

Richard Neutra, sketch of Cathedral of San Cristobal in Old Havana, 1945.
Courtesy of Richard and Dion Neutra papers, UCLA. Library Special Collections, Charles E. Young Research Library, University of California, Los Angeles (Box 1, Folder 48).

Opposite page:
Richard Neutra, Moore house, Ojai, California, 1952. Photo: Julius Shulman.

subjects with an unlimited sense of their own liberal imperatives. Neutra was chosen to exemplify this new kind of architect because his origin story included not only first-hand witnessing of technological innovation but also first-hand contact with Sigmund Freud.[14]

After WWII, Neutra increasingly and explicitly modeled himself on the kinds of psychotherapeutic practices becoming popular among the American middle class and described his architecture in terms of its therapeutic effects.[15] His psychologizing of the architectural design process began by having clients/patients keep diaries of daily activities and thoughts, and resulted in architectural spaces promising recovery from the experience of modern birth, an experience Neutra claimed had been rendered traumatic by industrialized hospital settings. Individual clients had individual desires: the Chueys sought to enhance their creativity and so commissioned a house that functioned

14 Neutra had been close friends with Freud's son, Ernst, also an architect, and later consulted with Freud about his own son.

15 For a detailed discussion of the impact on his mid-century work in Los Angeles of Neutra's reading of Otto Rank's *The Birth Trauma* in particular, see my *Form Follows Libido: Architecture and Richard Neutra in a Psychoanalytic Culture* (Cambridge, Mass.: MIT Press, 2004). For an economically framed reading of this psychologized architectural context, see Sandy Isenstadt, "Richard Neutra and the Psychology of Architectural Consumption," in *Anxious Modernisms: Experimentation in Postwar Architectural Culture*, Sarah Williams Goldhagen and Réjean Legault, eds. (Cambridge, Mass.: MIT Press, 2000), pp. 97-118.

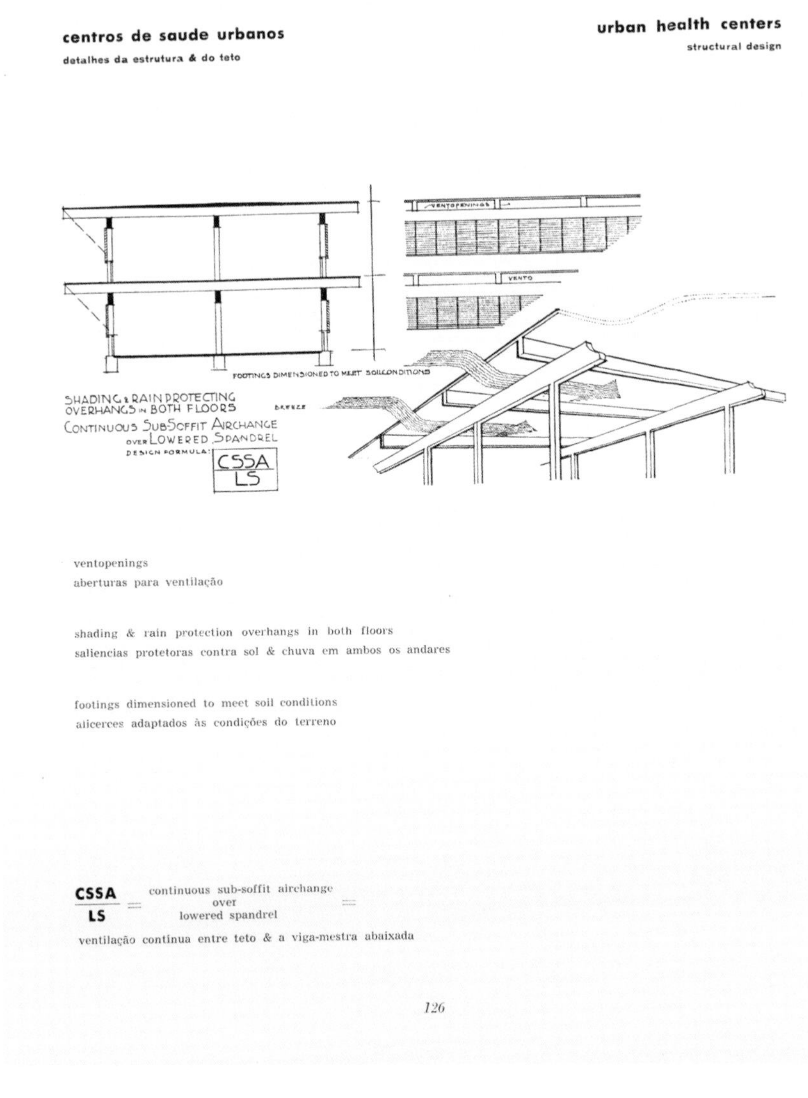

Structural design for urban health center showing continuous airflow through under the soffit. Air conditioning rendered this function of clerestory windows obsolete at the De Schulthess House. In Richard Neutra, ***Architecture of Social Concern in Regions of Mild Climate*** (São Paulo: G. Todtmann, 1948), p. 126.

Opposite page:
Richard Neutra, Chuey House, Los Angeles, 1956. Photo: Julius Shulman.

like a Reichian Orgone box, while the Moores wished to commune with the mystical aura of Ojai where Krishnamurti and his followers gathered. But the origin of neuroses lay in the birth trauma, according to Neutra, the archi-therapeutic solution for which was the provision of warm and constant temperatures across thresholds and especially in the passage between interior and exterior. Mitered glass corners enabled subjects to "feel" as if they were outside while remaining indoors; water features, heating and cooling devices and large glass walls that slid open and shut according to changes in weather, were designed to keep interior temperatures unvarying; and what he called spider legs, elements of architectural structure that began indoors under the roof and extended out into gardens, attenuated boundaries. All these elements worked together to eliminate sensory shock and neuralgic fatigue, allowing the inhabitant to repeat the process of moving from within (the womb) out into the world without trauma, and hence ready to realize their potential.

Neutra received the commission to design a house in Havana for Alfred and Harriet de Schulthess just as he was enjoying new celebrity following the publications of *Architecture of Social Concern* and *Survival Through Design*. As a pair, the books enabled him to generate a global audience by offering technical systems mitigating the backwardness and dysregulation of tropical societies to the Third World and design techniques unleashing psychic freedom to the First World. Although designing a house for a European in Cuba might have seemed an ideal opportunity to combine these architectural toolkits, the de Schulthess commission instead exposed the frailties of this dichotomized world view.[16] Cuba's economy was too closely connected to the "First World" to be subject to architecture generated from standardizing and regulatory specifications, and yet the territory was too agrarian and intemperate to be conceived as populated by liberated individuals in need of self-realization. Havana was an extreme instantiation of the undecidable status of Cuba as a whole—a city filled with European financial institutions and corporations, but one also associated with the uninhibited expression of carnal appetites unleashed by its tropical, tempestuous climate and the libidinous effects of sugar cane and tobacco. These disturbances in Neutra's understanding of what he called planetary order unsettled the architectural conditions of the De Schulthess House and helped shape a design organized neither by the pursuit of therapeutic effects or climatic integration, but rather by the fault lines undergirding the distinct imperatives of psyche and specification.[17]

The aporia was embedded in the De Schulthess House even before there was a building.[18] After joining the Banco Garrigó as an executive in 1953, de Schulthess, a Swiss national, wanted his wife and daughters to winter with him in Cuba from September to

16 For a discussion of the architectural context of modern Cuba before the Revolution, see Timothy Hyde, *Constitutional Modernism: Architecture and Civil Society in Cuba, 1933-1959* (Minneapolis: University of Minnesota Press, 2012).

17 For Neutra's "planetary" imagination and rhetoric, see his "Comments on Planetary Reconstruction," in *Arts and Architecture*, vol. 61, no. 12 (December 1944): 20-22. See also Barber's "The Form and Climate Research Group."

18 There is little theoretical literature on the De Schulthess House. What has been written is mostly concerned with establishing the chronology of the house's construction. See, for example, Eduardo Luis Rodríguez, *Modernidad Tropical: Neutra, Burle Marx y Cuba: La Casa de Schulthess* (2007); "Our Man in Havana: Richard Neutra's Incursion into Cuba's Tropical Environment," *Interiors* 153, 7 (July 1994): 42-43; *La Habana. Arquitectura del Siglo XX* (Barcelona: Blume, 1998); *The Havana Guide, Modern Architecture, 1925-1965* (New York: Princeton Architectural Press, 2000). On the history of the Garrigó bank and on banking in Cuba, see Luis Felipe Zegarra, "Bank Laws, Economic Growth and Early Banking in Latin America: 1840-1920," in *Explorations in Economic History*, vol. 53 (2014): 101-119; H. Bonin and N. Valerio, eds., "Colonial Banking: One Model, Two Histories: Cuba and Puerto Rico Before Independence," in *Banking, Money and International Finance*, vol. 4 (London and New York: Taylor and Francis, Routledge, 2016). See also historiacuba.wordpress.com/2017/02/15/banco-garrigo.

May but he did not want them to live in the old city, where the bank had established its headquarters in 1950. As a result, he purchased property in the Country Club Park of Havana, a new "development" zone that constituted an island on an island; in its very name the Park reflected allegiance not to Cuba but to the globalization of American-style housing and the forms of deterritorializing economic development on which it was predicated. Advertised as the most luxurious and urbanized residential neighborhood in Cuba, apartment buildings and commercial structures were banned there, to protect the sea views of large private houses and shield landowners from the surrounding economic and racial complexities. De Schulthess in fact purchased two adjacent lots, because he wanted a house grand enough to accommodate a guest wing and servants' quarters. The potential risk of developing a 9,000 square feet house in Cuba was offset by the kinds of exceptions offered by the Country Club Park: as the developer reminded buyers just a few years before the Revolution, "land brings with it the most solid guarantee that human ingenuity has ever imagined."[19]

Just as the real estate on which the house was constructed was simultaneously in the socially concerning climate of Cuba and in the deterritorialized space of global capitalism, the design of the house too reveals irresolution. On the one hand, as was typical of Neutra's mid-century residential designs in California, the main space of the ground floor lacks internal walls dividing living from dining rooms, and these public spaces are open to the outside garden through large sliding glass doors. On the other hand, the composition of the house as a whole is highly disciplined and formal: rather than a free plan generating a dynamic spatial distribution, as seen in the Chuey house, for example, the De Schulthess House is symmetrical and monumental. Its U-shaped plan, which recalls the geometries of French 18th-century *hôtels*, differentiates servants from owners, separates public and private areas and maintains distance between gender-specific rooms: Alfred's study, the butler's room, space for sewing and a room for the governess are all gender-determined.

Monumentality is produced not only by the compositional formality of the plan and the sheer size of the house but also by an uncharacteristic use of Neutra's characteristic elements. For example, the house does indeed have spider legs, but these are not deployed so as to activate what Neutra claimed as their therapeutic capacity: they do not go from interior to exterior, and hence fail to blur the bounded edge of the house; they are too numerous, self-similar, and aligned to operate as objects of psychological identification and individuation. In fact, these spider legs compose a colonnade for a porte cochère rather than constitute birth trauma mediators.[20] The pseudo-spider legs are, moreover, one of several

19 See the advertisement and development brochure, *Ventas a Plazos*, in the Neutra Archive, Box 310, Folder 11. (This and all further archival references are to the Richard and Dion Neutra Papers [LSC 1179], UCLA Library Special Collections, Charles E. Young Research Library, University of California, Los Angeles.) The language of credit and investment was one that Neutra knew well. He frequently argued that a "Neutra house" was a good financial investment and related the life span of their construction to the duration of modern mortgages. He even discussed visual characteristics in terms of value. For example, when attempting to convince de Schulthess to build a reflecting pool on the property, Neutra argued: "I believe when you look out of living quarters over this pool you would have an additional visual return on investment not just place to swim in." Letter from Neutra to de Schulthess, Dec. 14, 1954, Box 42, Folder 9.

20 Much of the discussion about design that affected the positioning of the spider legs concerned how many cars would be garaged and how much turning radius they would require.

LISTA DE PRECIOS DE LOS SOLARES DEL "COUNTRY CLUB PARK", PERTENECIENTES A LA SOCIEDAD "INVERSIONES RESIDENCIALES, S. A."

Sección 2 Lote	Superficie en varas	Precio por varas	Precio total	Primer pago	Precio aplazado	36 pagos mensuales, incluyendo capital e intereses	Precio de contado
42	3,572.51	4.00	14,290.04	3,572.51	10,717.53	326.04	13,575.54
50 P. 48 P. 47	4,918.80	3.25	15,986.10	3,996.52	11,989.57	364.73	15,186.80
Sescción 4							
B	5,790.18	3.50	20,265.63	5,066.40	15,199.22	462.37	19,252.34
C	4,622.65	3.50	16,179.27	4,044.82	12,134.45	369.14	15,370.30
F	4,865.73	3.50	17,030.05	4,257.51	12,772.53	388.55	16,178.55
G	4,135.66	3.50	14,474.81	3,618.70	10,856.10	330.25	13,751.07
Sección 5							
P. 159	4,404.19	3.50	15,414.66	3,853.66	11,561.00	351.70	14,643.93
160 y P. 159	4,404.19	3.50	15,414.66	3,853.66	11,561.00	351.70	14,643.93
117	3,950.04	3.50	13,825.14	3,456.28	10,368.86	315.43	13,133.88
118	4,001.55	3.50	14,005.42	3,501.35	10,504.07	319.54	13,305.15
Sección 11							
276	3,141.21	3.75	11,779.54	2,944.88	8,834.66	268.76	11,190.56
Sección 15							
326	2,887.97	2.50	7,219.92	1,804.98	5,414.94	164.72	6,858.92
329	3,436.31	2.50	8,590.77	2,147.69	6,443.07	196.00	8,161.23
330	3,276.46	2.50	8,191.15	2,04778	6,143.37	186.89	7,781.59
332 C	3,479.25	2.75	9,567.94	2,391.98	7,175.96	218.30	9,089.54
334 A	3,427.01	2.75	9,424.28	2,356.07	7,068.21	215.02	8,953.00
Sección 16							
338	4,738.72	3.00	14,216.16	3,554.04	10,662.12	324.35	13,505.35
344 y P. 345	7,296.41	4.00	29,185.64	7,996.41	21,889.23	665.89	27,726.35
P. 349 A.	5,398.26	4.00	21,593.04	5,398.26	16,194.78	492.66	20,513.38
350 y P. 349 A.	3,960.96	4.00	15,843.84	3,960.96	11,882.88	361.49	15,051.65
A	2,406.42	4.25	10,227.28	2,556.82	7,670.46	233.34	9,715.92
B	2,251.38	4.25	9,568.36	2,392.09	7,176.27	218.31	9,089.94
364	4,771.74	3.25	15,508.15	3,877.04	11,631.11	353.83	14,732.74
365	3,828.98	3.25	12,444.18				
Sección 17							
398	4,563.45	4.00	18,253.80	4,563.45	13,690.35	416.47	17,341.11
Sección 19							
A. y P. B.	6,600.00	3.75	24,750.00	6,187.50	18,562.50	564.69	23,512.50
Resto I.	3,500.00	4.00	14,000.00	3,500.00	10,500.00	319.42	13,300.00
Sección 20							
489 y P. 490	4,487.00	4.00	17,948.00	4,487.00	13,461.00	409.50	17,050.60
P. 491 y P. 492	4,338.62	4.00	17.554.48	4,388.62	13,165.86	400.52	16,676.76

Estos precios pueden ser alterados en cualquier momento.

Habana, Mayo 15, 1952

LOTES EN EL COUNTRY CLUB PARK

EL BARRIO RESIDENCIAL MAS LUJOSO Y URBANIZADO

El Country Club Park representa lo más bello como lugar residencial en Cuba. Hay invertidos en el Contry Club millones de pesos en lujosas residencias y su situación y altura lo hacen el sito mas fresco y más agradable de los alrededores de La Habana, donde existen limitaciones de que carecen otros Repartos y que le garantizan que allí sólo se construirán residencias privadas aisladas y nunca tendrá casa de apartamentos, comercios, cabarets, etc. La amplitud de los lotes trae como lógica consecuencia amplios jardines, rodeando cada casa.

Sus terrenos altos tienen preciosas vistas al mar.

Su cimentación es magnífica y su tierra excelente para parques.

Tiene un lago maravilloso y otros lugares de expansión.

Lo atraviesan dos Avenidas dobles con paseo central, y todas las otras Avenidas son muy anchas.

Está circundado en parte por los links de golf del Country Club de La Habana, los mejores de Cuba.

PRECIOS DESDE $3.50 POR VARA

VENTAS A PLAZOS

ABONANDO EL 25% DE ENTRADA Y EL RESTO EN 36 MENSUALIDADES, CON INTERESES DEL 6% ANUAL SOBRE LAS CANTIDADES PENDIENTES DE PAGO

5% DE DESCUENTO POR PAGO DE CONTADO.

En la actualidad hay muchas residencias en construcción y últimamente se han realizado ventas a personas que piensan fabricar inmediatamente.

Se han fomentado en los alrededores, clubs de recreo con miles de socios, se ha construido la Universidad Católica de Villanova, la Iglesia de Santo Tomás, donde es fácil la asistencia a las familias que viven en el Country Club.

La Parroquia del Corpus Christi está lindando con el Reparto.

El Sagrado Corazón de Jesús y el Merici Academy han construido sus planteles de enseñanza en las proximidades de este Reparto.

Se han urbanizado los terrenos entre este Reparto y el Vedado y se han construido cientos de residencias.

En las proximidades se han establecido modernos mercados, boticas y otros establecimientos.

RECUERDE QUE LA TIERRA ES LA GARANTIA MAS SOLIDA QUE EL INGENIO HUMANO HA IDEADO.

ADQUIERA UN LOTE AUNQUE NO LO CONSTRUYA DE MOMENTO

"COMPAÑIA DE INVERSIONES RESIDENCIALES, S. A."

ALBERTO G. MENDOZA

AMARGURA No. 205. TELEFONO M-9494.

Development brochure for the Country Club Park describing financial terms of property acquisition. Courtesy of Richard and Dion Neutra papers, UCLA Library Special Collections, Charles E. Young Research Library, University of California, Los Angeles (Box 310, Folder 11.)

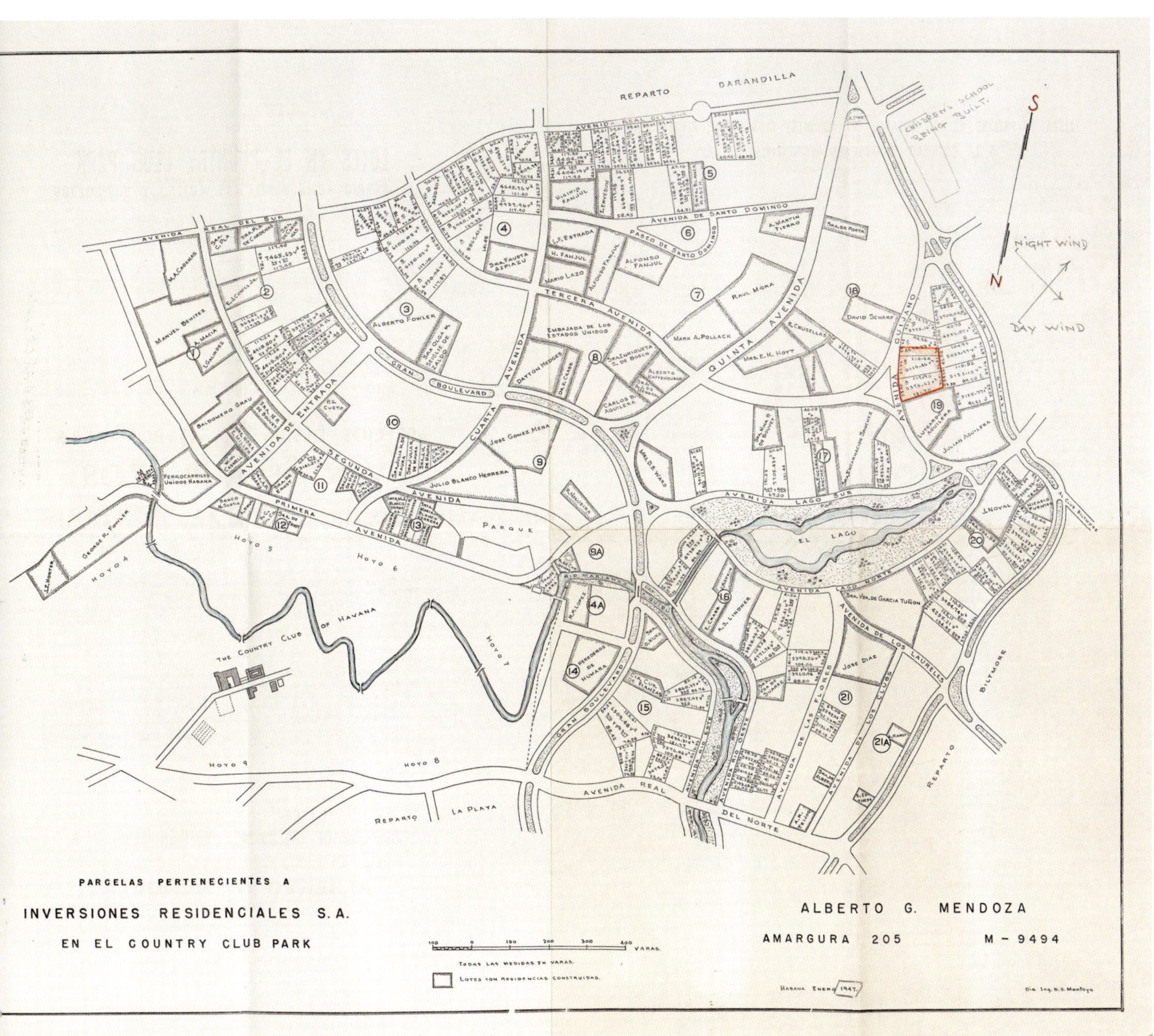

Development brochure for the Country Club Park showing lay-out of the subdivision. Highlighted section shows the double lot of the De Schulthess property. Neutra Papers (Box 310, Folder 11.)

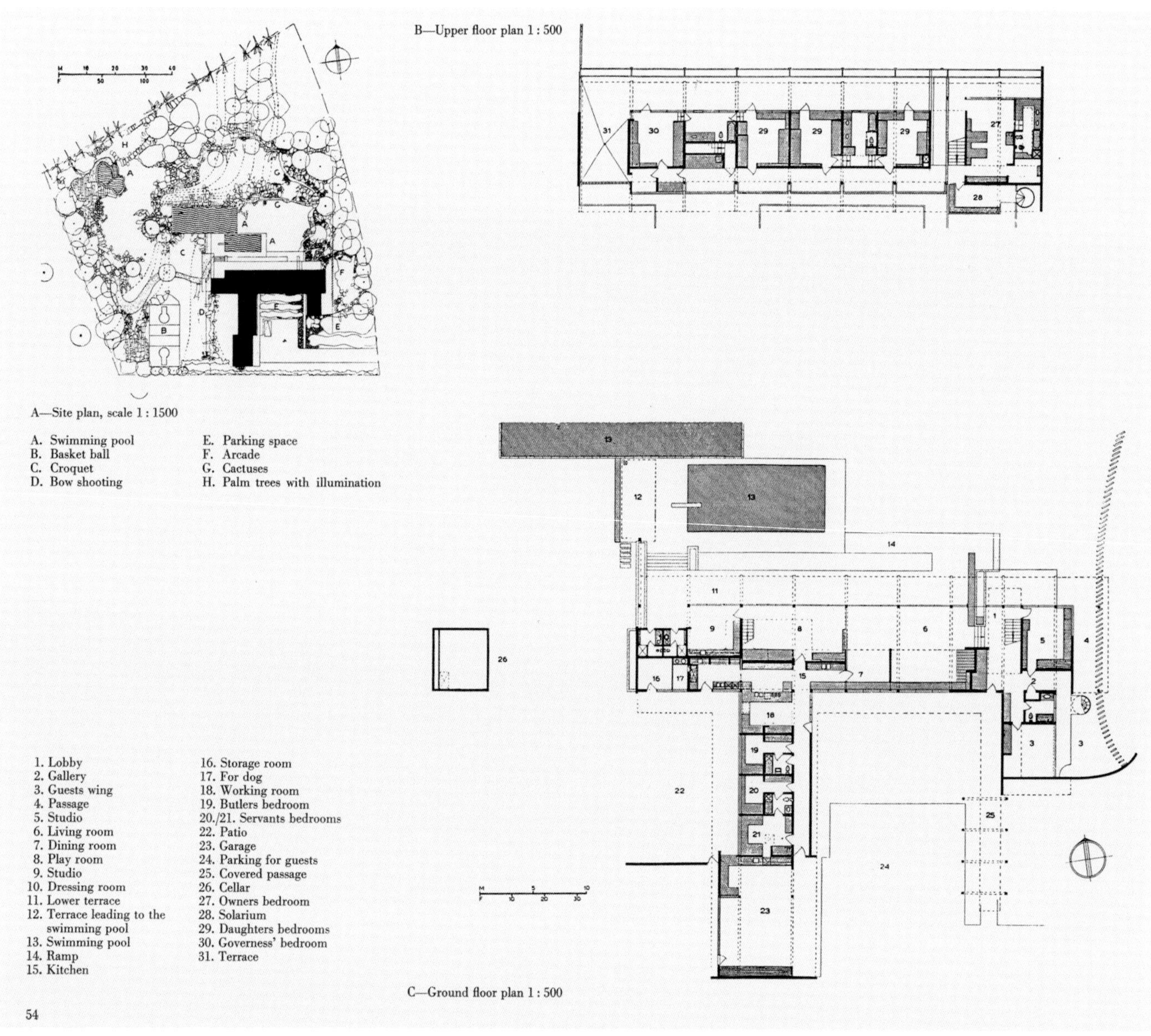

Richard Neutra (with Raúl Álvarez), De Schulthess House, plans and site plan, from W. Boesiger, ed. *Richard Neutra, 1950-60, Buildings and Projects* (Zurich: Girsberger, 1959), p. 54.

elements that together produce a fortification system engirding the house. Far from being open to the exterior, the De Schulthess House has rusticated stone walls on three sides and on all parts of the house at risk of allowing noise or sight to penetrate from neighbors or the street are screened by defensive landscaping. The De Schulthess House may at first appear to be a structure allowing fluid and free movement across barriers but it is in fact a hideout, battened down as if in anticipation of attack.[21]

Even though he had himself established them as geographically separated if not conceptually irreconcilable, Neutra did his best to maneuver between the demands of tropical management and individual self-realization. For example, he understood that de Schulthess expected the house to convey a sense of privilege and hence argued that the building, "for psychological reasons, should not be too low and lowly" or sited to "lose protected privacy."[22] On the other hand, positioning the house to serve these psychological, if narcissistic, goals, precluded optimal exploitation of air flows that would generate the kind of passive cooling systems he had specified for tropical regions.[23] Although climate conditions had a significant impact on the materials used (Neutra began with a steel structure, turned to wood when the cost of steel proved too high, and was eventually convinced that concrete was the only material able to withstand the combined effects of moisture and termites), they had little impact on the house's spatial organization and orientation.[24] Instead, Neutra and de Schulthess's solution to the climate question was air conditioning. From the very beginning of the design process, the principal discussion concerning environmental controls concerned what kind of air conditioning would work best—a central system that was more efficient overall, or individual room units that allowed more local control but impinged on interior space.[25] As a result, just like the spider legs that serve no psychological function, the clerestory windows between the exposed beams—so characteristic of Neutra's mid-century work and essential to his ideas about designs for hot climates—are mere vestigial remains of a cooling strategy rendered obsolete by mechanical systems. If the Country Club Park was walled off from the city, and the site was walled off against the Park, the house that appeared to embrace its tropical environment was in fact an autonomous zone of total control.

Paperwork is fundamental to modern forms of control and just as Neutra developed different kinds of architectural techniques for the "first" and "third" worlds, he developed different kinds of paperwork to manage psyches and specifications. Clients for single-family houses wrote detailed personal diaries about their domestic desires, while the Neutra office produced comprehensive specification books generic enough to apply to the whole tropical world in need of civilization.[26]

21 Contemporary reviews of the house emphasize this defensive quality. See "Tres obras de Richard Neutra/Three projects of Richard Neutra," *Arquitectura Cuba* 140 (March 1945); Jorge Mañach, "Neutra y su estela/Neutra's Inspiration," ibid., and Renato Pedio, "Villa de Schulthess a l'Avana, Cuba," *L'Architetettura: cronache e storia*, 4 (1958): 176-183.

22 Letter from Neutra to de Schulthess, Dec. 27, 1954, Neutra Archive, Box 42, Folder 9.

23 De Schulthess expressed more concern than Neutra about crosswinds and natural ventilation. To give just one example, in a letter from de Schulthess to Neutra, it is the client who suggests a reorientation of the entire house in order to "catch the day wind sufficiently." See letter from de Schulthess to Neutra, Dec. 20, 1954, Box 42, Folder 9.

24 Neutra's chief Cuban collaborator, Raúl Álvarez, played the pivotal role in the choice of a concrete structure, of many materials used inside the house, particularly local wood.

25 A continuous conversation about air conditioning runs through the entire correspondence. De Schulthess sent Neutra a punch list of key concerns: the first bullet point: "Design for Utmost in Privacy." Third bullet point: "Air Conditioning from Central Unit." Neutra asks for suggestions, in English, about what type of air conditioning would be best and if the decision can be handled via correspondence, Box 42, Folder 11. In February, letters are sent by the Neutra office to five different suppliers, including Carrier Cubana, the Havana office of Westinghouse, Victor G. Mendoza, Independent Electric Co and General Electric de Cuba, Box 42, Folder 9, memoranda dated Feb. 16, 1954. By early 1955, the decision is made not to use a central air conditioning system, out of concern that it would add too much height to the building. See letter from Dion Neutra to de Schulthess, Jan. 25, 1955, Box 42, Folder 10. The decision that all rooms, including the guest room, would have individual A/C units, led to a rearrangement that involved changes in the design of windows and the built-in cabinetry.

26 Neutra's specification books were popular with architects in Los Angeles, where they were often borrowed, copied, and circulated through projects around the city.

Conceived of in literary terms, the diaries were imagined to be stream-of-consciousness narratives awaiting translation into therapeutic architectural programs, while the specification books were office memoranda, written in an efficient and apparently non-rhetorical style. Because both Neutra and de Schulthess engaged in the design and construction of the house from a distance, the project generated an especially large amount of paperwork, even by Neutra's typically prolix standards.[27] But instead of expressing hopes for enhanced vigor or to commune with natural spirits, as other clients' diaries did, de Schulthess's writings reveal him to be a virtual caricature of the Swiss banker: his letters are dry, demanding, and fastidious. He offered "Dr. Neutra" little to work with that was not about privacy and defense, security against neighbors, against the weather, against Cuba. Utterly transactional, focused on percentages and returns, he revealed neither depth to plumb nor wildness to regulate.[28] Even his daughters could only muster a request for adequate space to organize their books and do their homework.[29] Few signs of emotion break through the tedium of their correspondence, and even those regard details. De Schulthess was thrilled, at least for a moment, during the design process, if only with the specification set he received from the Neutra office. He thanked Neutra with what, for him, was an urgent cable: "delighted with books containing such complete details impressed by thorough work of your staff."[30]

Try as he might to keep the world in its proper planetary order and to enlist the flow and categories of paperwork in that effort, it too resisted Neutra's regulations.[31] Although de Schulthess initially took some pleasure in discussing specifications, once the house was complete—the moment when many California clients sent letters to Neutra exclaiming how profoundly their life was changed by their house or how they (or at least their wives, according to Neutra) had fallen in love with him—de Schulthess sent only complaints, focused on failures in the house's ability to regulate climate conditions and on the "neuralgic" disturbances it caused.[32] If de Schulthess's expression of affect was paradoxical, a psychological response to apparently dispassionate specifications, Neutra's response to such "neuroses" was equally paradoxical: he offered the banker a way of understanding the house as a therapeutic device for overcoming the frustrations caused by the very house itself. "Irritations," he wrote to de Schulthess, "will eventually be hidden by either planting or the unconscious: at that point everything distracting, even property lines will disappear, together with all neighbors, every trace of them... Everything belongs to you up to the distant clouds, as far as the eye reaches..."[33] Tellingly, Neutra's therapeutic advice to his client is to imagine that the house will ultimately succeed in making Cuba itself disappear.

27 Although frequent worldwide travel had been key to the development of Neutra's expertise in building in tropical climates, illness increasingly kept him in Los Angeles by the 1950s.

28 Although de Schulthess engaged the design process with a virtually infinite attention to every detail, the sum total of the personal diary he gave to Neutra consisted of a short note inserted in the middle of a letter about other matters, saying: "I generally spend the mornings in my office downtown, the afternoons in my study, where I take care of my private correspondence." Letter from de Schulthess to Neutra, Dec. 26, 1954, Box 42, Folder 9. Although both he and Neutra were native German speakers, they communicated in English, except once when Neutra added a personal note in German.

29 The daughters sent individual, handwritten notes to Neutra, largely about needing desks and bookshelves. Harriet is much less visible in the archive than her husband, but when she does appear, she too is exceptionally specific, about her needs and in her way of communicating them: she added ruled drawings along with handwritten notes. See the notes from the children, Box 42, Folder 9, and Harriet's drawing appended to a letter to Neutra from de Schulthess, Feb. 6, 1955, Box 42, Folder 10.

30 See the cable sent on April 28, 1955, from de Schulthess to Neutra, Box 43, Folder 2.

31 No building code applied to the Country Club Park, which Neutra clearly found disconcerting, since Álvarez frequently needed to remind him of this, as did de Schulthess. The latter's remarks on the building code are interesting in that he quotes the advertising literature almost verbatim, making clear the various kinds of unwritten regulations about privilege and freedom that applied to those acquiring land in a supposedly unregulated zone. "We will not need a building code valid in Havana, as this code does not apply to residences in the suburbs. The only restrictions applying to the Country Club are... one cannot build Hotels, apartment houses, shops etc. There is a request to submit plans to the Country Club Association, but this is purely a formality. Moreover, I know the president personally." Letter from de Schulthess to Neutra, Dec. 19, 1954, Box 42, Folder 9.

32 "Neuralgic" may be a term de Schulthess learned from Neutra, who in turn learned it from Freud's writings on neurasthenic disorder. De Schulthess's complaints, focus on the master bedroom. According to him, the room did not get cool enough, could not be shaded adequately from the early morning sun, and was then too dark during other times of the day. For his use of the word neuralgic in particular, see his letter to Neutra, Aug. 9, 1956, Box 44, Folder 2.

33 Letter from Neutra to de Schulthess, Nov. 15, 1956, Box 44, Folder 2.

Above, left:
Richard Neutra (with Raúl Álvarez), De Schulthess House, view of servants' quarters. W. Boesiger, ed. *Richard Neutra, 1950-60. Buildings and Projects* (Zurich: Girsberger, 1959), p. 55.

Above, right:
Richard Neutra (with Raúl Álvarez), De Schulthess House, view of entry with spider legs. W. Boesiger, ed. *Richard Neutra, 1950-60. Buildings and Projects* (Zurich: Girsberger, 1959), p. 55.

Left:
Richard Neutra (with Raúl Álvarez), De Schulthess House, view of walled garden and private quarters. Barbara Mac Lamprecht, *Richard Neutra: Complete Works* (Köln, New York: Taschen, 2000), p. 31.

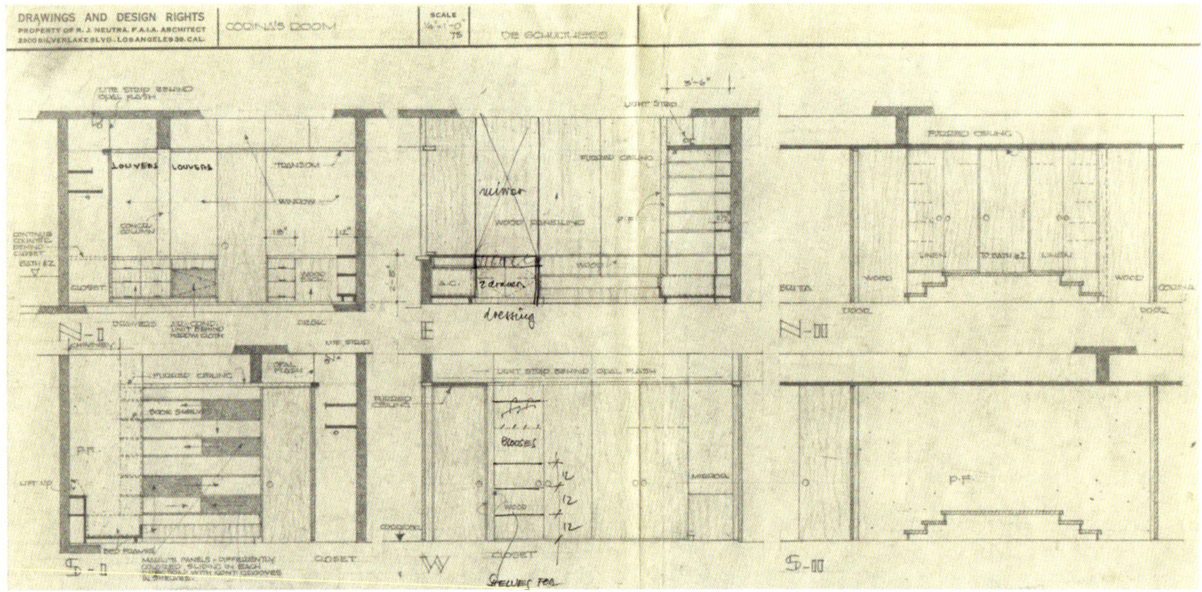

As an archive, the correspondence between de Schulthess and Neutra is most interesting not for the architecture it produced but for the overwhelming sense of disorder it symptomatically betrays. Since there was no psychological depth on which typically analytic attention could be focused, Neutra's letters to Cuba instead express his own anxiety over loss of control. Utterly dependent on Raúl Álvarez, the US-trained architect selected to serve as local architect after a lengthy process and chosen precisely because of his attention to detail and technical expertise, Neutra grew frustrated at Álvarez's increasingly slow response time, overly enthusiastic "corrections," and lack of appreciation for this opportunity to work with the American master.[34] From the outset, the letter Álvarez sent to Neutra accepting to serve as local architect provoked an immediate and disturbed response, expressing concern and surprise that details had been redrawn, suspicion that de Schulthess and Álvarez were working together outside of Neutra's sphere of influence, and insistence that only if they understood that "our specification book is 'the Bible'," and only by following its commandments would a "happy conclusion" be reached.[35] Towards the end of the process, Neutra complained that Álvarez did not respond at all.[36] Even greater chaos in communication plagued the landscape design. Neutra had taken some trouble to convince the de Schulthess couple to work with Roberto Burle Marx, but he too appeared and disappeared from the process, growing outraged when de Schulthess countermanded his planting decisions and threatening to remove his name from the project.[37] Nevertheless, Burle Marx also understood that his task was to "psychologically overcome the limitations... of the plot" by

34 The process of selecting an architect was a long one. De Schulthess recommended Roberto Pesant because they had met at a social function. (See letter from de Schulthess to Neutra, Jan. 12, 1955, Box 42, Folder 9.) Neutra sent an identical letter of inquiry to several Cuban architects, including Pesant, Eugenio Albarrán, Mario Romanach and Raúl Álvarez. Neutra eventually convinced de Schulthess to hire Álvarez, an architect who had received his degree from RPI. The other architects had all responded to Neutra's inquiry with a short note, but Álvarez's response was simultaneously highly detailed on technical matters and also very deferential. Álvarez to Richard Neutra, Feb. 14, 1955, Box 42, Folder 10. He also informed Neutra of "a new ruling by the Cuban Architect Assoc., that a foreign architect may not associate with a Cuban architect, in order to build in Cuba. A foreign architect may only be busy here in an advisory capacity." 1179, Box 42, f. 9 Dec. 19, 1954, letter from Álvarez to Neutra.

35 Frustration exudes from this letter, which in addition to insisting that Álvarez be faithful to the bible, underscores father and son's expectation that Álvarez is to "bend over backward to follow their lead." See the letter from Dion Neutra to de Schulthess, April 18, 1955, Box 43, Folder 2. Neutra also writes to de Schulthess asking that all communication go through him.

36 Álvarez eventually gives a range of excuses for his tardy responses, but often blames his delay on delays caused by the project itself. In addition to conflict and competition over credits and authorial control, Neutra and Álvarez also have financial disagreements. Neutra is furious to discover that a substantial contribution to the

designing a landscape able to "efface" or "camouflage" any signs of Havanese life.[38]

The dynamic and troubled interactions between a Swiss banker, the Country Club Park of Havana, a US-trained but Cuban-born architect, a landscape designer in Brazil and a Jewish, Hungaro-Austrian immigrant to California, clearly map an emerging "planetary" order while simultaneously revealing the untenable distinctions between civilized subjects—fully liberated from the mundane by technological and economic achievement—and rural subjects—in need of discipline and regulation—on which that map was predicated. The result was a building still celebrated for superficially appearing to confirm the worldwide spread of early 20th-century Internationalism, but fundamentally undermined by the disjunctions embedded in its foundations.

The history of the De Schulthess House is above all a tale of control systems and their failures. The paperwork on which its construction and design depended slipped in and out of order, the temperature and internal environment of the house failed to be regulated, privacy was seen as essential but always under threat, and the building's material constitution and behavior was made of an anxiety-provoking miscegenation: windows from Pittsburgh, plants from Brazil, a stereo system from New York and unskilled labor from Cuba. Even measurement, the *sine qua non* of architecture, was a source of disturbance: throughout the design process, conflict repeatedly arose over use of the imperial or the metric system, and whether drawing sheets should be sized according to US or Cuban conventions.[39] The two most telling instances of the chimerical constitution of the house are the two that most clearly fail to reinforce Neutra's self-fashioning as a planetary architect. The house is a fully air-conditioned rejection of the specifications he himself had produced for regions of mild climate,

Cuban Architects Association is expected, of which Álvarez is obviously a member. Neutra seeks to pass this fee onto de Schulthess. See Neutra to de Schulthess, June 30, 1955, Box 43, Folder 4.

37 Why Neutra wanted de Schulthess to hire a landscape architect is unclear: the most likely explanation for Neutra's insistence on bringing in Burle Marx was that he believed that the combination of Californian architect and Brazilian landscape gardener would attract international attention to a tropical project. Nevertheless, Burle Marx wrote to Neutra complaining that de Schulthess "misunderstands" his work and that "if the changes are made, I cannot be responsible for the results." Letter from Burle Marx to Neutra, June 21, 1956, Box 44, Folder 1. De Schulthess returned the favor, confessing that "we are beginning to regret our decision to have Mr. Burle Marx designing our garden." See de Schulthess to Neutra, Jan. 1, 1956, Box 44, Folder 1.

38 Burle Marx wrote: "before streets, property lines, neighboring projects clouded the basic appeal of the landscape... its unity can and must be recaptured." See document labeled "Garden of Mr. and Mrs. Alfred de Schulthess, Considerations, requirements and decisions on design," n/d., Box 43, Folder 12.

39 For example, on March 9, 1955, Neutra wrote to Mr. and Mrs. de Schulthess: "We feel that for reasons of 'politics' and to reduce the work of the Cuban Associates it would be better to draw and furnish 1 to 100 scale drawings, which we shall do, so as to pass the 'authorities.' We conclude from the information gathered that this hurdle has been set up so as to somewhat protect the local profession against foreigners." His emphasis, Box 43, Folder 1.

Photograph (5th of 8) documenting existing trees, telephone poles and other visual obstructions on site of the De Schulthess House before construction, 1955. Neutra Papers (Box 42, Folder 10).

Opposite page:
Wall elevations showing placement of air conditioning units, De Schulthess House. Neutra Papers (Box 310, Folder 11).

just as the spider legs, so fundamental to Neutra's sense of "First-World" architectural purpose, found no psyche to liberate and were instead absorbed into a uniquely Cuban logic of production. Designed initially to be in steel, they were redesigned for aluminum, then adapted to wood, which was ultimately covered in aluminum sheeting with a coating developed for the interior of 1955 Chevrolets—the cars that would come to be associated with the temporal and spatial isolation, as well as the extraordinary creative ingenuity, of post-revolution Havanese society.[40]

On the one hand, although de Schulthess occupied the house for several years, it only achieved the fully impervious status of the neutral territory it was designed to be once it had been appropriated to serve as the Swiss Embassy. On the other hand, the house's apparent neutrality is the architecture's most formidable defense against the defiant uncontrollability of life in Havana.[41] Neutra, like the house, was disturbed by many aspects of his Cuban experience, but the most distressing incident for him was the loss of his travel sketchbook recording his observations of Cuba, which is to say recording his effort to draw Cuba into his architectural perspective. Of all the kinds of paperwork to which he was attached—from the personal diaries of his mystical clients to the dry regulations he drew up for wet climates and the books he used to coordinate his credentials with shifts in architecture's political geography—he was most attached to his own travel sketchbooks, to which he could return after the fact to verify he indeed had a place in the

40 The choice of material for spider legs regularly plagued Neutra, no matter where he was building. He always wanted them in steel, and if not steel, aluminum, but the cost of both metals was always high. Clients understood them to serve no traditional function and therefore vigorously rejected the cost. Neutra had invented a work-around: using timber 2x4s nailed to wooden posts, he simulated the shape of a steel I-beam and then painted the wood silver. For the De Schulthess House, and despite much resistance from Neutra, the spider legs were built in sabicu wood. The beams were wrapped in an aluminum jacket that was then covered with Du Pont paint intended for car interiors. See cable from Álvarez to Neutra, July 11, 1955, and Neutra's cable in response, July 12, 1955, Box 43, Folder 4. See also the samples sent to the Sanfon Process Company in Los Angeles by Apex Steel Corporation with Du Pont samples, July 27, 1955, Box 43, Folder 4.

41 Many houses in the Country Club Park were converted into student housing after the Revolution, but the De Schulthess House was not.

Advertisement for Solex plate glass designed to absorb heat. This is one of many advertisements for building components, many of them designed for climate mitigation, made by US manufacturers, located with the papers on the De Schulthess House. Neutra Papers (Box 43, Folder 1).

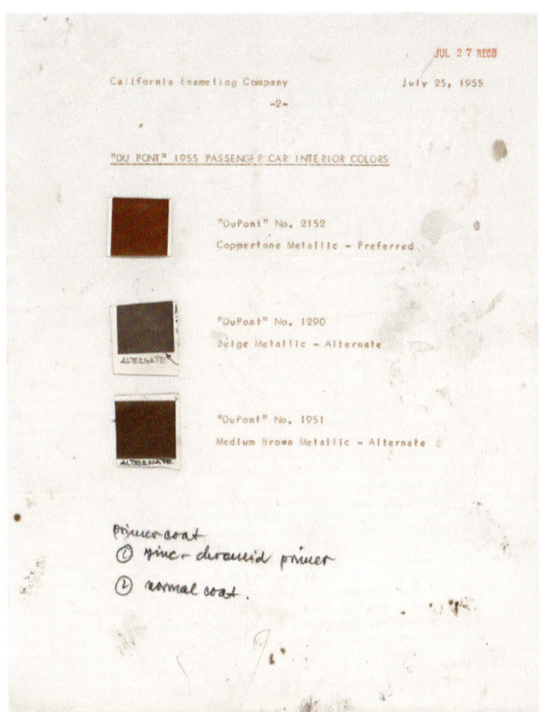

JUL 27 RECD

California Enameling Company July 25, 1955

-2-

"DU PONT" 1955 PASSENGER CAR INTERIOR COLORS

"DuPont" No. 2152
Coppertone Metallic - Preferred

ALTERNATE

"DuPont" No. 1290
Beige Metallic - Alternate

ALTERNATE

"DuPont" No. 1951
Medium Brown Metallic - Alternate

primer coat
① zinc-chromid primer
② normal coat.

Paint samples sent, along with samples of embossed aluminum, to be applied as veneer to the spider legs at the entry of the De Schulthess House. Neutra Papers (Box 43, Folder 1).

new planetary order. The last files of the de Schulthess archive are filled with desperate letters asking Álvarez to find the missing book. Álvarez searched high and low, indefatigably retracing Neutra's steps through Havana, but the book had been swallowed up by the deregulating life of the city.[42] Just as Neutra's architectural journey began on a ride beneath Vienna, his Cuban adventure ended somewhere along the Malecón, disturbing the poles of psyches and specifications, leaving a house torn between the vibrant heat of Old Havana and the neutral coolness of the Country Club Park, and exposing the racialized and classist biases undergirding the expertise of the global architect.[43]

42 Álvarez recounts his retracing of Neutra's steps in a letter to Dione, Neutra's wife. She encouraged the quest for the book in an effort to soothe Neutra, whose grief over the loss was exacerbated by illness. See the letter from Álvarez to Dione Neutra, Dec. 16, 1955, Box 43, Folder 4.

43 Neutra tried his best to return to Cuba in 1963, after an invitation to be a guest of the Colegio Nacional de Arquitectos in Havana. He appealed directly to Hubert H. Humphrey in his effort to secure a visa. His request was denied. See the letter from Humphrey to Diane (*sic*) Neutra, Aug. 21, 1963, Box 318, Folder 1.

REVOLT IN RADIOCENTRO: THE SAMPLE BAR, CAIGNET'S ANNOYING SILENCES, AND BATISTA'S RADIO-EXECUTION

Andrés Jaque

Cuba's Revolution happened as modern architecture; it was through the infrastructures, the inventions and the direct contribution of modern architecture that revolutionary ideas and actions were performed, broadcasted, funded, and assembled. Modern, pre-revolutionary architecture in Havana is often described as the enactor of Batista's regime—evidence of his US-run economic and cultural coloniality unfolding on the island. And yes, it was. But those descriptions often fail to explain how modern architecture dashed revolution. The July 26 Movement confronted ideologically the intentions of this modernity; but the societal entanglements that buildings mobilize always exceed the ideologies that motivate them in the first place. The Revolution grew through material and societal apparatuses, which buildings, infrastructures and ways-of-doing anticipated. The Revolution had an intimate relationship with Radiocentro CMQ that has never been explained. It was at Radiocentro's studios that Castro gave his first interminable speech.[1]

Both pages:
Radiocentro CMQ, Havana, Cuba. Architects: Martín Domínguez Esteban, Miguel Gastón and Emilio del Junco. Archivo Martín Domínguez Esteban, Museo Nacional Centro de Arte Reina Sofía, Madrid. All images in this chapter, unless otherwise indicated, are from this archive.

1 Pablo Sirven, "Goar Mestre, el rey de la televisión que apoyó a Fidel y terminó despojado," *La Nación*, November 29, 2016.

It was the radio station Circuito CMQ that provided the means for the Revolution to reconfigure as a media. It was through the narratives and the physical space of Radiocentro that Castro staged his confrontation with the Spanish colonial legacy.[2] It was the Revolution *as* Radiocentro when it simulated the execution of Fulgencio Batista.

Around 3:30 p.m., on March 13, 1957, the architecture student and revolutionary leader José Antonio Echeverría, known as "Manzanita," accompanied by a hundred armed revolutionaries, attacked the Master Control of the Radiocentro CMQ Building. Interrupting the national radio program Radio Reloj (Radio Clock), he addressed his fellow Cubans: "People of Cuba! Just now, Dictator Fulgencio Batista has been revolutionarily executed, while sleeping in his own lair of the Presidential Palace. The People of Cuba have gone there to settle accounts with him; and it is we, the Revolutionary Directory, who in the name of the Cuban Revolution have dealt the coup de grace to this regime of opprobrium. Cubans listening to me: It has just been removed."[3]

Batista, safe and well in the Presidential Palace, followed the news of his own death. Meanwhile, Manzanita, after leaving Radiocentro, tried to find shelter at the university, where he was eventually killed in a police raid. It was too late, though. Once the Revolution radio-killed Batista, it was only a matter of time before his dictatorship came to an end. At that time, Cuba was constituted as radio. Both the possibility and the end of Batista's dictatorship was in radio. The CMQ radio station was partnered with NBC. Cuba was the laboratory where CBS and NBC tested, from the 1920s, the creation of a Pan-American Radio Zone. The radio was the

2 Teresa Amiguet, "El español que retó a Castro," *La Vanguardia*, November 28, 2016.

3 Faure Chomón, "El ataque al Palacio Presidencial," in *La sierra y el llano* (Havana: Casa de la Américas, 1969).

4 Oscar Luis López, *La radio en Cuba: Estudio de su desarrollo en la sociedad neocolonial* (Havana: Editorial Letras Cubanas, 1981).

5 Ibid.

6 Ricardo Martínez Víctores, *7RR. La historia de Radio Rebelde. Testimonio* (Havana: Editora Política, 2008).

7 Sirven, "Goar Mestre, el rey de la televisión."

Radiocentro CMQ. Detail, theater entrance. Joaquín E. Weiss, ***Arquitectura contemporánea: colección de fotografías de los más recientes y característicos edificios erigidos en Cuba*** (Havana: Cultural, 1947), p. 45.

Radiocentro CMQ: first design. Joaquín E. Weiss, *Arquitectura contemporánea: colección de fotografías de los más recientes y característicos edificios erigidos en Cuba* (Havana: Cultural, 1947), p. 44.

means and the subject of colonizing the Americas. It propelled US industrial growth and expansion of its commercial and political domains.[4] In 1952, when the US-supported Batista dictatorship started, there were 500,000 radio receivers in Cuba, 200,000 in Havana alone.[5] Batista's radio-death was the beginning of the Revolution's intervention in Cuba's radio zone. On February 24, 1958, Radio Rebelde started to broadcast their twice-daily reports at 5 and 9 p.m. from the Sierra Maestra. Radio Rebelde not only coordinated the different sections of the Revolution and helped recruit fighters and supporters among the Cubans; it was also a fundraising channel that allowed international donors to support its cause.[6]

CMQ's chief executive, Goar Mestre, was concerned with Batista's local corruption, destabilizing use of violence, and impulsiveness, because they jeopardized the radio-colonial project Mestre was so intensively committed to through CMQ's association with NBC. He donated to Fidel Castro the mimeograph that was used to print *El Cubano Libre*,[7] the long-lapsed nationalist newspaper

DIARIO DE LA MARINA.—MARTES, 23 DE DICIEMBRE DE 1947

CRONICA HABANERA

Monseñor Alfredo Müller bendijo ayer tarde el Teatro Warner, cuya inauguración será esta noche

En la tarde de ayer el R. Padre Monseñor Alfredo Müller bendijo el nuevo cine Warner, situado en el edificio Radio Centro, en el Vedado, sirviendo de madrina de esta ceremonia la bondadosa dama Lily Hidalgo de Conill. Para hoy está señalada la inauguración del mismo, celebrándose con una gran función de gala dedicada generosamente por la empresa a los niños pobres de esta capital.

En representación de las instituciones benéficas que recibirán el producto de esta función de gala, aparecen en la foto, junto a Monseñor Müller y Lily Hidalgo de Conill, las señoras Gloria Montalvo de García Ordóñez, Lolita Barraqué de Del Monte, Ofelia Cortina de Arango, Sarah Giménez de Conill, Manolita Bravo de Cañal, Silvia Freyre de Fernández, Alicia Martínez de Mestre, esposa de nuestro distinguido amigo Goar Mestre; nuestra compañera Regina de Marcos y otras distinguidas damas.

Las instituciones benéficas que recibirán el aporte de la función son: Patronato Pro Hospital Infantil, Colegio San Vicente de Paúl y Asilo y Creche de la Habana Nueva y del Vedado.

Con "Radiocentro" se cumplió una hermosa y gigantesca jornada. El edificio podía albergar cuatro emisoras de radio, un teatro, restaurantes, establecimientos de todas clases, oficinas... Era una ciudad dentro de otra.

La inauguración de "Radiocentro" provocó el entusiasmo popular. Prueba de ello es esta fotografía, donde se ve al enorme público que hacía cola, impaciente, para visitar el nuevo edificio el día de su inauguración, en 1949.

Above left:
Monsignor Alfredo Müller blessing the Warner theater. "Crónica Habanera," *Diario de la Marina*, December 23, 1947.

Above right:
Bohemia (December 1953).

Right:
Bohemia (December 1953).

which revolutionary groups relaunched as a propaganda tool in 1957 from El Hombrito, in Sierra Maestra. Mestre, the son of drugstore owners from Santiago, a Yale graduate, and the proprietor (with his brothers Abel and Luis Augusto) of various businesses, had acquired 50 percent of CMQ by 1943, and became its CEO at a time when its signal did not reach beyond Havana. With the support of NBC, Mestre negotiated with the Central Trust of the Cuban Telephone Company, a subsidiary of the American International Telephone and Telegraph Corporation (ITT), to allow CMQ to develop a telephone network to send its live signal to seven antennas distributed over the island. This network of antennas expanded and synchronized the outlet's reach to the entirety of Cuba. Mestre mobilized the capacity of radio to unify a population divided by four centuries of colonial, racist, and classist rule by Spain. Under this new radiophonic regime, Cubans would be unified by a shared time, a shared consumption and shared promises (imported from America) of social and territorial mobility.

Radiocentro CMQ after the attack to Radio Reloj, March 13, 1957.

Radio Reloj was a crucial confirmation of this radio-rule. In 1947, six years before Manzanita's radio-attack, CMQ launched Radio Reloj—"the radio that serves punctuality," as it was advertised. It worked as a broadcasted clock. The announcement of each minute was followed by news, commercials, and the sound of a gong.[8] This was an alliance between societal coordination, commerce, and fact-making by which CMQ, in close collaboration with its US corporate partners, could unify Cuba's realities, consumptions and times. Both the expansion of CMQ as a national outlet, and its growing role in the societal and commercial coordination of Cuba, encouraged Mestre to lobby for an exceptional new building.

8 Enrique C. Betancourt, *Apuntes para la historia. Radio, Televisión y Farándula de la Cuba de Ayer* (San Juan de Puerto Rico: Apuntes para la historia, 1986).

This was Radiocentro. Sited on 23rd Avenue—La Rampa—between L and M streets, it was constructed between 1945 and 1947 and cost $3 million. The building was divided into five parts: a 1,650-seat theater open to the public and leased to Warner Brothers; a vertical back-house of technical machinery, which was equipped with the first centralized air conditioning system built on the island, to guarantee that the equipment would work in Havana's weather; seven floors of office space, mostly leased; a separate volume housing two large radio studios; and a commercial gallery with twelve shops, a bank, a two-story restaurant and an automobile showroom, all opening onto La Rampa. This mall constituted a podium and access point to the rest. It unfolded into several floors connected at different levels through a baroque and redundant system of ramps, staircases and balconies that directed La Rampa's intense pedestrian flows into the building. The building's expression did not rely on its broadcasting technology. During its pre-TV era, it did not even have a visible antenna. There was no need: the signal traveled from the

Radiocentro CMQ. View from across Calle 23.

building by telephone wires connected to the radio stations in Bella Vista and Playa Arena, from which it would be aired.

Most commentators of this building pay attention to what seems to be its most distinguished part, the theater. However, it is the entrance at the north-facing façade off La Rampa, rather than the theater, that engages most richly in the building's socio-political project. There, architectural components intended to enact specialized forms of societal construction, such as trading, news-making, management and entertainment, are brought together in what is really an architectural device, whose main function is to rearticulate Cuba socially. The US Kaiser-Frazer Car Gallery, the employee entrance to the Circuito CMQ offices and studios, the entrances to the shopping center and to the restaurant and bar—all are carefully interconnected by the complex series of staircases and walkways. (This manifold is actually the space where Tomás Gutiérrez Alea shot the famous scene in *Memories of Underdevelopment* [1968] in which his main characters negotiate their desire.) The plans of this part of the building show how much care and specificity were put into the design of the stairs. If the general definition of enclosed space follows standard design strategies, it is in stairways and walkways that singularity and specialization are packed. And the closer we get to the bar, the more the staircases seem to speed up. These staircases and their role cater to a project that remains unexplained. A project for societal articulation that would probably only work if it were never explicitly articulated.

The architect of Radiocentro, Martín Domínguez Esteban (alongside Miguel Gastón and Emilio del Junco) already had a prominent career in Spain when he went as an exile to Cuba in 1937. He was a member of the Generación del 25, a small group of architects who shaped the Spanish Second Republic in line with modern ideas found in the 1925 International Exhibition of Modern Decorative and Industrial Arts in Paris. His work, in association with Carlos Arniches, has been mostly studied through singular buildings, such as the Hipódromo de la Zarzuela or the Pabellón de Párvulos at the Instituto Escuela (both Madrid, 1935, though the hippodrome was only completed after the Civil War). Both feature spectacular cantilevered structures developed in collaboration with the structural engineer Eduardo Torroja. And yet Domínguez and Arniches did many other things that together give a better sense of their focus in architecture.

From 1926 to 1928 they published a weekly column, "La arquitectura y la vida" (Architecture and Life) in the progressive newspaper *El Sol*.[9] They designed filmmaker and playwright Edgar Neville's penthouse, a design that attracted Le Corbusier's attention during his visit to Madrid in 1928. They also built a reputation as

9 Concha Díez-Pastor, *La arquitectura y la vida. Los artículos de Arniches y Domínguez en El Sol y otros escritos* (Selfpublished, Safe-Creative, 2016).

Architects Martín Domínguez Esteban (below, left), Emilio del Junco and Miguel Gastón (middle, center), with engineers Manuel Padrón and Bartolomé Bestard (above, right), at the Radiocentro building site, 1946.

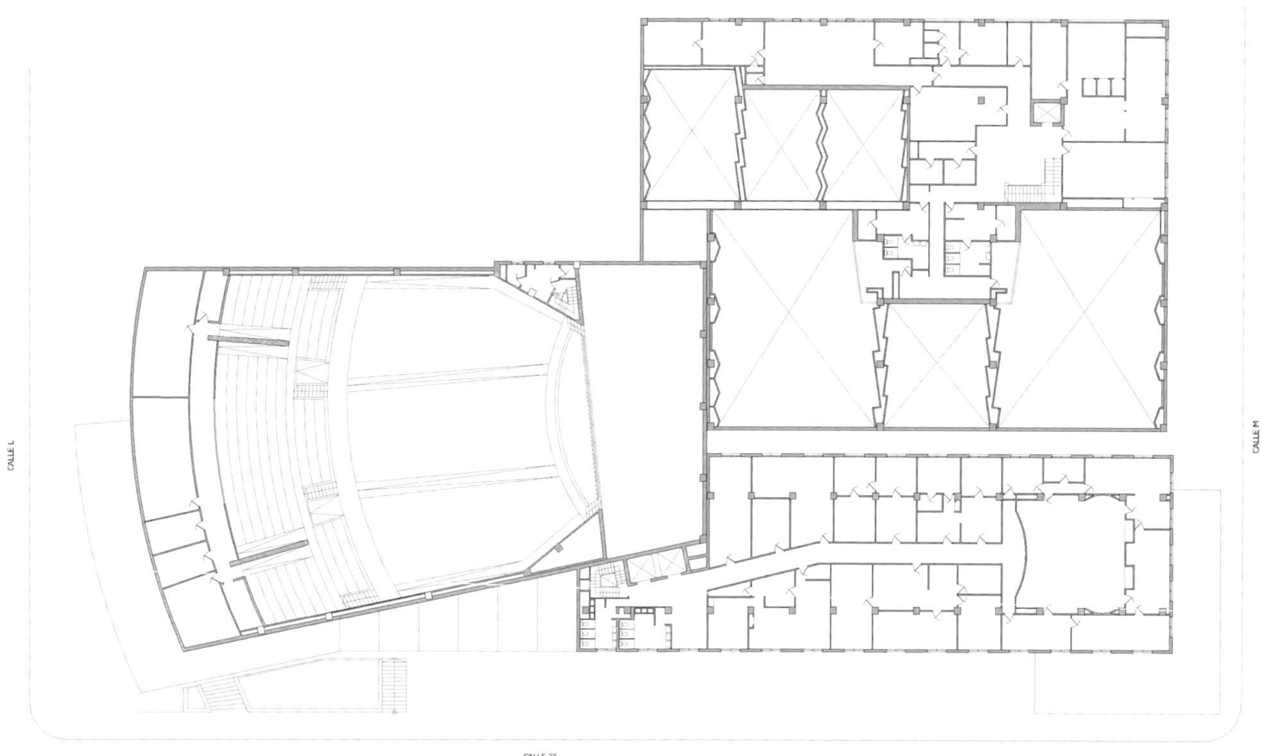

Radiocentro CMQ. First floor plan.

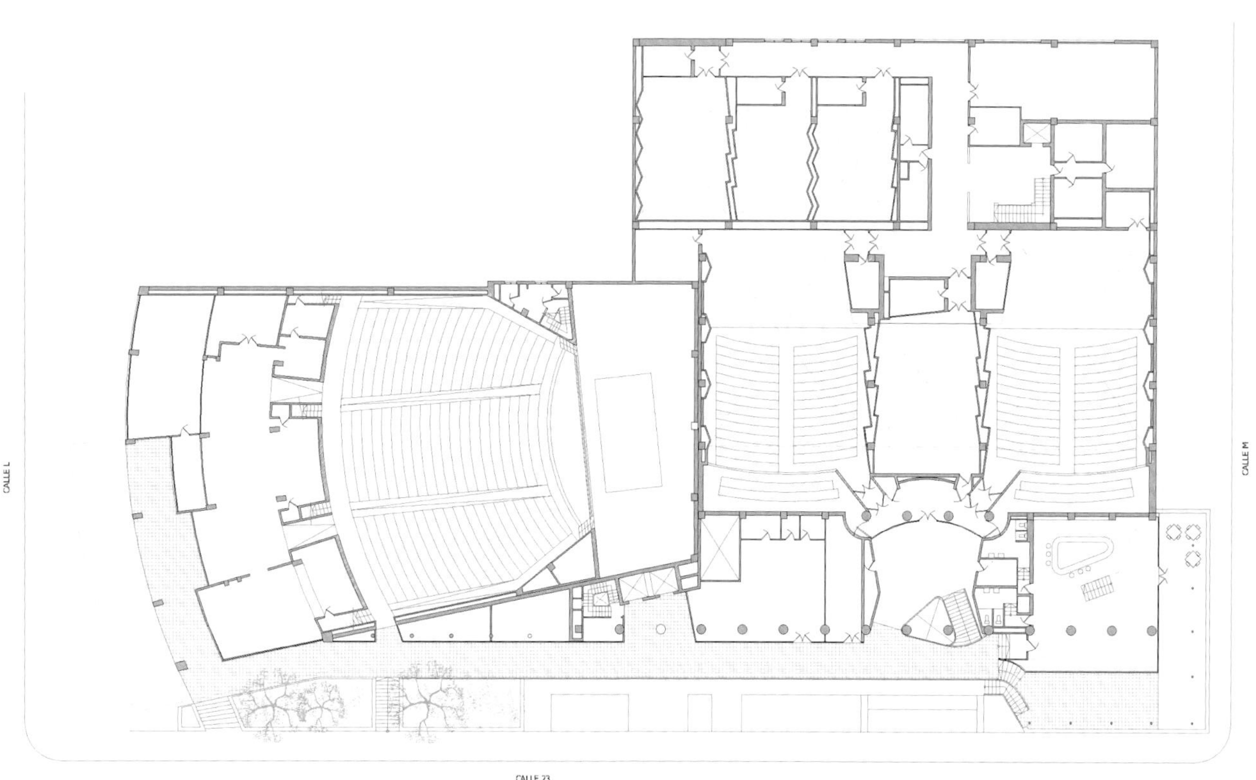

Radiocentro CMQ. Ground floor plan.

the designers of the most fashionable bars in the city. In 1924 they redesigned the Granja El Henar, a well-known cauldron for collective thinking.[10] They designed the Café Zahara on the Gran Vía in 1930, in collaboration with Secundino Zuazo, and the Hotel Palace's "Bar" (1925), a structure resembling a circus tent that eventually became an extension of their own architectural office. These all constituted an architectural enactment that operated across media, scale and materiality to render the Spanish Second Republic as a space for societal and political experimentations of modernity.

In 1937, the year Martín Dominguez arrived in Cuba, Cubans had the highest per capita consumption of soap in Latin America. This market became strategic for two US companies, Colgate-Palmolive and Procter & Gamble, which fought for this market through their Cuban subsidiaries, Crusellas and Sabates. These two companies saw radio as a great tool to reach their target of domestic soap buyers.[11] Crusellas worked with CMQ, and Sabates with CMQ's competitor, Radio Azul.[12] The need to scrutinize the effects of soap advertisement on potential consumers triggered the development of an unprecedented audience-survey industry in Cuba. Each survey consisted of more than 50,000 interviews, conducted by an army of interviewers who visited potential listeners at their homes.[13] One was the radio author, composer, and poet Félix Caignet, who at the beginning of his career made a living by running house to house to do these interviews. Being himself a radio scriptwriter, he was able to exploit the knowledge he thereby gleaned in his own work.[14]

This exceptional insight allowed Félix Caignet to revolutionize the format of *radionovelas* (also known as *novelas jabonosas*, soap operas, in reference to the soap companies that sponsored them) with his series *El derecho de nacer* (The Right to be Born). It was launched by CMQ in 1948 and aired live from the then brand-new studios of Radiocentro in La Rampa. The story begins with the daughter of a wealthy, respectable man. Unmarried and pregnant, she is pressed by her father to have an abortion, something she avoids with the help of her racialized servant, Mamá Dolores. This heroine takes care of her son and turns him into the prosperous and earnest Doctor Limonta, who later becomes an anti-abortion militant.

El derecho de nacer was an instant and unprecedented hit, adapted and broadcasted in almost all Spanish-speaking countries. It had an equally fertile life in multiple telenovelas and films, and continues to influence those media. The story structure is basic and effective: a virtuous, impoverished woman is moved by love and climbs the social ladder by fixing the mess that "morally loose," wealthy males can cause. In each episode, the virtuous woman faces a fork in the

Félix B. Caignet.
Reynaldo González, *El más humano de los autores* (Havana: Ediciones Unión, 2009).

10 It was here that Ortega y Gasset developed, in open discussion with other intellectuals who frequented the café, that landmark magazine of philosophy and science in Spain and Latin America: *Revista de Occidente*. Here, too, Ramón María del Valle-Inclán, Benito Pérez Galdós and Manuel Azaña hosted their weekly *tertulias* (Domínguez and Arniches also held a weekly *tertulia* there).

11 Jesús A. Chía Garzón, *El monopolio del jabón y el perfume en Cuba* (Havana: Ed. Ciencias Sociales, 1977).

12 Michael B. Salwen, *Radio and Television in Cuba: The Pre-Castro Era* (Ames: Iowa State University Press, 1994).

13 Ibid.

14 Reynaldo González, *El más humano de los autores* (Havana: Ediciones Unión, 2009).

Radiocentro CMQ. Ground floor view.
Archivo del Instituto Cubano de Arte e
Industria Cinematográficos.

Radiocentro CMQ. First floor view.

road; in her search for justice she has to choose between insisting on her natural goodness—that is to say, remaining compliant within a classist, sexist, colonial and racist order—or challenging and disobeying it. These two options are clearly marked by the episodes' structure. Two secondary characters offer advice to the lead (the virtuous woman), each of them polarizing their defense of either compliance or confrontation. A long—too long—silence follows. Then the main character invariably makes the wrong call, deciding not to challenge the repressive status quo.

The language of radio and telenovelas has been marked by the long silences Caignet introduced into the genre. These silences are actually the result of an architectural innovation located in the bar of the Radiocentro building. A careful inspection of the floorplan shows how complex are the circulations in the upper part of the two-story restaurant, where the ameba-shaped island-bar is located. This small space is filled by two very different publics, brought together by the passive action of two staircases. One public comes up a main staircase from the restaurant's lower floor, which is open to the people on La Rampa. The other public climbs the smaller stairs that connect with the lobby and allow access to the bar from the studios and the CMQ offices. These two staircases are designed so that in this tiny bar the workers of the radio station will mix with their audience (the people off the street). According to one expert on Latin American media, Caignet, in a technique based on his old interviews, would read aloud the part of the script where the challenge to the main character unfolds; then he would carefully listen to the reactions of the crowd at the bar. He would then rewrite the scene, amplifying those aspects that most riled the bar audience.[15] The silences, in radionovelas, are the moment when the audience at home debates what the main character is going to do: defy or obey. Even though Cuba was highly influenced by Spanish Catholic morality, abortion in Cuba was legal and broadly accepted at the time when *El derecho de nacer* was broadcasted. Day after day, Cuban audiences were annoyed by a show where Spanish actors, with Spanish accents,[16] imposed a dated morality on victims of the colonial power.

Architecture never works alone, and its designers' intentions are never that important. The architecture of Radiocentro came to be a messy overlap where Cuba's radio-reconstruction intersected with its bar, its multiplying staircases, Caignet's indignation-triggering-silences, and the soap-driven, Pan-American coloniality of Batista's radio-death fueled by anti-colonial anger. Radiocentro was constituted as the enactment of societal reconstruction, through media-triggered ire. That specific form of collective and scalable irritation resulted from the cooperation between a building

15 Jesús Martín-Barbero, *Oficio de cartógrafo. Travesías Latinoamericanas de la comunicación en la cultura* (Mexico City: Fondo de Cultura Económica, 2002).

16 The Spanish actors María Valero (Isabel García del Castillo) and José Goula (Don Rafael del Junco) would attract the lion's share of listeners' animosity.

Radiocentro CMQ. Interior view of the Warner Theater.

whose layout allowed for sampling and scrutinizing the emotions of large audiences (melodramatic radio silences), a networked infrastructure for radio coordination across Cuba, and a nascent storytelling industry drawing on the insights of massive media polling. The July 26 Movement confronted many of the interests, ideologies and forms of coloniality Radiocentro catered to, but it also grew as the material and performed reality that Radiocentro embodied. The Revolution grew as modern architecture, and through modern architecture.

BERLIN TO HAVANA; SANTIAGO TO BERLIN: MIES'S OFFICE BUILDING FOR CIA. RON BACARDÍ, SA, SANTIAGO DE CUBA

Bart-Jan Polman

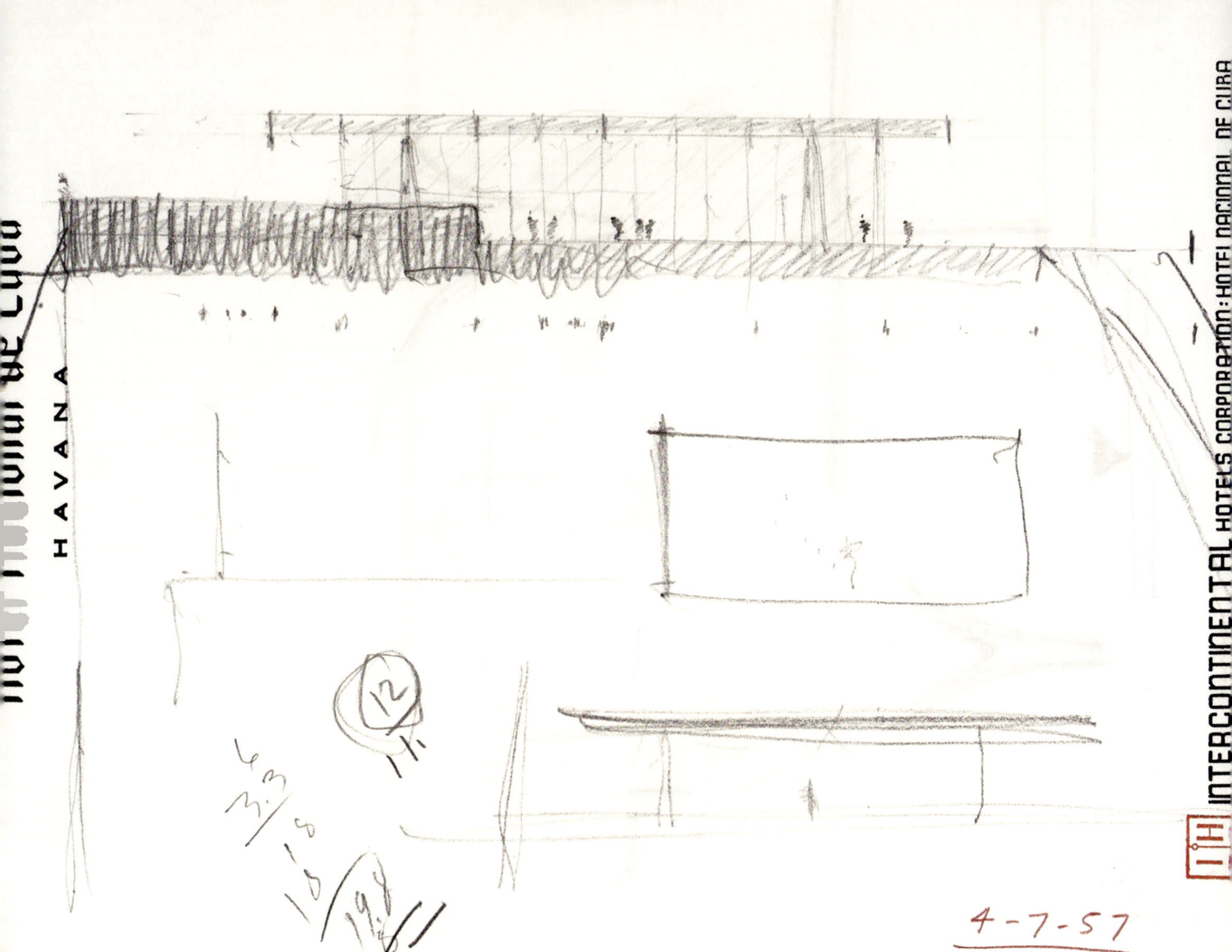

When Pan American Flight 436 landed in Havana, Cuba, on April 4, 1957, at 5:45 p.m., Havana's Hilton Hotel was already under construction. But it would not open until 1958, which made it too early for one of its passengers, Ludwig Mies van der Rohe, to stay in this key example of a corporate modernism that had come to define (not least through the visitor's own influence) large chunks of global architectural production during the 1950s.[1] With his assistant Gene Summers, Mies resided in the nearby Hotel Nacional instead.[2] Designed by the American firm McKim, Mead and White together with Ernesto Gómez Sampera in 1930, the eclectic neocolonial architecture of the Nacional featured a cloister-like courtyard enclosed on three sides. Situated on a slightly elevated plot of land wedged between Vedado and the Malecón, the courtyard opened towards the Gulf of Mexico, most of its rooms exposed to the salty ocean air. If, in a testament to the fluidity of architectural terminology, the

Both pages:
Mies van der Rohe and Gene Summers. Sketches for the Ron Bacardí y Compañia, S. A., Administration Building, project, Santiago, Cuba, 1957. Museum of Modern Art, Mies van der Rohe Archive.

1 I would like to express my gratitude to Rubén Gallo for his feedback and many of the insights given in this text, as well as for his invaluable help in accessing the archival material at MoMA. The flight details come from a telegram Mies sent to José Bosch on March 27, 1957. Mies van der Rohe Archives, Museum of Modern Art, New York, 5701 Bacardi Office building Cuba (Hereafter Mies Archive), Box 1, Folder 1.

2 The Hotel Riviera, another example, was also under construction and would open in late 1957, after Mies's arrival. The concrete Capri Hotel opened in November 1957 as well.

"neoclassical" architecture of Karl Friedrich Schinkel had been important for the "modernist" Mies, then the "neocolonial" features of the Hotel Nacional would also leave a mark on the architect's designs. Not so much because of an alleged universality but through a specific locality; an architectural ambiguity that aesthetically mirrored the very real twentieth-century fate of Cuba itself, hovering between implicit and explicit forms of colonialism, environmental abstractions, and revolution.[3]

Mies made at least two trips to the island: in April 1957, before the Revolution, and in February 1959, soon after.[4] He had come to Havana on the invitation of José Bosch, an executive at the Bacardí rum distillery in search of an architect for Bacardí's new headquarters in Santiago de Cuba.[5] Bosch would play a central role in the development of Bacardí as an increasingly international brand. Known as "Pepín," the Cuban-born executive had married into the Bacardí family and would head the company from 1944 until 1976. Instrumental to the company long before (his obituary in the *New York Times* credits him for pulling the brand through a near-bankruptcy during the Great Depression), he would oversee its eventual move away from Castro's Cuba in the early 1960s.[6]

Initially, for more than a year after Castro seized power on January 1, 1959, the company had a reasonable relationship with the revolutionary regime. Bacardí had long been linked to Cuban independence and Bosch, at first, supported the Revolution vehemently. As one of the engineers for the project, Luis Sáenz, describes in a letter to Mies on January 22, 1959 (three weeks after Castro had taken charge):

3 For a recent reading of the hotel's architectural significance in relation to Cuban politics, see: Erica N. Morawski, "Negotiating the Hotel Nacional de Cuba: Politics, Profits, and Protest," in *Journal of the Society of Architectural Historians*, vol. 78, no. 1 (2019): 90-108.

4 The first trip to Havana, which appeared to have also included a visit to the Santiago site, was April 4 until the 7th or 8th: "will arrive in Havana at 5:45pm Th April 4th by Pan American Flight 436." Telegram Mies van der Rohe to José Bosch, March 27, 1957. Mies Archive, 5701 Bacardi Office building Cuba, Box 1, Folder 1. And: "Mies and I arrive Havana Sunday Feb. 1, 5:45pm Pan Am 436." Telegram Gene Summers to Ignacio Martín, Saenz-Cancio-Martín, January 28, 1959. Ibid., Box 1, Folder 2.

5 Bacardí originated in Santiago and in the 1940s new laboratories were built by the architect Enrique Luis Varela. In the 1950s an addition to the plant was realized by Ermina Odoardo and Ricardo Eguilior. See: Victor Deupí and Jean-François Lejeune, *Cuban Modernism: Mid-Century Architecture 1940-1970* (Basel: Birkhäuser Verlag, 2021), p. 190.

6 *New York Times*, March 1, 1994, p. B-10.

Courtyard of the Hotel Nacional in Havana, Cuba, designed by McKim, Mead, and White.

> One of the happiest individuals among the millions of happy Cubans at present is Mr. Bosch, who made splendid contributions to the revolutionary cause. Mr. Bosch, in his great happiness, is enthusiastic about putting his ideas to work, convincing us of the advisability of taking the necessary steps to secure the authorization for building the Offices at Santiago de Cuba.[7]

Bosch's remarks are understandable given Castro's program would not take a distinct socialist turn until 1961. Mies's office, too, seemed in favor of the change. "*We all share with you the happiness you must have with the success of Castro and the people of Cuba,*" Summers wrote to Bosch on January 13, 1959. "*Our office was keeping up with every move these last few days.*"[8] Yet the first recorded issues between Bosch and Castro's regime appear around June 1959 already, and during 1960 it became clear that Bacardí's agenda was ultimately incompatible with the Cuban Revolution.[9] It represented too many of the "evils" that Castro wanted to banish from the island: American tourism; the casino industry; nightlife (with its connection to sex work). Ultimately, a wave of nationalizations—including the confiscation of Bacardí's facilities in October 1960—made Bosch leave the country together with the company he led.

Rum production persisted on the island, but now rebranded as an ideological, socialist commodity produced by the state; a commodity that as "Havana Club" or through "Cuba Libres" provided a way to generate foreign currency for the partially isolated regime.[10] To an extent, therefore, what Bacardí did before the Revolution could continue afterwards in altered form, as an almost identical means to a different end, with different optics and under different ownership. Similarly, continuation was ensured for the brand(ing) itself. Bosch had commissioned Mies in 1957 to design an administration building for Bacardí in Cuautitlán, Mexico. Work proceeded on both the Santiago and Mexico projects simultaneously for a time during 1958/1959, and the latter would be completed in 1962 (the year of Bacardí's centennial, and the year in which the Mies-developed scheme for the company's headquarters in Santiago was also scheduled to open[11]). While the Santiago project came close to construction—Mies's office billed for hundreds of hours during 1957, 1958, and 1959, and the project was specified in great detail, up to the light and bathroom fixtures—it would be abandoned sometime during 1960.[12] And Bosch, having left Cuba, continued to commission internationally operating firms, as he had done with high-profile architects including Philip Johnson and Félix Candela.[13]

The contentious years before, during, and after the Revolution—as well as the eventual instability of Bacardí's position in Cuba—obscure the fact that the company had long stressed the closeness

7 Luis Sáenz to Mies, January 22, 1959. Mies Archive, 5701 Bacardi Office building Cuba, Box 1, Folder 5.

8 Letter Gene Summers to José Bosch, January 13, 1959. Mies van der Rohe Archives, Museum of Modern Art, New York, 5701 Bacardi Office building Cuba, Box 1, Folder 2.

9 A letter dated June 17, most likely 1959, describes the intent by the government to cut through Bacardí's property with a new avenue. José Bosch to Gene Summers, June 17, 1959(?). By May 1960, there was talk of "disturbing events in Cuba." Robert Cooper to Gene Summers, 29 May 1960. Mies Archive, 5701 Bacardi Office building Cuba, Box 1, Folder 2 and Box 2, Folder 12.

10 Havana Club was originally another Cuban rum brand. While Bacardí owns the rights to distribute the name-brand in the US and its territories, the Cuban government, through a contested arrangement with Pernod Ricard, distributes its own Havana Club in other parts of the world. Historically it has been a way for the revolutionary regime to export, and therefore earn foreign currency, amidst various embargos.

11 The centennial was central to Bacardí's branding through architecture, and was planned well ahead. "In 1962 we expect to celebrate our centenary and this building also has the object to receive adequately our visitors from all parts of the World on that occasion." José Bosch to Mies, Feb. 14, 1957. Mies Archive, 5701 Bacardi Office building Cuba, Box 1, Folder 1.

12 At least, in May 1960 talks about construction were still going on, and the installation of the roof had originally been scheduled for June 1960. "I am sorry to say that the Cuba bldg. is not as yet under construction. We are still working on drawings but the date on which it will get under way is still not known to us." Gene Summers to Robert Cooper, France, May 31, 1960. And: "We expect construction to start next year but due to the political problems now in Cuba, I would advise your checking again around June 1960 as the roof should be in place at that time." Gene Summers to Robert Cooper, France, Dec. 16, 1959. Mies Archive, 5701 Bacardi Office building Cuba, Box 2, Folder 13.

13 1957 was a key year in this regard, as in addition to Mies, Bosch commissioned Félix Candela to design Bacardi a bottling plant in Cuautitlán, Mexico, as well as Philip Johnson to design Bosch's beach house in Varadero, Cuba. In 1958, in search of a Japanese pavilion for the Mexico plant, Gene Summers recommended the Japanese architect Junzo Yoshimura. Gene Summers to José Bosch, July 1958. Mies Archive, 5701 Bacardi Office building Cuba, Box 1, Folder 2.

of its ties to the island. As a benefactor of art and architecture it cleverly branded itself both culturally and commercially as a liquor-rich destination just south of the US. Like the company's first president, Emilio Bacardí, Bosch was a cultural promotor of sorts who used modern architecture to sell the brand before and after the Revolution. Recent scholarship has done much to show how Bacardí's architectural commissions had for a long time served as ways both to strengthen the family's role as benefactors of the arts and to expand the reach of the brand itself (to be sure, these goals are not mutually exclusive).[14] The Emilio Bacardí Moreau Municipal Museum in Santiago, for example, designed by Carlos Segrera in 1928 to house the Bacardí family art collection, illustrates the benefactor role. And the branding can be best understood through the 1930 Art Deco Bacardí building in Havana, designed by Rafael Fernández Ruenes, Esteban Rodríguez-Castells, and José Menéndez. Built before Vedado emerged as the city's tourist center in the 1930s, it was situated on the border of Centro Habana and Habana Vieja, then the business and financial center of Havana. Here, tourists could drink free cocktails in a bar on the ground floor, strengthening Cuba's image as a looser, more festive destination compared to its American neighbor. At the same time, as the architectural historian Kathryn O'Rourke has argued, the resemblance of the building to early American skyscrapers sought to reassure tourists that it was similar to the "trusted" companies back home in New York or Chicago.[15] In Cuba as elsewhere, Art Deco had become synonymous with a new and advanced wave of modernity in the second half of the 1920s thanks to its apparent lack of historical referencing.[16]

During those early twentieth-century decades, Bacardí also sought to actively promote itself through significant architecture abroad (perhaps not surprising for what was effectively Cuba's first multinational company ever since it opened a bottling plant in Barcelona, Spain, in 1910).[17] The company rented spaces in New York's Empire State building and, just like its competitor Seagram's Whiskey, in the city's Chrysler building. As the spatial practitioners Cooking Sections have demonstrated, while prohibition enabled Bacardí to flourish with its "clear" liquor to the south of the US, Seagram's "brown" whiskey was similarly advantaged to its North, in Canada.[18] Decades later, Bosch's commissioning of Mies—whose Seagram building in New York was by then already under construction—fits within Bacardí's consistent architectural engagement and offers a curious twist in architectural history: one in which two competing liquor companies eventually got to be associated with the office of Mies van der Rohe and the two main typological strains of his late work. Seagram's whiskey through its vertical Seagram building in Manhattan, and Bacardí's rum by ways of its

14 In particular, see the work of Kathryn O'Rourke and Allan T. Shulman. For example: Kathryn O'Rourke, "Mies and Bacardi: Mixing Modernism, ca. 1960," in *Journal of Architectural Education* 66, no. 1 (October 2012): 57-71; Allan T. Shulman, *Building Bacardi: Architecture, Art & Identity* (New York: Rizzoli, 2016).

15 Ibid.

16 Barry Bergdoll, Carlos Eduardo Comas, Jorge Francisco Liemur, and Patricio del Real, *Latin America in Construction: Architecture 1955-1980* (New York: Museum of Modern Art, 2015), p. 191.

17 The Bacardí company was officially founded in 1862 by Don Facundo Bacardí Massó, a Catalan immigrant who had developed some technologies that changed the existing rum-making process, including the use of a single strain of yeast to better control fermentation, as well as the use of oak barrels and charcoal filtration. For a more detailed history of the company as one of the earliest "multinationals" or globalized enterprises, see: Allan Shulman, "The Mixable One: Two Projects for Compañía Ron Bacardi. S. A.," paper presented at X Seminário Docomomo Brasil Arquitetura Moderna e Internacional: Conexões Brutalistas 1955-75, Curitiba, October 2013, p. 5.

18 Cooking Sections (Daniel Fernández Pascual and Alon Schwabe), "Architecture Inspirited: Mies in Bermuda Pants," in *Avery Review*, no. 8 (May 2015).

Mies van der Rohe, Neue Nationalgalerie, Berlin. Photo: Reinhard Friedrich.

horizontal Santiago project. And although the Bacardí headquarters in Santiago would ultimately not be realized, it remains significant due to its role as a precedent for Mies's last major work: the Neue Nationalgalerie in Berlin, commissioned in 1962, whose scheme was in large part based on the unrealized Cuban project.[19]

ENVIRONMENTS

Bosch decided on Mies after reading a profile on the architect in the March 18, 1957, issue of *LIFE Magazine*.[20] Mies had migrated to the US in the late 1930s to become the head of the IIT in Chicago, and the buildings he designed for its campus (in particular Crown Hall) impressed Bosch, who sought a scheme equally open and transparent. In April 1957, some twenty years after leaving Hitler's dictatorship behind, Mies—whether oblivious, apolitical, or simply opportunistic[21]—now found himself at the Hotel Nacional during the dictatorship of Fulgencio Batista.[22]

While a large and column-free open space, such as the one of Crown Hall, might have appealed to Bosch from the perspective of its fashionable open-plan layout, materially this particular precedent was ultimately a glass box with a steel structure, built for Chicago without any form of external shading. Cuba's climate, needless to say, is different, meaning constant exposure to tropical sunshine as well as to salty, corroding ocean air.

The structure of the office building for Cia. Ron Bacardí, SA, in Santiago de Cuba, was specified in concrete (rather than steel, which

19 The project enjoys a curious afterlife as the Bacardí headquarters in Hamilton, Bermuda (the topic of a study by Daniel Fernández Pascual and Alon Schwabe of Cooking Sections). This building, completed in 1972, is heavily inspired by Mies's scheme and is sometimes even wrongly attributed to the architect.

20 Franz Schulze and Edward Windhorst, *Mies van der Rohe* (Chicago: University of Chicago Press, 2012), pp. 348-349.

21 This is not the place to elaborate on Mies's postwar political positions in detail, as it is impossible to do justice to the intricacies and importance of such a topic in a small section like this. This does not mean dismissing the fact that Cuba, at the time of the commission, was effectively a brutal dictatorship. Many people, including those working for Bacardí, were living under precarious conditions. Mies could have known this, yet decided to take on the commission. While he did seem to support Castro's Revolution in its early stages, as discussed above, Mies's politics are notoriously complicated (ample scholarship has dealt with his ambiguities in relation to Nazi Germany in particular).

22 Mies was not the first Bauhaus director-emigré to visit Cuba. Walter Gropius had given an influential lecture in 1949 in the architecture school of the Universidad de La Habana. See: Bergdoll, *Latin America in Construction*, p. 191.

S. R. Crown Hall, College of Architecture, Illinois Institute of Technology, was designed by Mies van der Rohe and completed in 1956. Photographer: Unknown source: Chicago Historical Society (HB-18506-S2).

had been used in Chicago's Crown Hall). Although steel was available, its relative scarcity (and therefore its expense) could have been a factor in this. The contemporaneous FOCSA building, for example, was also done in concrete. Furthermore, import licenses for steel ran the likely risk of being rejected by the government.[23] The visible results of the Hotel Nacional's proximity to the ocean appears to have supplied an additional reason: Mies and Summers noticed how their rooms featured steel balcony railings that were rusty at the time. Phyllis Lambert (herself instrumental in the commissioning of the Seagram building to Mies) and Gene Summers reconstructed this narrative for the 2001 exhibition, "Mies in America," through oral histories, tracing how the Hotel's typological features informed parts of the scheme for Bacardí (Franz Schulze, in his biography of Mies, does something similar).[24] Quoting from an interview she conducted with Summers, Lambert tells how, while sitting in the courtyard of the Hotel Nacional, Mies proposed an inverted version of the cloister-like alleyway: rather than the alley being surrounded by the building, as in the hotel, the building would be surrounded by the alley. "*Mies leaned forward in his chair, in a very characteristic way, and said, 'What if we reverse it? Let's put a walk under the roof on the outside of the glass line.*'"[25]

Notwithstanding the risk of underwriting too much agency for the architect, early sketches for the project in the collection of the Museum of Modern Art in New York do somewhat support this narrative (as does Lambert in her book). Several are done on Hotel Nacional stationery in both Mies's and Summers's hands, and the drawings reveal some of the process that led to the scheme. Mies supposedly asked Summers to sketch what he called an "inverse" version of the courtyard of the hotel. One sketch in particular reveals a hastily drawn partial plan of a corner of the building, in Summers'

23 As Bosch wrote to Summers, "Am afraid that we cannot import the steel so it seems that it will have to be fabricated. The gvnt will not grant the import license." Telegram José Bosch to Gene Summers, March 25, 1958, Mies Archive, 5701 Bacardi Office building Cuba, Box 1, Folder 2.

24 Phyllis Lambert, "Space and Structure," in: Phyllis Lambert (ed.), *Mies in America* (New York: Harry N. Abrams, Inc., 2001), p. 480.

25 Schultze and Windhorst, *Mies van der Rohe*, p. 349.

hand, in which a multiple-column colonnade is shown in relation to the roofline and façade, exactly as one imagines what an "inverted" plan of the Hotel would look like. Various early sketches are studies of the grid-structure. They range from a 5 x 5 bay square order to a 10 x 15 bay rectangular arrangement, and from corner columns to column-free corners (as in the final design). While earlier schemes featured arrays of many columns, emphasizing the notion of a colonnade, the final post-stressed concrete version consisted of one large roof supported by eight columns; a single plane on pin connections above an interior space of 19,000 square feet. Particular attention is paid to the shape of these columns as well as to the design of its pinpoint connections, some of which seem expressive outliers in the more austere Miesian vocabulary. A few sketches suggest eight sets of double columns, and similar double columns can be traced in some of the most iconic collages of the project at MoMA (made after the sketches but likely before the scheme was finalized). In the final version, the roof extends 20 feet beyond the glazing, and columns were to be painted white or gray.

Gene Summers. Sketch for the Ron Bacardí y Compañía, S. A., Administration Building, project, Santiago, Cuba, 1957. Museum of Modern Art, Mies van der Rohe Archive.

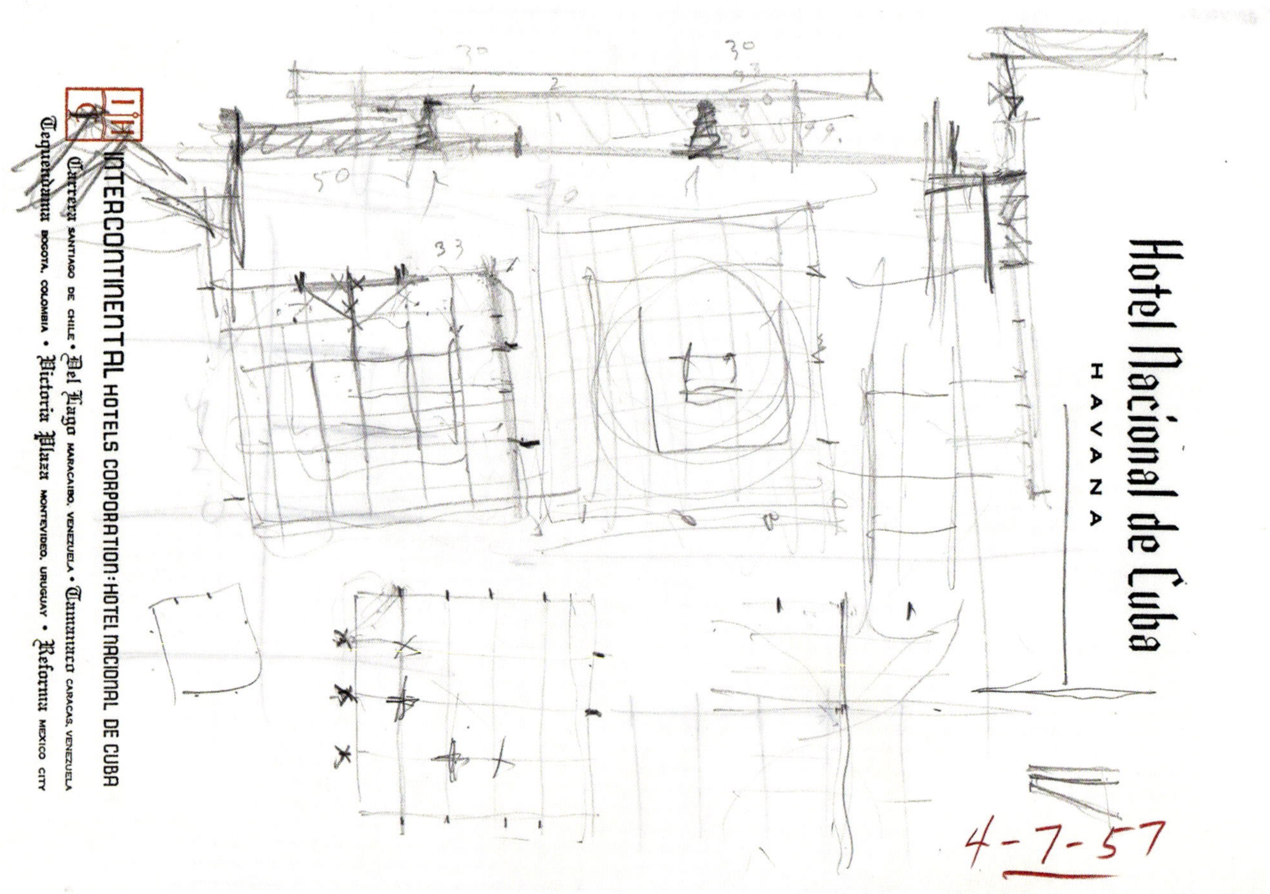

Hotel Nacional de Cuba

HAVANA

INTERCONTINENTAL HOTELS CORPORATION: HOTEL NACIONAL DE CUBA

Carrera SANTIAGO DE CHILE • Del Lago MARACAIBO, VENEZUELA • Tamanaco CARACAS, VENEZUELA

Tequendama BOGOTA, COLOMBIA • Victoria Plaza MONTEVIDEO, URUGUAY • Reforma MEXICO CITY

4-7-57

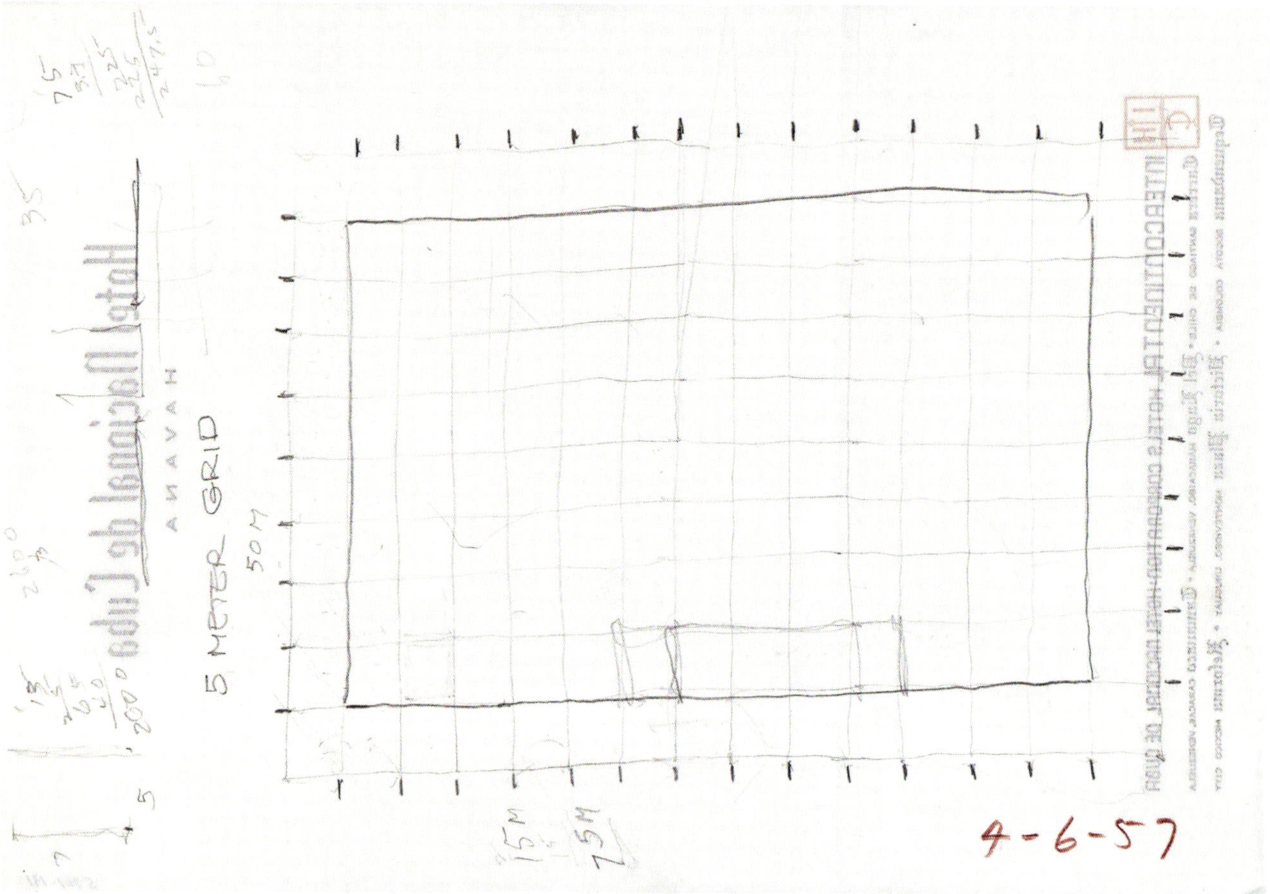

5 METER GRID

50M

4-6-57

Mies van der Rohe. Sketch for the Ron Bacardí y Compañía, S. A., Administration Building, project, Santiago, Cuba, ca. 1957-1958 (above) and ca. 1957-1960 (right). Museum of Modern Art, Mies van der Rohe Archive.

Opposite page:
Gene Summers. Sketch for the Ron Bacardí y Compañía, S. A., Administration Building, project, Santiago, Cuba, 1957. Museum of Modern Art, Mies van der Rohe Archive.

Mies van der Rohe. Ron Bacardí y Compañía, S. A., Administration Building, project, Santiago, Cuba, Elevation of column with roof and glass wall, final version, ca. 1957-1958.

Opposite page:
Mies van der Rohe. Interior Perspective of the Ron Bacardí y Compañía, S. A., Administration Building, project, Santiago, Cuba, ca. 1957. Museum of Modern Art, Mies van der Rohe Archive.

Mies van der Rohe. (Preliminary version) interior perspective of the Ron Bacardí y Compañía, S. A., Administration Building, project, Santiago, Cuba, 1957. Museum of Modern Art, Mies van der Rohe Archive (Ink, wood veneer, marbelized paper and cut-out reproduction on illustration board).

CIRCULATIONS

Never built, the Santiago project exists only through documentation, including its circulation in the media. The best contemporary images can be found in an issue of *Architectural Forum* from February 1959 (about a month after the overthrow of Batista's regime). The cover of the magazine featured a perspectival line drawing of the project, and under the header "Mies's one-office office building," an article described how "[t]*he champion of steel favors concrete and glass for Cuba's Bacardi building*" (a somewhat limited reading of the "American" Mies which disregarded his earlier brick and concrete works, and underplayed the significance of glass as a material throughout his career).[26]

The cover image reinforces the notion of a two-story project intended to be read as a one-story edifice, a single floor raised on a platform. It shows only the open structure of the upper space, with no hint of additional floors. Yet a lower level was very much part of the building's day-to-day operations. Home to a staff of about 20 (as opposed to ca. 75 on the upper level) the lower floor was to host detailed programs, including mechanical spaces; a bar; a retail shop; PR offices; storage spaces; conference and legal rooms. None of these

26 *Architectural Forum*, vol. 110, no. 2 (Feb. 1959). Although I would argue there are at least as many differences as similarities, Kathryn O'Rourke perceives a strong link between Mies's early 1923 concrete office project and the project for Bacardí. O'Rourke, "Mies and Bacardi."

Architectural Forum / the magazine of building / February 1959

FORUM

Above:
Architectural Forum (February 1959). Cover.

Right:
Model photograph of the Bacardí Santiago project, as published in *Architectural Forum* (February 1959): 97.

Model photograph of the Bacardí Santiago project, as published in *Architectural Forum* (February 1959): 94-95.

lower spaces suggest the presence of daylight, and the footprint of the lower level is significantly smaller than the upper one. That a shop and PR spaces are situated here, rather than in the defining upper space, indicates that unlike the Bacardí building in Havana, the Santiago project was not conceived as a material advertisement for a company that (American) tourists could visit and experience. Instead, it was always first and foremost an office building, and its role in helping to brand the company as a hyper-modern global firm was as an image, meant by association, by the circulation of the project in the media.[27] One of the sketches for the project even includes the letters B A C A R D I on the edge of the roof-slab, an unlikely addition within the office's work. (As mentioned above, in relation to Seagram's similar commissioning of Mies: the act of the commission itself cannot be seen as separate from the intention to strengthen Bacardí as an international brand, a corporate modernism in which the famous architect or the building-as-advertisement offer a purposeful mediatic performativity).[28] This nexus, this intersection of global circulation with local infrastructure (with both Mies and rum as examples of the former) was recognized by the Marxist critic Roberto Segre in 1967 as the ultimately visual symbol that the building was: a tangible representation of the unbreakable unity between art and capital, its materiality an advanced state-of-the-art, while its workers (both construction workers and workers for Bacardí) still found themselves living in precarious dwellings.[29]

ABSTRACTIONS (I)

Describing a "one-office office building" (as the 1959 article in *Architectural Forum* does) is an abstraction; a reduced understanding of an office as a single space with desks in which all supporting functions are nonexistent. Yet on both a human and non-human level, the building would have been defined precisely by the relationship between these floors; by the interplay of the (social) relations between the occupants as well as material, mechanical relations. Despite its sun-deflecting overhang, the building was to rely on climatization, its interior comfort levels artificially defined by the mechanical spaces in the building's basement, one ecosystem shaped by another. (This of course brings to mind Andrés Jaque's seminal study on the role the basement plays in the reconstructed Barcelona pavilion by Mies).[30] Countering the programmatically detailed lower level with its many distinct rooms, the abstract universality with which the upper floor is represented is commonly associated with Mies's later projects.

27 This is no surprise and has been recognized by the historian Allan Shulman in all of Bacardí's modernist commissions: "Although the Bacardi works employ no set style or mode of modernism, they do converge toward a single corporate strategy: the expression of an identifiable 'image,' a central aim as the company began to attach symbolic and cultural importance to its building activity." Shulman, "The Mixable One," 2.

28 On Mies in relation to advertising, see: Brett Steele, "ABSOLUT® MIESTM, ABSOLUTE MODERN: BUILDING GOOD COPY" in: *AA Files*, no. 48 (Winter 2002): 2-14. On the importance of corporate identity in commissioning Mies, see: O'Rourke, "Mies and Bacardi," 57-71. Illustrative of this is the fact that in the case of the Seagram building, as Felicity Scott has shown, the New York City Tax Commission levied an extra tax on the way the building embodied value as advertisement. See: Felicity Scott, "An Army of Soldiers or a Meadow: The Seagram Building and the 'Art of Modern Architecture,'" *Journal of the Society of Architectural Historians*, vol. 3, no. 70 (2011): 342. See also: Cooking Sections, "Architecture Inspirited," 3.

29 Roberto Segre, "Estética del prefabricado," *El caimán barbudo* (1967).

30 See Andrés Jaque's project, "PHANTOM. Mies as Rendered Society" (2012-2013).

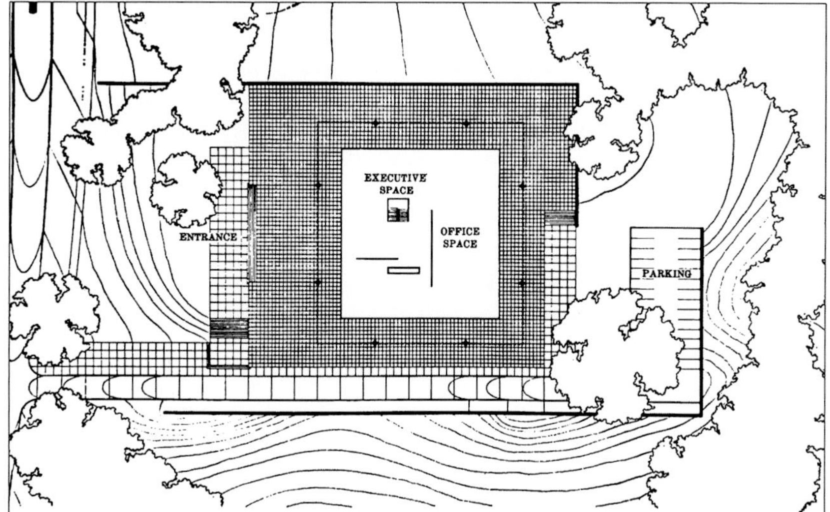

Floor plan (upper level) of the Bacardí Santiago project, as published in *Architectural Forum* (February 1959): 96.

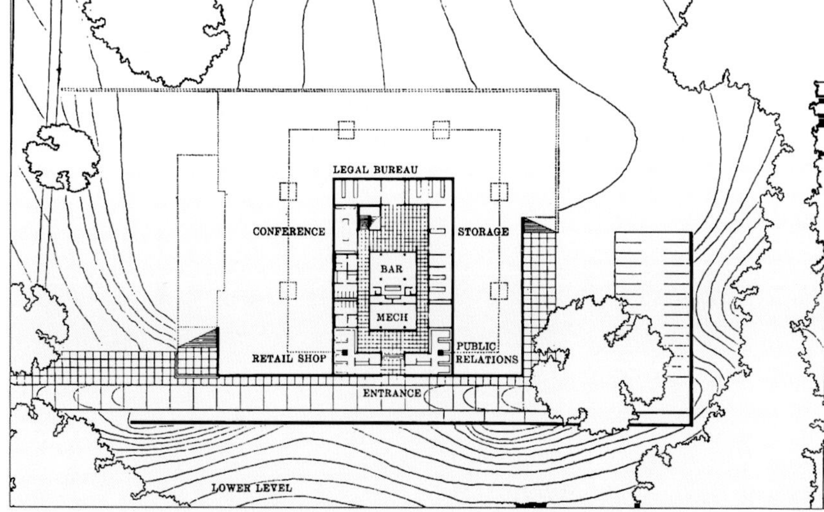

Floor plan (lower level) of the Bacardí Santiago project, as published in *Architectural Forum* (February 1959): 96.

Yet hierarchies were present here as well, between different ranks of staff. If a supposed universality existed at all, it would primarily be in the project's image. While this is not the place to offer an in-depth history of the developments in corporate office design in the mid-twentieth century, a brief detour will nevertheless help frame the project (especially as I write these words while a pandemic ravages the planet, not only challenging received ideas of open office layouts but also adding new terminology to our work-from-home vocabulary).[31]

The term "knowledge worker" was first coined in 1959, the year Mies's project was published in *Architectural Forum*. And what was called an "action office," which sought to reflect a more dynamic way of working that involved standing desks and hinged partitions, emerged a few years later, in 1964. Still, in the North American context in which Mies was mostly active at the time, the late 1950s were by and large a pre-cubicle era. While open-plan offices did exist, they existed in the understanding best reflected in Billy Wilder's film *The Apartment* from 1960—hardly a desirable space. Hierarchy between executives and regular office workers was a hierarchy

31 In fact (and for that reason) the examples that follow are taken from a *New Yorker* article discussing post-Covid office life: John Seabrook, "Office Space: The post-pandemic future of open-plan work," *The New Yorker*, February 1, 2021.

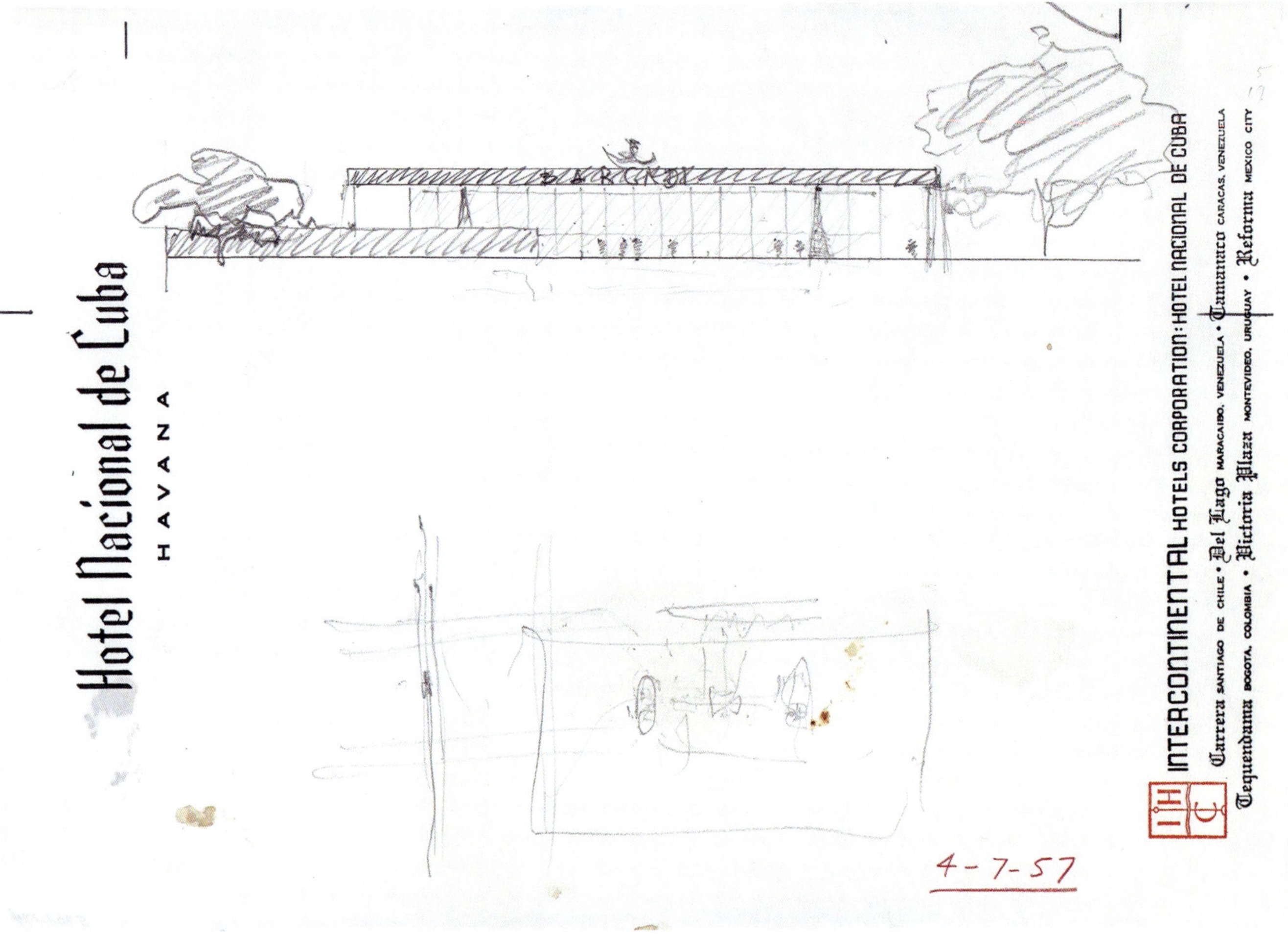

Gene Summers. Sketch for the Ron Bacardí y Compañía, S. A., Administration Building, project, Santiago, Cuba, 1957. Museum of Modern Art, Mies van der Rohe Archive.

between core and envelope: low- and mid-level staff would occupy open offices at the center of the floorplan, while the closed corner and perimeter offices—views, daylight, and privacy—were reserved for executives.

The Bacardí project challenges this notion by a suggested radical openness. Daylight everywhere. And Bosch pointedly described the ideal office as "one where there are no partitions, where everybody, both officers and employees, see each other."[32] At the same time, the only programmatic designation provided on the published upper-floor plan is that of a distinction between the "Executive Space" and the "Office Space." With existing corporate hierarchies thus left intact, its main contribution is to make the spatial qualities equal for both areas, introducing universality in spatial rather than social terms. Altogether, the programmatic intricacies and hierarchies of the project suggests that Mies and his staff were unaware of the very specific role Bacardí was playing in Batista's Cuba, designing—despite its spatial specificities—what functioned programmatically and hierarchically as a generic office building.

CONSTRUCTIONS

The building's vast open floorplan in its final iteration was covered by a large concrete roof-slab supported by eight columns total—two on each side. The roof spanned 177ft, and while the roof-plate becomes thicker towards the center (where forces are stronger) a hung interior ceiling flattens this perception and allows for a space in which ducts can be hidden from view. Much of this was likely enabled by the structural engineers and associate architects for the project—Sáenz-Cancio-Martín and Álvarez y Gutiérrez. The latter had worked with Bosch on previous projects, and Bosch had been instrumental in having both teams form the corporate firm SACMAG in 1958.[33] The Havana-based Sáenz-Cancio-Martín engineering firm had worked with Philip Johnson on his unbuilt design for the Riviera Hotel, and it is likely that Johnson endorsed them to Mies.[34] The firm also worked on Mies's Mexico project, and as of August 1960, still from Havana. (Luis Sáenz, like Bosch, in the first weeks after the Revolution was happy with Batista's departure.[35]) Yet like many others around 1961, the engineers and architects emigrated, and SACMAG would relocate to Puerto Rico. From here they would continue to serve as architects of record for Bosch's later projects, including the Mexico office project and those done by Félix Candela for the company.

Ducts would have connected the plenum to the machinery in the basement by means of a fixed interior column, abstract in appearance yet curtailing any understanding of the space as completely unobstructed. Stairs leading towards the basement and two low

32 Mies Archive, 5701 Bacardi Office building Cuba, Box 2, Folder 13.

33 Cuba did not know the type of corporate office that characterized SACMAG, which was becoming increasingly common in the US. See: Deupi and Lejeune, *Cuban Modernism*, pp. 190, 292.

34 In the MoMA archives there is a record of a phone call between Philip Johnson and Mies van der Rohe, in which Johnson recommends the firm as "very serious" (from handwritten notes of that conversation, Jan. 21, 1957); "Saenz is an excellent engineer, the best associate Johnson ever had... Johnson said his only trouble with Saenz was getting him to come to New York." Mies Archive, 5701 Bacardi Office building Cuba, Box 1, Folder 1.

35 "Dear Mr. van der Rohe: As you will have noticed in the news, matters came to a head in our country with incredible speed during the last few weeks, the result of which has been to reestablish the long sought freedom desired by everybody." Luis Sáenz to Mies van der Rohe, Jan. 22, 1959. Mies Archive, 5701 Bacardi Office building Cuba, Box 1, Folder 5.

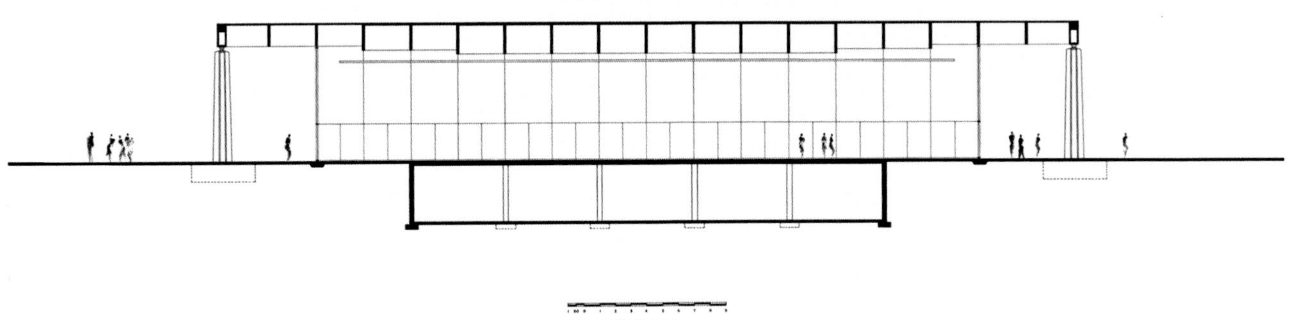

Mies van der Rohe. Longitudinal section of the Ron Bacardí y Compañía, S. A., Administration Building, project, Santiago, Cuba, ca. 1957-1960. Museum of Modern Art, Mies van der Rohe Archive (Ink on illustration board).

Opposite page:
Mies van der Rohe. Site plan of the Ron Bacardí y Compañía, S. A., Administration Building, project, Santiago, Cuba, ca. 1957-1958. Museum of Modern Art, Mies van der Rohe Archive (Ink over pencil on illustration board).

Mies van der Rohe. Neue National Gallery, Berlin, Germany (Floor plan of exhibition hall) 1967 (Pencil on acetate). Museum of Modern Art, Mies van der Rohe Archive.

partitioning walls are the other fixed elements in the otherwise open first-floor plan. A similar strategy would appear in the Nationalgalerie in Berlin, where the covered ducts and stairs are the only fixed elements in the open plan. Yet somewhat paradoxically, the scheme of the Nationalgalerie was symmetrical (in line with Mies's American work), whereas the Bacardí headquarters relied on asymmetric compositional strategies closer to Mies's earlier Berlin projects, such as the country house or Barcelona pavilion.

In the more classical Mies scholarship the project is considered part of a lineage of "universal-space clear-span buildings," generally described as starting with the Farnsworth House in Plano, Illinois (1945-51).[36] Mies's unbuilt Glass House on a Hillside (1934) and Resor House (1937-38) already featured the clear-span spaces and suggested connections with the landscape that reached a sort of residential apex in Plano. The distinction between these buildings and Bacardí, however, as has been observed, is that between Gothic and Classical types; the one-way span of Farnsworth, infinitely linear, and the two-way, self-contained one, as found in Bacardí.[37] Furthermore, both Bacardí's afterlife as the Nationalgalerie in Berlin, its programmatic-typological arrangement, as well as its "origins" in Chicago's Crown Hall do suggest a certain universality to Mies's architecture (an image that has been further cultivated by Mies himself, not least through his use of precisely such terms

36 Phyllis Lambert, "Space and Structure," 334.

37 Ibid., 424.

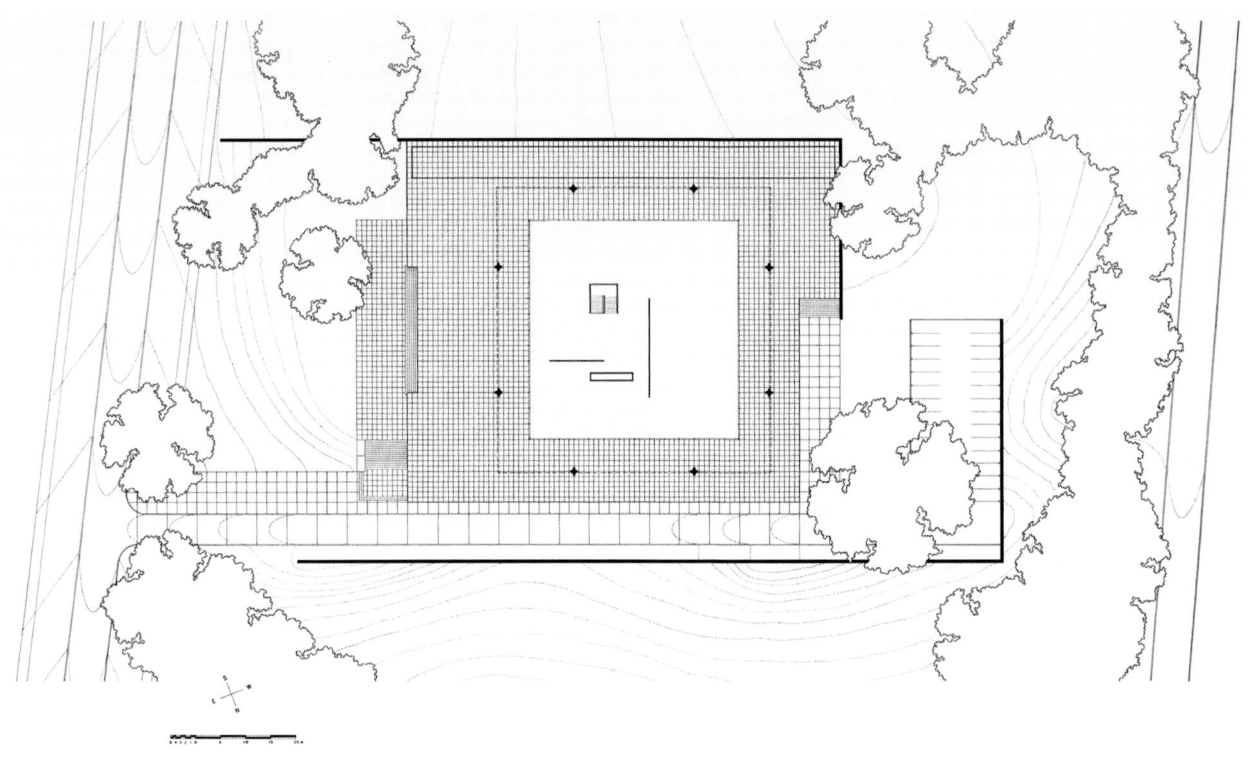

①　DETAIL DES ZULUFTGITTERS　M 1/1

②　GRUNDRISS DER ZULUFTSCHLITZE AN DER GLASWAND　M 1/20

③　SCHNITT DURCH DEN SPRUNG IN DER BETONDECKE　M 1/10

NEUE NATIONALGALERIE BERLIN

STIFTUNG PREUSS. KULTURBESITZ　BAUHERR

MIES VAN DER ROHE　ARCHITEKT

GRUNDRISS DER AUSSTELLUNGSHALLE M 1/100

A12

Pierre Huyghe
Mies Cuba Gets Cold, 2000
Unrealized project
Collage on paper, 65 x 50 cm / 25.6 x 19.7 in
Courtesy of the artist.

as "universal space"). But to believe in a universal validity of architectural forms is one thing, decontextualization is another. Just as certain qualities of the Seagram building are difficult to imagine without the dialogue with a very specific zoning law that exists only in New York (questioned by the building's setback, for example), details of the Bacardí building were the direct result of contextual, Cuban, conditions. Instead of an abstract universality enabled by the singular architect, this is an abstraction that serves as a starting rather than an end point of the architectural work. Crown Hall is abstracted into Cuba, where it encounters new environmental conditions and becomes the concrete Bacardí project; Bacardí is abstracted into Germany, where it becomes the steel Nationalgalerie. Abstraction-as-transformation.[38]

38 This specific understanding of abstraction as a technique in the context of specific ecosystemic environments (habitat) is thoroughly developed by Sven Lütticken, more on which below. Sven Lütticken, "Abstract Habitats: Installations of Coexistence and Coevolution," in: *Grey Room*, no. 59 (Spring 2015): 102-127.

ABSTRACTIONS (II)

Over 20 years ago, in 2000, the artist Pierre Huyghe proposed to turn the Neue Nationalgalerie—the museum designed by Mies for West Berlin during the 1960s as one of the last projects the architect had actively been involved in—into a Cuban rainforest. The upper level's open floor plan would be filled with native Cuban plants and other species, contained in the museum's glass box with its flat, black, overhanging metal roof. Titled "Mies Cuba Gets Cold," Huyghe's work was never realized, and what remains is only its proposal, materialized in a single collage that shows an image of a rainforest out of which a rectangular void is abstracted.[39] The triangular component of the Cuban flag, normally red, is rendered black (the same color as the upper bar of the German flag) and points down towards several scattered pieces of this abstracted ecosystem that suggest filling the boxy Nationalgalerie. In the background we can see buildings much harder to place into the Cartesian grid of Mies's Museum. First there is Hans Scharoun's Berlin Philharmonic, situated right next to the Nationalgalerie and equally part of the Kulturforum (the former West Berlin's cultural center). Behind that stands the Fernsehturm, the television tower that was the landmark highest building of the former East Berlin; as much an image of ideological (Eastern) superiority as the cultural forum was to be for the West.

The juxtapositions are not random. Not only was the Nationalgalerie based on the unrealized scheme for the Bacardí office in Santiago, but its distinct configuration was also—as the history around the Hotel Nacional shows—in part determined by distinct Cuban climatic conditions rather than abstract universalizations. These include both those in Havana as well as those in Santiago, where the climate can be more extreme. (While there is little hard evidence, it does seem that Mies visited the actual site on his first trip to Cuba in 1957.[40]) If a Chicago "Mies" was abstracted into the Cuban rainforest, the Cuban rainforest was now abstracted into Mies. If the color-swapping of the flag in Huyghe's collage merge Germany and Cuba on a symbolical level, and the inclusion of the television tower hints at the relation between the two countries on a historical-ideological level—in other words a shared history of socialism—then Huyghe's actual proposal for the gallery itself merges two ecosystems on a material level (irony holds that both Mies's Cuban project and Huyghe's Berlin proposal remain unmaterialized, yet gain significance through distinct material observations).

Like much of Huyghe's work, the jungle proposal is successful in discussing architecture as a socio-ecological project; a work consistently defined by the interaction of social, material, and interspecies aspects. Less directly, however, it also hints at the ultimate incompatibility of the project with Cuba. Not so much

39 Besides the plants and other species, the Nationalgalerie was to host an artificial weather system replicating Berlin's climate from 1957-68, and a film about insect life in Disney theme parks.

40 In a telegram to Mies, Bosch mentions a photograph: "... herewith a picture taken at the time of your arrival at Santiago de Cuba." Telegram José Bosch to Mies, April 9, 1957. Bosch had also written to Mies on February 14, 1957, that "it would be desirable to have you visit Cuba, both Havana and Santiago." Mies Archive, 5701 Bacardi Office building Cuba, Box 1, Folder 1.

because the project inserted a rainforest into Mies's glass box and created interior ecosystemic weather conditions that are completely foreign to its site; but rather by exposing, through its juxtaposition, the ideological incompatibility that exists between Bacardí (and by extension Mies) with Castro's project (an incompatibility already apparent in Segre's observations discussed above).

The work by Huyghe and related projects by other artists have been explained by Sven Lütticken as relying on forms of "abstraction" as a technique; a form of production that asks "*which forms of coexistence are possible beyond the dismal alternatives of maximum economic exploitation, on the one hand, and primitivist 'free the birds' screeds, on the other hand.*"[41] This begins with abstraction in its literal sense: the taking away of something (for example, the abstraction of a piece of native rainforest from Cuba in the case of Huyghe's "Mies Cuba Gets Cold") and placing it in a different context. To state the obvious, Mies's projects do not share in the critical abstraction-as-production such works of art provide from the outset. Yet such a reading of abstraction nevertheless offers the opening of a framework that provides an alternative way of reading Mies's projects—moving away from the tropes of "less is more," instead reading them as supposedly universal forms taken out of a specific context and left to encounter new socio-material conditions. If the former suggests revelation but more often than not conceals (as the hidden role of the basement shows), the latter suggests concealment but ultimately reveals material conditions by means of juxtaposed relationships. Particularly pertinent in the Cuban instance is how such ecosystemic abstractions fit within a long exploitative history of colonial and neo-colonial practices of abstraction, of the landscape abstractions by primarily American companies in the period of independence leading up to the Cuban Revolution (the sugar cane central to rum distillation, for instance), the offshore conditions of the island itself, and, in different econo-extractive form, of global corporations such as Bacardí operating through global tax havens.[42]

41 Lütticken, "Abstract Habitats," 103.

42 One could convincingly argue that the continuing "offshore" financial existence of the company in Bermuda is, like all forms of offshoring, a form of abstraction from the ground, an extraction with detrimental environmental and social repercussions like those laid out by Bruno Latour in his *Down to Earth: Politics in the New Climatic Regime* (Cambridge: Polity, 2019). On extraction and offshore existence in relation to Bacardí's Bermuda headquarters, see: Cooking Sections, "Architecture Inspirited."

TRANSFERS

The persistent idea that the realization of the Nationalgalerie was the epitomatization of certain universalist principles within Mies's late work is strengthened by another iteration of the scheme, one that had appeared between the first version in Cuba and the final version in Berlin. This was the design for a museum in Schweinfurt, Germany. Mies's grandson Dirk Lohan had married into a Bavarian industrial family and commissioned Mies to design the museum for the family's collection of nineteenth-century German art. This first proposed a steel rather than concrete structure for what was essentially a version

Mies van der Rohe. Georg Schaefer Museum project, Schweinfurt, Germany (Early scheme, scale model: 1:50 made by the Office of Mies van der Rohe) 1960-1963. Museum of Modern Art, Mies van der Rohe Archive.

of the Bacardí project, the office space now serving as an exhibition hall. Already in poor health in 1960, Mies put Gene Summers in charge of the job and the eventual scheme became, as they called it, a steel version of the "Cuba project" (no doubt informed by the ample availability of steel in the German Wirtschaftswunder and the vastly different climatic conditions in Bavaria) and almost identical in size. Work stalled when the client disliked the scheme, and the office was released from its obligations. This paved the way for its third and final iteration as the Berlin's Nationalgalerie, a commission that Mies's office received in 1962.

Mies scholar Detlef Mertins has pointed out that this transfer, from Santiago via Schweinfurt to Berlin, was pounced on by critics of Mies's "universal space" (or even of its universalist ideology) to illustrate how an overriding quest to eradicate differences in such architectures would ultimately lead to problems of functionality; a functionality that would always be perceived as secondary to universality.[43] Mertins counters these critiques by showing how Mies was well aware of the functional difficulties of the Nationalgalerie for hosting art in any traditional configuration, yet at the same time offered "*a great possibility for new ways to do it.*"[44] (Indeed, I would argue that one such possibility came with Pierre Huyghe's installation had it been realized.) One could hypothesize that Mertins' argument potentially holds true for the Santiago scheme as well: it is very difficult to have an office here. But a great possibility for new ways to do it.[45] The Nationalgalerie, however, offered a traditional gallery configuration on its lower level, creating a distinction from—an alternative to—the floor above. The lower level of Bacardí, as we

43 Detlef Mertins, "Mies's Event Space," in *Grey Room*, no. 20 (Summer, 2005): 61.

44 Ibid.

45 Other scholars have pushed back against a too-easy understanding of the scheme as a hand-me-down. Kathleen James-Chakraborty has pointed out that the idea of an uninterrupted lineage from the Bacardi headquarters to the Nationalgalerie should be approached with caution. After all, its materiality was substantially different in its concrete and then steel iterations. She also argues that what distinguishes the Nationalgalerie from the Cuban project is the influence of Karl Friedrich Schinkel on the former, as Mies developed the museum's design to relate to both Schinkel's Altes Museum and its urban context. See: Kathleen James-Chakraborty, *Modernism as Memory* (Minneapolis: University of Minnesota Press, 2018), p. 96.

have seen, was always mostly a support for its upper floor, not an alternative (and in that sense closer to a traditional office building than the museum was to a traditional museum).

Mies, of course, was never a functionalist. Rather, the scheme—whether in Cuba or in Berlin—illustrates some apparent contradictions in Mies that, as Fritz Neumeyer has argued, are the result of oversimplifications within an understanding of modernism itself.[46] If in such simplifications classicism equals authoritarianism and "free plan" equals democracy, then these projects, displaying both classical and free-plan features, contain both systems. While it might seem tempting to propose a retroactive reading of the building as a metaphor of precisely this contradiction in Cuba's or Germany's contentious twentieth-century history, such an alleged universality (or autonomy, even) is meaningless in and of itself, for it can only exist in relation to a myriad of social, technological, economic, political, and material actors that are beyond the architect's control. Precisely through such specificities can a reading of the project be made that would tie it to participating actors ranging from the smallest Cuban scale to the global networks in which Bacardí, Batista, or Castro partake, all of which to various extents informed the design and its afterlife.

This does not mean we cannot ask ourselves the larger question of the compatibility of Mies's architecture with Cuba on both a material and ideological level. If Huyghe with his work questioned the former through an exposé of the climatic (in)compatibility of the project, Segre exposed the latter through the contradictions within capitalism the building symbolized. Miesian modernism could certainly exist in the Global South, as ample built examples show. And we can imagine the building having been built. (We can even imagine it continuing to exist as a ruin, the fate of several contemporaneous built works in Cuba, or in pristine shape, such as the recently renovated Nationalgalerie.) But whether the architecture of Mies was compatible with the Cuban Revolution as an ideological project is a different question altogether. While it is hard to picture Mies as a rabid revolutionary, the letters and telegrams in MoMA's archive suggest his sympathies were with Castro during the early stages of the Revolution. Perhaps this was an understandable position. Despite his ambiguous departure he eventually witnessed the total destruction of his own country by Hitler's dictatorship. Ironically, however, it was precisely Castro's Revolution that ultimately made it impossible for Mies's and similar architectures to be realized.

The project did continue its virtual existence, briefly, in a move from authoritarian capitalism under Batista to Castro's early revolutionary project, before being rendered incompatible with the socialist project Castro wished to represent architecturally. Rum itself was incompatible with the Revolution only in its existing image, associated with tourism and sex; as a product, it was perpetuated by serving a different purpose for the state. Could the building, too, have been separated from its image, a signifier/signified disconnect, a rebranding of sorts? Perhaps, although it seems unlikely. As Felicity Scott has demonstrated with regards to the Seagram building, Mies failed to grasp the structural transformations that capitalism was undergoing—which would explain his apparent out-of-syncness with American consumerism.[47] Beyond his control, his building emerged into a media environment that encompassed global corporate forces and Cold War logics. The same might be said of the Santiago project had it been realized under Bacardí's corporate umbrella and its contemporaneous consumerism. But if these new conditions emerging in corporate America were partially informed by the logics of the Cold War, it was the very presence of Castro's regime that, in turn, informed the Cold War. Partially severed from these relationships after the Revolution, the building would either have been severed from the image of Mies or allow for the brand that he effectively was to exist simultaneously in relation to two ideological realities (which, nevertheless, at least in their modernism, were often two sides of the same coin).

Yet most of the projects realized under Castro adopted a different aesthetic altogether, one that served its ideological purpose in the mediatic battlefields of the Cold War through an architecture at first sight remote from anything Miesian, such as the art schools built on the former country club just outside Havana. While the project's realization under Castro would no doubt have helped expose a wide range of relationships, Mies, the brand, would have been an incompatible abstraction.

46 Fritz Neumeyer, *Mies van der Rohe: The Artless Word* (Cambridge: MIT Press), p. xix.

47 Scott, "An Army of Soldiers," p. 347.

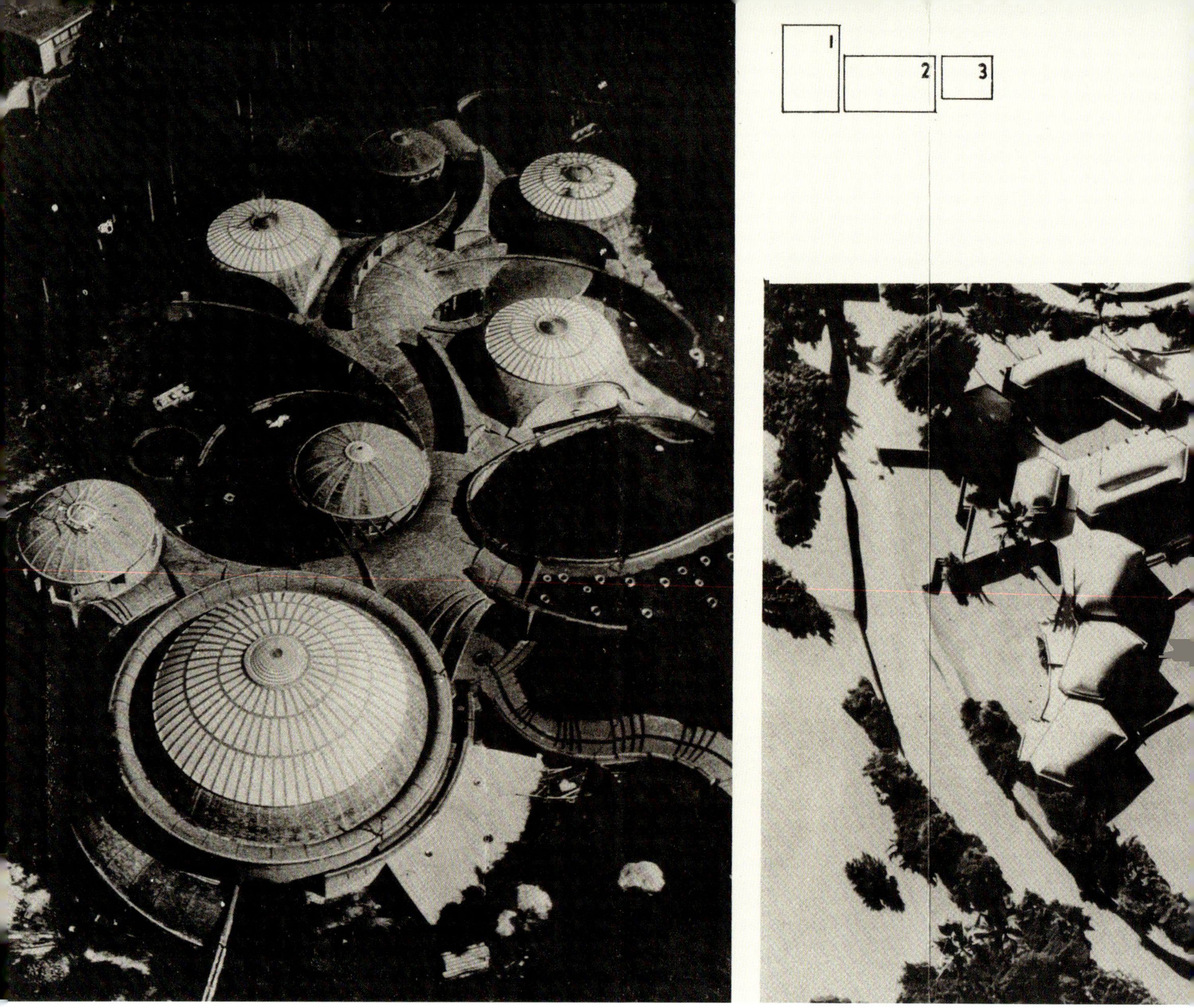

Photo spread from Roberto Segre, *Diez años de arquitectura revolucionaria* (Havana: Cuadernos de la Revista Unión, 1970) showing the three art schools:
Vittorio Garatti, National Ballet School, Cubanacán, Havana, 1961-1963. Aerial view. Photo: Vittorio Garatti.
Roberto Gottardi, National School of Dramatic Arts, Cubanacán, Havana, 1961-63. View of model.
Ricardo Porro, National School of Visual Arts, Cubanacán, Havana, 1961-1963. Aerial view. Photo: Ministry of Construction, Cuba.

EFFEMINATE ARCHITECTURE: DANCE, HOMOSEXUALITY, AND LITERATURE IN HAVANA'S NATIONAL ART SCHOOLS

Miguel Caballero

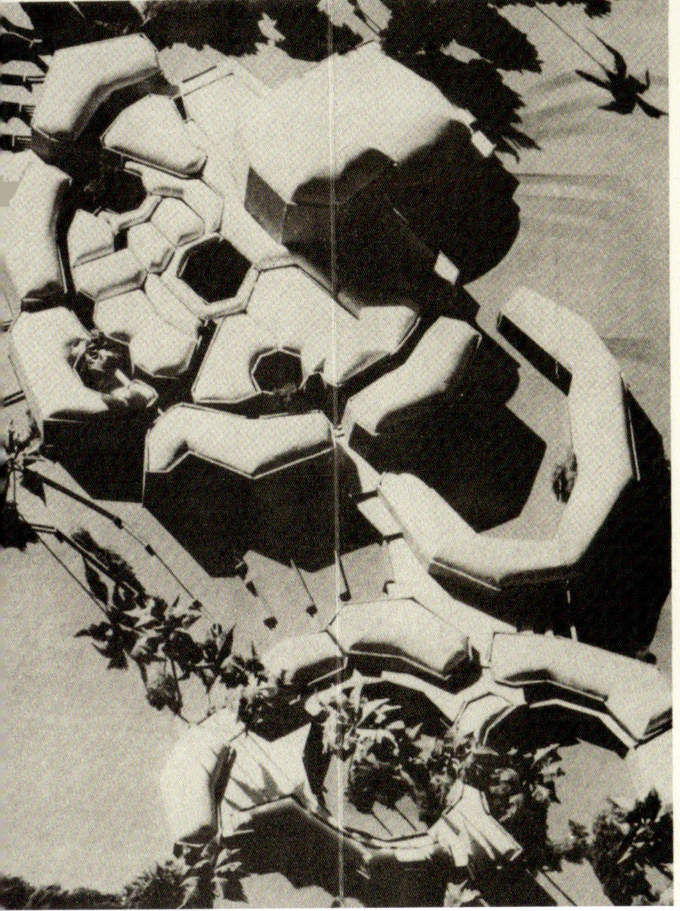

The National Art Schools in Havana, today known as the Superior Art Institute (ISA), were built, although not all completed, between 1961 and 1965. Together with the José Antonio Echeverría University Campus (CUJAE) and the housing projects of East Havana, they constitute one of the three great architectural undertakings that the Cuban Revolution launched in the capital or its outskirts during the early years of the new regime. Their foundational myth is the jocular anecdote about Fidel Castro and Che Guevara playing parody golf in one of the exclusive country clubs for bourgeois idlers that had thrived in pre-revolutionary Cuba. While trying to improve their swing, it occurred to them to turn the greens of Cubanacán Country Club into a set of art schools that would be a beacon for the whole anti-capitalist world.[1]

To design this project they commissioned the Cuban architect Ricardo Porro, recently returned home after partially training in France and then practicing professionally in Venezuela. There, Porro

1 In a corrective article from 2015 in *The New York Times*, it is pointed out that the famous photos of Che and Fidel playing golf were not taken in the Cubanacán country club, but in the one at Colinas de Villarreal, although Cubanacán was the site finally chosen for the Schools. Michael Cooper, "'Cubanacán' Images When Che and Fidel Compared Golf Swings," *The New York Times*, May 20, 2015, p. C-1.

had been professor of architecture at the brand-new University of Caracas, designed by Carlos Villanueva, which would exert a considerable influence on the Havana schools, above all in terms of the integration of the surrounding landscape.[2] In Caracas he had met the Italian architects Vittorio Garatti and Roberto Gottardi, whom he invited to join him on the Cuban project. Porro would design the Visual Arts and Modern Dance schools, Garatti was given the Ballet and Music schools, and Gottardi's brief was Dramatic Arts. The only buildings to be completed were Porro's, which opened in 1965, shortly before the architect was driven out of the country at the beginning of a long exile. The others remained unfinished, works in progress that have endured as ruins up to the present day.

Sidelined by the Revolution itself and virtually unknown outside of Cuba, the Art Schools have regained visibility in the last few years, sited at the heart of current debates around conservation and patrimony, postmodernity and architecture, art and revolution. John Loomis rediscovered them for global architectural circuits in 1999 through his book *A Revolution of Forms*, which stresses the originality of their formal conception and the successful incorporation of the telluric, not only in the fusion of the buildings with the landscape but also in the adaptation to modernism of native Cuban building techniques.[3] From then on, the ensemble has been acknowledged as a remarkable precursor of postmodern architecture and of what Kenneth Frampton has dubbed "critical regionalism."[4] It has secured the heritage prestige that eluded it for decades—both inside Cuba, with its belated inclusion in 2010 into the register of National Monuments, and internationally, since it is, at the time of writing, being considered by UNESCO for World Heritage status.

The fascination the buildings inspire owes something to the mysteries of their fall from grace. The very Revolution that dreamed them up so grandly ended up repudiating them, leaving them half-done, almost as if ashamed of them. The reasons for this must be sought in the political conjuncture of the time: the enthusiasm with which they were conceived belongs to the early months of the Revolution, characterized by unfettered creativity and ideological ambiguity. But this festival of liberation was undermined by Cuba's vulnerable position on the geopolitical map of the Cold War, which soon made itself felt in a string of serious showdowns that imperiled not only the small revolutionary island (as in the Bay of Pigs invasion of 1961) but also the world at large (the Missile Crisis erupted one year later, in 1962, the year the US trade embargo became almost total). The revolutionary regime reacted by closing ranks, imposing unquestioning unity and ideological orthodoxy. Although such rigidity may have permitted the country to survive, it did, among other

2 The key figure of modernist "*paisajismo*" (landscapism) in Latin America is Roberto Burle Marx, whose office opened in Caracas in 1956; he designed the Parque del Este during the period when Porro was teaching in the same city. MoMA devoted its first exhibition of a landscape architect to him. See: William H. Adams, *Roberto Burle Marx: The Unnatural Art of the Garden* (New York: Museum of Modern Art, 1991).

3 Although preceded by several scattered papers on the topic, John Loomis's book started a real wave of interest, manifest in publications but especially in documentaries, notably those by Alysa Nahmias and Benjamin Murray, by Francesco Apolloni, and by Florian Zeyfang et al. on Garatti. In the academic sphere, María José Pizarro Juana defended a doctoral dissertation on the Schools in 2012, while in that of contemporary art, references to the Schools appear in the works of Felipe Dulzaides and Reynerio Tamayo, among others. In 2014, Roberto Varela composed his opera *Cubanacán*, with a libretto by Charles Koppelman, about the construction of the Schools.

4 Porro was an avowed admirer of the Mexican architect Luis Barragán.

consequences, instill a profound mistrust of creative freedom and lead to the repression of those social sectors that failed to abide by revolutionary norms.

As well as seeing the partial and reluctant inauguration of the Schools and the expulsion of Porro, 1965 was also the year of the founding of the Military Units to Aid Production (UMAP): forced labor camps for elements of the population distrusted by the regime for their volatility and nonconformism, basically homosexual males and religious believers.[5] There followed years of censorship, ostracism, imprisonment or exile for the likes of Antón Arrufat or Heberto Padilla, writers whose cases were a watershed for the solidarity of intellectuals with the Revolution, both inside and outside Cuba. In the second half of the 1960s, there was no room for half measures or free verse; if you were not unconditionally with Castro's cause then you were against it, with a greater or lesser degree of hostility.

This essay sets out to cover all these contextual dynamics in a study of Havana's National Art Schools sited at the intersection of architecture, cultural history, and literature. I will explore the formal innovation of the Schools as well as their rapid relegation, inquiring into the views of students and teaching staff who were there during the tense period in question. If I have opted for a literary analysis, it is because literature is the best medium for delving into the experience of habitation, able to give rise to positive as well as demystifying accounts of buildings in that it facilitates the analysis of architecture in a wider sociopolitical context. My essay is therefore structured around the memoirs of the Mexican writer and journalist, Alma Guillermoprieto, *Dancing with Cuba* (2005); the memoirs of the modern dancer and dance teacher Lorna Burdsall, *More Than Just a Footnote: Dancing from Connecticut to Revolutionary Cuba* (2001); and histories of dance in revolutionary Cuba, chiefly Elizabeth B. Schwall's recent *Dancing with the Revolution* (2021).

The first of these works describes Guillermoprieto's experience in 1970 as a professor of modern dance, working in Ricardo Porro's building, and how she comes to terms with the end of her career as a dancer and a teacher. I was drawn to the book because it inquires with meticulous thoroughness into the relationship between dance and architecture. The author tells the story of a twofold defeat, at once personal and national-revolutionary. Trained at the most avant-garde dance academies of New York, when she was 21 Guillermoprieto realized she had to give up her studies under Martha Graham and Merce Cunningham, relinquishing her aspiration to become a top dancer and moving to teach full-time in Cuba. That was the first defeat. Meanwhile, Fidel Castro had set a chimerical target for that year's sugar harvest: 10 million tonnes of cane, requiring the

5 The 1984 documentary by Néstor Almendros, *Improper Conduct*, traces the persecution of homosexuals in those years and interviews some former UMAP prisoners.

wholesale mobilization of the country to achieve it. According to Castro, such an effort would be the definitive stimulus for overcoming underdevelopment once and for all. But even though the entire population threw themselves, willingly or otherwise, into the harvest, the results fell short. That was the second defeat. Guillermoprieto braids the two stories together, dance and harvest, to evoke a polarized period when manual work was exalted, the arts were decried, and collective depression prevailed.

Beyond the historical record it offers, this account based on the day-to-day life of the Schools sheds light on hitherto overlooked aspects of their design and subsequent abandon. It points out, for instance, that they were supposed to bring forth a new type of artist, faithful to the Revolution—something that implied not only an iron-clad commitment to the regime but also the cultivation of virility. These memoirs thus enable a fresh approach to the architecture of Porro, Garatti and Gottardi in light of how they incorporated or resisted the strict heterosexualizing discipline which, according to a conversation with Porro recorded in the book, the revolutionary leaders had demanded of them. The Schools can henceforth be studied in the context of the repression of homosexuality in the 1960s in Cuba and also, by extension, around the world, given that homophobia was endorsed at the time by the bulk of the psychiatric establishment in the capitalist sphere as much as in the socialist one. What's more, it transpires that the project's fall from grace may well be due in part to the fact that its design, far from discouraging homosexuality, tended to abet the effete by functioning like a huge anti-panoptic playground, celebrating deviation, dissimulation and play.

Opposite page:
Details of the three art schools. Hugo Consuegra, "Las Escuelas Nacionales de Arte," *Arquitectura Cuba* 334 (1965): 14; 18-19.

As well as tackling this issue head-on, Guillermoprieto also probes the tensions between architecture and habitability from the angle of her own failure to deal with such outlandish spaces. Despite being a teacher of avant-garde disciplines that query the relationship of the human body with architecture, she was unable to get these equally avant-garde classrooms to work for her. On the contrary, she felt they hindered her professional efforts. The account by her colleague Lorna Burdsall offers an alternative view. Her memoir uncovers a richer history of modern dance in Cuba than Guillermoprieto allows, one that is above all bolder in relation to architecture and more open to recycling; she conveys an understanding of revolutionary exigencies and Cold War restrictions not as a hindrance but as a spur to dig deeper into the relations between bodies, movement, and spaces.

LAS ESCUELAS NACIONALES DE ARTE

HUGO CONSUEGRA

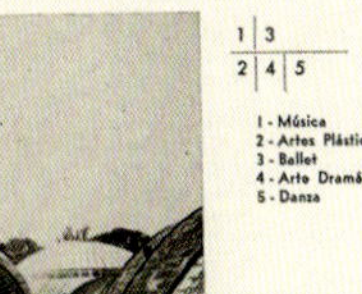

1	3	
2	4	5

1 - Música
2 - Artes Plásticas
3 - Ballet
4 - Arte Dramático
5 - Danza

Cuba, un pequeño país subdesarrollado, en el momento más difícil de su historia, cuando para sobrevivir debe hacer frente al coloso norteamericano, en medio del bloqueo económico y las agresiones armadas, se permite el lujo de construir —a un costo de más de 13 millones de pesos— unas escuelas de arte de tales proporciones como no se vieron en Londres, París, New York o Roma.

¿Qué sentido puede tener ésto? ¿Cómo explicárselo? Cinco escuelas de Arte (Ballet, Artes Dramáticas, Danza Moderna, Artes Plásticas y Música) con cinco sendas salas de teatro, cinco bibliotecas y cinco cafeterías, sin que —entre otros excesos económicos— se pensara en la utilización común de estos servicios. ¿No es evidente la desproporción? ¿Cómo justificar el estado de ánimo que mueve esta iniciativa? Se pudiera responder: ¿qué pensar de un pequeño país subdesarrollado que se declara "primer país socialista de América" a noventa millas de los Estados Unidos? Un pequeño país cuya economía, producción y mercados, era por entero controlada y orgánicamente dependiente de su colosal enemigo, y que, sin embargo, se atreve a romper esa dependencia y vivir en perpetuo desafío ¡David y Goliat! Un enorme sentido de la desproporción, sin duda.

El forastero que visita las escuelas de arte, independientemente de que le gusten o no —y lo más frecuente ha sido que se entusiasme con ellas— recibe una sensación de exceso y grandilocuencia, y ello naturalmente se presta a críticas, sobre todo entre aquellos arquitectos formados en los postulados de una arquitectura más directa y menos espectacular. También aquí cabe preguntarse: ¿no es grandilocuente y espectacular nuestro momento histórico? Una revolución que dicta para la historia una Segunda Declaración de La Habana, ante más de un millón de ciudadanos —entre una población total de seis millones— congregados en la plaza pública. Una revolución que durante la llamada "crisis de octubre", dispuesta a afrontar todos los riesgos, se produce con total independencia, haciéndose fuerte solamente en la razón moral que la asiste y en su disposición al sacrificio si fuere necesario.

Si la cultura cubana —en cualquiera de sus manifestaciones— aspira a reflejar la revolución, estimo que debe hacerlo con plena conciencia de cierta desorbitación; quiero decir: voluntariamente indiscreta y tremendista. No podemos ser suecos o finlandeses a noventa millas de los Estados Unidos, aunque tanta admiración sintamos por su arquitectura y aunque comprendamos que bien nos vendría un poco de su serenidad y su mesura. Las escuelas nacionales de arte, por arriba de la personal expresión de sus creadores —dos arquitectos italianos y uno cubano— es la expresión de este momento en la Cuba revolucionaria.

Se ha dicho que son "barrocas". El propio Ricardo Porro, autor de las escuelas de Artes Plásticas y de Danza Moderna, ha escrito: "Un sentido espacial clásico no se hubiera prestado a eso (se refiere a la caracterización de los espacios), ni a las imágenes que quería lograr. Necesitaba una riqueza de elementos arquitectónicos y espacios flúidos y variados. El resultado fue de un gran barroquismo". No estoy totalmente de acuerdo. Por supuesto que las escuelas, tanto las de Porro como la de Roberto Gottardi —Artes Dramáticas—y las de Vittorio Garatti —Música y Ballet— están muy lejos de lo que pudiera llamarse sentido clásico del espacio; pero yo propondría en lugar de "barroco", un

GARATTI

BALLET

MUSICA

GOTTARDI
ARTE DRAMATICO

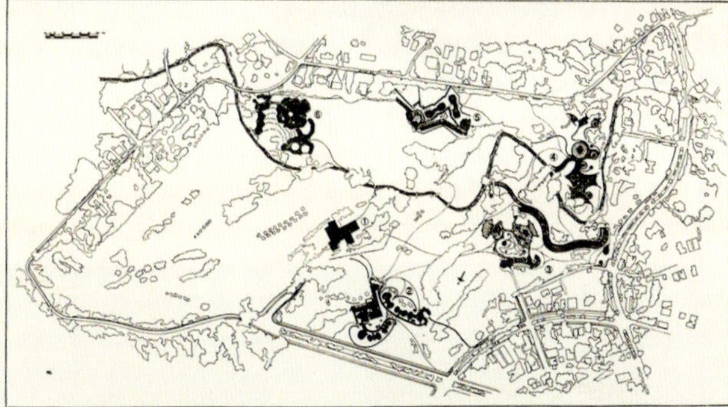

ESCUELAS DE ARTE/PLANTA

1 - ADMINISTRACION
2 - ARTES PLASTICAS/ARQ. PORRO
3 - ESCUELA DE MUSICA/ARQ. GARATTI
4 - ESCUELA DE BALLET/ARQ. GARATTI
5 - ESCUELA DE DANZA MODERNA/ARQ. PORRO
6 - ARTES DRAMATICAS/ARQ. GOTTARDI

Otra de las mejores correspondencias de forma-contenido la consigue expresar Garatti en su escuela de Ballet. El paseo arquitectónico es aquí musical, embriagante y envolvente: danzatorio sin duda alguna. Siempre a cubierto sobre ligeras bóvedas que se van foliando, acuchillando la luz, somos invitados a ondular, a girar, a resbalar sobre sus superficies. Fuentes y muros cuyos bordes superiores fungen de acueductos, crecen desde la tierra, dulcemente desarrollados, integrándose poco a poco en la danza de todos los elementos arquitectónicos, para luego, después de representado su papel, como en un ciclo vital, decrecer, morir y volver a la tierra de donde han salido. Su dulce intimidad, su genuino tropicalismo, la delicadeza de los detalles en el uso del ladrillo y la losa de barro, y su adaptación al paisaje de cuya frondosidad se hace eco, sitúan a esta obra entre las más refinadas que se hayan construido en nuestro país.

Soy optimista con respecto al futuro de estas obras. La realidad —por dura que sea ahora— y la esperanza —por fantástica que pueda parecer— se acercan, cada vez más vertiginosamente en la Cuba revolucionaria. La plenitud viene indefectiblemente. La "desproporción" de las escuelas de arte disminuirá con el tiempo. Para comprendernos hay que evaluar que somos un pueblo que compra muñecas españolas para la festividad de los Reyes Magos, en los momentos de su más intensa crisis económica. Las escuelas nacionales de arte, por su emplazamiento paradisiaco y su relación con los clubes marítimos —fabulosa inversión monetaria, rescatada para el uso popular— será sin duda, como apuntara Garatti, el núcleo del gran pulmón recreacional de La Habana y su función como centro intelectual irá mucho más lejos de la mera labor docente.

HOSTILE SCHOOLS

Alma Guillermoprieto records her first impressions of the Art Schools rather in the tone of a nineteenth-century archeologist, like a sort of Alice Dixon plunging into the jungles of Yucatán to discover fascinating, but unintelligible, ruins. She tells of arriving in Cubanacán by night after a long journey from New York and walking into what seems like a dark wilderness, full of creepy noises, from which loom, one by one, peculiar contours semi-smothered in undergrowth. This disturbing vision is poles apart from the sense of cosmic peace invoked by Georg Simmel at the beginning of the twentieth century to explain our attraction to archeological ruins. To Guillermoprieto, the shadowy buildings amid luxuriance are instead unsettling, for she intuits at once that she has come to live in a place she finds deeply *unheimlich*.[6] In intricate emotional detail, adopting the romantic technique of projecting inner turmoil onto the environment, she conveys the feeling of defeat that has shrouded her since deciding to stop training under Graham and Cunningham. Coming to Cubanacán means, then, stepping into darkness, literally and emotionally; an ominous premonition, for she had thought that any school, especially an art school, must always be dazzling rather than bleak or lugubrious.

Details of Gottardi's Dramatic Arts School. Consuegra, "Las Escuelas Nacionales de Arte,": 24-25.

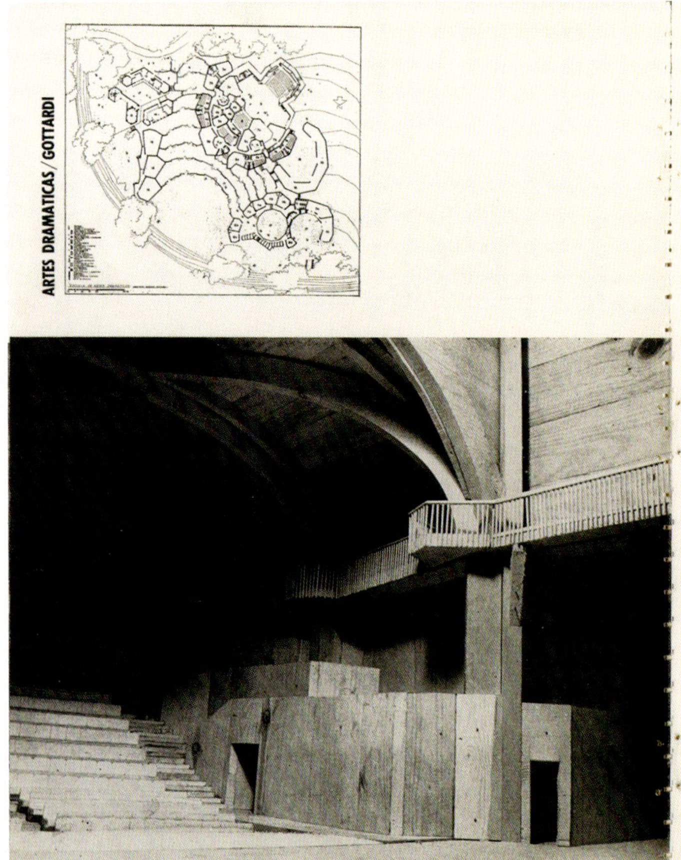

Paradoxically, the building she grows fondest of is the former country-club management office, now the rectorate. She calls it "a magical world in a bubble."[7] One of the strategies of the initial Cubanacán conversion was the old rhetorical gesture of erecting victors' symbols on top of the monuments of the vanquished, leaving their remains visible so as to emphasize the triumph over them. This gesture was one reason to reuse the office for administrative purposes while having it encircled by the five revolutionary art schools, as if besieged. Guillermoprieto, however, is unimpressed by the rhetoric, either because she is unwilling to meekly reproduce revolutionary discourse, or because she genuinely prefers white-cube modernism over the fantastical organicism of the schools. She does not see the country-club office as a captive foe, pardoned but forced to serve his captors. It is the reverse: she commends the building's beauty while, as we shall see, condemning the deficiencies of Ricardo Porro's Dance School.

Guillermoprieto spent almost a year living and working in Cubanacán, and her day-to-day experience of the place is recorded in rich detail. However, we should not forget that these are reminiscences of events that occurred thirty years earlier, so that subsequent experiences and ideas are bound to have seeped into her assessments. *Dancing with Cuba*, published five years after Loomis's book, demythologizes the iconic quality of Porro's building. It was inspired by the movement of dancers, something Guillermoprieto judges to be an esthetic success, but in her opinion makes for impractical, indeed hostile, teaching rooms. Her fundamental reproach to Porro is that he imposed his own visual creativity at the expense of the most minimal standards required by dancers to perform their best, especially when it came to the appalling acoustics: "every clap of the hands populated the space with echoes; every phrase from the teacher generated ghosts. Nevertheless, you had to shout in order to be heard by someone at the other end of the immense space."[8] The building played against the teacher, resonant close up and deadening at a distance, ignoring the acoustic requirements of an art form in which music, and sound generally, coexist with movement in harmony or tension. In the modernist context of a synthesis of the arts, the writer deplores the way an architect's delusions of grandeur forcibly marginalize the other arts that should have found an auspicious ecosystem in those spaces.

Guillermoprieto does comment on the unwelcoming, not to say aggressive, rehearsal spaces she had contended with in New York. And yet she seems unable to perceive the numerous ways in which the schools, inside and outside their classrooms, offered novel possibilities for spatial exploration: the winding medieval alleyways of Gottardi's drama building, the underground ramp of the Ballet

6 I recommend Anthony Vidler's study of the *unheimlich* (unhomely) in architecture, *The Architectural Uncanny: Essays in the Modern Unhomely* (Cambridge: MIT Press, 1992).

7 Alma Guillermoprieto, *Dancing with Cuba: A Memoir of the Revolution*, trans. Esther Allen (New York: Vintage, 2005), p. 48.

8 Ibid., p. 54.

Opposite page:
Above: Details of Porro's Visual Art Schools. Consuegra, "Las Escuelas Nacionales de Arte,": 20-21.

Below: Details of Garatti's Ballet and Music schools. Consuegra, "Las Escuelas Nacionales de Arte,": 22-23.

School, the shifting topographies enabled by the mobile ceilings of the Music School—both of these by Garatti—and the interminable, crisscrossing corridors of Porro's Visual Arts and Modern Dance buildings, dotted with light and shade like labyrinths merging with the verdant canopies of the banks of the Quibú River, near the creeks, lakes, and secret paths of the former golf course.

Guillermoprieto's dissatisfaction extends to the equipment and fittings. Unable to blame the architect for this, she castigates a Revolution steeped in extreme ideological inflexibility, to the extent that pianos and mirrors appear as capitalist vestiges that have no place in the educational spaces of the new regime. Or so the school board informs the new dance teacher. The author recognizes the ambiguity of this excuse: the lack of pianos and mirrors could well be down to the scarcity produced by the embargo, even though it is justified to her as a sovereign ideological decision in keeping with the Revolution.

Whether attributable to political purism or to shortages, Guillermoprieto takes these deficiencies as an affront to her work. She tries replacing the piano with Afro-Cuban percussion, only to conclude that such rhythms do not suit the type of movements proper to New York vanguardism. As for the mirrors, the directors forswear them as "symbols of vanity" and "decadence,"[9] which irritates Guillermoprieto beyond measure. Her solution to this problem provokes an incident. She decides to invite her students to her room, where at least the dressing table has a mirror. When the directors hear about it, she is reprimanded for the inappropriate presence of students in a teacher's bedroom. From that moment forward, her relations with students and colleagues deteriorate, it is the beginning of the end, the gradual acknowledgement of defeat not just as a dancer but as a teacher. The very title of the memoir in Spanish, *La Habana en un espejo* (Havana in a Mirror) is a nod to the centrality of this traumatic showdown around the absence of mirrors—an absence that leaves Havana incapable of seeing itself. The author must fill the gap. Thanks to her multicultural position (a New York Mexican) and her expertise (a foreign technician hired for an elite school), she can herself be the mirror; that is, she can offer an interpretation of the possible reasons that prevented the construction of a more open Revolution, more alive to the creative, the wayward, and the experimental.

9 Ibid., p. 51.

Guillermoprieto's colleague Lorna Burdsall, meanwhile, takes a very different view. The partner of an early revolutionary, Manuel Piñeiro, alias Barbarroja (Redbeard), whom she met when he was a student in New York during the 1950s, Burdsall underwent a similar formation to Guillermoprieto's. She too studied with Graham and Cunningham, as well as with the Mexican-American choreographer

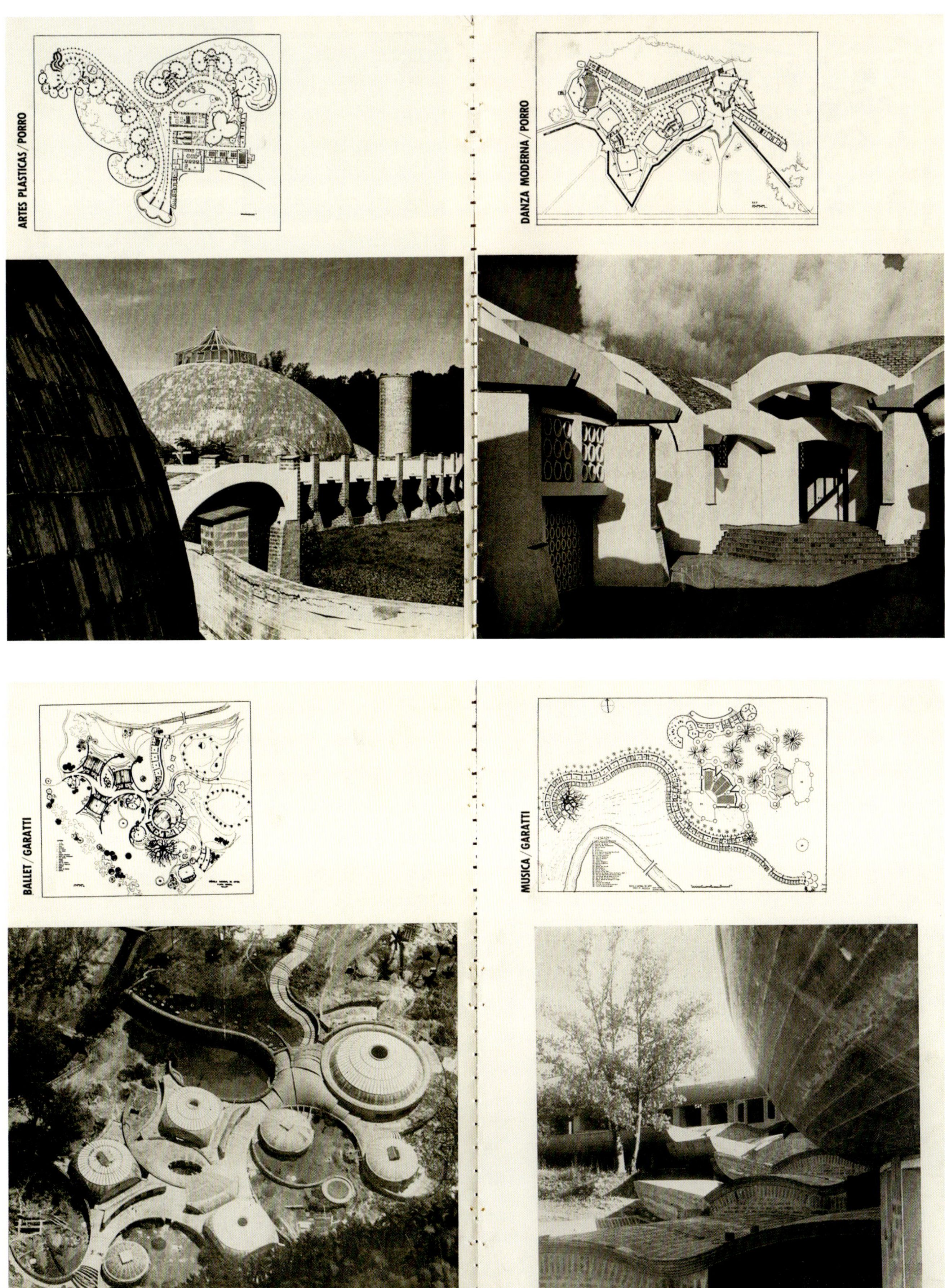
ARTES PLASTICAS/PORRO
DANZA MODERNA/PORRO
BALLET/GARATTI
MUSICA/GARATTI

José Limón. It was in Limón's class that she met Elfriede Mahler,[10] an American pupil of Graham's and a future antagonist of Guillermoprieto in her role as a director of the School of Modern Dance in Havana. Mahler brought Burdsall onto the staff in 1967 and Guillermoprieto three years later, in 1970. In contrast to the former's bemusement vis-à-vis the values of the Cuban regime, the latter was familiar with the ins and outs of revolutionary culture since before the Sierra Maestra, owing to her relationship with Piñeiro. She shared those values and lived by them, while supporting her husband unconditionally as, at that time, a top official in the Interior Ministry and the Cuban intelligence service, directly responsible for Fidel's security.

As befits this communion with the Revolution, Burdsall treated its constraints as so many opportunities to innovate, acting on the Castrist slogan about turning adversity into victory. She writes, for example, that the power cuts occurring in Cubanacán had nothing to do with shortages but were caused by the sabotage of students too lazy to rehearse, and that she, who taught the night class, responded with creativity and exigency. If the lights failed, she got her students to practice their balance in the penumbra outside, by the sole light of the moon.[11] Likewise the dearth of costumes and sets was countered by resourceful recycling, using lard barrels for props or torn parachutes to simulate heaving seas.[12] And if there was no rehearsal room available she would assemble her dancers in her own living room, sparking a run of "home performances"[13] at a time when international modern dance was similarly experimenting with unconventional locations.

Guillermoprieto castigates Porro and the Revolution for the same defect: both espoused lofty avant-garde notions, artistic or pedagogical, and then failed to properly execute them. Porro sought to build an iconic institution, the monument of a Revolution that called for new forms of habitation for a new regime and a new man, but he wound up imposing his ambition as a sculptor of buildings over the most minimal levels of functionality required by a dance school. The Revolution, aspiring to be in the educational vanguard, lured teachers of cutting-edge dance like Guillermoprieto herself, only to make them work in disgraceful conditions. And yet Burdsall's autobiography suggests, instead, that there was plenty of room for artistic innovation within revolutionary orthodoxy, because militant enthusiasm was able to forge new expressive possibilities. *Dancing with Cuba* describes the gulf between expectation and reality, project and practice, and the disappointments derived from the conservative turn taken by the notions of Revolution and avant-garde at a time of unusual geopolitical tension; but to read it alongside *More Than Just a Footnote* makes one aware of a certain incapacity in Guillermoprieto to identify the rich

10 Lorna Burdsall, *More Than Just a Footnote: Dancing from Connecticut to Revolutionary Cuba* (Havana: Lorna Burdsall, 2001), p. 112.

11 Ibid., p. 159.

12 Ibid., p. 186.

13 Ibid., p. 201.

14 Guillermoprieto, *Dancing with Cuba*, p. 231.

15 Ibid., p. 271.

16 Ibid., pp. 271-272.

potential of the uncommon spaces of Cubanacán and to dare explore them, revealing an imbalance between her avant-garde training and her traditionalist attitude even as some of her colleagues were embracing such risks.

A MASCULINE DANCE

Well into her book, Guillermoprieto mentions coming across John Loomis's work, *A Revolution of Forms*, and this discovery prompts a change of tone in her assessment of the Art Schools. She becomes slightly more understanding and appreciative, and at some points she practically reproduces Loomis's arguments. All the same, there remains the sense of a hostile architecture; "even the buildings are kind of disturbing,"[14] and this, as the narrative progresses, arouse a kind of Stockholm syndrome in the author. When her anxiety mounts, for instance, she repeats a compulsive ritual that helps to numb her senses: lying flat on her back in the middle of the Dance School, she counts all of the bricks in the cupola one by one. The abstracted observation of the very vault that oppresses her and hampers her teaching is what paradoxically enables her to escape from an adverse environment she does not understand, whose values she disapproves of, and whose intrusions she experiences as assaults.

Nevertheless, her reading of Loomis had the happy result of impelling her to seek out Porro, then living in Paris, for an interview. Although she does not say so in the book, to all intents and purposes the end of her dancing career launched her on the path to becoming a highly successful writer and journalist, one of the leading chroniclers of Latin America of the second half of the twentieth century and up to today. A contributor to the *Guardian*, *Newsweek*, the *New Yorker* and the *New York Review of Books*, among others, she has also won major international journalism awards. Guillermoprieto's conversation with Porro in Paris, recounted in *Dancing with Cuba*, casts an indispensable light on previously overlooked aspects of the conception and design of the Art Schools.

Why build a modern dance school at all, she asks Porro, when there was no modern dance to speak of in Cuba? Why not focus on the ballet, which enjoyed huge prestige inside and outside the country? Porro's answer is an eye-opener. He explains the creation of the Dance School as a strategy of the regime to render dancing wholesome, or to de-gay it, given that ballet had been infected by a kind of "virus of homosexuality."[15] The prestige of Alicia Alonso as director of the National Ballet of Cuba clearly ruled out simply banning the art. According to Porro, measures were taken instead to heterosexualize the ballet, such as recruiting new pupils from country farms and orphanages:[16] children raised at a remove from the city

A la izquierda: Planta general de la Escuela Nacional de Artes Plásticas, Cubanacán, La Habana, 1961/63. Arq. Ricardo Porro. Ala izquierda, abajo: Vista aérea de la Escuela. Se percibe la estructura compositiva libre, generada por los pasillos de circulación y los volúmenes cupulados de aulas y talleres. La zona corresponde a las aulas teóricas, oficinas y taller de grabado. En esta página: Vistas de los dos patios interiores circunscriptos por las circulaciones cubiertas, donde se realizan las exposiciones de los trabajos de los alumnos del taller de escultura. En el patio-plaza principal, una fuente-escultura constituye el centro visual de la composición.

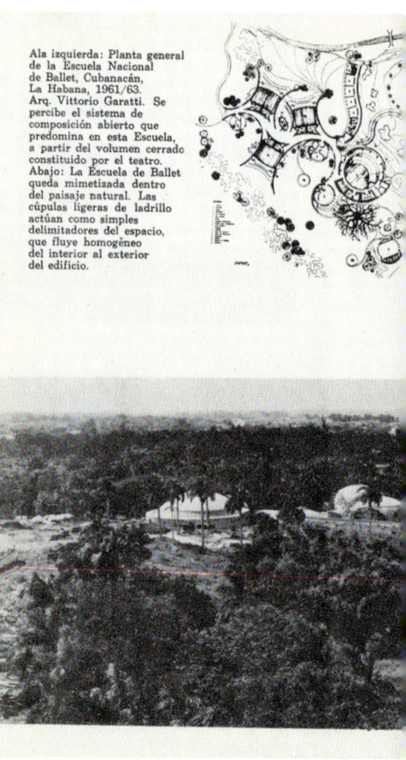

Ala izquierda: Planta general de la Escuela Nacional de Ballet, Cubanacán, La Habana, 1961/63. Arq. Vittorio Garatti. Se percibe el sistema de composición abierto que predomina en esta Escuela, a partir del volumen cerrado constituido por el teatro. Abajo: La Escuela de Ballet queda mimetizada dentro del paisaje natural. Las cúpulas ligeras de ladrillo actúan como simples delimitadores del espacio, que fluye homogéneo del interior al exterior del edificio.

and hence from its sexual deviations. Homosexuality, it seems, was an urban virus.[17] Modern dance, on the other hand, not as effeminate as ballet in the eyes of revolutionary officials, was a promising tool to combat what Fidel called *el fenomenito*, the "phenomenette" of homosexuality, which he saw as the legacy of urban capitalism with its cabarets, sequins and spangles, mirrors and pianos, thoroughly at odds with the manliness of the new regime.

Cuba was not of course alone in its acute homophobia. The war of repression of the 1960s was global and ideologically transversal, which is why the LGTBIQ+ movement kicked off precisely at the end of that decade. The relevant point with regard to Cuba and the topic that concerns us here is that, in Porro's opinion as recorded by Guillermoprieto, this homophobia impinged directly on the design of the Art Schools and their operation. For example, although the Revolution usually advocated functionalism and standardization, there was great pressure on the architects to replicate some rooms, however superfluously, so as to segregate the students in accordance with the sexual-orientation stereotypes espoused by the leadership. Porro tells Guillermoprieto: "For that reason, it was decided that a separate dining room would be built in each school. I thought it was ridiculous. The logical thing was for the Schools to function as a single vast center of communal life and artistic interchange, but no: it was best that each school should have its own dining room, so that the boys from the dance schools wouldn't endanger those from other schools."[18]

17 See, contradicting this assumption, the famous autobiography by Reinaldo Arenas, *Before Night Falls*, in which sexual activity between men is shown to be just as rife in the countryside.

18 Guillermoprieto, *Dancing with Cuba*, p. 271.

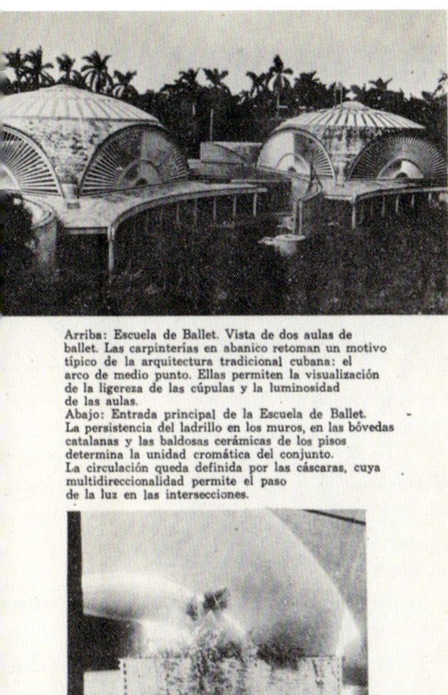

Arriba: Escuela de Ballet. Vista de dos aulas de ballet. Las carpinterías en abanico retoman un motivo típico de la arquitectura tradicional cubana: el arco de medio punto. Ellas permiten la visualización de la ligereza de las cúpulas y la luminosidad de las aulas.
Abajo: Entrada principal de la Escuela de Ballet. La persistencia del ladrillo en los muros, en las bóvedas catalanas y las baldosas cerámicas de los pisos determina la unidad cromática del conjunto. La circulación queda definida por las cáscaras, cuya multidireccionalidad permite el paso de la luz en las intersecciones.

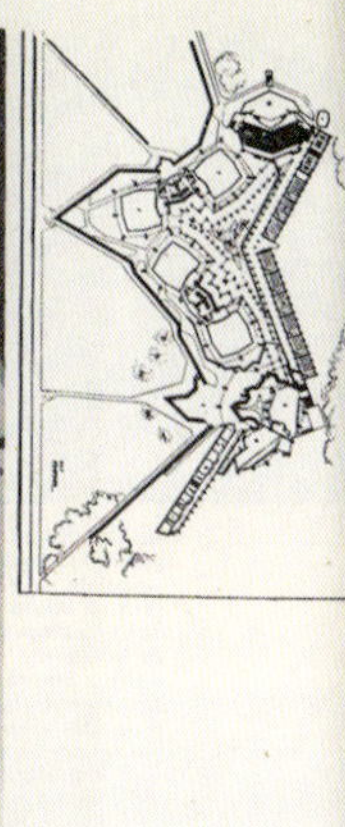

Escuela Nacional de Danza Moderna, Cubanacán, La Habana, 1961/63. Arq. Ricardo Porro. Arriba: Planta general de la Escuela. Las aulas de danza quedan pareadas y unidas por los servicios, articuladas libremente frente a la espina que forman las aulas teóricas. A la izquierda: las bóvedas que definen la entrada principal de la Escuela. Abajo: Vista parcial aérea; en primer plano el patio central y los corredores cubiertos de circulación.

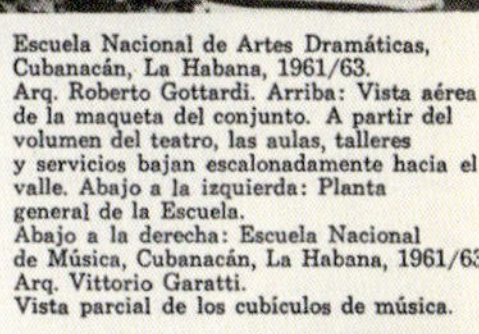

Escuela Nacional de Artes Dramáticas, Cubanacán, La Habana, 1961/63. Arq. Roberto Gottardi. Arriba: Vista aérea de la maqueta del conjunto. A partir del volumen del teatro, las aulas, talleres y servicios bajan escalonadamente hacia el valle. Abajo a la izquierda: Planta general de la Escuela.
Abajo a la derecha: Escuela Nacional de Música, Cubanacán, La Habana, 1961/63. Arq. Vittorio Garatti. Vista parcial de los cubículos de música.

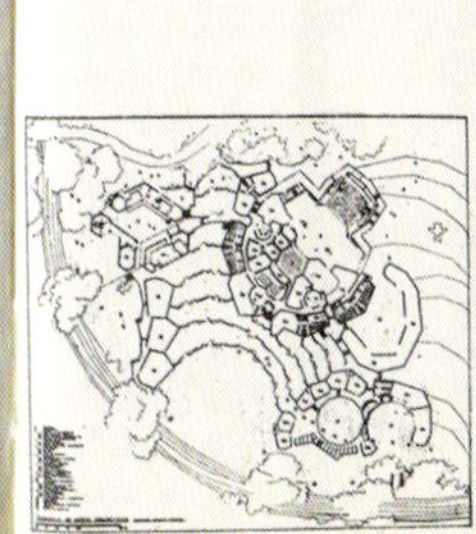

Both pages:
Roberto Segre, *10 años de arquitectura revolucionaria*, pp. 96-101.

The normalizing paternalism of the Revolution went in for spatial segregation in order to cure, not perhaps homosexuality root and branch, but at least its most conspicuous symptom, effeteness; in other words to stem the problem of "improper conduct," as in the title of Néstor Almendros's well-known documentary about the homophobia of the regime. The aim was to produce, on the model of the new man, a new dancer: free of affectation, virile, committed, and devoted.

The segregate-and-cure plan was not implemented for many reasons, chief among them the demands of material conditions; the shortages that plagued the Revolution as a result of the embargo and of the doomed attempts at humungous cane harvests made it necessary to maximize resources. To feed all the students in one hall was more efficient than to deal with several venues. In the case of the Dance School, the intended dining room was repurposed as a meeting room—which also happened to be the setting for the key scene in *Dancing with Cuba* that exposes the deep phobia of both gays and art that imbued the Revolution around 1970. The author reports a conversation in this room between the teaching staff and the students, who were preparing to go on strike against the inadequacies of their training and the poor prospects for developing a career after graduation. The meeting is chaired by Manuel Hidalgo, a baker by profession, lately promoted to the directors' board of the National Art Schools. In an earlier anecdote, Guillermoprieto has already indicated Hidalgo's disdain for the task assigned to him by the Revolution. She reconstructs a meeting between him and Burdsall's husband, Manuel Piñeiro, who asks: "I mean, is this school serving any purpose, in the end? We aren't too sure what artists are good for, in this country, we're not sure of their commitment to the Revolution, they continue to be the most unpredictable ... not to say vacillating sector, and from the beginning we've counted on this school to breed a new kind of artist. Good, clean people, without vices. So what do you think of these kids?"[19] After some beating around the bush, Hidalgo begs to be taken out of there and allowed to go back to baking, "because for this, for administering this shithouse full of artists and *patos* and intellectuals—I'm no good for this."[20] On top of his disparagement of art, homosexuality, and thought, Hidalgo seems to take for granted the failure of the Schools in forging a new sort of male dancer.

Given this background and returning to the scene in the dining room turned meeting room, Guillermoprieto is hardly surprised, though still outraged, by Hidalgo's belligerence toward her favorite student, Orlando, when he expresses his wish to drop modern dance and switch to ballet. Hidalgo scornfully suggests he go off to Miami: maybe over there people will pay for him to study "all that fancy prancing he's so attracted to."[21] For Guillermoprieto, this public humiliation of a student by a director is the last straw. She resigns from her job in Cubanacán. In narrative terms, this is the climactic event supporting one of the main themes of the memoir: By 1970, the Revolution had shut the door on creativity, casting artists, and gay artists in particular, as the enemy within. Feeling that in such conditions it would be unethical to remain involved in the revolutionary educational project, she decides to leave the island.

EFFEMINATE ARCHITECTURE

Guillermoprieto gives the impression that modern dance was virtually unknown in Cuba before the creation of the National Art Schools. However, Lorna Burdsall's autobiography concurs with the research of Elizabeth B. Schwall to make that an overstatement. From an insider's perspective and with a wealth of detail, Burdsall constructs a genealogy of modern dance on the island that reaches back to before the Revolution, and whose founding figure is the choreographer and dancer Ramiro Guerra. Trained in ballet in Cuba and then in Russia during the 1940s, Guerra moved to the US in the 50s to study with Doris Humphrey, José Limón, and Martha Graham, until his definitive return to the island a few years before the revolutionary offensive, planning to import a modern dance that would be enriched with the singularity of Cuban bodies, gestures, and folklore.

19 Ibid., pp. 133-134.

20 Ibid., p. 135.

21 Ibid., p. 239.

22 Carolina Riera Sanz, "Ramiro Guerra, bailarín, coreógrafo y maestro" (Santiago: Universidad de Chile, 2012), p. 26.

23 Elizabeth B. Schwall, *Dancing with the Revolution* (Chapel Hill: University of North Carolina Press, 2012), pp. 3-4.

24 Burdsall, *More Than Just a Footnote*, p. 173.

Guerra started off working with cabaret artistes, until the victory of the Revolution and foundation of the National Theater of Cuba led to the formation of a National Modern Dance Group in 1959. Guerra was appointed director, with Elfriede Mahler and Lorna Burdsall as his assistants.[22] In effect, this means that modern dance in Cuba predated not only the National Art Schools but indeed the Revolution itself, and recalls the direct yet paradoxical connection with the cabaret culture the Revolution so despised. The Soviet film *I Am Cuba* (1964) epitomizes this disapproval of nightlife in one of its four stories, focusing on an impoverished cabaret dancer and reluctant prostitute played by the Afro-Cuban Luz María Collazo, who was already one of the stars of modern dance on the island and married to the architect of the School of Dramatic Arts, Roberto Gottardi. According to Schwall, when modern dance largely replaced cabaret many choreographers and dancers used it to explore a range of mostly political themes, mostly toeing the official line, notwithstanding frequent tensions with the regime's contradictions around race, sexuality, and gender expression.[23] Although Guillermoprieto's text leaves out these precedents, her account of the Revolution's support for modern dance does not differ significantly from those of Burdsall and Schwall. The Revolution promoted modern dance, but with reservations and fluctuations. Its goal was to convert cabaret skills into a more politically aware type of dancing in tune with prevailing ideology, and this included efforts to make dance unambiguously heterosexual.

In Burdsall, the matter of homosexuality is less prominent than in Guillermoprieto, but the brief example she cites is particularly significant. She recounts how Ramiro Guerra, despite the prestige he had earned by the mammoth achievement of bringing modern dance to Cuba, was then ostracized by the regime for his use of elements that some regarded as phallic pornography in his work *Decálogo del apocalipsis*.[24] This happened in 1971, mere months after the situation described by Guillermoprieto. In the context of the late 60s and early 70s, with the UMAP camps operative until 1968, censorship of the arts at moments of high paranoia (1971 was also the year of the poet Heberto Padilla's arrest), and manly convocations to cane-cutting, the admission Porro made to his interviewer is hardly surprising. The brief to build a School of Dance whose students would be segregated for their supposed homosexual proclivities reveals the existence of discreet policies to counter the "*fenomenito*" from the very beginning of the Revolution, even if overt measures to combat it, such as the UMAP, were not planned and implemented until 1965.

The National Art Schools were conceived as part and parcel of these pro-heterosexual policies, but their design was paradoxical:

Both pages:
Details of Gottardi's Dramatic Arts School. Photos by Roberto Gottardi. Roberto Gottardi Papers, Special Collections, Princeton University Library.

while they were intended to segregate, cure, and re-educate, the plasticity of their forms and the playful possibilities they offered for habitation and transit positively compounded the affliction they were expected to remedy. Indeed, their architecture, unusually mannered for the modernism of the time, was like an invitation to a deviant sort of creative life. Guillermoprieto does not go as far as saying this, but she does describe the buildings as reproducing the very volatility for which gay people and artists were decried. Each ensemble, she writes, was "a variation on the form of a spiral at the moment it explodes,"[25] in other words a celebration of sudden, unpredictable motion. The Revolution had sought to turn a capitalist pleasure park into a school of rectification through art, to transform bourgeois leisure into revolutionary training in adherence to the norms; but this experiment turned out badly in the Revolution's own eyes, leading to the semi-abandon of the Schools and the banishment of their chief architect. Compared to the highly regulated, standardized layout of East Havana or the CUJAE campus, the National Art Schools are like a huge playground of curved, capricious forms, full of allusions to sex and the female body, as befitted the neo-baroque then in vogue.[26] Following

Roger Caillois's distinction in the ambit of play, they offer endless opportunities to combine the disciplined backbone of each art with the *Paideia* of everyday habitation—prompting improvisation, surprise, carefree movement, joy, queer circulation, shimmying, hiding, trying things out.

If Judith Butler defined gender as an imitation without an original, in the revolutionary Cuba of those years there was certainly an aspirational virile ideal codified in the figure of the bearded fighter, whose iconography and values scarcely ever changed. The Revolution also produced a number of contrary stereotypes or anti-models, among them that of the urban, effeminate male dancer associated with the casinos and parties of the bad old days. This character was thought to despise the hard work and ideological steadfastness required by the sugar harvest and the constant vicissitudes of a Cold War that always threatened to get hot. The notion that the Dance Schools could possibly correct these shortcomings testifies to the boundless biopolitical faith placed by the early Revolution in architecture and construction, not only to tackle pervasive socioeconomic inequality, but also as the "normalizing, genderizing, and racializing force"[27] extensively studied by Paul B. Preciado in

25 Guillermoprieto, *Dancing with Cuba*, p. 269.

26 *Paradiso*, by José Lezama Lima, is the paradigmatic case in literature. It was published just a year after the inauguration / semi-abandon of the Schools.

27 Paul B. Preciado, "Architecture as a Practice of Biopolitical Disobedience," *Log*, no. 25 (Summer 2012): 121-134.

Both pages:
Details of Gottardi's Dramatic Arts School. Photos by Roberto Gottardi. Roberto Gottardi Papers, Special Collections, Princeton University Library.

other contexts. But the designs by Porro, Garratti, and Gottardi subverted this aim, for, like time bombs going off, the Schools possessed the very traits which, says Guillermoprieto, Barbarroja ascribed to artists and Hidalgo, by extension, to gay men: they were whimsical, mischievous structures, unpredictable habitats for unpredictable artists, at a time when unpredictable was synonymous with counter-revolutionary.

CODA

Since their inauguration in 1965, the National Art Schools have operated without interruption but with a low profile, using just two (Visual Art and Modern Dance) of the five projected ensembles. Paradoxically, this semi-abandon contributed even more toward the deviant behaviors the officials were anxious to pre-empt. To fantastical architectures were added the ruins of unfinished mini-cities (Ballet, Music, Dramatic Arts), succumbing little by little to the encroachments of the wilderness; the fancifulness of the original designs was enhanced by the fancies induced by their fall into ruin.

At the same time this deterioration poses major conservation challenges, which Loomis's book succeeded in bringing to the attention of the international architectural community. There was widespread interest amid a realization that urgent intervention was needed to prevent the definitive destruction of the ensemble. The Revolution, too, has committed to the rescue effort: in 2010 the Schools were finally placed on Cuba's register of national monuments, once more becoming visible to the regime, in the acknowledgment of their great heritage value for the sense of being a Cuban and a revolutionary.

The same year of 2010 saw a sudden U-turn in the institutional stance toward homosexuality. Speaking of the persecution of the LGTBIQ+ community over past decades but especially during the 1960s, Fidel Castro declared: "It was a great injustice." His statement of apparent remorse and reparation launched a period in which the Revolution waved the banner of the LGTBIQ+ cause, though always within the vertical limits that characterize the regime. Once again, the history of the Schools and that of homosexuality unfolded in tandem: both were condemned to ostracism in 1965 and hailed as national emblems in 2010.

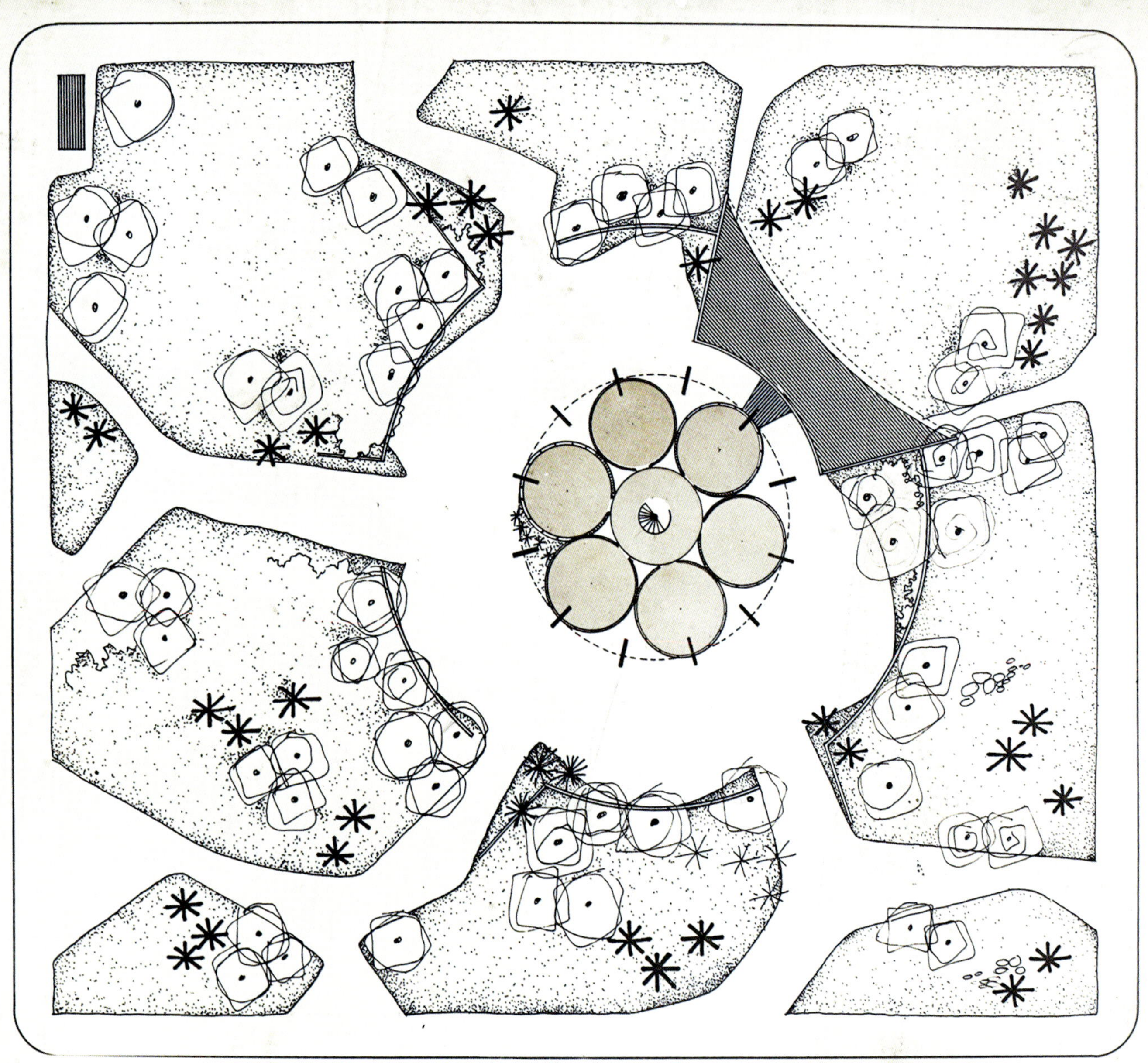

COPPELIA: REVOLUTIONARY ICE CREAMS

Iván L. Munuera

AN INFINITE LAND OF WHICH NO ONE HAD EVER SEEN THE END

In *The Infinite Island*, Gerardo Mosquera writes that the birth of Cuba in the Western imagination as an exotic and contradictory landscape can be pinpointed at the moment of its colonization.[1] When Spaniards landed on the northeastern coast of Cuba in the fifteenth century, the colonizers commanded by Christopher Columbus were uncertain whether the territory was indeed an island or *terra firma*. Its considerable size did not make this obvious to the gaze, so they asked the indigenous inhabitants, the Tainos, about its geography. The Tainos told them it was "an infinite land of which no one had ever seen the end, although it was an island." Cuba was thus born to the West as aporia, exoticizing its insertion in the canonical European corpus, overseeing its complexity, obliterating its inhabitants' right to narrate themselves.

Both pages:
Mario Girona, sketches for Coppelia Ice-cream parlor and park, ca. 1965. Mario Girona Archive. Image courtesy of Dolly Gómez. All images appearing in this chapter, unless otherwise indicated, are from the Girona archive.

1 Gerardo Mosquera, *Contemporary Art from Cuba: Irony and Survival on the Utopian Island* (Arizona State University, Delano Greenridge Editions, 2002).

Mario Girona, sketch for Coppelia.

The hyperbolic narrative of its territory continues, tinting the appreciation of its environment and understanding, and particularly its built environment and architecture, as an exotic and exoticized recipient of ideas developed elsewhere and then isolated from other relationships and genealogies. Cuban architecture has been analyzed through different lenses, frequently based on assumptions of its insularity—an insularity that is recognized from not only a geographical perspective (the island), but also a conceptual one (its isolation due to sociopolitical conditions). But the possibility of seeing it in connection with wider landscapes—let alone with a new understanding of what a landscape is, as the Tainos pointed out—has often been left behind.

The trajectory of Cuba's contemporary built environment in Western architectural theory and history can be traced from various angles, but mainly from that of its colonial history. This includes Spanish colonialism, which lasted until 1898; American imperialism, which continued until the 1959 Revolution; and then post- and de-colonial ideas put forth by Castro's regime and its dissenters: the blockade politics produced by the Cold War and Cuba's alignment with the Soviet Union and the solidarity movement, the international embargo, the public outcry coming from political prisoners within the country, and the economies of present-day tourism. What is certain is that the practice of contemporary architecture in Havana, particularly from the nineteenth century to today, is far from isolated, nor can it be merely bracketed under the umbrellas of "Tropical Modernism" or the Soviet influence. In fact, Havana's architecture is based on a continuous exchange, generating a liquid ecosystem of transaction, dialogue, friction, and ongoing debates: an infinite island. To understand the scope of these fluid transactions and their architectural-political approaches, the case of Coppelia—an ice cream parlor designed by Mario Girona, Rita María Grau and Candelario Ajuria in Havana in 1966—is revealing, as it is intimately tied to Cuba's contemporary history.

AT THE ZOO

One of the most famous images of Fidel Castro, taken by Alberto Korda during the Cuban leader's visit to New York in 1959, is of him enjoying an ice cream cone at the Bronx Zoo.[2] This image outlines the performative politics of the new Cuban regime, one that is shaped and prolongated by buildings such as Coppelia. Castro had traveled to New York in April, four months after the Revolution overthrew Fulgencio

2 *Korda: A Revolutionary Lens* (Gottingen: Steild, 2008).

Mario Girona, sketch for Coppelia showing patrons and upper galleries with tables.

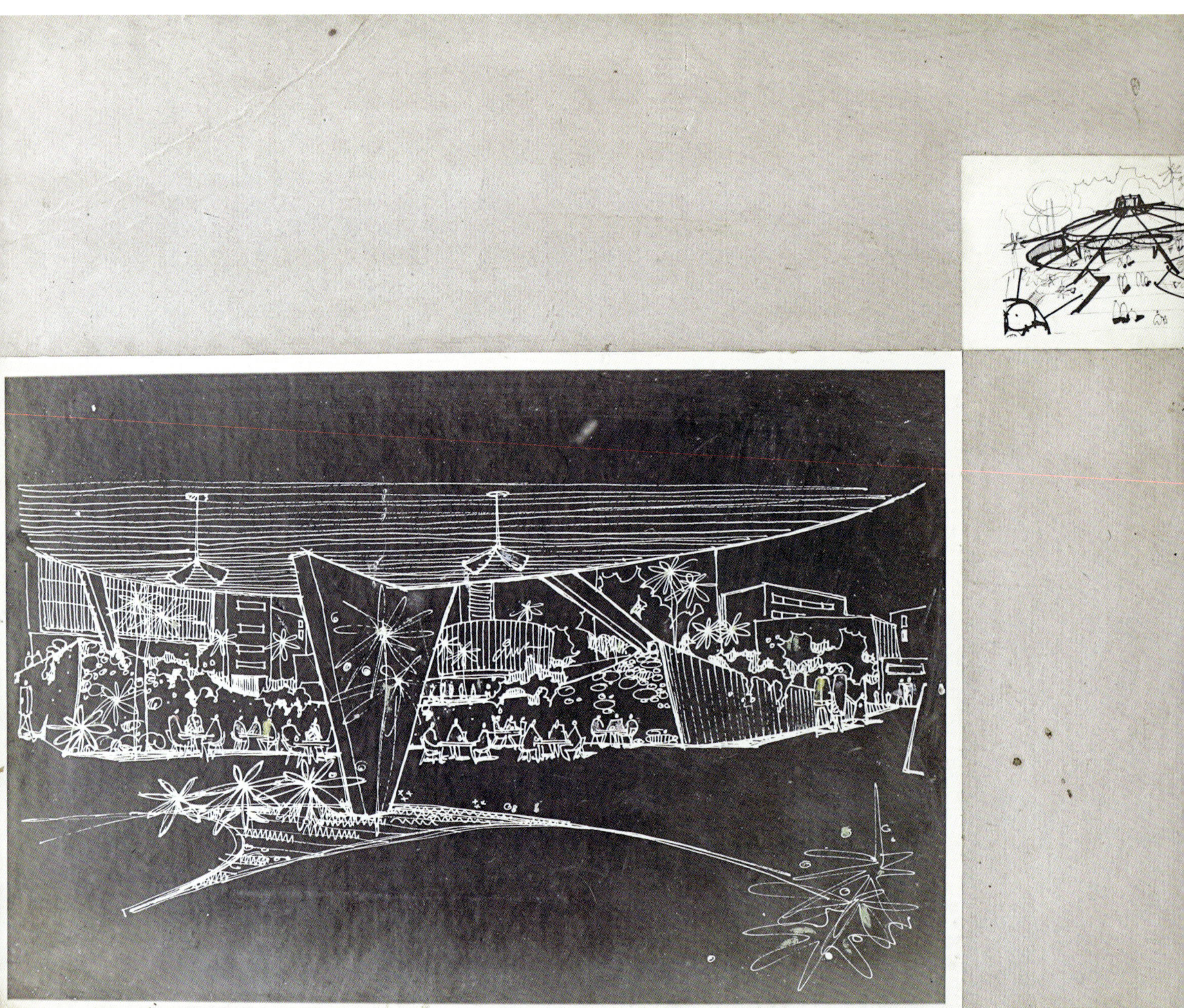

Pages from the Coppelia construction album:
Mario Girona, various sketches for Coppelia.

Batista's dictatorship, and was immediately celebrated by a captivated global audience as the image of a new way of understanding politics and revolution. Admired by the New Left and by crucial figures of the international intelligentsia such as Simone de Beauvoir and Jean-Paul Sartre (who visited Cuba in 1960), the revolutionaries were even esteemed in the United States, in the wake of a triumphant profile in the *New York Times* during their hideout in Sierra Maestra in 1957.[3]

For Eric Hobsbawm, this narrative had a cinematographic component: "The Cuban Revolution had everything: romance, heroism in the mountains, ex-student leaders with the selfless generosity of the youth—the eldest was barely past thirty—a jubilant people, in a tropical tourist paradise pulsing with rumba rhythms."[4] For others, at least at the beginning, the revolutionaries were "a bunch of Errol Flynns, theatrical brigands but not true revolutionaries," as Gamal Abdel Nasser, the leader of Egypt and pan-Arabism, described them. Their political alliances were not immediately clear, an ambiguity played on by Castro himself, who tried to tie the Cuban Revolution to the United States at a conference at Princeton University in 1959. There he stated that the Revolution was looking to 1776 (the year of US independence), and not to 1789 (the French Revolution) or 1917 (the Bolshevik Revolution). But everything changed a year after his lecture at Princeton.

When Castro was invited to speak at the United Nations in New York in 1960, the reception was rather different. Originally, the delegation was supposed to stay at the Hotel Shelburne on Lexington Avenue, but after being accused of cooking chickens in their rooms and destroying hotel furniture, they decided to switch their accommodation to the Hotel Theresa. Castro told the media that he was thinking of stringing up a hammock in Central Park or sleeping in the UN lobby if they were not treated with respect, understanding the powerful impact of images and narratives in a geopolitical context.[5]

Interviewed in his bed by Malcolm X (who declared Castro to be the "only white person I have really liked"[6]) at Hotel Theresa—located in Harlem, the pre-eminent cultural capital for African Americans—the Cuban leader criticized the structural racism of the United States. He also declared Cuba a place where everybody was welcome, regardless of their race, a site where everybody could work together for a better society. These ideas, immediately directed to denounce US policies, were further developed in Castro's four-and-a-half-hour speech at the UN Assembly, where he blasted international imperialism (particularly American), drew his position closer to the Soviet Union, affirmed the rights of nations to full sovereignty, and mooted alliances with the solidarity movements across Africa, Asia, and Latin America. This stance was also illustrated by the changes in his itinerary in New York: instead of

3 Herbert L. Mathews, "Cuban Rebel Is Visited in Hideout: Castro is still alive and still fighting in mountains," *New York Times*, February 24, 1957.

4 Eric Hobsbawm, "The Cuban Revolution and its aftermath," in *Viva La Revolución: Eric Hobsbawm on Latin America* (London: Little, Brown, 2016), p. 262.

5 Simon Hall, *Ten Days in Harlem: Fidel Castro and the Making of the 1960s* (London: Faber and Faber, 2020).

6 Rosemari Mealy, *Fidel & Malcolm X: Memorias de un encuentro* (Havana: Letras Cubanas, 2018).

attending lobbyist parties, he decided to visit popular destinations or neighborhoods in the city where marginalized communities gathered, from Harlem to the Bronx Zoo to Central Park. All this infuriated Eisenhower's government. It proposed the embargo in 1960 and cut diplomatic ties with Cuba in 1961.

HYPERCALORIC LANDSCAPES

After this, the photograph of Castro eating an ice cream cone at the Bronx Zoo became more than just anecdotal. For Castro, ice cream became part of his revolutionary project of social reconfiguration. Immediately after the Revolution, Castro ordered his ambassador in Canada to send him twenty-eight containers of ice cream from Howard Johnson's, a US restaurant and hotel chain. After trying all the flavors, he decided that Cuba needed to respond on a revolutionary level by creating something bigger and tastier, yet still affordable enough so that everyone could enjoy it, subsidizing its manufacture and the final product.

The bet on subsidized ice cream had three facets: First, it was an obvious challenge to one of the quintessential capitalist brands, combining political activism with light-hearted enjoyment. Second, it was a means of introducing dairy products into the Cuban diet, which would help to combat the rampant malnutrition and infant mortality that had prevailed during the years of Batista's dictatorship—the hypercaloric consumption of ice cream serving as a festive weapon against these deficiencies. Third, the production of ice cream required sugar, which made sugarcane cultivation respectable again. Sugar production in Cuba was politically charged—it was, after all, the result of brutal, enslaved labor practices, and was also connected to the pre-revolutionary regime's exploitative ways and destruction of nature.[7] With Castro's new endeavor, sugar transformed the productive and agricultural landscape of the island, as well its economy and trade relations. Cuba became one of the primary exporters of sugar to the Soviet Bloc.[8]

This manifested into the ice cream served at Coppelia. Today, Cubans and foreign visitors still enjoy ice cream at different prices, more expensive for tourists and international visitors, cheaper for Cubans. Located in the Vedado neighborhood on a site previously occupied by a nineteenth-century children's hospital—Hospital Reina Mercedes, demolished in 1958, a year before the Revolution—Coppelia showed off the new face of Castro's government. Just a few meters away from the former Havana Hilton (now the Hotel Habana Libre, designed by Welton Becket, Arroyo, and Menéndez), the Edificio Radiocentro CMQ (responsible for the regime's radio communication), the Cine Yara, and the university, Coppelia stands at the very end

7 Lillian Guerra, *Visions of Power in Cuba: Revolution, Redemption, and Resistance, 1959-1971* (Chapel Hill: University of North Carolina Press, 2012).

8 Louis A. Pérez Jr., *Cuba: Between Reform and Revolution* (New York: Oxford University Press, 2006).

9 Richard E. Feinberg and Claudia Padrón Cuota, "Frozen Inequality," *Quartz* (July 29, 2018).

10 J.R. Curtis, "Havana's Parque-Coppelia: Public Space Traditions in Socialist Cuba," *Places*, vol. 8, no. 3 (1993): 62-67.

Mario Girona, Sketch for Coppelia showing patrons and upper galleries.

of La Rampa, a street rising up from the Malecón. This street is the site of most governmental and institutional offices, meaning that Coppelia became the intersection of Cuba's possible futures.[9]

The building was designed by Mario Girona, Rita María Grau, and Candelario Ajuria, and engineered by Maximiliano Isoba and Gonzalo Paz. Before Coppelia, Girona was mostly known for his work with Aquiles Capablanca in designing houses for the rich in the Vedado neighborhood, and for hotels like the famous Hotel Capri. For Coppelia, he decided to work with an open concrete structure surrounded by a lush tropical garden.[10] This construction signaled a change in Havana's architectural conception: in contrast to the soaring vertical towers that had marked the previous regime (such as the US embassy, designed by Harrison and Abramovitz, with Mira and Rosich [1953], or the Hotel Riviera [1957], by Polevitsky, and Carrera), Coppelia proposed an expansive horizontal structure in the form of a spider. This was a response to the embargo, which had caused a steel shortage and hence a retreat from the construction of tall buildings (evident, too, in the National Art Schools, by Porro, Gottardi and

Page from the Coppelia construction album.
Above: Mario Girona, sketch showing buttresses, roof, and crown.
Below: Model.

Garatti).[11] It also signified a symbolic change: instead of the vertical, hierarchical society of Batista's regime, the new building embodied a horizontal and egalitarian political system.[12]

Coppelia's name and logo (the legs of a dancer in red slippers) were inspired by Léo Delibes's ballet, one of the signature pieces performed by Cuba's National Ballet under the direction of Alicia Alonso. Under the new regime, the bodily discipline produced through dance was regenerated by means of diet. Coppelia was also the favorite ballet of Celia Sánchez Manduley, a Sierra Maestra revolutionary and close collaborator of Castro's, who was particularly concerned about nutrition-related issues and became a champion of the ice cream parlor. The circular structure opened to the public on June 4, 1966, and quickly became famous for its long lines, though it was capable of hosting more than 1,000 people. The Coppelia menu offers twenty-six flavors, in honor of the failed revolutionary attack on the Moncada Barracks on July 26, 1953, preceding and fueling the Cuban Revolution.

If the mammoth structure could be seen as a macho gesture, the legislations prosecuting the queer community at the time could be seen as an extension, both physically and metaphorically, of Coppelia itself, epitomizing a new regime that condemned queer practices. In 1965 the UMAP (Unidades Militares de Ayuda a la Producción) camps were introduced in the country. These detention camps particularly targeted gay men, along with other groups seen as deviant from the Revolution's corpus (from Jehovah Witnesses to political objectors)—bourgeois degenerates. Yet Coppelia oversaw an increasing queering process. In this time of state-sanctioned persecution of gays, Coppelia became a cruising spot where flavors were symbols of sexual orientation. In a well-known scene from the film *Strawberry and Chocolate* (1993), the two protagonists meet at Coppelia.[13] One of them, Diego (a gay man) orders a strawberry ice cream (chocolate being the most popular flavor); this choice is a coded way of communicating his sexuality. The scene pays homage to the essential role of Coppelia as a venue for social contact, a queer-encountering space, which remained coded for decades.

Nowadays, its role as a space for interaction has been redefined by the emergence of free Wi-Fi zones throughout the city, of which Coppelia is one. Different social media allow dissident bodies to make contact with each other, continuing Coppelia's queering history into present times. Moreover, in the radius of Coppelia you can obtain the "Weekly Package" (*Paquete Semanal*), a terabyte collection of contraband material from abroad replete with television series, from *Game of Thrones* to *The Wire*; music, from Rihanna to Maluma; newspapers, from the *New York Times* to *Le Monde*; software; and other media, from *Vogue* to *Cosmopolitan*.

11 Ricardo Porro, "Cuba! Cuba!," *L'Architecture d'Aujourd'hui*, no. 350 (January-February 2004): 64-69.

12 Susana Torre, "Architecture and Revolution: Cuba, 1959-1974," *Progressive Architecture* (October 1974): 84-91.

13 *Fresa y Chocolate*, 1993, dir. Tomás Gutiérrez Alea and Juan Carlos Tobío.

NON-HUMAN REVOLUTION

The constellation of bodies and politics embodied in Coppelia's architecture and ice cream is closely linked to the reconfiguration of Cuba's productive landscape and international relations. Milk was needed to produce ice cream, and the dairy industry needed a symbol that it could apply to the new social engineering. This was found in Ubre Blanca (White Udder).

The genetically modified cow, Ubre Blanca, who lived from 1972 to 1985, became the symbol of agricultural modernization and a prodigious biodesign project: she was able to produce 109.5 liters of milk per day.[14] Castro was obsessed with this project, publishing daily photos and news about the cow in *Granma*, the Communist Party newspaper. When Ubre Blanca died, Castro dedicated a stamp and a marble statue to her. At the same time, he ordered geneticists to cryopreserve samples of her tissues in a (failed) bid to clone her at Cuba's Center for Genetic Engineering and Biotechnology. Ubre Blanca was finally stuffed and placed on permanent exhibition at the National Veterinary Center.

Crisis hit Cuba again in 1990, during the so-called Special Period following the collapse of the Soviet Union. When the German Democratic Republic (Cuba's second most powerful ally in terms of commercial exchange) was reunified with the Federal Republic of Germany, millions of dollars in aid for powdered milk and other food staples were cut. Almost simultaneously, the Soviet Union stopped sending butter.[15] Faced with a lack of foreign currency to buy these products abroad, and insufficient cows to provide milk domestically, Cuban authorities had to make a choice: butter or ice cream. They chose ice cream.

Coppelia still stands at the same location in Havana, with franchises in places like Varadero, an international tourist destination. The building in the Cuban capital maintains its powerful image as the place where different futurities and possibilities could be enacted. A place where politics, bodily practices, and social discussion could be performed in contradictory, aporistic, but also joyous, hypercaloric ways.

14 Rubén Torres Martínez, "Les bêtes dans le discours politique. 'Pis blanche' et la Révolution Cubaine," Studii de Ştiinţă şi Cultură, Editura Universitatii Vasile Goldiş, 3 (2014).

15 Medea Benjamin, Joseph Collins and Michael Scott, *No Free Lunch: Food & Revolution in Cuba Today* (San Francisco: Institute for Food and Development Policy, 1989).

Page from the Coppelia construction album. Above: Mario Girona, sketch showing the crown. Below: Photograph of Coppelia, ca. 1966.

Page from the Coppelia construction album. Clockwise: crane lowering prefabricated concrete slab; roof made of pre-fabricated concrete slabs; interior view of vaulted ceiling.

Page from the Coppelia construction album. Clockwise: crane lowering prefabricated concrete beams; detail showing vaulted ceiling and upper galleries with concrete buttresses; crane placing prefabricated concrete beam as buttress.

Page from the Coppelia construction album. Clockwise: Exterior view, showing concrete piers and buttresses; exterior view showing upper-floor galleries; street view from Habana Libre, with Radiocentro complex on the right.

Previous pages:
Page from the Coppelia construction album. Clockwise: Installation of stained-glass windows in upper-floor galleries; view of vaulted ceiling with neon lights; exterior view showing upper-floor galleries and concrete buttresses.

EXPORTING THE REVOLUTION: THE CUBAN PAVILION AT EXPO 67, MONTREAL

Guillermo S. Arsuaga

Left:
Patrice Lumumba poster. Second floor, Cuban Pavilion, Expo 67. Courtesy of Vittorio Garatti. Università IUAV di Venezia, Archivio Progetti, Vittorio Garatti Archive. All photographs reproduced in this article, unless indicated otherwise, are used by permission of the Garatti Archive.

Center:
Mural "Fight/Victory." Cuban Pavilion.

Right:
Detail, photomural. Cuban Pavilion.

Hurry to the Cuba pavilion, where the spicy fragrance of the restaurant black bean soup, sprinkled with rice, oil and vinegar and grated onions, hangs over the entire pavilion like a protective aura, so that the platoon of swarthy security men in baggy, oversized black suits really isn't needed. That aroma would dissuade the most determined bomb toting anti-Castroite.[1]

Rigoberto Rodríguez, one of the Cuban bartenders at the Cuban Pavilion in Expo 67, never thought that he would ever again serve rum to an American tourist after the Revolution ended.[2] Nor did he think he would again put on the white uniform he used to wear when he worked as a waiter in Old Havana during Batista's day. Nevertheless, here he was, in the middle of Montreal, eight years after the Revolution, serving rum to an American tourist at the terrace of

1 "The Smells," *The Gazette*, June 17, 1967.

2 Rigoberto Rodriguez is a fictional name, representing one of the waiters serving at the Restaurant at the Cuban Pavilion in Montreal, Expo 67. See: "Hacia Cuba el 'Pino del Agua' con periodistas y trabajadores del Pabellón de la EXPO-67," *Granma*, May 5, 1967. "Y en Canadá también venceremos. Una visita a la escuela donde se preparan los trabajadores cubanos que participaran en la exposición internacional de Canadá," *Granma*, March 29, 1967. "Llegaron los Gastronómicos de las Expo-67," *Granma*, November 1, 1967.

Cover, ***Arquitectura Cuba*** 336 (1966).

Cuban pavilion model.

the Cuban Pavilion. The sounds of the propagandistic films projected in the pavilion invaded the space. Rigoberto set off another sound: that of cracking ice while he—dressed all in white—served rum on the Pavilion terrace, a crackle muffled by the live Cuban band. What was an American-looking bar doing in the middle of the Revolutionary Cuban Pavilion at Expo 67?

"What does the name CUBA suggest to you? Sunny beaches... Afro-Cuban rhythms... the world's best rum and tobacco? Or a revolutionary people who sacrifice and struggle for a better life?" With this, the official guide of the Expo 67 began its description of the Cuban pavilion. In 1965 Vittorio Garatti, Hugo D'Acosta, and Sergio Baroni won the competition to design the Cuban pavilion for Montreal's Expo 67. Designed a mere six years after the culmination of the Cuban Revolution, this building was the first Cuban contribution to appear in an International Fair following Castro's victory.[3] The designers faced an intense query that has been a constant preoccupation of the Cuban Revolution:[4] How could architecture export this revolution? In this case, more specifically, how to communicate the Cuban Revolution beyond the country's borders in a geopolitical environment dominated by the Cold War? In short, how could architecture be mobilized to present the Cuban Revolution in the way the Cuban government wanted to show it?

In a context where the US embargo marked almost any geopolitical communication and trade from Cuba, Expo 67 was a unique opportunity for Cuba—the first socialist country in the western hemisphere—to internationally showcase its achievements among Western countries.[5] On the one hand, Cuba wanted to portray its commitment to fight against hegemonic imperial

3 Luigi Alini, *Vittorio Garatti: Opere e Progetti* (Naples: Clean Edizioni, 2020), p. 91.

4 On the export of Cuban revolutionary aid, see: Margaret Randall, *Exporting Revolution: Cuba's Global Solidarity* (Durham: Duke University Press, 2017), pp. 1-21.

5 "Y en Canadá también venceremos." Ibid.

6 On Cuban internationalism, see: Randall, *Exporting Revolution*, pp. 98-111.

7 However, the pavilion was ultimately given to the City of Montreal. See: "Cuban Pavilion Handed Over to Montreal," *The Gazette*, October 13, 1967. On the original plan to return the pavilion to Havana, see: "Cuba en la Expo 67," *Granma*, August 9, 1967.

Cuban Pavilion model, side view.

Garatti and his team during a design meeting.

powers, its international revolutionary commitment;[6] on the other, it wanted to present Cuba as a friendly and likable country, in opposition to the anti-communist propaganda of the North American discourses.

In this export task, the architecture at the Cuban pavilion was conceived as a media device capable of juxtaposing those two messages (revolutionary internationalism and affable tropical life) and communicating them effectively to the visitors at the Expo and the international community.

The pavilion was imagined as a prefabricated structure housing film projections, photographic murals, live music, and a bar space to interact with the visitors. Prefabrication was a perfect architectural approach to the export discourse: a design that could be quickly assembled, transported, and expanded without any geo-national determination. Indeed, the pavilion was designed to be dismantled and returned to Cuba at the end of the Expo.[7] At the same time, it reflected the growing interest of Cuban architects in prefabrication as a way to tackle the housing shortage in a country plagued by lack of materials and technical resources.[8] As Roberto Segre put it: "Prefabrication in architecture is a constant component of the architectural evolution of the revolutionary process."[9] [10]

In the first carboard design models, the pavilion was conceived as a series of stacked geometrical volumes; these were quick to assemble, easy to transport, and aesthetically surprising to the public due to their geometrical bluntness. The building was constructed from industrialized materials such as steel frames and vinyl-coated aluminum panels mounted on-site: prefabrication and modularity governed the pavilion from the beginning.[11] Construction

8 Roberto Segre, *Arquitectura y urbanismo de la revolución cubana* (Havana: Editorial Pueblo y Educación, 1989), p. 87.

9 "Una constante de toda la evolución arquitectónica del proceso revolucionario," ibid., my translation.

10 Indeed, one of the pavilion's architects, Hugo D'Acosta, was already experimenting with prototypes for expediting the housing agenda of the Cuban Revolution through prefab and modular housing. See: Barry Bergdoll et al., eds., *Latin America in Construction: Architecture 1955-1980* (New York: Museum of Modern Art, 2015), pp. 201-202.

11 María Victoria Zardoya Loureda, "La Habana," in *La arquitectura de la revolución cubana 1959-2018*, ed. Manuel Cuadra (Kassel: Kassel University Press, 2018), p. 18.

was completed three days before schedule and *Granma* celebrated the project as the first Cuban victory at the Expo.[12]

The metal frame was cladded with aluminum panels coated in white vinyl.[13] The top floor, marked by sharp angles, makes the building appear like a periscopic projection machine The only elements emerging from the white surfaces was the word "CUBA," identifying the national pavilion to the visitors; a series of round, convex colored windows; and rectangular openings at the end of the volumes.

The pavilion's metal frame was anchored on concrete footings, a solution that reinforced the idea of the pavilion being movable, not rooted in the land but simply placed upon it. The building barely touched the ground, as if wanting to emphasize its transportable vocation.[14] The footings also acted as a buffer between the Cuban pavilion and this foreign soil. In fact, in the early floor plans and models the concrete footings are as important as windows, doors, and other spatial elements.

The visitors took part in this separation of the building from the earth. Access was through a series of raised metal platforms that guided visitors from ground level to the elevated entrances. Once the visitor entered the Cuban Pavilion, he or she was also parted from Canadian ground.

Here and there the planes were punctured by round, tinted windows that functioned like lenses, affording a magnified or fish-eye view of the interior from outside.[15] When a visitor approached the entrance from the elevated metal gangway, the round windows would offer a preview of the inside. Before the extremities of the main volumes, the metal paneling was substituted by glass, making the prisms "open-ended," as if they were rectangular pipes. The pavilion

12 At the same time the newspaper highlighted the unlikeliness that the American, West German or Venezuelan pavilions would be finished on time. See: "Antes del plazo fijado concluye la instalación del pabellón cubano en la Expo 67," *Granma*, April 25, 1967.

13 Expo (International Exhibitions Bureau), *Expo 67: Official Guide Officiel* (Toronto: Maclean-Hunter, 1967), p. 129.

14 Vittorio Garatti in 2020 compared the footings of the Cuban Pavilion with the footings of the US satellite that landed on the moon, no doubt referring to Surveyor 1 in 1966. See: Florian Zeyfang, Alexander Schmoeger, and Lisa Schmidt-Colinet, *Pavilion-In-Parts*, 2020.

15 Described in: Satish Dhar, "The Cuban Pavilion at the Expo," *The Gazette*, August 12, 1967.

16 "Cuba en la Expo 67." Ibid.

17 Ibid.

Workers painting the word "CUBA" on the Pavilion's façade.

Cuban Pavilion. View from the top of a neighboring building.

used these end windows to project part of the interior exhibition to the audience outside.

THE EXHIBITION: THE SPACE

The main aim of the exhibition was to present the Cuban Revolution in its complexity: national and international, struggle and celebration, oppression and victory. What was the Cuban Revolution about?[16]

More than communicating an image, the exhibition wanted to "communicate a feeling."[17] The curator, Enrique Fuentes, was in charge of conveying the Revolution in all its complex reality. He conceived the show as a dynamic, multimedia experience centered on history and articulated through space, photographic murals, and film projections on walls, floors, and ceilings, with electro-acoustic music throughout—a sort of continuous chronological storyboard

Cuban Pavilion. View from the outside. Notice the round window allowing visitors to peek inside.

“This is Cuba.” Entrance to the Cuban Pavilion. Reception desk on the right.

towards Cuban liberation that culminated in the progress achieved by the Revolution in the areas of education, industrialization, health, and more.[18]

The exhibition started on the ground floor. On crossing the threshold, to the left, was a reception desk where a Cuban guide would help visitors stamp their "Expo Passports." The tiny corner desk was placed against a backdrop of wallpaper made from blown-up newspaper clippings describing Cuba's geopolitical situation, emphasizing US aggression and the triumph of the Revolution.[19] Opposite the entry door, a vinyl text on one of the round windows announced: "THIS IS/VOICI CUBA" flanked by an introduction in verse to the exhibition, in French and English:

Visitors getting their Expo passports stamped at the Cuban Pavilion.

> This is Cuba.
> discovered by Columbus, conquered by Velázquez:
> Indian, Spanish, African.
> For four centuries Cuba holding out to the world
> its colors, rhythms, joys.
> Years of sorrow did not weaken us,
> years of oppression did not diminish us,
> the freedom gained while fighting
> does not make us arrogant.
> This is our life, this is our story:
> a people yearning to build
> a new life in peaceful labor.
> In the oldest diary in America
> you can read
> "The most beautiful land beheld by human eyes."
> But beauty cannot always be
> An unending jubilee.

Commencing the tour, visitors would turn right into a room dominated by a banner announcing "VOICI NOTRE VIE / NOTRE HISTOIRE" and featuring high-contrast black-and-white photomurals illustrating the history of slavery in Cuba, including an oversize reproduction of the famous slave-ship hold packing diagram that slanted from the wall onto the floor. The photomurals continued on the right, illustrating Spanish colonial rule and the horrors of the Batista regime.

Opposite the slavery mural, under the staircase leading to the second floor, a series of twelve posters featuring images and text (in English and French) directly interpellated the visitor. One of the posters announced: OBSERVER UN CRIME EN SILENCE C'EST LE COMMETTRE. Striking slogans included: MAN'S LONG JOURNEY THROUGH CENTURIES OF EXPLOITATION AND MURDER COMES

18 Enrique Fuentes already had experience in curating post-Cuban-Revolution exhibitions for an international audience. Indeed, he curated a similar exhibition in the Pabellón Cuba in 1964 in Havana for the International Union of Architects, in which photography, murals, and a mixed media approach were also prominent. See Lisa Schmidt-Colinet and Alex Schmoeger, eds., *Pabellón Cuba: 4D – 4Dimensions, 4Decades* (Berlin: b_books, 2008), pp. 58, 74.

19 From the available images, reproductions from the *New York Times*, the Italian Communist newspaper *L'Unità*, the French Communist organ *L'Humanité*, and Venezuela's *El Nacional* could be identified, among others.

TO AN END; ATOMIC BLACKMAIL; AGGRESSION, INVASION, AGGRESSION; THE TURNING POINT OF HISTORY HAS COME; HUNGER, DEATH, C.I.A., NAPALM...

Other posters featured the United Nations General Assembly, a portrait of Bertrand Russell (who publicly advocated for an end to the US's aggressive policies towards Cuba),[20] and photos of schoolchildren and revolutionary prisoners. One displayed a series of numbers—50 54 56 58 60 61 62 63 64—a sort of ciphered message, highlighting the dates the last two digits of the years of important revolutionary and anti-colonial events in the Third World.[21]

Still in the first exhibition room, on the next wall, the visitor encountered one of the largest photomurals of the exhibition, celebrating the victory of the Revolution while emphasizing the struggle. The photos, applied on cubes that evoke the pavilion's structure, included images of Fidel Castro and Che Guevara in the Sierra Maestra, and the slogans LA VICTOIRE/VICTORY, FIGHT/LA LUTTE, TYRANNIE-RESISTANCE. While the images depicting the colonial era and Batista's dictatorship were printed with high contrast in order to create a dramatic effect, the photos of Revolutionary struggle were unretouched and presented as historical documents.[22] The next mural in this room showed another

20 Victoria Martin, "Bertrand Russell's Role in the Cuban Missile Crisis," *Historian*, no. 74 (Summer 2002): 25-29.

21 The term "Third World" was introduced in 1952 by the French economist Alfred Sauvy to describe countries that were not part of either NATO or the Warsaw Pact. Regarding the dates: 1950: Puerto Rican Nationalist Party revolts; attempt on the life of US President Harry S. Truman. 1954: Algerian War of Independence. 1956: launch of Cuban Revolution led by Fidel Castro. 1958: Iraqi Revolution. 1960: April Revolution erupts in South Korea, leading to the end of the First Republic of South Korea. 1961: the Angolan War of Independence begins. 1962-74: the leftist African Party for the Independence of Guinea and Cape Verde (PAIGC) wages a revolutionary war of independence in Portuguese Guinea. 1963: the Bale Revolt in southern Ethiopia. 1964: Simba Rebellion in the Congo.

22 Interview with Mayito, "Cuba en la Expo 67."

Cuban Pavilion, first room of the exhibition.

Detail on the stair from the ground floor to the second floor.

revolutionary hero, Camilo Cienfuegos, and Fidel Castro delivering a speech on the themes of "Freedom" and "Revolution."

Opposite the Revolutionary Mural and flanking the stairs leading to the second floor, there was an "Electronic World Map."[23] This installation highlighted the main "historical processes" that had taken place since 1868 across the globe.[24] The date 1868 marked the beginning of Cuba's ten-year independence struggle against Spain. The map would light up for seven seconds each of the countries where the selected events took place, as well as photos of the most prominent freedom fighters and explanatory texts in English and French. The first floor ended here, pointing the visitor towards a metal stair behind the electronic map that led to the second floor.

This staircase between the two levels constituted a spatial and narrative transition, from past struggles on the first floor (slavery, colonialism, dictatorship, revolutionary victory) to contemporary struggles, illustrated on the second.

The second floor presented the advances achieved by the Revolution, showing workers at various tasks and portraying post-revolutionary Cuba as a productive industrial country. The exhibit highlighted the human element with collages of agricultural workers, new factories, hospitals, and education facilities, presided by photos

23 "Técnicos cubanos construyen máquina y mapa electrónico para la 'Expo 67,'" *Granma*, March 9, 1967.

24 Ibid.

of Castro, Guevara, and Cienfuegos and accompanied by exhortations such as: "MAKE FRIENDS / GIVE BOOKS / A BOOK A FAITHFUL FRIEND / GIVE POETRY BOOKS OF LOVE."[25]

The second floor also transmitted the Cuban government's commitment to Third World solidarity and international struggles against imperialism,[26] by featuring high-contrast portraits of revolutionary leaders like Sandino, Lumumba, and Nguyễn Văn Trỗi, alongside evocative revolutionary proclamations.[27]

One eighteen-foot-tall poster (placed in a double-height space that rose to the floor above) offered multiple portraits of the Congo independence leader Patrice Lumumba, crowned by the phrase: "IMPERIALISM never ceased to make the WAR."[28] At the bottom of the image, "LE MOMENT DECISIF DE L'HISTOIRE EST ARRIVE" and "TIME TO FIGHT TO REVOLT" was followed by, again, the dates "1950 54 56 58 60 61 62 63 64," along with a list of countries: "Vietnam Guatemala Laos Lebanon Iraq Congo Panamá Cuba."

Another double-height space featured a floor-to-ceiling photo of Nguyễn Văn Trỗi repeated three times (in a way similar to the Lumumba poster), accompanied by the phrase "THE TURNING POINT IN HISTORY HAS COME."[29]

Nearby, a dramatic late addition to the line-up of sacrificial heroes was a huge cylindrical display featuring a picture of Che Guevara, accompanied by these words attributed to him: "Wherever death should surprise us, welcome be it as long as our war cry creates a perceptive ear, and another hand stretches out to take our weapon."[30] It is important to note that Guevara had been murdered in 1967 in Bolivia, while attempting to organize another revolution.

The same quote appeared in *Granma* the day after Guevara's death, together with an image of raised rifles.[31] This portrait-cum-slogan strategy was used in Cuba for mass-media communications campaigns featuring the images of Fidel Castro, Camilo Cienfuegos, and Che Guevara.[32]

Guevara's image at the pavilion coincided temporally with *Granma*'s publication of a full-page back cover of the famous image *Guerrillero Heroico* by Alberto Korda, which was also used as the background for Fidel Castro's eulogy to Guevara in Havana. Though the portrait presented at the pavilion was not the *Guerrillero Heroico*, it aligns with the image of Guevara as a courageous and tragic revolutionary.[33]

The third floor was spatially dominated by two large shafts that opened to the floor below. One of those double-height spaces offered a view of the oversize portraits of Lumumba and Nguyễn Văn Trỗi, along with revolutionary slogans against "Atomic Blackmail." This floor was mainly devoted to film projections on two screens at either end of the room (also visible from the

25 "Haga amistad / regale libros / un libro un amigo fiel / regale libros poesías de amor."

26 "Informa Van Ba a los cubanos que trabajan en EXPO'67 sobre acuerdos del FNL de Sudvietnam," *Granma*, September 4, 1967.

27 On the presence of international revolutionary leaders' posters at the Pavilion, see: Ernesto Menéndez-Conde, *Trazos en los márgenes: Arte abstracto e ideologías estéticas en Cuba* (Independently published, 2020), p. 149.

28 On Cuba's ongoing support for the Congolese revolutionary movement, see, for instance: "Llamamiento al pueblo de Cuba para expresar solidaridad con la lucha del Congo," *Granma*, February 12, 1967.

29 Description according to photograph in: "Hacia Cuba el 'Pino del Agua' con periodistas y trabajadores del Pabellón de la EXPO-67."

30 "Cuba Honors Dead Revolutionary As Pavilion Adds Photograph," *The Gazette*, October 25, 1967.

31 "Contra el Imperialismo," *Granma*, October 16, 1967.

32 On the use of portraits of revolutionary leaders in Cuba, see, for example: "¡Todos a la Plaza! ¡Viva el VIII Aniversario!," *Granma*, January 2, 1967.

33 María-Carolina Cambre, *The Semiotics of Che Guevara: Affective Gateways*, Bloomsbury Advances in Semiotics (London: Bloomsbury Academic, 2014), p. 9.

Opposite page:
Installation under the staircase.

US Marine visiting the Cuban Pavilion. "Cuba en la Expo 67." *Granma*, August 9, 1967, p. 4.

"Cuba Honors Dead Revolutionary As Pavilion Adds Photography." *The Gazette*, October 25, 1967, p. 42.

Nguyen Van Troi poster, Cuban Pavilion. "Hacia Cuba el 'Pino del Agua' con periodistas y trabajadores del Pabellón de la EXPO-67." *Granma*, May 5, 1967.

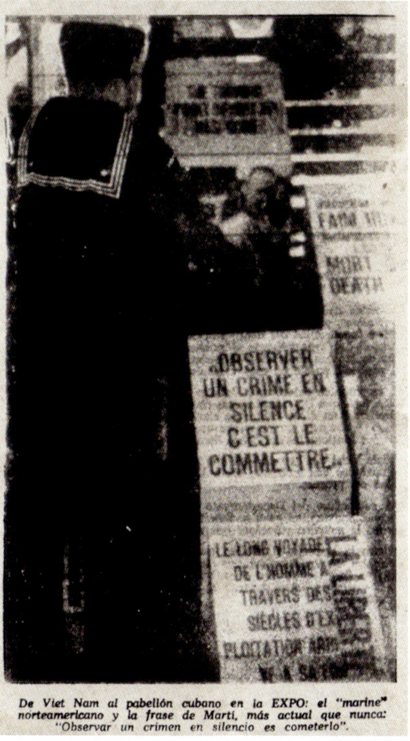

De Viet Nam al pabellón cubano en la EXPO: el "marine" norteamericano y la frase de Martí, más actual que nunca: "Observar un crimen en silencio es cometerlo".

Cuba Honors Dead Revolutionary As Pavilion Adds Photograph

A grim note has been added at the Cuban Pavilion.

Visitors who entered the pavilion yesterday were greeted by a huge photograph of Che Guevara, a former lieutenant of Fidel Castro, who was recently killed in Bolivia.

Before disappearing from Cuba more than two years ago, the 39-year-old revolutionary served as Fidel Castro's finance minister.

Bold letters written across one wall facing the suspended cylindrical display read: "Wherever death should surprise us, welcome be it as long as our war cry creates a receptive ear and another hand stretches out to take our weapon . . ."

When the Argentine-born revolutionary disappeared from Cuba there were reports that he had been executed by his former comrade in arms.

But soon many South American newspapers began carrying conflicting reports as to the whereabouts of the guerrilla warfare expert.

He was killed by Bolivian army soldiers while leading a local revolutionary group.

Guevara was born in Argentina of Spanish and Irish descent and as a teen-ager was an avid reader of leftist and Marxist literature.

He was involved in a number of left-wing revolutionary groups in South America before joining the Castro brothers in Cuba in 1956.

RATTLING OF MACHINE GUNS AND
NEW CRIES OF WAR AND VICTORY

ARMES ET QUE D'AUTRES HOMMES SE LEVENT POUR ENTONNER DES CHANTS LUCTUEUX AVEC LES REPITENTS DES MITRAILLEUSES ET DE NOUVEAUX CRIS DE GUERRE ET DE VICTOIRE

CHE

(CP Photo)

Che makes appearance at Cuban pavilion

Film projection, Cuban Pavilion, third floor.

Cuban Pavilion, third floor.

outside) and seats for the public. The films, made by Santiago Álvarez, Pastor Vega, and other filmmakers from the Instituto Cubano del Arte e Industria Cinematográficos (ICAIC) highlighted the progress and achievements of the Cuban Revolution.[34] Film production, regarded by the government as an efficient and powerful propaganda tool, experienced a significant boom in post-revolutionary Cuba. This cultural push was institutionalized with the foundation of the ICAIC in 1959, weeks after the victory of the Revolution. At the ICAIC, film directors experimented with new formats, giving rise to a rich cinematic culture.

THE EXHIBITION: THE MEDIA

Vittorio Garatti, one of the pavilion's architects, defined the whole undertaking as a "Projection Machine."[35] Projections were used throughout the pavilion, including on the exterior walls.[36] Jorge Fraga was in charge of designing these cinematographic experiences.[37] The violent effect created by the exhibition's images was softened by the moving pictures and the music.

Films were projected onto six strategically placed screens, visible from both inside and out. Two of these screens were used for slides, and the other four for documentaries and films; images could also be projected over the photos presented at the exhibition.[38] In the slide shows, two loops of eight minutes each showed three slides at a time, in a triangular arrangement that changed constantly. These projections were envisioned as a sort of "visual entertainment with the images as raw material."[39] The other four screens projected films and documentaries, some produced especially for the exhibition. There were two screens per floor, and the top floor functioned as a cinema, where people could sit down and watch the projections at greater leisure.

The mobilization of cinema and architecture as an immersive multimedia device juxtaposing moving images as political propaganda had already been used a decade earlier, in the US Pavilion for Moscow in 1959. There, the famous designer couple, Charles and Ray Eames, had projected a short film called "Glimpses of the U.S.A." to show an idealized suburban American life that focused on domestic space.[40] The duo designed an enveloping cinema show in which multiple related images appeared on several screens.[41] The films and slideshows at the Cuban pavilion were not only interrelated, but also projected over the photographic murals and accompanied by electro-acoustic music, thus creating a complex media environment in which music, photographs, film, and architecture collaborated to tell the story of the Cuban Revolution.

One of the most original elements in the Cuban pavilion was the montage of films projected onto posters and photomurals.[42] In Moscow, the Eames team had produced a new kind of architecture marked by film production and projection.[43] In Montreal's Cuban pavilion, the projection determined the architecture: witness, for instance, the early design of the rectangular windows conceived as a projection surface. The projections themselves were also modified by the architecture, as the images were superimposed on the posters, photos, ceilings, and walls. For example, returning to the rectangular windows used as projection surfaces, the same image was projected in the interior and exterior, but it was inverted on one of the sides. From the inside, spectators would watch a front projection and from the outside a rear projection.

In this multimedia experience, photography stands out as the medium that most bluntly presented revolutionary struggles.[44] The photographs were designed and produced by Mario García Joya (Mayito) and then retouched and organized into exhibition format by the curator Enrique Fuentes together with María Eugenia Haya.[45] Mayito told *Granma* that "there is no single space [in the exhibition] where the spectator can escape from watching even if he does not stop. To make an analogy with cinema: instead of moving images on screen, we have a moving spectator."[46]

The curatorial team considered the visitor's gaze when planning the spatial disposition of the photographs. How would the public receive and rearrange the information that the pavilion was communicating? The visitor's gaze was crucial in the design of this montage. A large-scale model was built to immerse the

34 Zeyfang, Schmidt-Colinet and Schmoeger, *Pabellón Cuba*, p. 75.

35 Manuel Cuadra, *De Primera Mano* (Kassel: Kassel University Press, 2019), p. 64.

36 Expo (International Exhibitions Bureau), *Expo 67*, p. 129.

37 Schmidt-Colinet and Schmoeger, *Pabellón Cuba*, p. 74.

38 Menéndez-Conde, *Trazos en los márgenes*, p. 149.

39 Expo (International Exhibitions Bureau), *Cuban pavilion = Pavillon cubain: Expo'67, Montréal, Canada* (Montreal, 1967).

40 On the multimedia architecture by the Eameses and the Moscow exhibition, see: Beatriz Colomina, "Enclosed by Images: The Eameses' Multimedia Architecture," *Grey Room*, no. 2 (2001): 7-29. For more on the Cold War and domesticity, see: Beatriz Colomina, *Domesticity at War* (Cambridge, Mass.: MIT Press, 2007).

41 On the multiple screens and their credibility, see: Jean-Louis Cohen, *Building a New New World: Amerikanizm in Russian Architecture* (New Haven: Other Distribution, 2021), pp. 480-487.

42 Menéndez-Conde, *Trazos en los márgenes*, p. 149.

43 Colomina, "Enclosed by Images."

44 Órgano Oficial del Comité Central del PCC, "Exposición Internacional de Fotografías," *Granma*, September 23, 1967.

45 Zeyfang, Schmidt-Colinet and Schmoeger, *Pabellón Cuba*, p. 74.

46 "Y en Canadá también venceremos."

curatorial team into the space and to allow them a previous walk-through among the images. The mobilization of photography in an architectonic and spatial way in exhibition spaces (and especially the inclusion of the spectator as part of the exhibition) recalls El Lissitzky's projects at the Soviet Pavilion during the International Press Exhibition (*Pressa*), held in Cologne in 1928.[47]

In fact, the photomurals at the Cuban pavilion evoke El Lissitzky and Sergei Senkin's photo-frieze at the *Pressa* show. The spatiality and dynamism achieved by the montages at the Soviet Pavilion in 1928 were replicated at the Cuban Pavilion by the three-dimensional murals, which would unfold and protrude from the wall, and sometimes intersect with the windows in an effort to expand the frame.[48]

The architectural design of the pavilion facilitated the continuous and progressive narrative of the exhibition as an ascending spatial promenade in a "continuous multimedia box" designed to communicate the achievements of the Revolution.[49] The spatial continuity of the exhibition was reinforced by the continuous soundtrack by Juan Blanco, a pioneer of Cuban electro-acoustic spatial music, traveling through the entire pavilion.[50] The sound design was a complex system, created by Eugenio Vesa from the ICAIC Sound Lab, which took advantage of the spatiality of the exhibition. Instead of being heard simultaneously across the pavilion, the sound transitioned from speaker to speaker and from room to room.[51]

The dynamism characterizing the film projections and music was emphasized by *Cosmorama*, a kinetic sculpture by Sandú Dairé. This was a set of three abstract sculptures mounted on revolving bases, lit by intermittent projectors and enclosed inside a screen-box. The rotation of the sculptures and the lighting threw shapes onto the screens.[52] The effect of these shadows was also defined as "electro painting" in the pavilion's catalog.[53]

Lastly, the pavilion also mobilized nearly 200 Cuban workers, who traveled to Montreal for the occasion. The Cuban government trained the personnel in advance; they were instructed in "human relationships" and how to promote the products offered for sale at the pavilion.[54] In August *Granma* reported on the women working in the kiosks in front of the Cuban Pavilion that sold Cuban products were there to answer questions about Cuba and the Revolution: these stalls were also spaces for ideological debates.[55]

The Cuban Delegation promoted its vision of women as an active and indispensable part of the revolutionary process.[56] The guides to the Cuban pavilion were exclusively female. *Granma* wrote: "They will surely fulfill, as ever, this new task indicated by the Revolution. They, on behalf of our people, will know how to honor the name of revolutionary Cuba at Expo 67."[57]

47 Jorge Ribalta, "Introduction," in *Public Photographic Spaces: Exhibitions of Propaganda, from Pressa to The Family of Man, 1928-55* (Museu d'Art Contemporani de Barcelona, 2008), p. 17.

48 For more on the Soviet Pavilion at Pressa, see: Jeremy Anysley, "Pressa Cologne, 1928: Exhibitions and Publication Design in the Weimar Period," *Design Issues* 10, no. 3 (1994): 53-76.

49 Roberto Segre, *Diez años de arquitectura en Cuba revolucionaria*, Cuadernos de la revista Unión; 1 (Havana: Ediciones Unión, 1970), p. 214.

50 On Juan Blanco, see: Helio Orovio and Project Muse, *Cuban Music from A to Z* (Durham: Duke University Press, 2004), p. 29.

51 The sound design was controlled by a "music box" where a cylinder with sound contacts rotated activating the speakers across the exhibition. "Técnicos cubanos construyen máquina y mapa electrónico para la 'Expo 67,'" and Schmidt-Colinet and Schmoeger, *Pabellón Cuba*, p. 386.

52 Ibid., p. 77.

53 Expo (International Exhibitions Bureau), *Cuban pavilion = Pavillon cubain*, p. 24.

54 "Y en Canadá también venceremos."

55 "Expo'67. Aquí Montreal Canadá. Las 'Boutiques' Cubanas," *Granma*, August 23, 1967.

56 See, for example: "Con Relación a la Mujer se ha producido dentro de la Revolución una Revolución," *Granma*, August 23, 1967; "Seguiremos siempre el ejemplo de la mujer Vietnamita," *Granma*, March 9, 1967; "Inauguró Villa Espín anoche la exposición La Mujer y La Revolución," *Granma*, April 29, 1967.
For more on Third World solidarity and women, see: Lani Hanna, "Tricontinental's International Solidarity: Emotion in OSPAAAL as Tactic to Catalyze Support of Revolution," *Radical History Review*, no. 136 (January 1, 2020): 169-184.

57 "Están seguras que en esta nueva tarea señalada por la Revolución, también cumplirán. Ellas, en representación de nuestro pueblo, sabrán poner en alto el nombre de Cuba revolucionaria en la Expo 67." "Y en Canadá también venceremos."

Vittorio Garatti inside the large-scale model of the Cuban Pavilion.

Vittorio Garatti discussing one of the murals inside the large-scale model of the Cuban Pavilion.

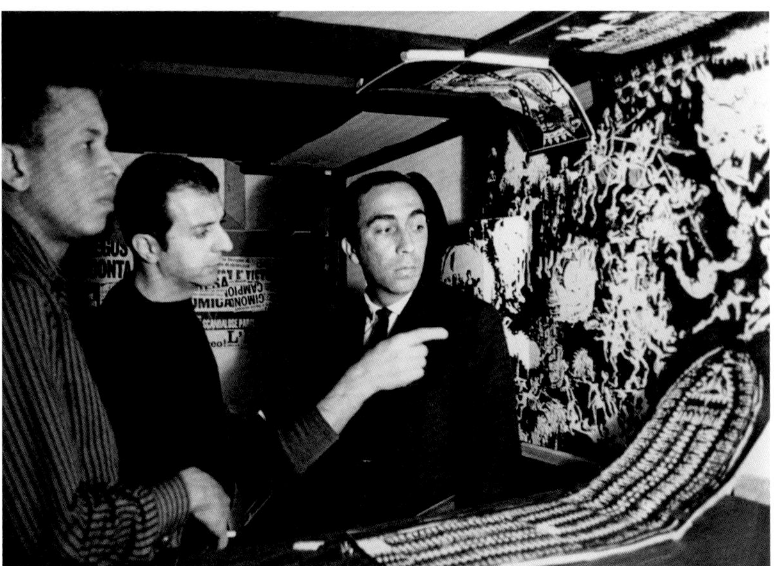

Vittorio Garatti discussing the slavery mural inside the large-scale model of the Cuban Pavilion.

Both the Canadian and Cuban press of the time highlighted the role of the female attendants at the Cuban pavilion. Montreal's *The Gazette*, picturing an attendant holding a "REVOLUTION" poster, described her role as to explain the Revolution to the public while ready to fight any counterrevolutionaries who might come to the pavilion.[58]

The Canadian press largely criticized the pavilion as a propaganda machine. While this might be true, the bar, at least, offered an ideology-free oasis. It was celebrated as the pavilion's most interesting place.

The idea of including a bar to lure reluctant visitors came from Enrique Fuentes, the exhibition's curator. Fuentes convinced Celia Sánchez (Fidel Castro's right-hand woman since the Sierra Maestra) to use the bar to balance the starkness of the exhibition's political content.[59] Indeed, the growing influx of visitors during the first months of the Expo to the bar was closely followed by the Cuban press and celebrated as part of the pavilion's success.[60] The Canadian *Gazette* itself praised the gentle and accommodating demeanor of the male waiters at the bar, described as "suave," smiling and waving "*hasta la vista*."[61]

The bar mediated between the official government message and the public's hostility toward communism. Drinks and tropical vibes seduced visitors while inserting them into the "revolutionary" space of the building, though not coercively. The pavilion had two main access points from the exterior: one led into the exhibition areas,

REVOLUTION
REVOLUTION
REVOLUTION
REVOLUTIO

(Gazette Photo Service)

Carmen Quintana explains the Cuban Pavilion in a single word

"Cuban Hostesses Have to Handle the Antis," *The Gazette*, June 17, 1967, p. 37.

View from the exterior.

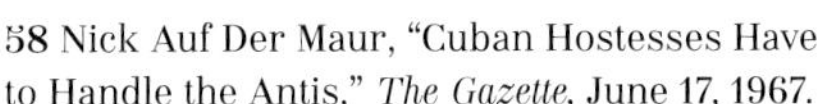

58 Nick Auf Der Maur, "Cuban Hostesses Have to Handle the Antis," *The Gazette*, June 17, 1967.

59 Menéndez-Conde, *Trazos en los márgenes*, p. 149.

60 "Llegaron los Gastronómicos de las Expo-67," *Granma*, November 1, 1967. On the success of the Cuban Bar: "Creciente Afluencia de público al restaurante del Pabellón Cubano," *Granma*, May 23, 1967.

61 Harry Bruce, "The Feel."

Dining room, Cuban Pavilion.

while a second ramp connected the exterior directly with the bar without crossing the exhibition, thus allowing visitors the possibility of bypassing the propagandistic interior space.

As befits a mediator, the bar's forms differed from the rest of the exhibition spaces.[62] If the latter exploited sharp angles and industrialized aesthetics, the bar recreated the flavor of old Havana under American rule: curvy hand-crafted wooden furniture, tropical plants, live music, daiquiris, cigars, seafood, and waiters in white uniforms designed by Fernando Ayuso.

The bar also incorporated architectural projections: it had a movable wall that retracted and opened the space completely to the terrace and the adjacent canal. From this canal, visitors could also observe the interior of the Cuban bar and terrace while being ferried across the Expo by boat.

The bar was a critical spatial element at the pavilion, a double agent. Disguised as a pre-revolutionary Havana venue, it attracted nostalgic Americans and inserted them into a revolutionary container. Although struggle and political determination were present, so was the "the Cuban way of life." The architecture reflects the more significant questions of the Cuban revolutionary movement and its possibility of exportation. How might an international global revolution be pursued while preserving the liberated peoples' geographical determination and national identity? As an architectural mediator, the bar was able to articulate these two realities.

62 See the sociopolitical dynamizing program at the Radiocentro cafeteria in Havana by Andrés Jaque, "The Interior and the Polemic: Rearranging the Tele-Urbanism of Some Moderns," in *Superpowers of Scale* (New York: Columbia Books on Architecture and the City, 2020), pp. 303-317.

LA BURLA YANQUI EN LA EXPO 1967

EL BURLON GLOBO

2 GRANMA Internacional

CONCLUSION: GEOPOLITICAL SCALES AT THE PAVILION

The Montreal Exhibition was, besides a celebration, a geopolitical archipelago of national pavilions that reflected the tensions of the time. The Cuban pavilion (like all the others) operated in a heavily loaded context, and there was pressure, especially from the US and Canada, to portray the Cuban pavilion as a potential threat.[63] Cuba's design cannot be understood as an isolated action but rather a reaction to the exhibition's geopolitical network.[64]

Preoccupation in the US with the Cuban presence at Expo 67 surfaced early, especially in Miami, home to a large number of anti-Castro Cuban Americans. The Miami press described the pavilion as "a chamber of horrors," and warned that "seen from outside, [it] Is as innocent as the ice-cream they sell," but in reality "their presence here is dynamite."[65]

And it was not only the US that saw the Cuban pavilion as a menace to its sovereignty. The Canadian press portrayed the building as a communist Trojan horse. Quebec had been thrown into turmoil by the Front de Liberation du Québec, and a section of the Canadian press interpreted the Cuban presence as a threat that could extend the project of socialist revolution to the francophone province. In an article published in July, *The Gazette* reported that the guards at the Cuban Pavilion were guerrillas who, after their shift was done, would spend their time "imparting guerrilla warfare tactics to subversive groups." The rhetoric of communist menace was emphasized, noting that Cuba was transmitting daily broadcasts in French, and that their news "bulletin and commentary was slanted to the Communist viewpoint."

What was feared was the export of the Cuban–US "conflict" to neutral Canadian territory. The local press used a violent and weaponized language to paint the possibility of a terrorist outrage in which anti-Castro groups could "blow up the building [the Cuban pavilion]."[66] Ever since the announcement of the Cuban participation, concerns about such terrorist attacks had multiplied, especially as Castro was planning to visit Montreal (though the visit never materialized).[67]

In contrast, Cuba's participation in Expo 67 was reported as a roaring success by *Granma*, which commended the "friendly and popular" image that Cuba had brought to the international fair, avoiding conflicts.[68] In the same article *Granma* described the US pavilion as a "*burla*" (joke), and claimed that the US had made little effort to create an interesting pavilion, except for the grandiloquent geodesic dome by Buckminster Fuller which the paper called "*El globo burlón*" (the joker balloon): "Same as the 'American way of life,' the North American Pavilion is just façade."[69]

The Montreal Expo offered a clear architectural reading of the Cold War: the two blocs (the USSR and the US) were materialized in

63 "Cuba Puts Chamber of Horrors in Expo 67," *Miami Herald*, May 9, 1967; "Cuban Plans Pavilion for Fair," *New York Times*, March 6, 1967.

64 As a clear illustration, the exhibition was sited on a group of artificial islands, created, enlarged, and stabilized to create a new sort of almost heterotropic environment for the fair.

65 "Cuba Puts Chamber of Horrors in Expo 67"; "Cuban Plans Pavilion for Fair." See also: Jay Clarke, "Cuban Exhibits Sell Revolution at Expo," *Miami Herald*, May 26, 1967.

66 Eddie Collister, "Shell Find in City Sparks Precaution At Cuban Pavilion," *The Gazette*, April 10, 1967; Bill Bantey, "Conflict and CUBA," *The Gazette*, October 27, 1967, sec. Expo 67.

67 Arthur Blakely, "Cuba Acepts with Great Pleasure," *The Gazette*, March 30, 1967.

68 "Cuba dejó en la Expo'67 una estela de simpatía y popularidad," *Granma*, October 31, 1967; "Satisfecha del deber cumplido en Expo'67 la delegación cubana dice el comisionado Cossio," *Granma*, November 3, 1967.

69 "Al igual que el 'American way of life', el pabellón norteamericano es solo fachada." "La Burla Yanqui en la Expo 1967," *Granma*, May 24, 1967.

two prominent buildings, built on two opposed islands, with a bridge in between. In this context the Cuban pavilion introduces another axis along which to read the geopolitical arena: imperialism vs. anti-imperialist struggle.

The Cuban pavilion's explicit support for Third World movements came at a time when the USSR was rethinking its support of anti-imperialist struggles in the Third World, to focus its energies on outdoing the US. The Cuban bid to portray the Revolution as an anti-bureaucratic struggle—the term was *Lucha contra el Burocratismo*—was also an effort to distance itself from the Soviet model.[70] [71] In making Third World revolutionary movements visible, Cuba presented itself not as an isolated revolutionary country but rather as a crucial player in a network of emancipatory anti-imperialist global movements.

The Montreal exhibition was developed under the overarching title "Man in His World" ("Terre des Hommes" in French) The possessive article "his" is essential to understand how "the world" was understood by the hegemonic powers at the Expo: as part of "men's property and resource towards development." As the *Miami Herald* wrote:

> With technological and artistic achievements all around them—the pavilions of Czechoslovakia, Algeria, and the United Arab Republic [Egypt], for instance, are models of good taste—it is a pity that Castro's underlings have ignored the key to Expo's theme, "Man and His World."[72]

On the one hand, the US and USSR compete in showcasing their latest technological and aero-spatial advances. Lunar modules, astronauts'

70 On the divergence between Cuba and USSR, see: Mervyn Bain, "The Glasnost Effect on Soviet/Cuban Relations," *Journal of Transatlantic Studies (Edinburgh University Press)* 2, no. 2 (September 2004): 125-142, and Mervyn Bain, "Moscow, Havana and Asymmetry in International Relations," *Cambridge Review of International Affairs* 29, no. 3 (July 2, 2016): 1044-1060.

71 During 1967, *Granma* published several articles hailing the Cuban Government's "struggle against bureaucratism." See, for instance: "Lucha Contra el Burocratismo. Reanudan en La Habana los juicios en la Lucha contra el Burocratismo," *Granma*, May 9, 1967.

72 "Cuba Puts Chamber of Horrors in Expo 67."

Cuban Pavilion, view from the canal.

Opposite page:
"La burla yanqui en la Expo 1967," *Granma*, May 24, 1967, pp. 2-3.

¿Uno más...? Esta es la pregunta de una de las compañeras que están a cargo del Salón de Coppelia. Y en el rostro de esta niña checa hay una respuesta: ¡Cómo no...! ¡Cuando termine este...!

Sabroso... ¿verdad? Por vez primera muchos de estos niños prueban las frutas tropicales a través de los helados Coppelia. Y ellos saben que los niños cubanos, también disfrutan de esos riquísimos sabores. Porque Coppelia es un helado para el pueblo.

"Cuba en la Expo 67." *Granma*, August 9, 1967, p. 4.

outfits, and satellites were exhibited as part of a dominant techno-utopia: faith in technology and progress was shared by the two hegemonic powers of the cold war.

On the other hand, while the leading economic powers at the exhibition mobilized all their technological achievements in their pavilions, Cuba opted for simple materials and opted instead to impact on the visitors through the continuous experience of photographs, films, and montages of images. The Cuban pavilion was a counter-technological artifact, disparaged on this account by some observers: "In this pavilion little effort has been made, either in the exterior or the interior, to achieve constructional neatness."[73] But the Canadian press also recognized its effectiveness in communicating and its spatial attractiveness:

> For sheer visual impact brought about by economy of exhibit techniques, there are few pavilions that beat this one. [...] Here is a buoyant and spirited building with a blunt and brutal tale to tell. It is not to be hamstrung by small matters. Once you get this idea you will like this pavilion, although you might not agree with the propaganda that it blatantly dishes out.[74]

In an interview in 2020, Vittorio Garatti described the pavilion as a lunar module arriving in an alien land: "It reaches the destination and tack! it launches in that world [the Expo] its satellite and starts to bombard *la Revolución*."[75] The pavilion operated as a sort of satellite, extending its operational field to the city and the country beyond Expo's borders.

The public was also seduced through the distribution of Cuban goods (cigars, rum, the famous Coppelia ice-cream, crafts, etc.) and Cuban culture (dance shows, film and documentary projections, fashion parades).[76] With this strategy, the Cuban pavilion effectively bypassed the US embargo on the importation of Cuban goods and reached out to the American and international public in a metaphorical way, narrating the revolutionary message, promoting Cuban culture, all while selling goods for profit.[77] Indeed , as we have seen, there were kiosks at the Expo, beyond the limits of the pavilion, that also sold such goods.[78] In response, the US government introduced stringent inspections on Americans returning home, to make sure no Cuban product entered the US.[79] The blockade targeted Canada as well as Cuba. Large-scale geopolitical tensions were imported into the exhibition grounds.

As part of the cultural export, Montreal's Théâtre Maisonneuve hosted a "Fiesta Cubana," featuring contemporary and popular music performances, movie screenings, modern dance, a fashion show, and a street conga.[80] Cuban filmmaking also had a strong

73 Dhar, "The Cuban Pavilion."

74 Ibid.

75 From an interview in Florian Zeyfang, Alexander Schmoeger, and Lisa Schmidt-Colinet, *Pavilion-In-Parts*.

76 Menéndez-Conde, *Trazos en los márgenes*, p. 149.

77 In fact, when presenting the "Pino del Agua" that would carry the workers and goods from Havana to Montreal, *Granma* described it as the ship "that already sails the seas around the world smashing the imperialist block imposed on our land." See: "Una visita al buque en el que irán a la Exposición Internacional de Montreal los trabajadores cubanos," *Granma*, April 1, 1967.

78 "Miles de visitantes en el Pabellón Cuba en Montreal," *Granma*, April 29, 1967.

79 See John M. Lee, "Cuban Goods Pose Expo 67 Problem," *New York Times*, March 23, 1967. Nick Auf Der Maur, "Cuban Cigars Could Fire Up Border Points," *The Gazette*, June 22, 1967.

presence beyond the national pavilion. There was a Cuban Film Festival at the Youth Pavilion (a neutral, non-national venue)[81] and a Cuban Cinema Week in one of the city's main movie theaters.[82] Finally, the Galerie Libre hosted a show featuring works by Cuban artists.[83]

Third-World solidarity was patent in the interaction with other national pavilions. For example, during the National Day of Algeria, the celebrations extended to the Cuban pavilion, together with the Quebec and United Arab pavilions.[84]

The Cuban pavilion in Montreal was a multidisciplinary space, where architects, filmmakers, photographers, curators, costume designers, artists, baristas, guides, and musicians participated in creating a space that would communicate the ideals of the Cuban Revolution.[85][86] The pavilion had a strong focus on history and a people's struggle against oppression. It also promoted the importance of arts and culture, and its commitment to Third World solidarity and internationalism. Cuba came across as a dynamic, fun-loving country, in contrast to the drab and monolithic Soviet socialism displayed in the USSR pavilion.[87]

The mobilization of film and photography were not new in the exhibition context. Indeed, the most significant superpowers of the time, the USSR and the US, had already mastered these mediating techniques to transmit their political message to a broad public audience. However, Cuba introduced a great innovation: the bar as a spatial mediator. While the pavilion consisted of metal structures and sharp forms that evoked an internationalist modernity, the bar was designed as a traditional, tasteful space, featuring classy dark wood furniture that evoked pre-revolutionary Havana under US influence. And while the Cuban exhibition was criticized for its political content, the bar was celebrated in the local press. Indeed, the bar was a geopolitical space for the Cuban delegation: the waiters, the musicians, the seafood, the rum for mojitos and daiquiris, and the cigars had been shipped from Cuba, and here, Western fairgoers had access to them regardless of the US embargo.

The architecture at the pavilion articulated the representation of the Cuban Revolution and social achievements combined with the joy of rum and artistic riches. By this means, the pavilion avoided reducing Cuba to either a folkloric touristic destination or a purely industrial society. With its acknowledgments to Third World revolutionary leaders, Cuba portrayed itself as a Latin American, Third World socialist country: a country emancipated from hegemonic powers, that threw off its victim condition and took up its own agency in history.[88]

Rigoberto Rodríguez tirelessly served daiquiris to thirsty Americans after their hot day at the fair. Everything looked like in

80 See: "Fiesta Cubana," *The Gazette*, July 22, 1967; Menéndez-Conde, *Trazos en los márgenes*, p. 150; and "Declarado el 26 de Julio como 'Día Nacional de Cuba' en la 'Expo-67' del Canadá," *Granma*, March 29, 1967.

81 On the Cuban Film retrospective: "Cuban Films at the Expo," *The Gazette*, August 19, 1967.

82 "Declarado el 26 de Julio como 'Día Nacional de Cuba'."

83 The artists representing Cuba at the gallery were: Amelia Peláez, Raúl Martínez, Umberto Peña, Mariano Rodríguez, Pedro Martínez, Salvador Corratgé, Fayad Jamís, Antonia Eiriz, and Wifredo Lam.
See Irene Heywood, "Cubans Exhibiting Exciting Art Growth," *The Gazette*, July 29, 1967.

84 "National Day of Algeria," *The Gazette*, October 5, 1967, section Expo 67 Today.

85 The list of artists and multidisciplinary specialists who participated in the pavilion: Vittorio Garatti (Architect), Sergio Baroni (Architect), Hugo D'Acosta (Architect), Enrique Fuentes (Curator), María Eugenia Haya (Designer), Mario García Joya (Photographer), Sandú Duré (Artist), Juan Blanco (musician), Fernando Ayuso (Costume Designer), Raúl Martínez (Painter), Félix Beltrán (Designer). See Schmidt-Colinet and Schmoeger, *Pabellón Cuba*, pp. 74-77.

86 The definition of the Cuban Pavilion as a multidisciplinary work was mentioned by the Italo-Cuban architect Roberto Gottardi in a 2007 interview with Lisa Schmidt-Colinet and Alex Schmoeger. See: ibid., p. 92.

87 Menéndez-Conde, *Trazos en los márgenes*, p. 150.

88 Manuel Cuadra, *Aspiraciones y Espacios de una Revolución. Arquitectura y urbanismo en Cuba 1959-2018* (Kassel: Kassel University Press, 2019), p. 108.

Llegada de los obreros gastronómicos que integraron la delegación cubana a la exposición internacional de Montreal (Expo 67) al aeropuerto "José Martí", de Rancho Boyeros, ayer a las 12:30 del día.

LLEGARON LOS GASTRONOMICOS DE EXPO-67

CON dos horas de antelación a la señalada para su arribo a Cuba, llegó al aeropuerto internacional "José Martí" de Rancho Boyeros, el segundo grupo de miembros de la delegación cubana a Expo-67. Este contingente estaba integrado por los trabajadores gastronómicos.

Al bajar las escalerillas del avión Britannia de Cubana de Aviación que los trajo de regreso a la Patria, los obreros ejemplares abrieron una tela con una leyenda impresa que decía: "Los gastronómicos cumplimos en Montreal y siempre venceremos por la Revolución"; otros saludaron a familiares y amigos que se concentraron en la terraza del aeropuerto, portando pequeñas banderas cubanas.

El director del INIT, compañero Armando Rivas, y el compañero Nivaldo Herrera, en representación de la COR del Comité Central del Partido, dieron la bienvenida a los compañeros de Expo-67. La recepción que se había organizado para expresar a los delegados la felicitación del pueblo por su magnífica labor en la exposición de Montreal, no pudo ofrecerse por la anticipación en la llegada del avión. Con los gastronómicos arribó a Boyeros el funcionario del INIT, Abraham Masique, que estaba con ellos en Canadá.

El arribo del tercer y último grupo que integró la delegación a la Feria Mundial del Canadá, está anunciado para el día 2 de noviembre.

"Llegaron los Gastronómicos de Expo-67," *Granma*, November 1, 1967. Banner reads: "We fulfilled our mission in Montreal and will always win for the Revolution."

Cuban Pavilion restaurant.

Opposite page:
Bartender at the Cuban Pavilion bar.

Cuban Pavilion bar.

an Old Havana Bar, Rigoberto's and his colleagues' uniforms, the cocktail glasses in which he served the drinks, the round metal tray he used, the ceramic jugs that the tourists drank from, the round marble tables, the four round, curvy café chairs per table with their woven cane backrests, the live band playing rumba, and the ceramic tiles on the floor. However, what made the place feel like Havana was the sinuous grace of Rigoberto and his colleagues moving between the tables.

When the Expo was over, in November 1967, Rigoberto and his colleagues boarded a Bristol Britannia aircraft flown by Cubana de Aviación to return to Havana, where they were welcomed by Armando Rivas, director of the Instituto Nacional de Industria Turística, and Nivaldo Herrera, from the Communist Party's central committee. Rigoberto and his colleagues descended from the Britannia and extended a banner before the journalists covering their arrival: "We the gastronomical workers fulfilled our task in Montreal, and we will always win for the Revolution."[89] The bar workers had accomplished their task: the Cuban Bar had been a total success. For their mission there was not simply to serve customers, like in any other bar. It was a revolutionary task: to mediate the bluntness of the revolutionary message in a capitalist country with the warmth of Cuban hospitality.

89 "Los gastronómicos cumplimos en Montreal y siempre venceremos por la Revolución." See: "Llegaron los Gastronómicos de Expo-67," *Granma*, November 1, 1967.

HAVANA SYNDROME: RETRANSMITTING THE “EDIFICIO EXPERIMENTAL”

Mark Wigley

In November 2016, a number of people working at the United States Embassy in Havana started complaining about intensely painful, high-pitched noises, followed by debilitating mental and physical symptoms of what turned out to be brain damage. Strangely, those immediately nearby were unaffected, as if it was only happening in certain heads, or was simply not to be believed. The traumatizing intrusions into brains typically occurred in streets, homes, and hotel rooms. Yet the media reports constructed the impression of a mysterious weapon able to pass through the seemingly solid, mini-fortress-like, US embassy perched on the city's famous waterfront edge. Every piece featured an image of the building's crisp façade, with its austere grid of windows punched into a smooth, creamy-white marble monolith—making it the most famous embassy on the planet.

The building had opened to much fanfare in early 1953 as an image of US pride and control—only to reappear in the international

"Edificio multifamiliar de viviendas de 17 plantas," *Arquitectura Cuba*, 338 (1971).

media every time there was a diplomatic crisis, which means often. Yet this new viral circulation of façade images greatly magnified and complicated the already convoluted role of any embassy as the political façade of a nation outside the nation, an exterior inserted into the interior of an exterior, the mark of an inside floating in the outside, sitting on a small piece of land that no longer belongs to the land in which it sits. A particular building—more precisely, a particular image of a building's self-assured exterior—became an avatar of brooding geopolitical uncertainty. It channeled a deeper uncertainty about buildings, boundaries, ground, air, and property.

US embassy, Havana, ca. 1955.
Max Abramovitz Papers.
Avery Architectural and Fine Arts Library
Columbia University, New York.

The polemically self-contained and proudly fully air-conditioned building had been designed by the New York office of Wallace Harrison and Max Abramovitz in 1951 to look like an occupiable façade—symbolically positioned as a kind of signal of authority broadcast from the most visible site on the Malecón, that strip of roadway, promenade, esplanade, and concrete seawall across which the United States can always be sensed less than a hundred miles away. The refinement of the modern architecture conveyed by the perfected façade had been sent across the water from the supposedly superior North in order to reiterate and defend that superiority—only to be challenged by a mysterious sonic intruder that didn't care about reinforced concrete, travertine marble skins, whiteness, or crisp geometry.

If an embassy represents a nation and its capacity to protect its own, then the damage to the brains of US citizens abroad represented a failure of that image, and therefore that façade. The building, and the force it represents, was insufficient protection. In the coldest war of fantasies, an invisible enemy was using invisible means to inflict hidden damage on the brains of national subjects. The nation was being undone by some anti-architectural device. And Cuba was not by chance the laboratory of this experiment to bypass architecture, or at least the site in which such a threat could be publicly discussed.

Similar incidents have since been reported in many different countries around the world, including the United States itself and the very grounds of the White House, but it is still referred to as "Havana Syndrome"—with lingering uncertainty as to whether it is a physical or mental incident, or, more precisely, a physical attack on the mental. Officially the cause is still unclear, but the comprehensive report by the National Academies of Sciences in December of 2020 concluded that the most plausible explanation was "directed, pulsed radiofrequency energy."[1] Radio waves, most likely microwaves, flowing through walls, penetrating buildings and bodies to trigger shock waves in the brain that permanently alter mental functioning—even if humans are likely not the real target but the electronic brains of their prosthetic devices, the phones and computers nestled in hands, laps, backpacks, or bags. It is as if the kind of weapon so vividly imagined in science fiction over the last century, and the focus of huge military research projects for decades, had finally been perfected and operationalized.

Yet this violation of buildings and bodies didn't simply subvert a stable physical world of self-contained structures and subjects. All buildings are incubated in the space of radio waves. Ever since humans became insects at the end of the nineteenth century—as they added antennae to their bodies to network their brains with the invention of radio—architecture has been in the air and on air. Buildings are structured by the radio signals that so uncannily pass through them. This is nowhere more obvious than in Cuba. Or, more precisely, the expression "in Cuba" or even "on the islands of Cuba" presupposes a physically delimited territory that has never, in fact, been clearly delimited. The original indigenous Taino word *cubanacan* is said to mean "place in the middle." Cuba is defined by what is outside and around it. The very idea of an interior to Cuba has long been constructed in the radio waves sent towards and from that mythical middle. Better said, it is constructed in the particular ways those waves are tuned into. Cuba itself is suspended in a sea of competing radio signals. Cuba is the name of a radio contest. And this contest negotiates the relationship of the Caribbean to the world beyond in which the spatial order of that wider world is at stake. As Alejandra Bronfman puts it:

> The Caribbean is not a firmly bounded place but rather a set of claims about space. ...wireless and broadcasting helped generate the very idea that the Caribbean and the wider world ought to be imagined as distinct and distant even if increasingly connected.[2]

Every building "in" or "on" Cuba must be seen in terms of its simultaneous obliviousness to radio and dependence on it. No building in Cuba simply rests on the ground. Everything floats, even the islands themselves. The astonishing force of the ocean waves that have done so much to shape the histories of the place is matched by equally stormy radio waves. All the extractive colonial occupations and rebellions forming the islands, plus the international commerce in goods, bodies, and ideas over centuries, has produced nested confusions of inside and outside with a unique density of hybridity now sustained by overlapping transmissions, counter-transmissions, jamming, eavesdropping, and interference patterns. No building simply arrives from some outside. Nor is any building simply born there. In the end, no building is simply built in Cuba. In reverse, Cuba haunts international architectural discourse in ways that have never been fully accounted. Whatever Cuba is—or the many Cubas—it has

1 National Academies of Sciences, Engineering, and Medicine 2020, *An Assessment of Illness in U.S. Government Employees and Their Families at Overseas Embassies* (Washington, DC: National Academies Press, 2020), p. 2.

2 Alejandra Bronfman, *Isles of Noise: Sonic Media in the Caribbean* (Chapel Hill: University of North Carolina Press, 2016), p. 14.

never simply been the victim of its outside. It continuously radiates disruptive signals. Cuba is a challenge to normative understandings of what it means to build.

The embassy building deposited on the Malecón as the formal representative of the not so "good neighbor" to the north—based on a then-new US Government strategy of deploying architecture itself as a "good ambassador"[3]—stands alongside buildings launched as it were from the hypothetical interior of Cuba, sent to the front as a counter-signal. Consider for example the so-called Edificio Experimental, the 17-story housing structure standing a few blocks further along the waterfront in the same Vedado neighborhood. If the embassy was embarrassed by its concrete core—the naked, gridded, reinforced-concrete frame that stood on view as a new kind of see-through monumental sculpture for almost two years during the construction, before being dressed in a smooth skin of marble and sealed with glass—the newer building celebrates the concrete doing all the work. It is not dressed or sealed. It flaunts its nudity and even conveys the sense of being unfinished, a work in progress like some kind of huge kitset with new elements yet to be plugged on. This polemically brutalist structure for social housing was designed in the late 60s as a counter-capitalist and counter-US propaganda statement by the architects Antonio Quintana and Alberto Rodríguez and a team of colleagues including the engineers Sixto Ruiz, Hugo Wainshtok, and César Rivero. Supposedly built by the workers for the workers, the structure was itself a kind of worker standing over the ocean in front of all the towers, luxury residences, and institutions that exemplified US influence in Cuba with their pose of a relaxed modern architecture seemingly relieved of social responsibility to now embrace light, shape, color, pattern, plants, and play.

US embassy, Havana, in construction, ca. 1955. Max Abramovitz Papers. Avery Architectural and Fine Arts Library Columbia University, New York.

Ever since its conversion from farmland in the 19th century, the Vedado neighborhood has been the largely bourgeois white neighborhood of Havana, home to the newly rich and playground for tourists. Architecture too had seemingly been on vacation there, echoing the buildings of Miami on the other side of the water and thereby creating a kind of architectural bridge that matched, marked and glamorized all the financial and political contracts that subordinated most Cubans.

The new building was intended as an icon of the new communism and the necessary industrialization of building construction in order to distribute affordable housing to the working poor, as a right, rather than cater to the needs of the rich minority. It was a manifesto for the program Fidel Castro presented in detail in a February 16, 1959 speech to the National College of Architects, just five weeks after arriving in Havana to declare the victory of the

3 "U.S. Architecture Abroad: Modern Design at Its Best Now Represents this Country in Foreign Lands," *Architectural Forum* (March 1953): 102.

4 Castro's speech made a lengthy analysis of the flaws in existing buildings and urban organization, calling for "scientific," economic, less exploitative designs that resisted the "monotony" that typified worker's housing, while focusing on details like the positioning of toilets, ventilation, hygiene, lighting levels, and play areas, along with radio and television. All building materials needed to be produced in Cuba rather than imported, starting with new factories to make cement for concrete, and the entire logic of property needed to be transformed, replacing architecture "as business" with architecture as public service. More than 100 architects were needed so that more than 100 new buildings could start construction on the Malecón within two months. Fidel Castro, speech to Colegio Nacional de Arquitectos, February 16, 1959.

Leonardo Finotti, 2014. Photo of Edificio Girón. *Latin America in Construction: Architecture 1955-1980*, ed. Barry Bergdoll et al. (New York: Museum of Modern Art, 2015), p. 10.

Revolution. It was his first speech to any professional organization, even though, as he ironically noted, few architects had been involved in the revolutionary struggle. The new building was a belated but almost point-by-point response to the speech's call for social revolution to be architectural revolution—including the urgent call for more than a hundred new buildings to rapidly occupy the Malecón that had been the playground of the rich isolated from the majority of Cubans, areas for children's play, shorter distances between housing and work, ventilation, a new local concrete industry, efficiencies of prefabrication, architects to always be thinking in terms of the design of cities rather than isolated buildings, and even the call for 5 percent of the budget of all projects to be devoted to aesthetics, since beauty itself was the right of all Cubans.[4] Castro later insisted that architects had to redesign themselves to produce such structures, performing an almost biological shift away from their long-internalized role as exploiters.[5]

Most of the leading architects of the 1950s promptly left Cuba. Antonio Quintana, however, who had been responsible for some of the most internationally celebrated buildings for the elites in the very same Vedado neighborhood, was now at the center of the new project to rebuild wholesale. He was appointed as the National

5 In 1961, Castro berated architects for being so well adjusted to the "society of exploitation" that they had difficulty countering the "inhuman" environments it produced, because they too had become exploiters: "A good technician would necessarily end up in that situation, because that man did what the others did. That man adjusted himself to that exploitative environment, that inhuman environment, that selfish environment, in the midst of which he been raised and his mind had been formed. The social milieu has a decisive influence on the conduct of men, and in that society of exploitation and robbery, the technicians wound up being exploiters." Fidel Castro, "Discurso del Comandante Fidel Castro a los trabajadores de la construcci April 6, 1961," in "Cronología de la revolución a la arquitectura (1953-1969)," *Ensayos sobre Arquitectura e Ideología en Cuba Revolucionaria* (Centro de Información Científica y Técnica, Universidad de La Habana, 1970), p. 93.

CONTENIDO

Revista.
Normas y tipificación.
Gran Panel
su tecnología y ejecución II
Edificio multifamiliar multiplanta.
Sistema de eliminación de polvos industriales.
El hormigón y el mar.
Naturaleza de la Industrialización III
Ultimas publicaciones recibidas.
Hacia la industrialización de la construcción (separata).

CONTENT

Review.
Standards and tipification.
Large Panel
it's technology and assembly II
Multi-familiar multi-storey building.
Industrial dusts avoiding system.
Concrete and the Sea.
Nature of the industrialisation III.
Last publications received.
Towards Building Industrialization (reprint)

TABLE DE MATIERES

Revue.
Normes et typification.
Grand Panneau
technologie et exécution II.
Bâtiment multifamilier á plusieurs étages.
Systèmes pour l'élimination des poussières industrielles.
Le betón et la Mer.
Nature de l'industrialisation III.
Denières publications reçues.
Vers l'industrialisation du bâtiment (separata).

Portada: Dibujo de la fachada sur del Bloque B del edificio multifamiliar de vivienda que se construye en Malecón y F, Vedado.

Contraportada: Ejecución de la obra del edificio experimental de 17 plantas que se construye en el Vedado.

cubaconstruye

ORGANO OFICIAL DEL MINISTERIO DE LA CONSTRUCCION
EDITADA EN LA HABANA, REPUBLICA DE CUBA

Año 4 - Números 3 y 4 - 1967

Revista trimestral inscripta en la Administración de Correos de La Habana, acogida a la tarifa de impresos periódicos. Redacción: Centro de Documentación e Información Técnica de la Construcción. Avenida Carlos Manuel de Céspedes, Plaza de la Revolución. Teléfonos 7-4052, 79-1293 y 70-7791 Extensión 161, La Habana, Cuba. Precio por suscripción anual: $5.00. Apartado de Correos número 6111.

DIRECTOR: **José Respall Arana**
JEFE DE REDACCION: **Jesús Pulido Millán**
FOTOS: **Humberto Michelena**
CONSEJO ASESOR: **Enrique De Jongh Caula**, **Juan Vega Vega**, **Luis Felipe Luaces**, **Eduardo Ecenarro**, **Armando Pascual**, **Armando López Callejas**, **Eduardo López**, **Luis Pérez C'd**, **René Saladrigas**, **Gonzalo Quesada**, **Pablo Hernández Matos**, **Francisco Borrero**

Cuba Construye, vol. 4, nos. 3-4 (1967), cover and index page.

Project Director, then Technical Vice-Minister for the newly formed Ministry of Construction (MICONS), organizing a vast program in which architects worked in teams to produce housing, schools, hospitals, factories, parks, and urban infrastructures. Much of the work was architecturally and politically ambitious, while increasingly prioritizing standardized solutions over "unique" structures now demonized as elitist. MICONS literally took over the schools of architecture and engineering in 1965 and teachers and students of both schools were part of the team that designed the Edificio Experimental—idealized as a collective laboring for the collective.

UNIQUELY STANDARD

Paradoxically, this building called on to represent standardization was completely unique. Its innovative slip-mold system of construction—where the metal formwork for pouring a rapidly setting concrete for the walls is continuously moved by hydraulic jacks up the very walls it is forming—was a mechanism for efficiently manufacturing successive floors as a kind of on-site factory. It could vertically repeat the layout of apartments any number of times to form a tower block,

18

EDIFICIO MULTIFAMILIAR MULTIPLANTA EXPERIMENTAL

En Cuba, al igual que en otros países con mayor desarrollo técnico, se plantea la construcción de edificios multifamiliares multiplanta, que responden entre otras a las siguientes motivaciones:

—Las viviendas concentradas en edificios en altura (12 a 14 pisos, para nuevas urbanizaciones) demuestran índices técnico-económicos superiores a los que arrojarían esas viviendas agrupadas en edificios de cuatro plantas, con igual volumen de fabricación, debido principalmente a la economía que se obtiene en las redes de instalaciones, trazado de vías y concentración de servicios básicos.
En nuestro caso es admisible llegar hasta 17 plantas, por encontramos en una urbanización ya construida, con sus redes de instalaciones, etc., en funcionamiento.

—La mejor utilización del suelo, aumentando la densidad de población y limitando al mismo tiempo el crecimiento horizontal desmesurado de las ciudades.

Arq. Antonio Quintana Simonetti
Arq. Alberto Rodríguez Surribas
Ing. Sixto Ruiz
Ing. Hugo Wainshtok Rivas
Ing. César Rivero Lage

19

Antonio Quintana and Alberto Rodríguez, "Edificio Multifamiliar Multiplanta Experimental," *Cuba Construye*, vol. 4, nos. 3-4 (1967), model photo, pp. 18-19.

which could then be repeated on the same site or any number of other sites. Yet the building was one-of-a-kind, and unambiguously sculptural. The very relentlessness of its polemic against unnecessary excess produced a distinct form and esthetic.

The horizontal and vertical circulation is separated away from the two blocks of apartments as a kind of plumbing system for humans—minimized to horizontal tubes only every three floors, suspended between two vertical shafts per block, and all connected to just one elevator tower. There are no added layers of plaster or paint to soften the rough concrete—although the horizontal tubes are smoother and whiter, as are the water storage structures that float above the roof. Both tubes and tanks were assembled from precast elements lifted by crane and joined in place with matching white cement. The overall effect is of two perforated slabs of concrete connected by a vertical grid standing in the gap between them. Glass is subordinated and the horizontal windows strips have the same dimensions as the bands of concrete between them, accentuating the sense of a relentless system. The thin planes and glassy boxes of the surrounding neighborhood, with their implied air conditioning systems, have given way to a sense of solidity and cross-ventilation by sea breezes.

From a distance, the structure reads as a single solid, like some impenetrable medieval fortification. Closer up, it breaks into two thick overlapping and interconnected planes pierced by the bands of windows. The internal walls dividing the four nine-meter-wide apartments on each floor can clearly be read running down the façades, and have large, inverted V-shapes cut out of them as they emerge below to form legs. Even the vertical shafts holding the horizontal walkways have an angled notch cut out as they meet the ground. The circulation system and apartment blocks are suspended on these angled legs, a floating effect that is paradoxically accentuated by the apparent weight of all the exposed concrete above, freeing up a landscaped surface for plants and play underneath. The thicker block closer to the water, hosting 64 three-bedroom apartments, floats higher than the other to create a sense of entrance. The thinner block, with 68 two-bedroom apartments, floats lower, to shelter the children's play area. The building itself is playful as it meets the ground. The space underneath the two relentlessly systematic blocks anticipates regular flooding and has an idiosyncratic, complex geometry of stepped plinths, floating horizontal and vertical planes, stairs and angles. Catching the eye even before the building does,

Both pages:
Expansion concept, apartment plans, structure, and circulation plans. Antonio Quintana and Alberto Rodríguez, "Edificio Multifamiliar Multiplanta Experimental," *Cuba Construye*, vol. 4, nos. 3-4 (1967): 22-24; 27.

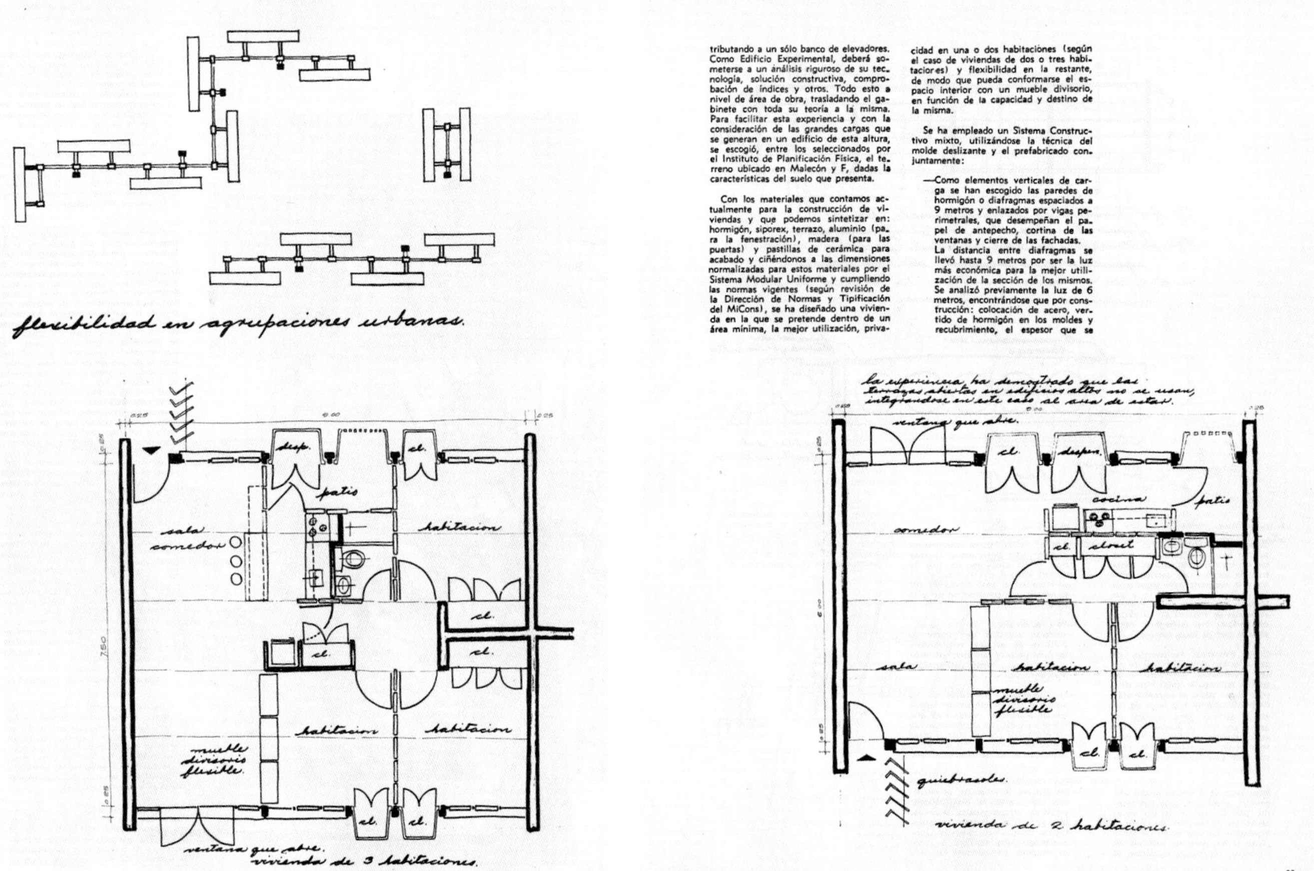

tributando a un sólo banco de elevadores. Como Edificio Experimental, deberá someterse a un análisis riguroso de su tecnología, solución constructiva, comprobación de índices y otros. Todo esto a nivel de área de obra, trasladando el gabinete con toda su teoría a la misma. Para facilitar esta experiencia y con la consideración de las grandes cargas que se generan en un edificio de esta altura, se escogió, entre los seleccionados por el Instituto de Planificación Física, el terreno ubicado en Malecón y F, dadas la características del suelo que presenta.

Con los materiales que contamos actualmente para la construcción de viviendas y que podemos sintetizar en: hormigón, siporex, terrazo, aluminio (para la fenestración), madera (para las puertas) y pastillas de cerámica para acabado y ciñéndonos a las dimensiones normalizadas para estos materiales por el Sistema Modular Uniforme y cumpliendo las normas vigentes (según revisión de la Dirección de Normas y Tipificación del MiCons), se ha diseñado una vivienda en la que se pretende dentro de un área mínima, la mejor utilización, privacidad en una o dos habitaciones (según el caso de viviendas de dos o tres habitaciones) y flexibilidad en la restante, de modo que pueda conformarse el espacio interior con un mueble divisorio, en función de la capacidad y destino de la misma.

Se ha empleado un Sistema Constructivo mixto, utilizándose la técnica del molde deslizante y el prefabricado conjuntamente:

—Como elementos verticales de carga se han escogido las paredes de hormigón o diafragmas espaciados a 9 metros y enlazados por vigas perimetrales, que desempeñan el papel de antepecho, cortina de las ventanas y cierre de las fachadas.
La distancia entre diafragmas se llevó hasta 9 metros por ser la luz más económica para la mejor utilización de la sección de los mismos. Se analizó previamente la luz de 6 metros, encontrándose que por construcción: colocación de acero, vertido de hormigón en los moldes y recubrimiento, el espesor que se

some large mounds of rough weathered limestone are exposed at the leading edge of this constructed landscape on their own plinth, as if to convey that the building behind is an almost geological extension of the rock below. These incongruous craggy lumps act as avatars of its uncompromising, even confrontational, toughness.

The basic strategy, once the foundations had been sunk one meter into the rock, was to cast all the vertical elements on-site in one extended slip-mold pour. As the walls steadily rose a meter and a half per day, a single crane lifted up all the precast horizontal elements and they were joined together in the air between the verticals. It is as if the rougher verticals host the smoother horizontals that host the even smoother interiors of the apartments. Each apartment maximizes efficiency and flexibility, with divisions between rooms made of standardized prefabricated furniture elements that don't reach the ceiling so the air flows over and around them. One dividing wall can potentially be eliminated, to turn a three-bedroom apartment into two, or a two-bedroom into one, with correspondingly larger living areas. All door frames, aerated concrete panels, sanitary and kitchen fittings were prefabricated. The entire building was a vast kitset of standardized components—so relentlessly standardized

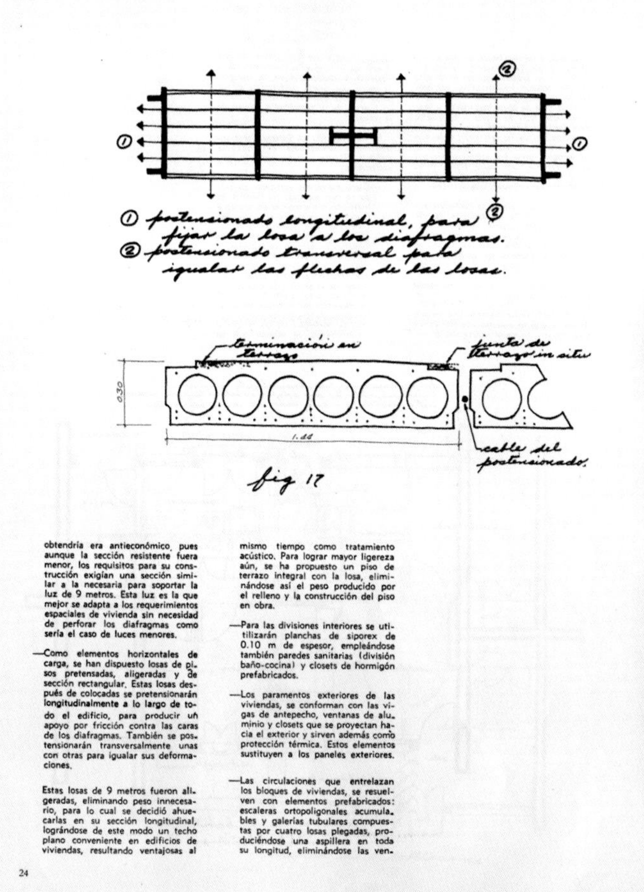

obtendría era antieconómico, pues aunque la sección resistente fuera menor, los requisitos para su construcción exigían una sección similar a la necesaria para soportar la luz de 9 metros. Esta luz es la que mejor se adapta a los requerimientos espaciales de vivienda sin necesidad de perforar los diafragmas como sería el caso de luces menores.

—Como elementos horizontales de carga, se han dispuesto losas de pisos pretensadas, aligeradas y de sección rectangular. Estas losas después de colocadas se pretensionarán longitudinalmente a lo largo de todo el edificio, para producir un apoyo por fricción contra las caras de los diafragmas. También se postensionarán transversalmente unas con otras para igualar sus deformaciones.

Estas losas de 9 metros fueron aligeradas, eliminando peso innecesario, para lo cual se decidió ahuecarlas en su sección longitudinal, lográndose de este modo un techo plano conveniente en edificios de viviendas, resultando ventajosas al mismo tiempo como tratamiento acústico. Para lograr mayor ligereza aún, se ha propuesto un piso de terrazo integral con la losa, eliminándose así el peso producido por el relleno y la construcción del piso en obra.

—Para las divisiones interiores se utilizarán planchas de siporex de 0.10 m de espesor, empleándose también paredes sanitarias (división baño-cocina) y closets de hormigón prefabricados.

—Los paramentos exteriores de las viviendas, se conforman con las vigas de antepecho, ventanas de aluminio y closets que se proyectan hacia el exterior y sirven además como protección térmica. Estos elementos sustituyen a los paneles exteriores.

—Las circulaciones que entrelazan los bloques de viviendas, se resuelven con elementos prefabricados: escaleras ortopoligonales acumulables y galerías tubulares compuestas por cuatro losas plegadas, produciéndose una aspillera en toda su longitud, eliminándose las ven-

24

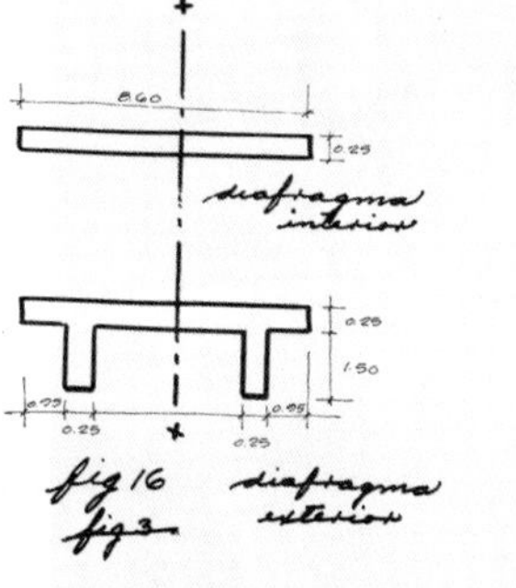

El refuerzo resultó mínimo excepto en la zona entre las ramas, que se supuso actuando como viga pared, siendo reforzada consecuentemente según esta suposición.

CIMENTACION DE LAS TORRES, DE ESCALERAS Y ELEVADORES

El esquema de análisis del conjunto, seguido durante el cálculo, fue el siguiente: el bloque de habitaciones rígido en los dos sentidos, las torres rígidas en uno y apoyadas en los bloques por medio de las escaleras en otro, de ahí que mientras las torres son casi cuadradas, sus cimentaciones tengan una forma rectangular con una dimensión del orden de los nueve metros y la otra de aproximadamente tres metros.

En las torres, la carga llega al cimiento por cuatro zonas bien definidas, dos a cada lado, lo que determinó dimensionar el cimiento con una configuración similar (Fig. 15).

Esta forma produjo una economía de más de 13 metros cúbicos de hormigón en cada uno de ellos, pues en las zonas abiertas no se excavó la roca, limitándose ésta a la forma de doble H. En definitiva son dos cimientos unidos por vigas muy peraltadas que obligan al trabajo en conjunto; el refuerzo como en el anterior fue mínimo.

DIAFRAGMAS

Cada bloque consta de seis diafragmas, cinco transversales y uno longitudinal, aunque en los exteriores aparecen pequeños alletones que ayudan a este último a tomar los efectos del viento a lo largo del edificio, así como aumentar la estabilidad del conjunto durante la construcción. Uniendo los diafragmas, existen vigas perimetrales muy peraltadas (debido a condicionales arquitectónicas), cuya función estructural consiste en soportar las escaleras, ventanas, closets exteriores, etc., así como durante el proceso de construcción servir de arriostramiento a los diafragmas que, como se aprecia por sus dimensiones, son muy esbeltos.

Para la distribución de las cargas de viento se utilizó el método de las deformaciones, que en este caso particular de diafragmas paralelos, las distribuye proporcionalmente a la inercia de cada uno. Así a los exteriores corresponde tomar la mayor parte, pues su inercia es más de un 50% mayor que los interiores (Figs. 16 y 16A).

En la determinación de las cargas se usaron las normas dadas por la NOCAE, a causa de que en la distribución de las

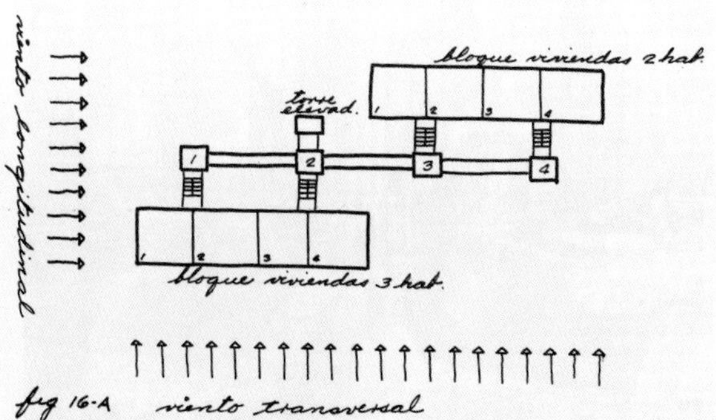

27

Detalle del deslizamiento del tímpano.

Cimiento y estructura de los tímpanos.

28

Plataforma del molde deslizante.

Vista del bloque de viviendas de tres habitaciones en proceso de fundición.

29

Construction photos. In Antonio Quintana and Alberto Rodríguez, “Edificio Multifamiliar Multiplanta Experimental,” *Cuba Construye*, vol. 4, nos. 3-4 (1967): 28-29.

as to produce non-standard effects. Prefabricated concrete storage closets, for example, protrude through the façade to maximize interior space, provide thermal insulation, and an articulated pattern on the exterior visible from afar. They have different colored ceramic tiles cast into their outer planes that makes the closer view, looking up the façade, more varied, and even more so when looking across from the walkways or stairs while moving through the building. Similar precast protrusions extend the internal patio spaces and are punctuated with an explicitly decorative pattern of square holes for ventilation that produce a more complex internal light and external effect.

The imperfections and rough texture embraced throughout the building is smoothed over on the floors by terrazzo that has been cast into the concrete floor slabs. When the 1.5 x 9-meter slabs were hoisted up to be laid in place across the width of the apartments, the strip of terrazzo added to cover the joints between them had a slightly different color and density, producing a striped pattern on the floor—with the block of three-bedroom units being just one stripe wider.

These minimal but insistent decorative effects extend beyond the apartments with a flower-like pattern of colored ceramic tiles covering the intersection between the metal elevator doors and their concrete shaft. The terrazzo continues on the precast stair landings, and the prefabricated concrete steps themselves produce a zig-zag pattern accentuated by the precast L-shaped vertical concrete fins floating between them to provide safety, cross-ventilation, and a kind of gauzy see-through effect of layered screens. Even the longitudinal post-tensioning steel cables—the hidden strengthening of the whole structure than runs between all the floor slabs—terminate in concrete studs that form a grid pattern on the end walls between the concrete fins that strengthen the overall structure and mitigate the effect of the wind. Every decision to do the most with the least, and build the most for the least, generates some kind of unique visual texture.

The overall effect is tough—braced against the ocean and the previous political economy as an unambiguously brutalist building, perhaps the most brutal possible—but not austere, simple, or harsh. There are clear relationships with the monumental concrete shafts and organizational division of served and serving spaces of Louis Kahn, the formal strategies of the so-called Team 10 architects in the late 50s and early 60s to turn housing blocks into interlinked urban nets, and the expandability concepts of the Japanese Metabolists. But the particular interlinking system, construction method, structural system, ventilation, internal organization, and on-site assembly are unique. More importantly, the overarching narrative is no longer the supposed egalitarian hospitality of architecture as the embodiment of the welfare state, but the toughness of architecture as a form of reparation to laboring workers—building as a form of justice. The fragment of ceramic tile pattern exposed on the side of the stairs that come down to lightly touch the ground, as if from the underbelly of a spaceship, hints that the tough exterior has a softer interior, while reinforcing the other-worldly sense of a building from the future, a society where the workers have the best view.

Fidel Castro celebrated "the famous building that was built on the Malecón" in an October 18, 1969 graduation ceremony speech at the university in Santa Clara, insisting that the "amazing" results of such innovative construction techniques carried out by roving construction brigades were essential to the country's social, industrial and economic future—as were architects.[6] *Granma*, the official government organ, published a lengthy article a few weeks later affirming that the "edificio experimental" was so progressive that it would be "historic." The article began with the provocation: "Is it possible to erect the wall and beam structure of a 17-story building in 10 days and two hours?"[7] 151 workers, organized in quasi-military "platoons" and "squads," had apparently accomplished the unlikely "feat" by laboring day and night using the extreme system combining slip-mold walls with prefabrication of all other components. The two accompanying images of the formwork for the reinforced concrete walls being steadily pushed up as the building grows up on top of itself was an unambiguous metaphor of the revolutionary government building a nation up out of itself.

In fact, as the article acknowledged, construction on the project had really started more than two years earlier, in April 1967. The first block had gone up in a continuous night-and-day effort for 30 days (as Castro's graduation speech reported, without saying when it happened) and the initial framework for making the legs of the second block was already assembled before the first block reached the second floor, but the result was never fast. For more than two years, the waterfront exhibited a new kind of conspicuously empty monument—the single block with empty holes for the windows and closets, one vertical shaft unconnected to the block by stairs, no horizontal walkways and the ghostly beginnings of the second block. Only in September of 1969 did the construction of the second block begin. *Granma* showed the structure on the third day of construction and its current state without any explanation of the extended time of incompletion, only saying that the plan was to complete the circulation system and outfit all the apartments by the "glorious day" of July 26, 1970, to celebrate the anniversary of the Revolution. Eventually it would be known as Edificio Girón, as the word "GIRÓN" was constructed in large concrete letters and placed on its own podium at the base of the building to be seen by passing cars and cameras, fusing revolutionary architecture to the defense of the Revolution at

6 "Recently, too, the sliding-mold brigade, which built the tower here and has been busy with some major engineering works, built the structure of a 17-story building in 11 days. It's that famous building that was built on the Malecón, they started and built the first structure in 30 days. Now they have built the second building in 11 days with the sliding mold system, the concrete in trucks! And it didn't stop for a minute from the time they started, and in 11 days they reached the 17th floor. You can see that if we want to solve housing, the housing of industries and the economic plans of the country, we must use techniques of this type. Then the cranes come and bring in the prefabricated floors and put them in place from the top. All these techniques have been analyzed and studied. And some of the results are amazing. When a work is started by a brigade, it has to stay there to the end, from the removal of earth to the completion of the buildings." Fidel Castro, speech at the graduation ceremony of agronomy students and mid-level technicians of the Agricultural Technological Institutes held at the Central University in Santa Clara, October 18, 1969, quoted in "Cronología de la revolución a la arquitectura (1953-1969)," p. 151.

7 Raimundo Rodrigues, "Un Edificio de Viviendas que será histórico en Cuba," *Granma*, November 25, 1969, p. 4.

UN EDIFICIO DE VIVIENDAS QUE SERA HISTORICO EN CUBA

¿Es posible levantar la estructura constituida por muros y vigas de diecisiete pisos de un edificio en diez días y dos horas?

Parece inverosímil contestar afirmativamente, pero se logró en La Habana. La proeza la realizaron los trabajadores que construyen un edificio multifamiliar, multiplanta experimental, en Malecón y F, en el Vedado. Para levantar los 17 pisos laboraron ininterrumpidamente 242 horas: desde las 3 de la tarde del día 29 de septiembre hasta las 5 p. m. del 9 de octubre, lo que representa un promedio de 4.80 metros de altura diarios.

El comandante Fidel Castro, en su discurso del 18 de octubre, en Santa Clara, se refirió elogiosamente a este gran trabajo.

La construcción de los 17 pisos en las 242 horas fue posible por la utilización de un sistema que tiene como ventaja principal la rapidez, y que está en boga en los países más desarrollados para edificar viviendas en el menor tiempo posible: el de moldes deslizantes, que se emplea por primera vez en Cuba para la producción de viviendas.

El nombre del sistema se debe a que el molde o cofre de los elementos verticales de carga, como son las paredes de hormigón o diafragmas, vigas de antepecho de los bloques de viviendas y las paredes de la torre de los elevadores y de las cuatro torres rectangulares donde se apoyan las galerías y escaleras, se deslizan.

Conjuntamente con la técnica del molde deslizante se utiliza la técnica del prefabricado para los elementos horizontales de carga, tales como las losas de pisos.

Para el montaje de los diversos elementos prefabricados se emplea una grúa torre, francesa, telescópica, de 70 metros de altura y 40 metros de brazo y una capacidad de carga de 120 tonometros, o sea, tres toneladas a 40 metros de distancia.

El inmueble se comenzó a construir el 19 de abril de 1967. Su origen se debe a una decisión de la Dirección del Ministerio de la Construcción de confeccionar un proyecto de edificio multifamiliar, multiplanta experimental, con una tecnología progresista y acorde con nuestras condiciones actuales y con miras a la industrialización de la construcción. Se escogió el lugar debido a características particulares del suelo.

Con los materiales existentes actualmente para la construcción de viviendas se diseñó una vivienda en la que se pretende, dentro de un área mínima la mejor utilización, privacidad en una o dos habitaciones (según el caso de casas de dos o tres habitaciones) y flexibilidad en la restante, de manera que pueda conformarse el espacio interior con un mueble divisorio, en función de la capacidad y destino de ella.

El edificio tendrá 132 viviendas con el máximo de aislamiento al no haber pasillos; ventilación cruzada por el norte y el sur, dos elevadores, escaleras, dos tanques de agua con capacidad para 10,560 galones cada uno y una cisterna para almacenar cien mil galones; "chuter" o canal para la basura, instalación sanitaria sobre el piso (oculta debajo del mueble de la cocina), tubería empotrada en la unión de dos losas e inodoros de descarga por atrás. También contará con zona de parqueo, áreas verdes con bancos y área de juego infantil.

La expresión total del edificio corresponde a dos bloques —A y B— de viviendas, interconectados, cada uno con una altura de 53 metros.

El bloque A tiene 16 plantas —cada una con un área de 275 metros cuadrados— con un total de 64 apartamentos de tres cuartos (cada Apto. tiene una superficie de 67 metros cuadrados). El bloque B dispone de 17 pisos —cada uno mide 242 metros cuadrados— y 68 viviendas de dos habitaciones (cada apartamento abarca 54 metros cuadrados).

Además de los cuartos, los apartamentos tienen sala, comedor, cocina, patio y servicio sanitario. Asimismo, dispone de closets de hormigón prefabricados calados para aumentar el área de colgar la ropa y permitir la ventilación; y para ahorrar espacio el fondo sale al exterior, y esto sirve de protección térmica y como estética para el edificio, ya que están forrados con pastillas de cerámica de distintos colores.

Así se encontraba el edificio, al tercero de los diez días en que se levantó la estructura, constituida por muros y vigas de 17 pisos. (Foto: MICONS).

El entrepiso está formado por losas prefabricadas, las cuales después de colocadas se postensionan a todo lo largo del edificio por medio de cables situados entre las juntas de las losas.

Para las divisiones interiores se usan planchas de siporex de diez centímetros de espesor; se emplean también paredes sanitarias (división baño-cocina) y los citados closets de hormigón prefabricados.

Los paramentos —cara de una pared o muro— exteriores de las viviendas se conforman con las vigas de antepecho, ventanas de aluminio y los closets, que se proyectan hacia el exterior. Estos elementos sustituyen a los paneles exteriores.

Como el costo de mantenimiento de este tipo de edificio es elevado en cuanto a los exteriores, se ha eliminado totalmente la pintura de la fachada, dejando a los materiales su textura y color.

Debido a que en Cuba la solución óptima para obtener la mejor ventilación es la de edificios por galería, se proyectaron las circulaciones horizontales y verticales separadas del bloque de apartamentos, correspondiendo las primeras con las paredes de elevadores.

La circulación vertical está constituida por los elevadores y las escaleras ortopoligonales acumulables. La circulación horizontal, o sea, la comunicación entre las torres de escalera, se resolvió con una galería en forma de tubo con una aspillera de veinte centímetros a todo lo largo, lo cual favorece el disfrute de las vistas, y elimina las ventanas de cristal, lo que significa economía en el mantenimiento.

La confección del programa de ejecución para la obra se realizó por el Departamento de Matemática Aplicada del MICONS, en colaboración con el Centro de Cálculo de la Universidad de La Habana, mediante el método de la Ruta Crítica. Asimismo, el Instituto de Viviendas desempeña la función de inversionista y la Escuela de Arquitectura actuó como proyectista general. Otras empresas también brindan su ayuda.

Actualmente, hay en el edificio 151 trabajadores de la Unidad de Obras Varias del Ministerio de la Construcción, organizados en pelotones y escuadras. Laboran 8 horas, pero cuando es necesario aportan horas voluntarias. Así, durante los diez días dedicados a la construcción de los 17 pisos, su contribución gratuita ascendió a 8,679 horas.

Para cumplimentar los grandes planes de viviendas que se contemplan se desarrollarán fundamentalmente edificios de cuatro plantas. Pero con este inmueble de Malecón y F podrían lograrse índices técnico-económicos mejores a los que arrojarían esos apartamentos agrupados en edificios de cuatro pisos, debido principalmente a la economía que se obtiene en las redes de instalaciones, trazado de vías y concentración de servicios básicos.

Es decir, que por su carácter experimental de una nueva técnica constructiva, este edificio será histórico. Por eso el responsable de la obra, Julio Sosa; el ingeniero César Rivero, los arquitectos José Licea y Avelino Macías, el técnico José Flores y los dirigentes y responsables obreros Rolando Roig, Miguel Angel Hardy, Jorge Olmo, Homero Espinosa, Ezequiel Domínguez, Evelio Valdés, Fernando Alonso, Carmelo Crespo y Adolfo Iglesias, y todos los trabajadores en general, se esfuerzan en su construcción, y tratan de terminarlo el 26 de Julio de 1970, como saludo a la gloriosa fecha.

Estado actual en que se encuentra el edificio de Malecón y F, al que se refirió Fidel en su discurso en Santa Clara.—(Foto: Emilio Argüelles).

● Raimundo Rodríguez

the Playa Girón (Bay of Pigs). The Malecón was once again the front line in a propaganda campaign. There was never any doubt that this building was a signal.

The Malecón itself had been self-consciously constructed as the façade of Cuba in 1901, during the first occupation of the country by the United States. The concrete sea wall and wider roadway were designed by US Navy civil engineers as part of a massive project of public works addressing infrastructure, communication, sanitation, and disease. It was to be the main transportation artery, a shield against the ferocity of waves, winds, and potential enemies, but also a representation of nationhood. The US military government had imposed itself in 1899, after the US had finally stepped into the fray so that the three decades of rebellion against Spain could succeed at last. It officially left in 1902, with the formal establishment of the Republic of Cuba—but infamously never left its naval base at Guantánamo Bay, where it had participated in a key defeat of Spain in 1898. The architecture of the Malecón is inseparable from the image of a supposedly independent self-governing nation and the barely repressed fact that this very image is the artifact of ongoing external force. The Malecón literally allowed Cuba to face the outside world. More and more architecture came to the water's edge as it was gradually completed over half a century, collaborating to form a vertical face.

The US embassy building, constructed just as the Malecón reached its full eight-kilometer length, was therefore a façade inserted into a façade, strategically turning itself at right angles to the water to look along the arc of buildings towards the Fortaleza de Los Tres Reyes del *Morro*, designed by the military engineer Battista Antonelli toward the end of the 17th century to defend Spain's colonial conquest against privateers and rival colonial powers.[8] These defenses had huge strategic and symbolic force, since Cuba was never just an example of colonialization in the Americas but its very origin—the first mistaken "discovery" of the mythical Orient by Columbus—and its fortifications were regarded as defending the entire colonial project. Not by chance was Cuba the first victim of US nation-building efforts, with the American attempt to control the outcome by depriving most black Cubans from voting on who would assemble to form a constitution, or voting for the government itself. Tying the right to vote to property ownership guaranteed that the new world would be based on the inequities of the old. In forcing its own right to intervene into the wording of the constitution itself, the US effectively guaranteed inequity, establishing a new kind of colony and sowing the inevitable seeds for rebellions to come.

8 Olimpia Niglio, "Geometry and Genius Loci: Battista Antonelli's Fortifications in Havana," *Nexus Network Journal*, 16 (2014): 723-735.

Opposite page:
"Un Edificio de Viviendas que será histórico en Cuba," *Granma*, November 25, 1969, p. 4.

RADIO WARS

The history of the republic that emerged from the defeat of Spain is a radio history. The first proposal of a wireless link between Cuba and the United States was already made at the end of 1899, the year the US military government installed itself. The idea was to build matching antennas in Havana and Key West, and have the mobile antenna on the steamship *Grande Duchesse* act as an intermediary to transfer the signals each time it was halfway across its regular transit between Cuba and Florida.[9] In fact, the same ship had been chartered by the US Government as a military transport between the US and Cuba during the Spanish–American war and had just been outfitted with radio equipment that September, so that Marconi could demonstrate the feasibility of land-to-sea and sea-to-sea wireless communication to the US military.[10] The official project to create a wireless link between Havana and Key West was announced in Cuban newspapers just 11 days before the formal declaration of independence on May 20, 1902.[11] The idea of independent nationhood was tied to the idea of a new kind of connection. Lee de Forest, Marconi's main rival, promptly shipped radio equipment from New York to Havana and soon signed agreements with the newly formed Cuban government to make the connection.[12] Marconi signed a similar agreement, but it was de Forest who first established the international link in early 1905 with the construction of a commercial wireless station on the Vedado waterfront.

A 57-meter-high antenna, held in place by four cables, rose up just a block away from the future site of the Edificio Experimental, with only a flimsy wooden hut to house the equipment—as if embodying the dramatic shift in the status of seemingly solid buildings. This prosthetic extension of the city, reaching up so much higher than any building and creating new kinds of intimacies with lands and ships in all directions, was the first of its kind in the Caribbean, with a range of 200 miles networked to stations in the US, Mexico, Puerto Rico, and Panama.

9 José Altshuler, "La telegrafía sin hilos en Cuba (1899-1916)," *LLULL- Revista de la Sociedad Española de Historia de las Ciencias y de las Técnicas*, vol. 20 (1997): 443-463.

10 Linwood S. Howeth, *History of Communications-Electronics in the United States Navy* (Washington: Government Printing Office, 1963), p. 26.

11 "Telegrafía sin hilos," *Diario de la Marina*, April 9, 1902, p. 2.

12 "Wireless System for Havana," *New York Times*, June 15, 1902.

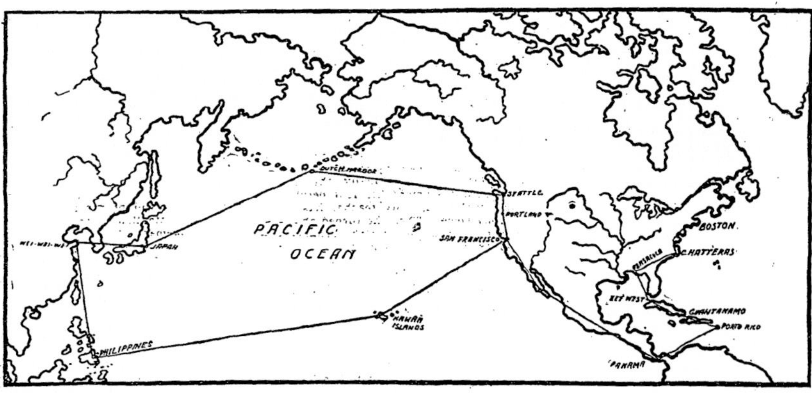

Chain of De Forest radio stations "spanning the seas," *New York Times*, July 10, 1904.

Postcard of Malecon and Morro antenna, ca. 1920.

Morro Wireless Station, 1908. Cuban Heritage Collection, University of Miami.

Yet the station was never simply commercial. Within a couple of months, de Forest completed two 76-meter-high radio antennas for the US base at Guantánamo Bay. The agreement was that he could also pass commercial traffic through them, just as military traffic could pass through the Vedado antenna, in a typical blurring of commercial and military ambition.[13] In fact, de Forest had been contracted by the US government to construct a whole "chain" of radio stations ringing both the Caribbean and the Pacific Ocean, interconnecting all US Navy ships to create a vast territory and surveillance system that was immediately publicized in the *New York Times* as a new geopolitical map.[14] Its vast "circuits" transcended land masses, being larger than any continent, and the antennas in Havana and Guantánamo acted as crucial nodes in the network, literally engineering a new world.

It is not simply that radio transformed Cuba. Cuba gave to radio more than it received. During the second US military occupation from late 1906 to early 1909, the all-too-frankly named "Cuba Pacification," the army installed an antenna at its base near Havana to connect with the huge antennas just completed on the waterfront at Key West and tested mobile "field wireless platoons" for the first time. Portable radio stations made by Berlin-based Telefunken connected to a new net of fixed stations around Cuba, interlinking all units.[15] Some of the maneuvers were even the first experiments by any military of guiding all troop movements by wireless.[16] The Republic of Cuba was an experimental radio laboratory from the start.

The Cuban government was itself actively involved in radio experiments throughout the second occupation, and in 1906 formally commissioned its own network of eight large antennas to be built on strategic sites interlinking the islands. The largest was

13 Frank E. Butler, "How Wireless Came to Cuba," *Radio Broadcast* (March 1925): 916-925.

14 "Spanning the Seas with De Forest Wireless," *New York Times*, July 10, 1904, p. 32. Not only would commercial stations participate in this military network, but the contract required all US Navy ships using de Forest equipment to pass commercial traffic.

15 George A. Wieczorek, "Field Wireless Operations in Cuba," *Journal of the United States Cavalry Association*, vol. 17 (Jan. 1907).

16 "Army of Cuban Pacification," *War Department Annual Reports, 1908* (Washington: Government Printing Office, 1908), p. 317.

finally completed in Havana in 1908. The 74-meter-high structure, erected immediately next to the Morro fort, used Telefunken’s usual triangulated metal structure made of identical elements assembled as a kind of kitset that elegantly rests on a single point. It was held in place by one set of wires, while another set carried the signals bringing the world into Cuba and Cuba into the world. The antenna (upgraded with much more sensitive and powerful equipment from de Forest’s company in 1916) is rarely referred to but can be seen in historical postcards and films until the 1930s, presiding over all major events of urban life—from the arrival and departure of warships to carnivals, car races, Sunday promenades, and everyday traffic—with the continuous façade of the buildings that line the Malecón seemingly culminating in its massive yet delicate metal frame reaching up to the sky. It was by far the tallest structure on the horizon, visible from almost everywhere in the city, and seemed to be part of the fortifications that guard the entrance to the harbor and hence protect Cuba itself. The defense of Cuba, even the defense of the idea of Cuba, was by radio. A new architecture, even a new kind of monument, had arrived to simultaneously reinforce and disrupt geopolitical boundaries and ecologies of desire.

Antennae multiplied exponentially with the arrival of commercial broadcasting in the 1920s. Wireless interaction between US and Cuba was soon denser than that between the East and West of the continental US. The New York-based radio station WEAF opened the PWX station in Havana in 1922 by adding two antennas on top of the Cuban Telephone Company building at the intersection of Zulueta and Dragones streets in the heart of the old city. These extensions—rising up only to seemingly dissolve into the clouds and the night sky—again became a crucial part of the visible city and its new invisible spatial order. It is as if buildings had developed delicate sensory organs to reach up into the sky to launch a new kind of conversation with the world. The idea of a nation suspended in water gave way to the idea of being suspended within and permeated by signals. Within a year, there were 30 more commercial radio stations. Antennas could be seen in every direction, like a whole new layer of the urban fabric, enabling the city to send and receive itself. Havana in and on the air. The historical weight of the dense buildings was perforated and mobilized by radio waves. As the number of stations doubled again within the next half decade, Cuba had more stations per population than any country in the world. Houses sprouted their own antennas as the price of radio receivers dropped and do-it-yourself kits became popular. Buildings without antennas became a rarity, even an impossibility.

Radio waves were already the primary medium of both authority and dissent, with entertainment, politics, commerce and culture being

Photograph of Malecón with the Morro and PWX radio antennas, ca. 1920.

tightly interlaced in the air. By the 1950s, the biggest antennas for radio and TV were still reaching up from the Vedado neighborhood to define lived political space by broadcasting inland and to the US. Symptomatically, the new US embassy building faced the tallest antenna of all, that had just been erected close to the Malecón behind the Ambar Motors building adjacent to the Hotel Nacional. It dominated the skyline from land and sea with its bands of red and white to warn aircraft of its towering yet see-through metal presence, acting as a kind of massive urban statement conspicuous in numberless images of the canonic modern buildings of the 1950s yet seemingly invisible to conventional architectural historians—as if it were a ghost. It was constructed by an ally of Fulgencio Batista shortly after his military coup of 1952 and equipped with the most powerful transmitter yet able to broadcast the new Telemundo television Channel 2 over 125 miles, to reach the US and a string of six other antennae across Cuba in the first national TV network. After the Revolution, the network was naturally appropriated as a key instrument of government and inevitably renamed Televisión Revolución.

Countless clandestine radio stations had sprung up as Batista's US-backed dictatorship attempted to control radio space. Each had a different political perspective, music, and audience.[17] Not by chance was the Revolution a radio revolution, with each brigade of rebels having its own portable station and each day's highlights broadcast in a nightly show on Radio Rebelde, the umbrella station set up in 1958 on shortwave so it could be heard throughout the Caribbean basin.

17 Lawrence C. Soley and John Nichols, *Clandestine Radio Broadcasting: A Study of Revolutionary and Counterrevolutionary Electronic Communication* (New York: Praeger, 1987).

Radio didn't simply report on the struggle but was a decisive weapon. Castro was already a radio personality, with a 15-minute daily show in Havana. His mentor Eduardo Chibás had committed suicide in August 1951 during one of his regular live broadcasts in the hope of inciting revolution—unaware that the microphones had been turned off at the usual time of ending the show, just seconds before he shot himself. Che Guevara was likewise insistent on the tactical use of radio, having personally experienced the US use of radio broadcasts from Swan Island in the Western Caribbean to overthrow the elected government in Guatemala. The antennas on Swan Island masquerading as the commercial station Radio Swan that relentlessly broadcast anti Castro programming, were used to coordinate the failed Bay of Pigs invasion in 1960, and provoked the continuous counter-programming since 1961 by Radio Havana, specifically targeted at the US.

Cold War Cuba was an epicenter of radio surveillance, and surveillance of surveillance, involving arrays of massive antennas, galaxies of micro antennas and multiple media technologies from the most secret to the most public. The US relentlessly broadcast anti-government programming into Cuba and the government there equally relentlessly tried to jam it and counter-broadcast. After the failure of the Bay of Pigs invasion, the US considered using airplanes that would pick up TV signals with an antenna in their tail and resend them from a 28-feet-long retractable antenna hanging under their fuselage to broadcast live TV to Cuba from 30,000 feet up—using the so-called Stratovision technology developed in the immediate post-war years as a possible way to beam TV across rural America.[18] A few months before the Bay of Pigs assault, *Popular Science* already reported that the ability of airplanes to broadcast television across a radius of 200 miles was considered a technology that could change the course of the Cold War.[19] The idea was revived in 1990 when the Miami-based Radio Martí propaganda station run by the US government was supplemented by TV Martí's 30 hours of weekly broadcasts delivered across the sea from balloons tethered 3000 meters over a military base in Key West.

Meanwhile, the Lourdes intelligence site set up near Havana in 1962 was Russia's biggest outside Russia, covering 28 square miles with more than 50 buildings and countless antennae operated by 1500 engineers to monitor all supposedly private, commercial, military, and governmental US communications from basic telephone calls to shipping, satellite systems and space programs; not just surveilling every kind of signal but jamming them, and actively directing spy satellites. In other words, its cluster of massive antennas bred a whole ecology of other antennas in a vast net eventually interconnecting the most distant spacecraft to the cell phones in people's pockets. The Cuban government at one point boasted that

18 The original idea was that a fleet of such aircraft could send the signal to each other and blanket entire continents with television without any infrastructure on the ground. According to its inventor, just 14 aircraft, for example, could simultaneously broadcast nine programs across 78% of the United States. C. E. Nobles, "The Stratovision System for Television, FM," *International Projectionist* (December 1945): 16-17, 34.

19 "Schoolroom in the Sky," *Popular Science* (January 1961): 94.

more than 75 percent of Soviet "strategic intelligence" passed through Cuba. The base was itself networked to other surveillance bases on the island, including the two dozen massive antenna of the Cuban government's own spy station at Bejucal. The Guantánamo radio station originally set up by Lee de Forest had meanwhile grown exponentially and all the stations tracked each other in an endless cat-and-mouse game in which Cuba itself was only the ground on which rival antennas carried out a proxy war between distant superpowers. It was inevitable that an Asian country would add its own antennas to the island as it reasserted its own status as a superpower. It started to share use of the Lourdes station. The largest parabolic antennas to date started to appear there and at Bejucal as recently as 2018.

As the antennas attached to every person, object, building, and vehicle on the planet steadily multiply, shrink, and interconnect in a vast ecosystem of invisible radio waves that mirrors, affects, and even directs the visible physical world, the underlying infrastructure that sustains and monitors that ecology has become ever more massive. The commercial antenna that de Forest erected on the waterfront of Vedado to connect the island to the world beyond in 1905 was just the start of the exponential growth of an architecture of radio that completely transforms the status of the land on which it is built, the buildings on that land, and the lives that are lived there and elsewhere.

Cuba bristles with antennas, ranging from the massive arrays installed by would-be superpowers to the do-it-yourself aerials made of aluminum TV dinner trays protruding from buildings all over the island. Cuba is an artifact suspended between ocean waves and radio waves. The very idea of Cuba hangs in the interferences between the voice of government, which has always been very much a radio voice—whether channeled as information, education, or entertainment—and counter-governmental transmissions. Cuban architecture is constructed in this space. It is not simply that sites, buildings, bodies, and vehicles have antennas attached to them, each antenna acting as the delicate intersection between the visible world and invisible waves. Nor is it just about the mirage-like architecture of the antennas, present in every vista but never discussed, or the architecture that might be conveyed in radio and TV signals, or those architects who try to dissolve buildings into the space of electromagnetic waves.[20] It's not even about the very specific spatial and political effects of the expanding official and unofficial Wi-Fi nets in Cuba which may be shaping urban space more decisively than any street or building. Rather, it is about the simple fact that visible buildings are constructed and received in an invisible space of radio. A building with an antenna is not more in radio space than one without. Nor is a building that tries to dematerialize itself to, as it were, meld with the waves or accept its ultimately insubstantial status

20 See, for example, Mark Wigley, *Buckminster Fuller Inc. – Architecture in the Age of Radio* (Zurich: Lars Müller, 2015) and Mark Wigley, *Konrad Wachsmann's Television: Post-Architectural Transmissions* (Berlin: Sternberg Press, 2020).

in network space. Any form of building is networked. Not only do the signals make the space but the buildings themselves are ultimately signals, broadcasts in their own right that are received by a radio species.

Furthermore, it is never clear that either the invisible signals or the visible ones in the form of structures are self-consciously shaped by a particular agency. For all the machinations of governments, resistance movements, extractive commercial opportunists, and military strategists, the actual signals that so densely fill so many frequencies of the electromagnetic spectrum are a form of agency in themselves that shapes the thoughts and actions of "senders," "receivers," "jammers," "engineers," "entrepreneurs," "authorities," "personalities," and what today would be called "influencers." Radio itself, if such a singular word can be used to refer to such an immeasurable, ungraspable, ever-shifting ecology, is an architect.

OUT OF TIME

A building like the Edificio Experimental rises up in the space of radio, even, if not especially, when the brute defensive force of its concrete seems to be the opposite of the delicate, barely visible architecture of antennae hovering between visible and invisible. In a sense, most buildings in the radio age (all 125 years of it) act as a form of denial of radio. Some, like the Edificio Experimental, magnify this denial only for the denial to paradoxically become the signal. Indeed, one way to rethink the wave of brutalist architecture that transcended most political boundaries in the 1950s and 1960s is as an attempt to reassert the materiality of visible structure as a last stand against the unseen and ever more pervasive world of information—recovering the idea of architecture as fortress in a kind of militarization of everyday life. The point here is that Cuba's unique history as a geopolitical radio laboratory and battlefield means that this building is not simply brutalist in the sense of being one of the most remarkable and sophisticated examples of a global architectural movement—or counter-movement, in the refusal of the lightweight pseudo-mobility of canonic modern architecture. It is not that Quintana and Rodríguez simply picked up the signals of brutalism emanating from Europe, the US, and Russia to retransmit them yet again in a faithful colonial outpost. Even less does it exemplify this subordination by presenting itself as an exotic tropical variation on ideas from the never-that-distant North. Cuba is the focus of North–South, North–North, and South–South constructions. Or, to say it the other way around, the labels North and South cannot exist without Cuba. They are even, as it were, made in Cuba. Indeed, the strength of this remarkable building lies in the way it is ultimately unable to be absorbed by the voices of either supposed North or supposed South. It slips through, while continuously sending a signal that wasn't picked up and in that sense was paradoxically always a signal from both the past and the future, as if the building had never had a present.

After all, the building has always had a disjointed relationship with time. It is seemingly forever out of sync, marked from the start by the fact that this supposedly fast-track project, usually referred to as having been built in 1967, actually took more than three years to go up and was not really occupied for even longer. Likewise, the allusions to it at the time and since ignore the fact that the industrialization of building that it supposedly represented had already been taken over, in late 1965, by a huge Soviet-gifted factory in Santiago de Cuba. Quintana himself was very involved at MICONS with this facility for mass producing concrete-paneled housing, which had since multiplied to more than 20 such factories across the island. Whole new cities were going up at the time the building was being made, and all the new structures were celebrated for making a new kind of human. It is hard to be impressed by a solitary concrete building on the Havana waterfront when Castro was devoting whole speeches to the future of cement and detailed architectural drawings of each of the five new cement factories were being published locally and internationally, feted as transformative incubators of architecture and nationhood.[21] Castro argued besides that the need for a genuinely horizontal society meant that most of the new concrete capacity was earmarked for the rural poor, not for existing cities.

The innovation of the Edificio Experimental was to make a vertical version of the argument, breaking through the four-story limit that defined the majority of prefabricated concrete panel buildings. Even so the scale of the new building was unlikely to impress too much, when, for example, a huge housing and social services "city" had just been made for 1,600 family members of the construction workers in Havana.[22] The project on the Malecón was launched in a propaganda space, and treated as a form of built propaganda, with an awareness of its disconnect conveyed in the word "experimental." Even the fact that the name now used—"Edificio Girón"—only arrived decades later, speaks of the ongoing lack of sync. The building's current condition, visibly eroded by weather and chronic neglect, yet fully and vibrantly occupied, resonates with it always having been, as it were, a preemptive ruin, but a ruin of the future precisely, as captured in the permanently provisional name: "Edificio Experimental."

The experiment first appeared in a 1967 issue of *Cuba Construye*, in an extended presentation credited to the architects Quintana and Rodríguez.[23] The cover featured a colored elevation rendering of the façade of one of the blocks conveying the sense of system, a

21 See, for example, the report and drawing of MICONS' new plant for increasing national cement production by 40% and prefabricating building elements. Joaquim Oramas, "Nuevitas: City of the Future," *Granma Weekly Review*, April 3, 1966, p. 7. See also the drawings of the largest cement plant under construction by 700 workers and intended to be operated by 500 workers continuously in three shifts. José R. Vega Díaz, "Cement Factory Being Built at Siguaney," *Granma Weekly Review*, December 24, 1967, p. 9.

22 Marta Rojas, "Construction Workers' City Is Reborn," *Granma Weekly Review*, March 5, 1967, p. 6.

23 Antonio Quintana and Alberto Rodríguez, "Edificio Multifamiliar Multiplanta Experimental," *Cuba Construye*, vol. 4, nos. 3-4 (1967): 16-32.

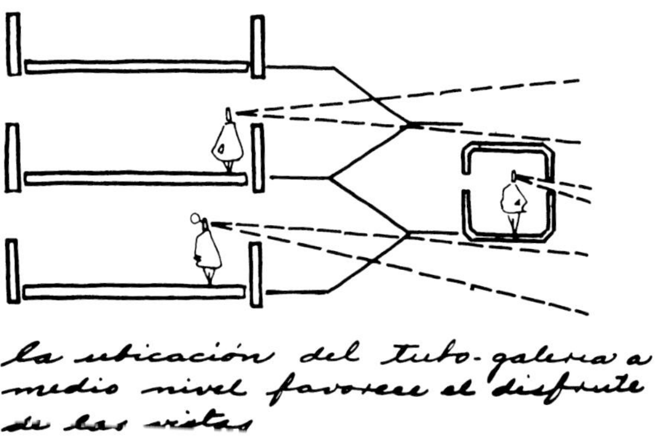

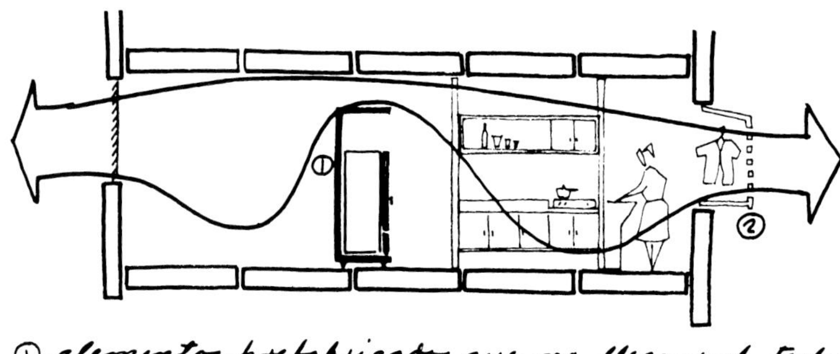

Section of views and air flow. *Cuba Construye*, vol. 4, nos. 3-4 (1967): 25.

mass of identical apartments, but also the variation of colors in the closets that punctuate the black bands of windows, as if to insist that systemization does not mean regimentation [p. 176]. The effect is like an abstract painting—but also the hint of a communication system of dots and dashes, or even the flickering lights monitoring the activity of a computer or some kind of control panel. The background color of the cover is the same as that of the exposed concrete of the building, as if the structure itself is embedded in concrete, emerging from concrete, or the most minimal articulation of concrete. The label of the magazine below becomes the effective label of the façade, savoring the ambiguity about whether this is what Cuba constructs or this is what constructs Cuba. The implication was: both. Symptomatically, the building on the cover was not the subject of the first article. It followed a series of highly technical reports from a recent congress focusing on control, mechanization, panels, and prefabrication grouped under the title “Towards Industrialization.” The colorful façade is the façade of the very idea of standardization, the promise of a new kind of beauty born out of industrialization.

It was an unambiguously aesthetic statement. Yet the 15-page article never mentions aesthetics. On the contrary, it insists on every technical detail of design, material, technology, construction and performance. All design decisions are diagramed by hand, as if drawn just for the reader by a friendly technician, and rationalized from the exact positioning of all the post-tensioning cables to the angles of view—with the horizontal walkways and their horizontal slits for looking out positioned between floors so as not to block the view from the apartments. The section showing the airflow through the apartment evocatively conveys the sense that all elements (including the furniture units, kitchens, and floor slabs) have been assembled in the air, with the slabs drawn as still disconnected, like a large dotted line echoed in the smaller dotted lines for windows and closets. The three successive positions for the construction crane, exactly fitting between the blocks and shafts, are drawn with the respective arcs of movement. Efficiency is the guiding principle throughout. Even the cast-in terrazzo is rationalized as a way of avoiding the extra cost and weight of adding a floor to the slabs that are already internally reduced in weight, as they are cast around sets of cylindrical cavities running through their length that are of course drawn in sketched sections. The fact that the design was done in collaboration with the school of architecture where Quintana was teaching at the time, along with the school of engineering, underlines the collective character of designing for the collective. Daytime and nighttime photographs of the construction are combined with photographs of the presentation model with detailed roadway, cars, planting, and sky, to give a sense of the final effect.

The back cover of the magazine issue features a construction photograph. It is as if the article tries to be a bridge between that scene and the façade effect on the cover. In reverse, the back cover image that so directly resonates with the expression "Cuba Construye" might be the real façade of the building. There is an almost cinematic sequence of eight images of construction, from the foundations already sprouting out of the ground, to the sliding metal frame seemingly airborne as it begins its work, to day and night images as the frame keeps climbing, four then five then seven floors, as if extruding the building. The main idea of the project is construction itself, a way to combine standardized prefabricated elements into blocks, and even the idea of combining blocks into a bigger assemblage. A crucial drawing shows the megastructural ambition that the circulation system of walkway tubes suspended between vertical shafts can simply keep growing, turning corners and bifurcating to gather more and more blocks of apartments into a single network of lived collectivity. The system grows to collect and grows onto and out of itself. The image of the building under construction was the image of a nation building itself.

Edificio Experimental under construction. *Cuba Construye*, vol. 4, nos. 3-4 (1967): 30.

The more than three years of standing so patently uncompleted on the Malecón might be seen as a polemical image of the aspiration for experimental construction that was as urgent an image as that of successfully housing workers. This housing was anyway already happening on a massive scale, with hundreds of prefabricated concrete panel buildings. The decentralized factories producing the panels were feeding a quasi-military campaign all across the islands that was carried out by an ever-growing number of newly trained brigades of construction workers "who already know that with cement and rebar they can build not only houses but also communism."[24] The images of construction crucial to the whole political project increasingly celebrated the anti-aesthetic condition of whatever was being made, as a kind of badge of socialist pride unlikely to be

24 "Construir: No Solo Casas," *Cuba International* (May 1968): 62.

Edificio Experimental under construction. *Cuba Construye*, vol. 4, nos. 3-4 (1967): 20.

featured in any international architectural magazine, and anyway had no aspiration to be so celebrated by any suspect capitalist other. The importance of a few unique symbolic architectural projects immediately after the Revolution had given way to a remarkable series of hundreds of ambitious buildings, particularly schools—all different but based on standardized techniques—that had in turn given way to countless self-consciously anonymous projects that were captured better in statistics. Ultimately, construction itself was the great object of celebration—the island, nation, and human species being rebuilt.

The image of the Edificio Experimental under construction—seemingly at the very epicenter of the demonized regime of colonial occupation, extraction, exploitation, and information in Vedado—was able to represent this whole project of which it was never simply a part. The building rose up in magazines and newspapers simultaneously with its rising on-site, and uncannily remained in this moment of rising as an enduring image of a nation itself rising rapidly, radically, and in resistance. It already appeared in *L'Architecture d'Aujourd'hui*'s October-November 1968 survey of architecture in the "Third World" alongside works from Ghana, Egypt, and Algeria, and curated portfolios from India, Cuba, and Turkey. It was one of the small set of projects selected by the Havana-based historian and critic Roberto Segre to represent Cuba after the Revolution.[25] The construction photograph showed the first block at full height alongside a single detached stairway shaft—like a huge minimalist sculpture. A model photograph, taken by Segre himself, shows the intended effect—with a bus in the foreground perhaps unconsciously suggesting that the building aspired to be

25 Roberto Segre, "Architecture, sous-développement et révolution," *L'Architecture d'Aujourd'hui*, no. 140 (1968): 76-87.

A.A. 140

bâtiment collectif expérimental

antonio quintana
et alberto rodriguez
architectes
école d'architecture

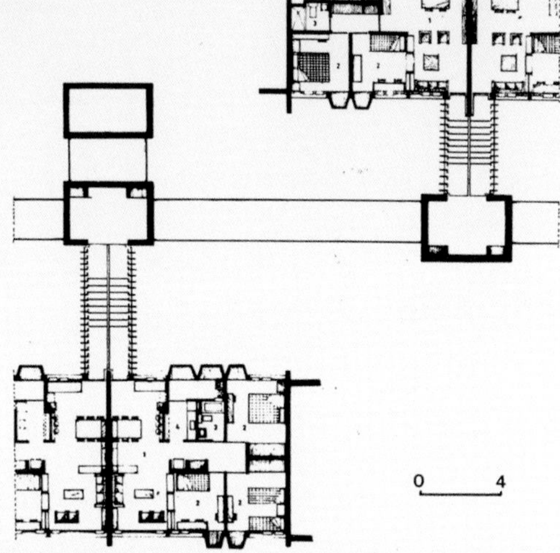

Ce projet expérimental, maintenant réalisé répond à deux critères de base : utiliser, pour la première fois à Cuba, des systèmes de moules glissants et concevoir des logements à double orientation.

Tous les éléments intérieurs ont été préfabriqués : dalles de plancher creuses de 9 m de portée, cloisons en Siporex.

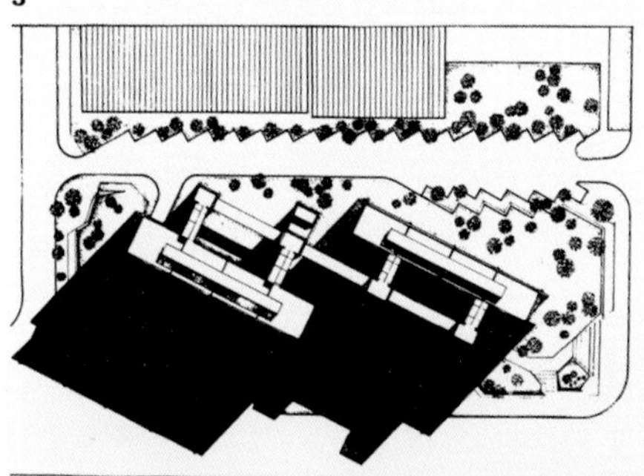

1. Détail des logements types (1. Salle à manger. 2. Chambres. 3. Salle de bains. 4. Cuisine). 2. Maquette du bâtiment. 3. Plan d'ensemble. 4. Le premier bâtiment en construction.

81

Plans, model photo, and construction photograph. Roberto Segre, "Architecture, sous-développement et révolution," *L'architecture d'aujourd'hui*, 140 (1968): 81.

the architectural equivalent of public transportation (and making the fact that a bus is passing by the building in the first construction photograph in the *Cuba Construye* article seem less coincidental).

A year later, the government weekly newspaper *Granma* reported on the "experimental" construction of the second block without referring to it as the second block. The lengthy article repeated the same basic arguments about the building from two years earlier, but without reference to Quintana and Rodríguez, as if the very idea of the individual designer had to be stripped away from a collective work. The prospect of this unfinished work being historic internationally is explicitly embraced, even in the title of the article, "Un Edificio de Viviendas que será Histórico en Cuba"; but almost as if it was an image of the future of industrialized construction in the knowledge that that particular future would never come—acting in that sense as a façade. Again, the uncompleted façade was the real façade. Consistent with this, the actual completion seems to have been anti-climactic, seemingly invisible at the time or in any subsequent history. The building seemingly ghosted into use long after its projected completion. Symptomatically, the interior of the apartments at the heart of the project, the true living spaces of the workers being honored, was never shown.

The building was published as the leading example of the industrialization of housing in a 1971 issue of *Arquitectura Cuba* when Segre was chief editor, with a pair of side-by-side photographs crossing the fold of the magazine. One shows the late stages of construction of the second block before the rooftop structures and circulation system were added, and the other looks up the allegedly finished building ("edificio terminado") at a constructivist angle that foregrounds the aesthetic effect of the successive layers in the surface of one of the slip-molded vertical shafts, the geometric pattern of screened stairs connected to it, and the adjacent protruding storage units, including the ones punctuated with square holes, with even the thin lines in the surface revealed by the angle of the light [pp. 170-171].[26] Not by chance, the photograph of the construction process comes after the one of its effect. The process itself is what is meant to linger. A 1976 essay in *Arquitectura Cuba* on all the lessons learned about the industrialization of housing since the Revolution wound the clock even further back. It featured an image of the construction of the first block as it reached the 10th floor before even the first shaft to support the walkways and stairs was poured. The crane is lowering the next bucket of concrete for the vertical walls that protrude from the latest set of prefabricated horizontal slabs that it had recently lifted into place. More than any other, this construction image crisply lit by the late afternoon sun conveys the sense of a one-story-high metal building construction factory that is a hive of non-stop activity lifting

26 "Proceso de industrialización de la vivienda," *Arquitectura Cuba*, 338 (1971): 52-53.

Las técnicas constructivas en el marco de la Cuba Socialista. La técnica tradicional mejorada

Nuestros primeros pasos en las transformaciones socio-económicas comenzaron a incidir también en la estructura de las construcciones, y es así que la madera y el acero, materiales básicos en esta actividad, se volvieron deficitarios a medida que el bloqueo económico se hizo sentir, por lo que rápidamente se buscaron vías que salvaran esta situación para no detener las construcciones.

Surgió así la prefabricación a pie de obra de elementos pequeños (0,50 × 1,50) que pudieran montarse con equipos de izaje de poca capacidad, siendo las últimas expresiones de este sistema modelo E-14 y SP-72, la viga y la losa que hoy se emplean en zonas rurales donde no hay equipos de izaje que alcancen las 25 t/m.

En cuanto al sistema SP-72 no solamente se ajustó a las características descritas, sino que es un sistema que se diseñó siguiendo la línea de desarrollo de la construcción de viviendas de la prefabricación abierta, lo que permite la utilización de elementos catalogados y una mayor flexibilidad en el proyecto urbanístico.

De un lado, la introducción de elementos prefabricados a pie de obra nos permitió un gran ahorro de madera de encofrado y también el empleo de aceros de menor graduación y de más fácil elaboración, y de otro lado, a causa de su repetición, al tipificar los modelos de edificios, poder imprimir los documentos de proyectos y utilizar fuerza técnica menor de alta calificación, arquitectos e ingenieros, se llegó a dominar el conocimiento de los detalles constructivos por personal menos calificado.

El empleo de estas técnicas no desaparecerá totalmente con el desarrollo, pues existen factores materiales que determinan su uso, tales como fábricas de ladrillos, bloques, empleo de fuerza de trabajo menos calificada, flexibilidad en las necesidades de equipos, bien sean de la obra o de transporte, etc., aunque cabe señalar que en los lugares donde ha sido posible por contarse con medios, se han prefabricado a pie de obra o en planta las losas de entrepisos de mayores dimensiones (4,42 × 3,15) o de (3,52 × 1,19), dependiendo de la serie en cuestión E-14 o SP-72. Empleando este sistema constructivo, se han construido edificios de doce plantas.

La técnica de los pequeños paneles

La prefabricación de los distintos elementos de una vivienda en pequeñas dimensiones y de poco peso constituyó para nosotros una etapa necesaria que aún no ha concluido, pues el empleo de la misma para determinadas condiciones es satisfactorio.

Las características generales de esta técnica, conocida como Sandino, son que se compone de pequeños elementos con los cuales se puede construir una vivienda de uno a dos pisos; el peso de los mismos varía desde 63 kg, que son los más numerosos, hasta 740 kg, de los cuales unos se pueden colocar manualmente y otros con el empleo de mecanismos de izaje ligeros. Las uniones de estos elementos son a tope o por medio de juntas húmedas.

En cuanto a fuerza de trabajo, proporcionalmente emplea menos fuerza calificada que otras técnicas. La transportación de los elementos en los casos que se requiere, es muy flexible y se adaptan a cualquier medio de transporte.

44

Edificio Experimental under construction. *Arquitectura Cuba*, 345 (1976): 44.

itself steadily into the sky, almost as if excreting the building beneath it—with yet another solitary bus symbolically passing by on the Malecón below.[27] Again, building as nation and nation as building, with the water dividing Cuba from imperial capitalism in the background as the unspoken real spatial and political context.

Segre, the party-line historian of post-Revolution architecture, and for decades the main critic comprehensively describing designs in Cuba for an international audience, devoted a page of text and three images to the "Edificio Experimental" in his key 1970 book, *Diez años de arquitectura en Cuba revolucionaria*. But he argued that it never fully escaped the typological precedents of the 1950s, and its value as a test of the future was uncertain. The experimental combination of a "total prefabrication" concept (where buildings are assembled from a kit of factory-made components) with the slip-mold concept (where the

27 "El campo y la ciudad: hacia una dimensión especial única de las condiciones de vida y de trabajo del hombre," *Arquitectura Cuba*, 345 (1976): 44.

Roberto Segre, *Diez Años de Arquitectura en Cuba Revolucionaria* (Havana: Ediciones Unión, 1970), p. 150. Photograph of the Edificio Experimental under construction.

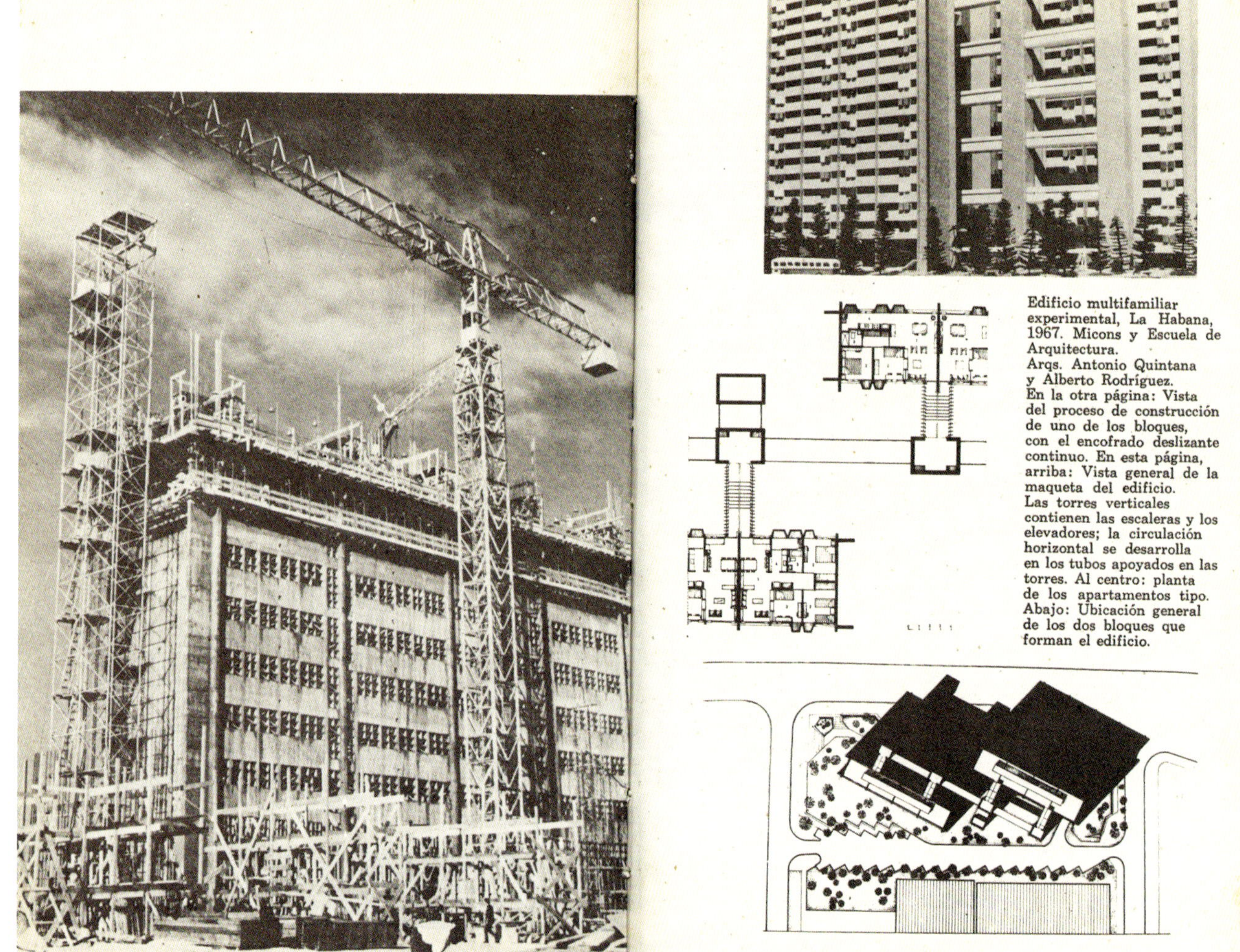

Edificio multifamiliar experimental, La Habana, 1967. Micons y Escuela de Arquitectura.
Arqs. Antonio Quintana y Alberto Rodríguez.
En la otra página: Vista del proceso de construcción de uno de los bloques, con el encofrado deslizante continuo. En esta página, arriba: Vista general de la maqueta del edificio. Las torres verticales contienen las escaleras y los elevadores; la circulación horizontal se desarrolla en los tubos apoyados en las torres. Al centro: planta de los apartamentos tipo. Abajo: Ubicación general de los dos bloques que forman el edificio.

Roberto Segre, ***La vivienda en Cuba en el siglo XX: República y revolución*** (Mexico City: Editorial Paz, 1980), p. 68.

factory is effectively on site) called for lighter materials to perfect the prefabrication strategy. Since these were unavailable because of economic isolation, the details could only be "prefigurative forms of a solution achievable in the near future."[28] The text of the book was finished in 1969, before work on the second block began that September, but its account of the building's ambiguous relationship to the future pointed to an even more remote past. A full-page photo of the first block only halfway up is presented—with the initial formwork for second block emerging below in the foreground, and the crane suspended against the sky above. The facing page shows the intended result, with Segre's photograph of the model along with the apartments plan and site plan as before. But again the main point was construction itself, the promise of construction, the experiment of building in a new way. For Segre, the building negotiated between what was learned in the 1950s and what might come in the 1970s, yet its own status remained unclear—as if it was trapped between decades just as it was trapped in seemingly perpetual construction.[29] It is not given any special status in the book. It was no longer one of the ten exemplars of architecture in Cuba after the Revolution, as it was in *L'Architecture d'Aujourd'hui*, and didn't even appear in some of Segre's key surveys, like the substantial March 1970 special issue on "Arquitectura Cubana" that he edited for the Buenos-Aires based magazine *Cuadernos Summa–Nueva Visión*.[30] The project had interestingly not been included in Segre's very first book on the architecture of the Cuban Revolution, published in Uruguay in June 1968, even though the text was completed in August of 1967, when

28 Roberto Segre, *Diez años de arquitectura en Cuba revolucionaria* (Havana: Ediciones Unión, 1970), p. 130.

29 Segre would later position the project in a "short" second stage that explored new systems of housing between the first major symbolic projects immediately after the Revolution, and a third stage from 1971 onwards, dominated by more widespread use of standardized concrete panel techniques and "anonymous" four-story blocks. Roberto Segre, "Nuevos caminos en la arquitectura de la revolución," *Bohemia* (November 14, 1975): 210-213.

30 In contrast, the projects receiving the most attention in *Diez años* are featured in special fold-out arrays of photographs to open the book—with the most images given to the National Art Schools and the José Antonio Echeverría University. The same images appeared in the central essay of the special issue of *Cuadernos Summa–Nueva Visión*, but the Edificio Experimental is never referred to, even in the lengthy essay on prefabrication in housing that was originally published in the December 1968 issue of *Auca*. "Arquitectura Cubana," special issue edited by Roberto Segre, *Cuadernos Summa–Nueva Visión* (March 1970): 46-47. Roberto Segre, *La arquitectura de la Revolución cubana* (Montevideo: Universidad de la República, Facultad de Arquitectura, 1968).

Edificio Experimental under construction. Roberto Segre, ***La vivienda en Cuba en el siglo XX: República y revolución*** (Mexico City: Editorial Paz, 1980), p. 73.

Opposite page:
Roberto Segre, "Continuita e rinnovamento nell'architettura cubana del XX secolo," ***Casabella***, 446 (1981): 16.

the first block was already up, and could all too easily have been the end of a narrative that begins with the 1950s buildings of Vedado, including those of Quintana.[31]

Segre would publish many different images of the building under construction in various books and essays during the 1970s, each time showing a different phase, even in different editions of the same book published in the same year, as if insisting ever more on the process rather than the result.[32] Only in 1979 did the book on housing in Cuba before and after the Revolution include a photograph of the completed building.[33] The uncanny image looks across a Malecón completely empty of vehicles or people, like a ghost town, or a town of which the buildings are the only real inhabitants. It appeared again in a longer version of the book, published a year later in Mexico; yet now only the location was identified, not the name, architects, date, or technology—despite initiating a series of images illustrating the advanced industrialized construction techniques based on the idea of "open systems" that started to be developed at the end of the 1960s.[34] The image appears separately from the same one-paragraph discussion of the building that includes the plans and model photograph Segre used in 1968, but begins with a new photograph taken from ground level showing the second block under construction, with the first block and its still disconnected vertical shafts visible behind.[35] This layering of the two blocks in different phases of going up accentuates the polemical image of process and the sense of a kind of organism or machine expanding itself independently of humans. Yet the photograph also shows 10 of

31 Segre, *La arquitectura de la Revolución.*

32 The Italian edition of the 1970 *Diez años*, for example, was published in the same year but updated the construction image with another photo by Segre himself, still showing only the first block having reached the 17th floor with its adjacent concrete shaft. The photograph appears to have been taken on the same day as the one in *L'Architecture d'Aujourd'hui*, but from a slightly lower angle. Roberto Segre, *Cuba, l'architettura della rivoluzione* (Padua, Marsilio, 1970), p. 252.

33 Roberto Segre, *La vivienda en Cuba. República y revolución – Premio Ensayo 1979* (Havana: Departamento de Actividades Culturales Universidad de La Habana, 1979), p. 126.

34 Segre had already argued in a December 1972 interview in Buenos Aires that the Edificio Experimental launched the research into high-rise buildings that tested a variety of prefabrication techniques, with the ultimate goal of "prefabricación abierta," combining extreme industrialization with social participation as users, rather than architects combining standardized elements that are interchangeable across different construction techniques—prefabrication as a source of difference rather than sameness. Roberto Segre, "Planeamiento, educación y diseño en Cuba – Entrevista al arquitecto Roberto Segre," *Summa*, 59-59 (1973): 20.

35 Roberto Segre, *La vivienda en Cuba en el siglo XX: república y revolución* (Mexico City: Editorial Paz, 1980), pp. 68, 73.

36 Roberto Segre, "Continuitá e rinnovamento nell'architettura cubana del XX secolo," *Casabella*, 446 (1981): 16.

37 Roberto Segre, "20 Años de Arquitectura en la Revolución cubana," *Revolución y Cultura*, no. 114 (February 1982): 45.

the never-discussed horizontal cables, reaching deep into Vedado, that had to pull on one end of the rapidly ascending second block to correct a severe problem with it twisting and rising at the wrong angle. The 1981 survey article for *Casabella* showed the completed building but didn't refer to it in the text.[36] The 1982 follow-up article on "20 años de arquitectura en la Revolución cubana" even began with another photograph of the completed building, now looking steeply up the façade right under the title of the article—as if it finally represented the 20 years—but again, the building is never mentioned in the text.[37] It paradoxically represents what cannot be placed within. Like the exception that confirms the rule, an image detached from the argument it represents.

Segre repeatedly affirmed that Quintana was a "great" designer and remained loyal to the work in a 50-year stream of texts. This loyalty cannot be separated from loyalty to the regime—or at least to the promise of its first two decades. After all, Segre's early texts can never be described as simply relaying the architectural work of the new government, since they were effectively part of the workings of that government, regardless of which country they were published in. Yet their de facto status as official works doesn't detract from their sophistication and insight. On the contrary. Segre drew on a very wide scholarly landscape and sustained a uniquely intense and perceptive analysis of projects and geopolitical effects. Besides, the workings of government were never simply monolithic, even in an environment so intolerant of dissent and controlling of all publications.

Segre retroactively portrayed himself as laboring against mediocrity by working in the "cracks" between misguided decisions, whether by government or university colleagues, including the collapse of the distinction between the two with the imposition of Quintana and MICONS on the university in 1965.[38] With time, he would revise the weighting of some of his early judgements and acknowledge, like most colleagues, that Quintana was an acidic, relentlessly opportunistic and self-isolating personality who was often dismissive of the work of others in a way that was censorship, given his official position. Furthermore, Quintana imposed standardized solutions on students and colleagues while granting himself the right to produce unique works—strictly enforcing the rules of MICONS while personally generating exceptions.[39] Yet Segre continued to praise the work, and the building on the Malecón always lurked in his texts even as their scope steadily widened beyond Cuba and Latin America. Indeed, it continued to paradoxically act as an avatar of the very regime in which it was an enigmatic exception.

Segre's series of celebratory articles about Quintana in the mid-80s included a full page in *Revolución y Cultura* devoted to his own framed color photograph of the finished building that symptomatically

38 "Fortunately in Cuba, the traditional political and ideological rigidity of the socialist system had its cracks and there were possible alternatives to the wrong decisions imposed by the leaders. When the MICONS occupied the Faculty in 1965 and Salinas was replaced by Antonio Quintana, and at the same time Mario Coyula resigned as director of *Arquitectura Cuba*—the College of Architects having imposed on him a *political commissioner* who reviewed the texts to be published in the magazine, and later emigrated to the United States—a *black* period took place in the Faculty..." Yasser Farrés Delgado and Roberto Segre, "Cinco Decenios de Teoría de la Arquitectura en Cuba (1963-2013) y un Diálogo Intergeneracional: Entrevista a Roberto Segre," *ACE: Arquitectura, Ciudad y Entorno*, vol. 8, no. 23 (2013): 84.

39 "The architects of the 'generation of 1980' trained at the Faculty of Architecture in Havana, in a technocratic and standardizing climate. It was almost impossible to draw up an original project for a house, agricultural facility, industry, or urban ensemble by applying the typified elements and the building regulations established by the MICONS. The renowned architect Antonio Quintana, whose own 'special' works violated the prevailing rules, forced the students to make repetitive planimetric and typological proposals." Roberto Segre, "Encrucijadas de la arquitectura en Cuba. Realismo mágico, realismo socialista y realismo crítico," *AAA: Archivos de Arquitectura Antillana*, nos. 9-10 (1999): 68.

Photograph of the Edificio Experimental by Roberto Segre in *Revolución y Cultura* (1984).

takes the point of view from Vedado towards the water, seemingly as a local perspective reversing the usual presentation as imagined to a visitor along the seafront.[40] The building looks the same from front or back because the two blocks sit on opposite sides of the shafts and walkways that link them. There is, in a sense, only one façade. Yet precisely because of this, Segre's photograph gives the sense of seeing the façade shown to the world, but from behind—as if the outer representation of communism itself is seen or seen through from the inside.

INSIDE-OUT

Segre's own view was literally an inside one. In an extended retrospective interview a few months before his death in 2013, he said that his only completed architectural work in Cuba, since arriving from Argentina in 1963 to teach history at the school of architecture, was to design the handrail for the stairs of the Edificio Experimental.[41] It turns out that he was part of the project that he couldn't position.

Following student demands to radicalize the faculty, all teachers, including theorists and historians, were expected to be active in production. Segre's assigned responsibility was to supervise all the prefabricated elements of the building. In fact, he wrote *Diez años de arquitectura en Cuba revolucionaria* during his spare time on that job.[42] Uncannily, he prepared the book in the nearby library of Casa de la Américas that in 1960 had taken over a 1947 Art Deco building located one block over on the Malecón, on the very site where the antenna of Lee de Forest's radio station that made the first international wireless link had once stood. In fact, he wrote a key theoretical-philosophical polemic there, arguing that a genuinely revolutionary architecture would be a form of mass media broadcast.

The lengthy text embraced the socialist role of radio and television in keeping with the perspective of Marshall McLuhan, rejecting Umberto Eco's insistence that media is invariably alienating to the community, even when it belongs to the community. The goal was an architectural media effect without the gratuitous symbolism that had shaped the first projects of the early 60s through which Castro had sought to showcase the progressiveness of the Revolution—whether the symbolism of function and construction, as in the huge Havana Este housing projects, or the symbolism of nature and Afro-Cuban roots, as in the permanently unfinished National Schools of Art. Only an anti-formalist, anti-monumental, revolutionary architecture based in the "concrete reality" of functions, techniques, and social relations, without expending the extra effort of representing them, would produce the much-needed "architecture conceived as *mass media*."[43] It is precisely by stripping away representational layers

40 Roberto Segre, "Quintana: ¿Arquitecto o Paisajista?" *Revolución y Cultura*, no. 3 (1984): 41.

41 "My only material work in Havana is the handrail of the staircase of the 17-story building on the Malecón, by Antonio Quintana and Alberto Rodríguez, which still resists the ravages of time." Farrés Delgado and Segre, "Cinco Decenios de Teoría," 80.

42 "Those hard years, when we *intellectual* professors were sent *to production*, was one of the most peaceful periods of my life in Havana, working with Antonio Quintana on the 17-story building where nobody cared whether I did any useful work—I was appointed inspector of prefabricated parts—perhaps distrusting my hidden talent as an architect. This allowed me to take refuge in the library of the nearby Casa de las Américas and calmly write my book, *Diez años de arquitectura en Cuba revolucionaria*, published by the National Union of Writers and Artists of Cuba (Uneac) and also in Spain and Italy," ibid., 85.

43 Robert Segre, "Significación de Cuba en la cultura arquitectónica contemporánea," *Pensamiento Crítico*, 32 (September 1969): 217.

44 The first version of the article was published in the May 1969 issue of the Italian journal op. cit. - *Selezione della critica d'arte contemporanea*. The journal's editor, Renato de

that the very fabric of architecture becomes a communication system in its own right. Such a mass medium would reject the lubrication of capitalism seen in the recent, consumerist associations of architecture and mass media by figures like Reyner Banham, Denise Scott-Brown, Robert Venturi and Archigram. Cuba could thereby assume a key strategic role in disrupting and transforming international architectural discourse.

Segre immediately published numerous variations on this essay in journals of architecture, art, culture and theory across Latin America and Europe—effectively conducting an international media campaign to promote the revolutionary value of recent Cuban architecture as itself a new form of mass-media broadcast, without addressing specific examples.[44] All of Segre's countless subsequent essays and books on particular projects would be underpinned by this theory and strategic mission that had first been sketched out in the 1968 issue of *L'Architecture d'Aujourd'hui*. His introduction to the selection of projects had invoked the idea of architecture as mass media for the first time, presenting it as a new phase of industrialization in which the isolated aesthetic monument gives way to collective form. Segre posited that designs that refuse to be based on "easily communicated" aesthetics paradoxically generate a more advanced aesthetic that communicates more broadly, even as a kind of "linguistic system"—as he had already argued in an article on "The Aesthetics of Prefabrication," celebrating one of the selected projects in a 1967 issue of the cultural magazine of the Union of Young Communists.[45] The visual effect of prefabrication itself—where structure, function, and construction are inseparable, with all elements standardized—broadcasts communist values in conveying collective working life rather than isolated individuals and regimes of private property. Segre had found a way to argue that communism itself could be broadcast by buildings that refused to send the usual signals.

The slow-motion construction of the image of rapid construction with the Edificio Experimental turns out to be the very construction site of the theory of sustained subversive architectural media transmissions from the Caribbean. *Diez años de arquitectura en Cuba revolucionaria* even began by referring to McLuhan, to argue that one of the potential effects of contemporary mass media—"radio and television universalized with artificial satellites, thus configuring the era of instantaneous interrelation of thought and knowledge"—is to reverse the usual subordination of once distant and supposedly "undeveloped" places like Cuba. The center–margin relationship can be inverted. Long-marginalized places of the so-called Third World can challenge and change the discourse of the supposedly "developed" places that routinely subjugate and exploit them.[46] The margins are no

Fusco, had published his book *Architettura Come Mass Medium* in 1967, which is a key reference in Segre's argument. De Fusco likewise argued for a tactical reappropriation of mass media from the interests that control them, and control with them. Other versions of Segre's article include "Signification de l'architecture cubaine dans le monde contemporain," in the January 1970 issue of *Espaces et sociétés* and the lead essay in Segre's March 1970 issue of *Cuadernos Summa – Nueva Visión*.

45 Segre's article celebrated the implicitly communist sensibility of the methods introduced by the Soviet concrete panel factory in Santiago de Cuba—in contrast to the unique "visual symbols" made in the same city for the defense of the Spanish empire and the defense of private companies with no interest in the housing of their workers, as when Mies van der Rohe designed the headquarters for Bacardí. Segre argued that the José Martí housing project for 50,000 people produced by the factory was "the most technically and aesthetically advanced" housing in the continent. It was aesthetically advanced precisely because it was not just a "superficially communicable" visual symbol, disconnected from function and the daily working lives of humans. Segre explicitly dismissed the idea that such techniques "annul" the aesthetic dimension of architecture, as well as the fear that people could lose their personality in the same way as the buildings they inhabit. Simply, architecture no longer communicated the individual will of the architect or of the property owner; instead, the building "communicates a function within a community," with its elements operating as a "linguistic system." It is as if Segre were arguing that communism itself radiates from a coordinated set of structures in which nothing stands out, including, especially, the buildings themselves. Roberto Segre, "La estética del prefabricado," *El caimán barbudo*, no. 16 (1967): 21-22.

46 "It is as a result of the possibilities opened up by the mass media and contemporary technology—radio and television universalized with artificial satellites, thus configuring the era of instantaneous interrelation of thought and knowledge—that it has been possible to reverse the center-margins structure of diffusion coming from the technically advanced countries, which relegated the underdeveloped countries to a simple receptive function. The effect of this inversion has been not only to project the vital and persistent existence of the Third World into the global arena, but also, by the implicit value of the content of its ideas, to violently impinge on the so-called 'developed world' by highlighting its internal contradictions, awareness of which among progressive and revolutionary forces has impelled a frontal struggle, not only in the Third World, but also at the very heart of neo-capitalism, of the 'opulent' society." Segre, *Diez años*, p. 13.

longer passive receivers but active transmitters.[47] The whole narrative of the book is to survey and analyze the decade of architectural production after the Revolution as itself a single, ongoing, disruptive transmission. The Edificio Experimental exemplifies this disruptive signal, but is assigned no special status. All projects are treated as equal parts of the broadcast, even when they mark directions no longer followed, or only indirectly followed, as when the slip-mold technique introduced by the project was used extensively in Cuba in the 1970s.

While most of Segre's many survey texts refer to the project, there is no experimentation with the description. The argument simply moves from text to text, focusing on the way the project undoes the pervasive "isolation" that is said to typify the capitalist ecology based on private property, in a belated echo of Castro's 1959 speech to architects.[48] What is at stake in the building is precisely the ground. Yet there is no reference to the actual conditions, labor, or discoveries in the construction (including the major difficulties that arose) of this project that Segre was actually part of, other than the external image of the building being made, an image in which no workers are seen—as if the building is making itself. Nor is there a single reference to the subsequent life within the building in any of the media coverage, by Segre or anyone else. No human is ever seen in relationship to the building for decades. In all the published images, there is at most a single bus or car passing by; nobody appears on the street, below the building, on the stairs, or at the windows, and there is never an image of the interior. It is as if the project remained uninhabited, suspended in the moment of its greatest promise, and was seen to still radiate that promise from the water's edge in its particular way of insisting that a social revolution is necessarily an architectural revolution.

One of the key symptoms of this is the very name, "Edificio Experimental," that lingered for decades. To live in the building was to live in a perpetual experiment that echoed and represented the triumphs and tragedies of the political experiment of the nation itself. In 1976, for example, the Havana magazine *Bohemia* published a photograph of the Edificio as seen from the window of a small plane over the water. The building catches the sun in a way that accentuates its geometry as it floats over its unique planted landscape, at a different angle to all the buildings behind it, which are made to look obsolete. This echoes the ambition of the photo essay to show how all the architecture of the city will be replaced and "slowly, but surely, we will remodel the work of man. The future will be more beautiful." The caption preserves the feel of experiment, even taking advantage of the original meaning of the word Vedado (from *veda*, closed) to present the building as an unlocking of the

47 There is an echo here of Frantz Fanon's 1967 discussion of how radio went from being the embodiment of French colonial control in Algeria to being a tool of rebellion against that control. Fanon's work is a key reference for Segre's essay.

48 The text accompanying Segre's 1984 photograph, for example, explains that the horizontal and vertical circulation system stitches individual cells to ever larger collectives without the isolation implied by private property: "In this block, the experience achieved in the field of housing in the 1950s evolved and adapted to the conditions established by the Revolution: on the one hand, the possibility of using an advanced construction technology, the sliding mold system; on the other, the study of the urban scale and the unity of the cell, in accordance with the social needs of the great majority. While, in the capitalist stage, the building was isolated on the ground, because of the private ownership of the land, the liberation of this link in socialist society allows us to conceive the model of the block in terms of a multiple unit at the scale of the whole. This is achieved through the system of towers and galleries of horizontal and vertical circulation, whose independent structure allows the coupling of various housing blocks placed in different directions." Segre, "Quintana: ¿Arquitecto o Paisajista?," 40. A year later, Segre argued that the project exemplified the conversion of "the isolated model under capitalism" into an "evolutionary type" representative of socialist society. Roberto Segre, "En busca de una arquitectura con vocación estética. La trayectoria de Antonio Quintana," *Casa de las Américas*, vol. 25, no. 149 (1985): 61. Segre's 1994 survey of three decades of architectural work since the Revolution portrayed the project's rejection of "autonomous form" as a fundamentally "environmental" strategy. Roberto Segre, "Tres décadas de arquitectura cubana," *Revolución y Cultura*, vol. 33, no. 3 (May-June 1994): 40.

Alberto Pozo, "La Habana desde el avión," *Bohemia* (June 11, 1976): 69.

inequitable regime of private property, a political experiment but also an experiment with beauty:

> Giving a lesson of beauty to the sumptuous columns of apartments manufactured for the bourgeoisie, the experimental building on Malecón and F stands out in the foreground, pioneer of the chain of tall buildings that, with the technique of the sliding molds, are progressively being erected throughout the country. In the background, the Vedado—of closure, of prohibition—a closed preserve in its early days, today a free territory open to the people, like all of Cuba.[49]

49 Alberto Pozo, "La Habana desde el avión," *Bohemia*, June 11, 1976, p. 69.

An image of the building was included in the comprehensive official bilingual survey publication on "Architecture and National Development," prepared for the 13th Congress of the International

Bohemia (January 3, 1985): p. 16.

Union of Architects (UIA) held in Mexico City in 1978. Appearing a few pages after the usual image of the villainous "luxurious" residential towers of the 1950s in Vedado, it is simply captioned (without title, location, date, or designers) as an example of the slip-mold construction technique that is highlighted in detail later in the book with a number of more recent examples.[50] The building was now associated with the phase between 1959 and 1975 when 22,000 housing units a year were being built that fell short of the perceived demand for 35,000 units, requiring an ever more efficient use of prefabrication and slip-mold techniques. It had launched the experiment to produce high-rise housing worthy of the Revolution and continued to represent that experiment, even if no later building resembled it.

Bohemia's early 1975 survey of the new wave of tall buildings, for example, overlaid its title, "EDIFICIOS ALTOS," on a full-page photograph of the Edificio Experimental seen from across the Malecón—even if the image is uncaptioned and the text only mentions later, in passing, that the building at the intersection of Calle F and the Malecón inaugurated the use of slip-molds.[51] The structure was superseded by taller, less ambitious, more repeatable projects that had absorbed its basic construction strategy but omitted the key concepts of interior design through furniture systems, ventilation, suspended circulation, and interconnection between blocks. The 20-story slip-molded and semi-prefabricated concrete building type—first constructed in 1972 and repeated with little variation in many sites across Havana and other cities around Cuba for over a decade—was smoother, more self-contained, and might be described as "rationalist" but never "brutalist."[52] A defiant structure insisting on its difference from everything else had given way to structures embracing their normality.

Hugo Wainshtok, the young structural engineer of the Malecón building, who became Cuba's foremost expert in ferrocement construction, retrospectively regarded the project as 20 years ahead of its time, "a building of the future"—insisting that the later buildings did not develop the technique well, using too much concrete and lacking the "experimental" spatial organization.[53] Quintana himself relished the paradoxical status of the "experimental building"—arguing in a 1978 interview that an "atypical" building like the one on the Malecón tests new approaches that can inform later buildings, while being as unlike those buildings as it is unlike the ones that came before. In fact, all typical buildings "must" be the product of such atypical experiments.[54]

But finally, or perhaps from the beginning, the project eluded conventional narratives for and against the national experiment, because it was always a double revolt. It emphatically rejected the

50 *Arquitectura y Desarrollo Nacional, Cuba 1978* (Havana: Comité Estatal de la Construcción, 1978), p. 119.

51 Maggie Marin, "Edificios altos," *Bohemia*, January 3, 1975, pp. 16-21.

52 The innovation of the slip-mold technique was credited to the Edificio Experimental up to the mid-1970s, for example in coverage of the 20-story housing tower going up on the corner of Loma and Tulipán in Havana by José M. Cortinas, Nelson Martínez and María Garcilaso de la Vega, that was repeated in several other sites in Havana and Santiago de Cuba. See: "Los moldes deslizantes. Una técnica sorprendente," *Bohemia*, July 25, 1975, p. 85. But it is soon not referred to, for example, in the official 1977 publication (devoted to the "dignity" of construction workers as national heroes) that offers extensive coverage of all types of building, and even describes the combination of slip-mold and prefabrication techniques opposite an image of one of the 20-story buildings under construction. *Construir la vida: Homenaje a los dignos hombres de los cascos blancos* (Havana: Centro de Información Técnica de la Construcción, 1977). The four celebratory pages that *Bohemia* devoted to the latest version of the 20-story type in 1985 likewise does not mention the earlier precedent. Obviously the other, simpler, less experimental model had taken over as the blueprint. Gregorio Hernández, "Las 20 plantas de la esquina de Tejas," *Bohemia*, September 6, 1985.

architecture of the repressive, quasi-colonial occupation of the "pseudo-republic," the version of quasi-tropical modernism that effectively extended the slave trade, the architecture of which Quintana himself had been such a leading proponent. But equally, if less obviously, it rejected the other new architectures of concrete in Cuba that had supposedly left that exploitative elitism behind, again including projects in which Quintana played a key role. It was never simply bypassed by a more radical embrace of industrialized building, since that industrialization was already well underway before it was designed. The building makes a very particular claim on the association between concrete social-material-technological-economic conditions and concrete buildings. It was always a unique signal.

In the 1990s, the structure started to be featured in international exhibitions and books celebrating post-revolutionary architecture. But it had, symptomatically, lost its all-important name, Edificio Experimental, in favor of Edificio Girón, the name that didn't actually arrive for decades and in a sense marked the end of the experiment—revolution itself becoming history, and the regime having long since become something quite different from what was promised. The building is usually presented in the form of high-resolution photographs of its current state—simultaneously heroic and eroded, like an elderly soldier—accompanied by minimal descriptions that merely echo some of the most basic claims originally made for it. A reference to the use of slip-mold construction is usually seen as sufficient—no mention of the extreme test of prefabrication and spatial organization—with never a sense that the reader might need to know what the slip-mold system consists of, or what its use might mean. Writers are careful not to link what they say to what readers can see. The building is not burdened by the text. It is there but not there—haunting the narratives within which it cannot be pinned down.

That Quintana was, in Segre's own words, "Fidel's architect" might explain some of the reluctance to engage with the building, yet many of his other post-Revolution projects have often been discussed in some detail and in a positive light, as if unmarked by the politics of the very system they were explicitly designed to celebrate.[55] The question, even dilemma, of what might constitute revolutionary architecture remains open. This is especially accentuated by the fact that the Edificio Experimental was itself left behind by the regime—as if it was not standing there so visibly on the waterfront, housing workers as originally planned. Even during the hiatus of its original construction, it had likely seemed too much of an investment for too few workers in the name of doing more with less for more. Yet a decision was clearly made to go ahead, a decision from the top to send the signal, as marked by Castro's celebratory speech of 1969.

53 Orlando Inclán Castañeda and Claudia Castillo de la Cruz, "Entrevista al Dr. Hugo R. Wainshtok Rivas," *Hablando de Espacio* (radio program on design, architecture, and urbanism), February 25, 2011.

54 *Cuba International*: "You have worked on various housing projects, in particular, in the last few years, on the 17-storey building on the Malecón. Its scheme seems rather atypical to us; what has been the value of that experience?" Quintana: "The residential building at Malecón and F is experimental and, of course, atypical. In this experience some functional conclusions were reached, such as: the separation of circulations and housing, giving greater privacy and improving ventilation. The feasibility of using several building blocks with a single elevator tower, which results in significant savings. On the structural and technological side, the technology of sliding molds was used for the first time in Cuba in multi-family multi-story housing, a technology that is currently being applied in several constructions. The floor slabs were fixed to the vertical load-bearing elements (concrete walls) by means of prestressing technology—also for the first time in Cuba—demonstrating this possibility for future development. Precast, post-tensioned and hollowed slabs were used, a precursor of those currently used in great numbers and produced by highly developed machinery. In conclusion, the typical project has to emerge from an experimental one, which gets tested; later it is developed, or cherry-picked for whatever suits the construction industry." Antonio Quintana, "Temas de una nueva arquitectura," *Cuba International*, 88 (1978): 14. The name "Edificio Experimental" persists when Quintana was interviewed by the same magazine in 1984, with a new photograph of the building. Quintana again insists on the need for experimentation to develop a new architectural language, arguing that technological innovation is what shapes buildings—using the example of how the space between the two blocks and the shafts of the circulation bridges had to accommodate the crane exactly. Ciro Bianchi Ross, "Cara a cara con Antonio Quintana," *Cuba International* (1984): 71-72.

55 The most discussed projects include the Parque Lenin (1972), the Casa de los Cosmonautas (1975), and the Palacio de las Convenciones (1979). The most detailed information on Quintana's life and work is supplied by Carlos Alberto Odio Soto. See, for example, Carlos Alberto Odio Soto, "Antonio Quintana Simonetti: Las edificaciones multiplantas de El Vedado en el contexto de su vida y obra," PhD dissertation, Universidad de Valladolid and Universidad de La Habana, Instituto Superior Politécnico José Antonio Echeverría, 2011.

56 Barry Bergdoll, Carlos Eduardo Comas, Jorge Francisco Liernur and Patricio del Real, *Latin America in Construction: Architecture 1955-1980* (New York: Museum of Modern Art, 2015), p. 12.

The resulting statement is stubborn. The building lingers on after the party, or after all the party talk. The brevity and disengagement of the references to it is somehow true to this sense of an object that just remains, and remains strange. It keeps transmitting itself both out to sea and into the land, but no one knows what to make of the message.

No text at all was deemed necessary when the project was given the special status of appearing as one of the twelve commissioned photographs that open the catalogue of MoMA's major New York exhibition of 2015, *Latin America in Construction: Architecture 1955-1980* [p. 175].[56] The building stands, as it were, at the waterfront of the massive survey book, once more at the cutting edge of the South seen from the North, but without explanation or even label, while its companions from other countries enjoy additional attention and affection further inside the book. The point here is not to insist on such text. Even less is it to offer these reflections as a belated caption to what has become little more than a globally rebroadcast façade image. Rather, it is to suggest that the building was always a unique kind of façade and remains experimental precisely in evading categorizations based on established geopolitical, aesthetic, and historiographic disputes. It is a brilliant building worthy of celebration in the traditional sense—possibly one of the least boring buildings of the last century—but it is also a kind of glitch, or cross-channel interference effect, a symptom yet to be pinned down. Conventional receivers are unable to tune into it. It is a floating signifier, not empty but fully active, only according to protocols as yet unseen—hopefully never to be fully pinned down and reinserted into the disputed ground over which it so uncannily and persistently hovers.

Opposite page:
Roberto Segre, "20 años de arquitectura en la Revolución cubana," *Revolución y Cultura*, no. 114 (February 1982): 45.

20 AÑOS DE ARQUITECTURA EN LA REVOLUCION CUBANA

Roberto Segre **Fotos: Grandal**

No resulta fácil, en pocas líneas, resumir la complejidad del proceso seguido por la arquitectura cubana, a partir del triunfo revolucionario en 1959. Fueron gigantescas las responsabilidades que debieron afrontar urbanistas, arquitectos y constructores al materializarse los programas sociales planteados en el sector de la construcción. No sólo por su carácter cualitativo y cuantitativo —se trataba de acometer la concreción de industrias, viviendas urbanas y rurales, hospitales, escuelas, centros recreativos, etc.—, sino por las dificultades creadas por el imperialismo para frenar el desarrollo de la Revolución. Estas se manifestaban básicamente a través del bloqueo económico que impidió el abastecimiento de materiales, equipos y componentes técnicos de la construcción y la huida de los profesionales, quienes no comprendieron el valor social de las nuevas tareas que debían acometer. Prefirieron seguir en su éxodo a la comitencia burguesa que afrontar las exigencias impuestas a la arquitectura y el urbanismo por el campesinado y el proletariado. No aceptaron los nuevos términos del trabajo profesional, concebido como una tarea colectiva, interdisciplinaria, organizado dentro de las estructuras técnicas del estado; ni realizar indistintamente el diseño, la ejecución o la solución de los problemas técnicos, cualesquiera que fuesen los recursos disponibles; ni construir no ya en los restringidos límites de La Habana, sino en los sitios más recónditos del país.

El escaso número de arquitectos, urbanistas e ingenieros que se identificaron con los objetivos del Gobierno Revolucionario, contaron con la participación de las nuevas generaciones de estudiantes universitarios, técnicos medios y obreros calificados, quienes afrontaron responsabilidades concretas muy superiores a su experiencia técnica, asumidas paralelamente a su proceso formativo. Las difíciles condiciones del punto de partida fueron superadas paulatinamente y se concretaron, en las tres escalas del diseño —planificación, urbanismo y arquitectura—, a través de un sin-

REVOLUCION Y CULTURA Febrero 1982 45

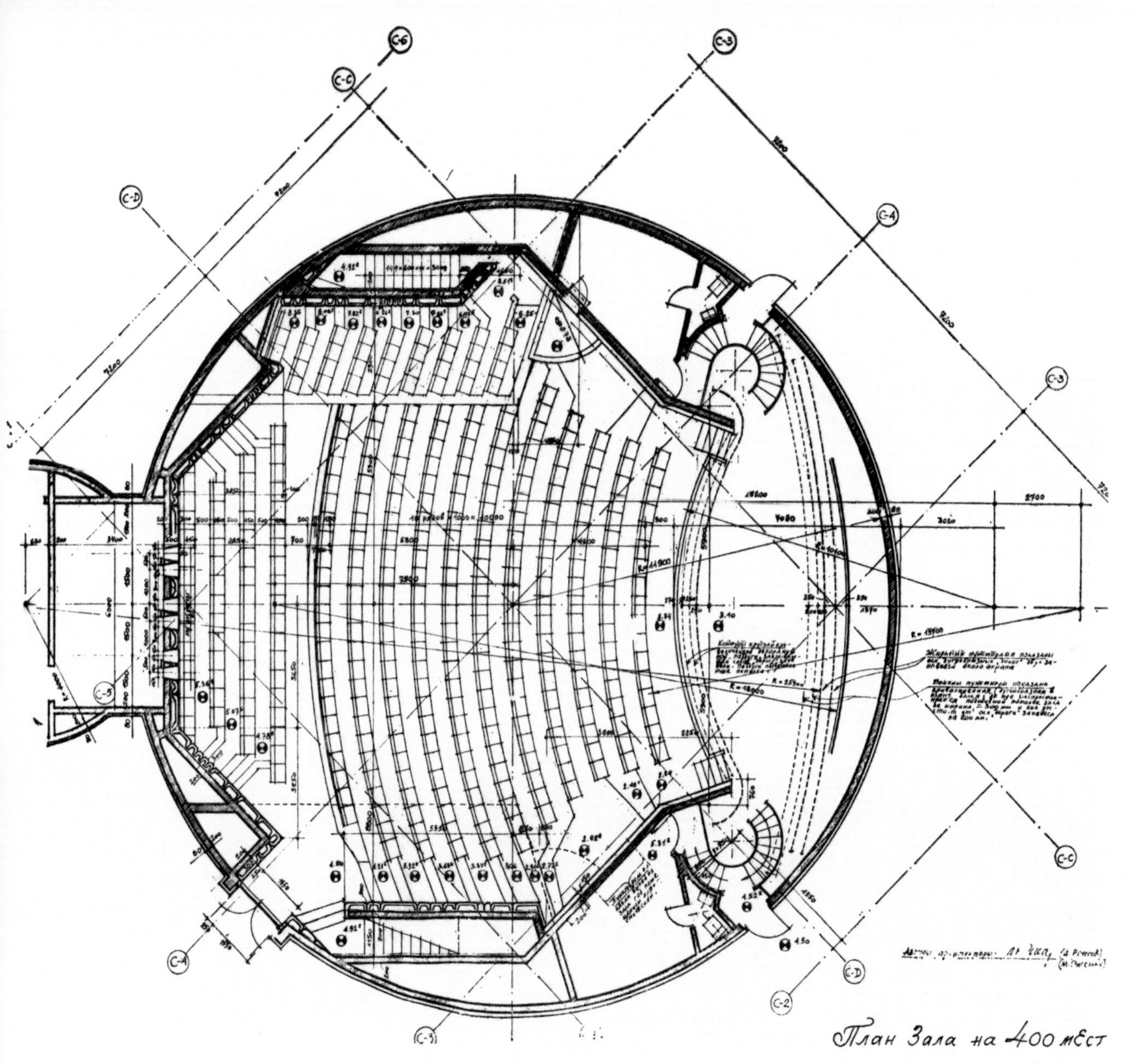

ARCHITECTURE OF REVOLUTIONARY BELATEDNESS: THE USSR EMBASSY IN HAVANA, CUBA

Darja Filippova

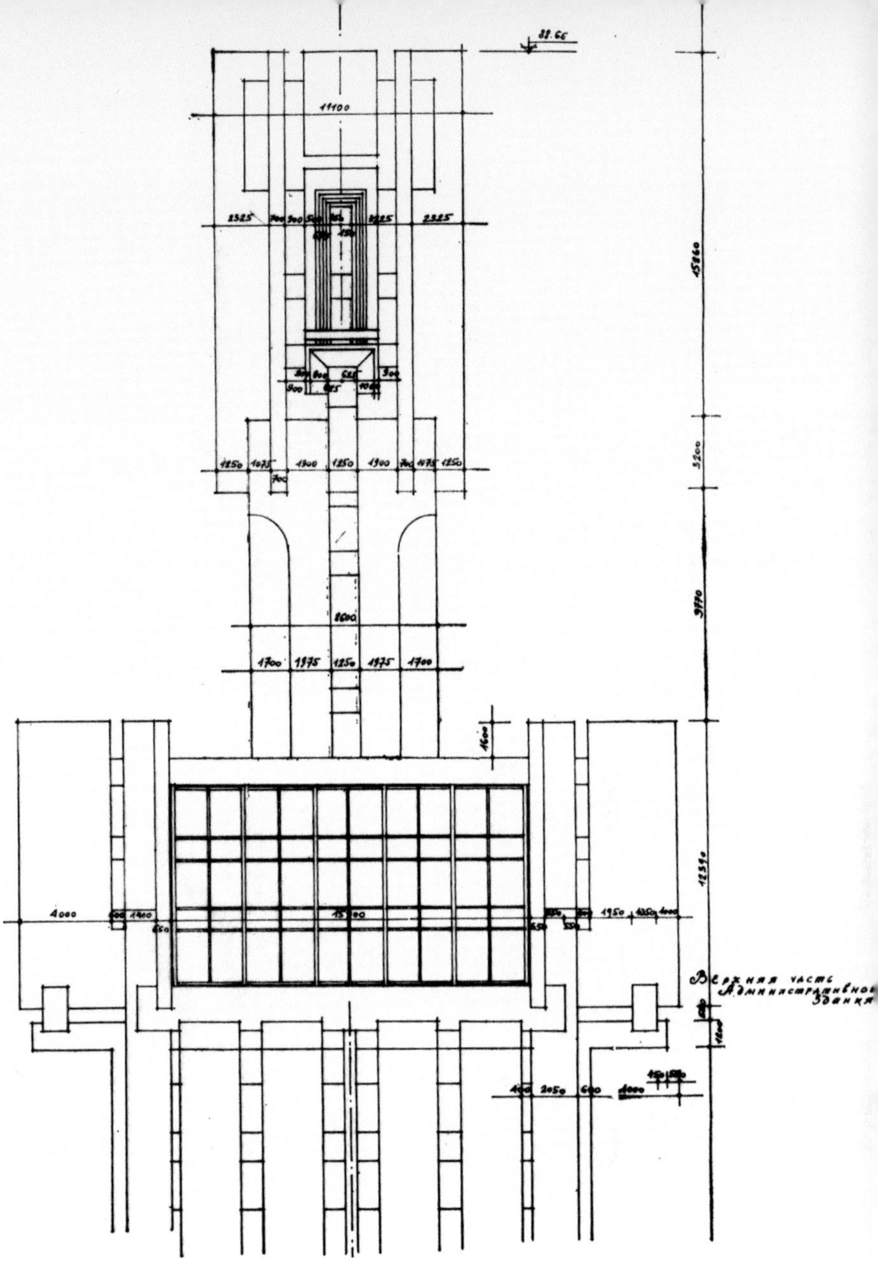

If it—learning to live—remains to be done, it can happen only between life and death. Neither in life nor in death alone. *What happens between the two, and between all the "two's" one likes, such as between life and death, can only maintain itself with some ghost, can only talk with or about some ghost.*

Jacques Derrida, *Specters of Marx*

I don't even know how many floors there are. I certainly haven't been to all of them. It's just a lot of offices and old cables, I think.

Andrei V. Mitrofanov, assistant to the Russian consul in Cuba, when asked about the height of the embassy building.

Author interview, Havana, March 2017

Left:
Rochegov's original design for a 400-seat auditorium at the Embassy. Aleksandr Grigorievich Rochegov, *Arkhitektura: Prospekt k vystavke rabot* (Moscow: 1982).

Center:
First design for Embassy tower, 1975. Note the differences between this design and the built project.

Right:
Design for embassy tower. Aleksandr Grigorievich Rochegov, *Arkhitektura: Prospekt k vystavke rabot* (Moscow: 1982).

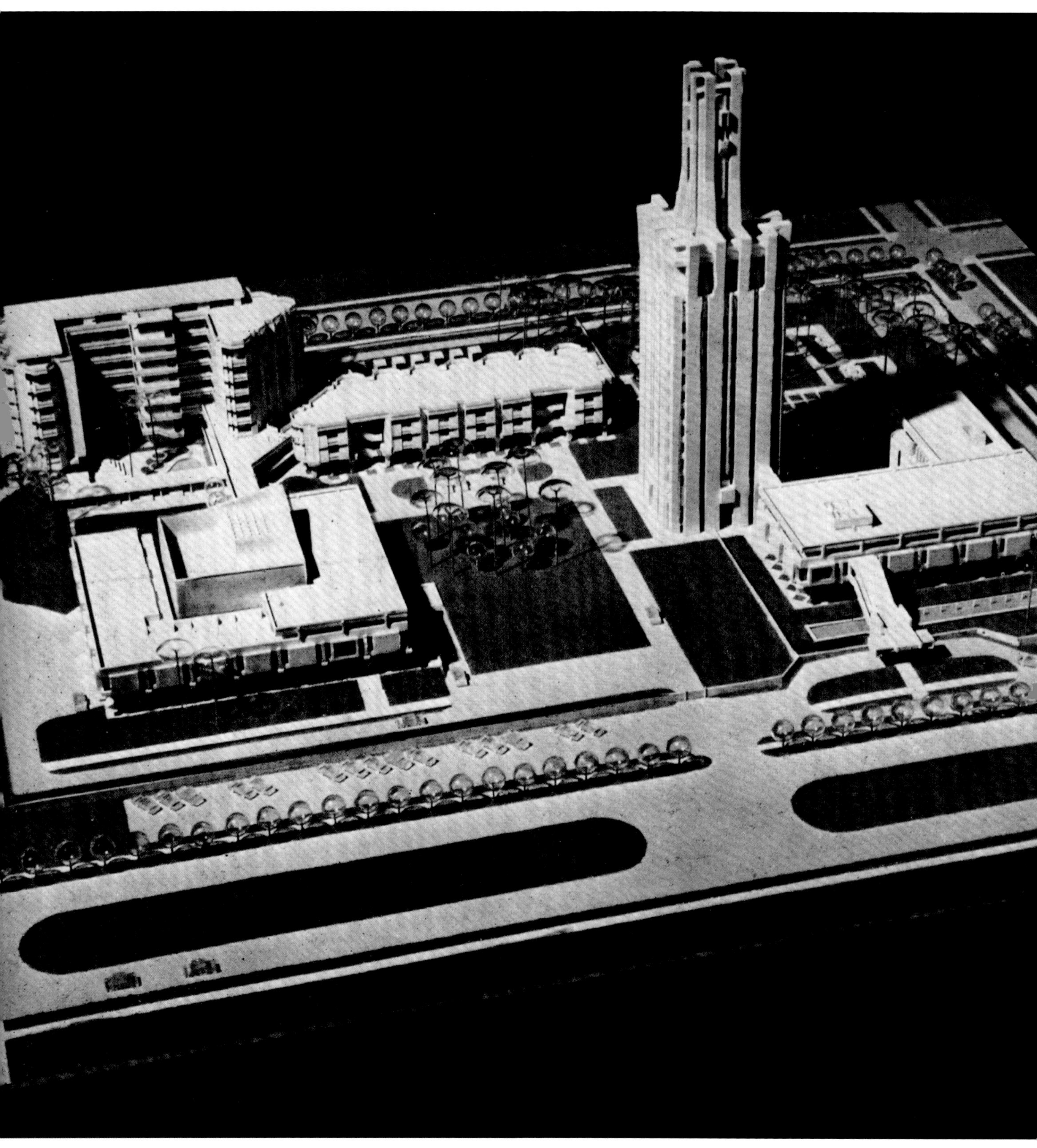

A large, dark band of tinted floor-to-ceiling windows stares down over Havana. These are a distinctive architectural element of the tower of the Soviet, now Russian, embassy compound, endowing it with a somber, omnipresent feel. One of the tallest buildings in Havana, the tower is a skyscraper in the Miramar district with views of the significantly smaller embassy of the United States, a sleek six-story glass-and-concrete building by Harrison & Abramovitz constructed in 1953 on Havana's famous eight-kilometer esplanade and seawall, the Malecón. The windows, circulating around the rectangular shape positioned on the upper half of the tower, look like a set of eyes; panopticon-like, the ghost of the dissolved USSR is watching over the "*Ostrov svobodi*"—"Island of Freedom," as the island was popularly referred to in the Soviet Union.

Opposite page:
Mosproekt-1 design for the Soviet Embassy complex in Havana. Aleksandr Grigorievich Rochegov, *Arkhitektura: Prospekt k vystavke rabot* (Moscow: 1982).

A close ally of Cuba, the Soviet Union built many structures on the island, but the embassy—as the symbolic representative of the USSR—erected on such an imagined "Island of Freedom" uniquely speaks to the nature of the projections of the Soviet Union on Cuba. Conceived at the height of Cuban–Soviet alliance, but inaugurated just before the collapse of the USSR, the embassy manifests an architecture of revolutionary belatedness—coming too late, for both the USSR and Cuba. This paper proposes that the *untimeliness* of the Soviet Embassy in Havana enacts many future-oriented returns, and these in turn mask the desire for redemption of a vision of Soviet monumental architecture that was no longer feasible in the post-Stalin USSR. The multiple historic references of the embassy read as a crypt—housing cultural relics to be preserved in a faraway place and parallel revolutionary temporality—further making visible the out-of-jointedness of time in Cuba itself, a place that is on the cusp of being swallowed into the homogenizing aesthetic of the neoliberal present.

MARIA ENGELKE AND ALEKSANDR ROCHEGOV

A project by Aleksandr Rochegov and Maria Engelke, the Soviet embassy design was bilaterally approved in 1976. On-site construction began in 1978 in collaboration with the No. 6 Cuban Ministry of Construction,[1] and lasted nearly ten years. The building compound was inaugurated in November 1987 in Havana, the month of the 70th anniversary of the October Revolution—a momentous occasion at the time, which also marked the last ten-year anniversary jubilee of the USSR. The stylized rectangular shape on top of the monumental tower nods to 1920s Soviet Constructivist design, while its unique height—this is one of the tallest embassies in the world—positions the embassy in relation to Stalinist-era *vysotki* (Moscow high-rise buildings). While the design was clearly not referential of Cuban

1 The chief architect on the Cuban side was V. Pjasetskii (В. Пясецкий).

2 www.st-gridasov.ru/history

architecture, many of the construction materials were locally sourced: the walls of the tower are rendered in Cuban porous limestone. Local marble was used in the interior halls, which are exemplary of the total-design element—the coordination between the shape of the lamps, doorknobs, floor design, etc.—that is the hallmark of Maria Engelke's interior work. The relationship between the embassy tower's exterior and interior—like that of the embassy and Havana architecture—is tenuous; the embassy looms over the city like a shape lost in time; similarly, while the ground floor interior halls of the tower are lighted with custom-made chandeliers in the shape of the embassy tower hung in reverse, other elements of interior décor—such as the explicit use of pre-Revolutionary Russian aesthetic in the murals and paintings, appear historically misplaced and clashing with the Constructivist exterior. Apart from the tower, the 4-hectare compound includes a sports pavilion, a volleyball court, a tennis court, two swimming pools with ocean water and residential staff buildings. The embassy ran a "Russian school" for the Soviet and post-Soviet expat population, which continues to this day.

Speaking to the design of the embassy, the architect Rochegov is said to have wanted to make an independent microcosmos—a part of Russia in Cuba—like an Orthodox monastery with a belltower.[2] The size of the compound itself enhances the feeling of having a miniature of the Soviet project outsourced to be preserved on a distant land. Although an outlier in some sense, the embassy can be compared with the Soviet embassy in Paris, France. Designed by architects I. A. Pokrovskij (in 1991 recognized as "People's Architect of the USSR," along with Rochegov), A. V. Klimochkin and D. A. Lisichkin, this embassy was inaugurated during Leonid Brezhnev's state visit to Paris. The structure is a closed parallelepiped with an internal courtyard. Like the Havana embassy, the compound is not only meant to house the consul and the staff, but also has an auditorium with 3,000 seats and a concert hall for 450 guests. It also runs a school. Both buildings are large in size and explicitly reference early Constructivist design in their stylized geometric exterior shapes, which was popular in the 1970s. However, the embassy in Paris does not dominate the landscape, thus further querying the reason for building such a towering structure in Havana.

USSR embassy in Paris, 1974-1976. Architects: I. A. Pokrovsky, A. V. Klimochkin, D. A. Lisichkin. Like the complex in Havana, this embassy marks a return to constructivism in 1970s Soviet modernism. The embassy was inaugurated during Brezhnev's official visit to France in 1977.

Officially, the embassy project was led by Mosproekt-1, the massive Moscow collective of architects and engineers that was administering city planning projects in and out of the capital, specifically in the sector of multi-sectional panel housing. From 1963 to 1982, Mosproekt-1 was directed by the architect Aleksandr Rochegov. Rochegov (1917-1998) and the designer-painter Maria Engelke (1918-2011), his wife, were the co-authors of the embassy project. The more recognized of the two, Aleksandr Rochegov was a distinguished Azerbaidjan-born Soviet Russian architect, recipient of the State Prize of the USSR (1990), among many other medals and awards. A graduate of the Ilya Repin Leningrad Institute for Painting, Sculpture and Architecture, Rochegov gained widespread recognition for his work as the architect of a section of the Volga-Don Canal (1952).

Rochegov and Engelke both rose to prominence through their work in the workshop of the renowned Soviet architect, Leonid M. Polyakov. While working for Polyakov, Rochegov designed a series of residential and administrative buildings in central Moscow (1945-55). His career milestones include the Hotel Leningradskaya (1949-54), Moscow Central Bus Station (1971) and Moskovsky department store (1984), three structures that significantly contributed to the architectural landscape of the capital. While director of Mosproekt-1, Rochegov designed and implemented massive panel-housing compounds that were built in Moscow and throughout the USSR (*KOPE;* 1979-82) and oversaw plans for their renovation in 1994-96. As an important commission outside of the capital, Rochegov was project lead for the reconstruction of Tashkent city, Uzbekistan SSR, after the devastating 1966 earthquake. Other than the role of director of Mosproekt-1, in 1968 Rochegov chaired the international group "Zhilische" ("housing"); from 1982 to 1992 he was chair of the Architects' Union; from 1993 until his death in 1998 he was President of the first (post-Soviet) Russian Academy of Architecture.

Living in Leningrad, where Engelke was born, Rochegov and Engelke relocated to Moscow by invitation of L. M. Polyakov to work together for Polyakov's state commission—Hotel Leningradskaya (1949-53). A graduate of Ilya Repin Leningrad Institute, Maria Engelke supervised the massive ground-floor interior design of

Arbatskaya Metro station designed by Maria Engelke, 1954.

Leningradskaya; other projects quickly followed—the interior designs of metro station Arbatskaya (Moscow, 1954) and metro Pushkinkya (Leningrad, 1957), the interiors of the GUM (state department store) in Moscow (1954), and the concert hall of the Hotel Rossiya, then the largest hotel in the world (1964; now destroyed), for which she won the State Prize Award in 1976. After the commission for the USSR embassy in Havana, Engelke received commissions to design the interiors of important government structures—symbolic seats of power: the interiors of The House of the Government ("The White House," 1981; now destroyed) and clergy-use interiors of the Cathedral of Christ the Savior, the central church of the Moscow Patriarchate (2000); Engelke was also a distinguished painter.

Rochegov and Engelke were widely acclaimed in their lifetime, making them the likely recipients of the Havana Embassy commission. However, Maria Engelke had only recently been recognized as co-author of the embassy project, her name being added side-by-side with that of Rochegov. Their work as a couple is gaining recognition through the 2008 publication of the monograph *Maria Engelke*, co-authored by Elena Lisenkova and Natalia and Anna Rochegova (the Engelke-Rochegov daughters) and the 2018 exhibition *Four Generations: Architecture, Painting, Graphic Arts* in Moscow, organized by Natalia Rochegova (also a professor of architecture at MArkhi, Moscow Architecture Institute), dedicated to the four generations of Rochegov and Engelke family practice in the field of arts, design and architecture.

FROM BREZHNEV TO GORBACHEV: THE EMBASSY AND THE CHANGING LANDSCAPE OF THE COLD WAR

The embassy tower is one of the most distinctive government buildings built on foreign soil. Its peculiar shape invites a simple question: Why would the USSR commission such a project in 1976? Information about such an order is difficult to locate in the archives of Soviet architecture, largely because the details of a strategic embassy compound in close proximity to the United States remain classified. In addressing these questions, one notes that, as an embodiment of a country's projected self-image, the highly symbolic architecture of an embassy often takes one of two approaches: it can either showcase the vernacular style of the country it represents, or it can refer to the local architecture. Despite some use of local marble (for the interior) and local porous limestone for the exterior walls (*jaimanitas*), it is obvious even to the untrained eye that the embassy project was not meant to reflect Cuban architecture or the local landscape, while its relationship to Soviet architecture of the 1970s and 80s remains unestablished.

Left:
Moskovsky Supermarket and
Hotel Leningradskaya
on Komsomolskaya Square, Moscow.

Right:
Aleksandr Rochegov and Maria Engelke in 1957. in E. A Lisenkova, Anna Rochegova, and Natalia Rochegova, ***Maria Engelke*** (Moscow: Bely gorod, 2008), p. 9.

There is a history of Soviet architecture in Cuba that predates the embassy. In the early 1960s, Cuba adopted Soviet prefabricated panel construction as a solution to its housing crisis. One district in Havana—Alamar—is still colloquially termed the "Russian *barrio*." This expedient and efficient mode of construction was implemented in the Soviet Union as a pragmatic post-war extension of the materialist dialectic: the forming of the new socialist community through the built environment. However, given its explicit aesthetic of excess and monumental height, the embassy cannot be seen as referential of the "Russian *barrio*," but perhaps as antithetical to it in its desire to rise above the limits of material conditions. The form of the structure may be placed within the Modernist turn in Soviet architecture post-1955—a relatively new term elaborated in Felix Novikov's *Soviet Modernism 1955-1985* (2010)—referring to a set of peculiar buildings, many of which were built in the Soviet satellite states, that are seen as "futuristic" and "utopian" today; such as the Ministry of Highways in Georgia (built 1977) or the "Friendship" sanatorium in Yalta (built 1985).[3] Some Soviet embassies built during this period—most notably the one in Paris (1977), discussed previously—bear a formal resemblance to the one in Cuba. Lastly, the embassy displays striking analogies with the Moskovsky department store, which Rochegov was working on concurrently.

The Moskovsky department store (co-designed with Oleg Gridasov, 1976-83) was a realization of Rochegov's interest in French raw concrete, or brutalist, architecture, of which Rochegov published a compendium in 1979.[4] The store is situated on Komsomolskaya Square, which it shares with the Leningradskaya Hotel as well as

3 Felix Novikov, *Soviet Modernism 1955-1985* (Yekaterinburg: Tatlin Publishers, 2010 [Russian and English]). Novikov is a Soviet-Russian architect and architecture theorist.

4 www.st-gridasov.ru/history

with a series of other architecturally notable buildings. Looking closely at the façade of the department store on Komsomolskaya Square, one notes a formal resemblance between it and the embassy; the upper part of the embassy tower is strikingly similar, in its use of Constructivism-derived elements of geometric design, to the façade of Moskovsky. However, within the context of the Cold War, the architecture of the embassy first and foremost speaks to an environment of competition with the United States: it is as if the dramatic withdrawal of the missiles from Cuba, following the Cuban Missile Crisis in 1962, created a power vacuum that could only be filled by the erection of this monumental building. It is likely that the embassy's oversized scale was an attempt to compensate for a diminished political relationship. Incidentally, the Cuban embassy in Moscow is just a two-storied building, painted in demure pastel yellow and pink.

The changing historic context between the 1970s and 1980s colors the embassy project. While the Cold War continued as the major divisive force in the world, the USSR underwent profound ideological changes between the leadership of Leonid Brezhnev (in office 1964-82) and Mikhail Gorbachev (in office 1985-91)—one being the longest chairman in office after Stalin, the other, its last. The embassy project was among the myriad of joint ventures that resulted from the tightening of Cuban–Soviet relations following Brezhnev's eight-day visit to the island in 1974. Brezhnev was the first Soviet leader to travel to Latin America, and his visit was celebrated with a mass rally in Havana, said to have been attended by a million Cubans. During this visit, a flurry of bilateral agreements were reached to increase trade between the two powers and the Soviet Union committed to investing in the island. A year later, Cuba ratified a new constitution modeled on the Soviet one and implemented the Soviet-directed System for Economic Planning and Management, embarking on a path that is referred to as the Sovietization of Cuba.[5] This departure from the 1960s model of revolutionary development initiated a complex relationship of unequal material dependency on the USSR that Cuba could only have accepted grudgingly, given the legacy of anti-imperialism and independence that continued to drive Fidel Castro's vision of socialism.

By the mid-1980s, 8,000 Cubans had studied in the USSR and 140 educational centers had been built by the Soviet Union in Cuba.[6] When Mikhail Gorbachev became General Secretary in 1985, trade between the two countries was at a peak, accounting for 70 percent of Cuba's total trade; however, the USSR bought many Cuban products above market price, at a loss. After 1985, Gorbachev chose to address the fundamental economic and ideological problems facing the Soviet Union with radical reforms—*perestroika* and *glasnost*. The pages of

5 Mervyn Bain, "Cuba-Soviet Relations in the Gorbachev Era," *Journal of Latin American Studies* 37, no. 4 (2005): 773.

6 Ibid., 774.

Left:
L. M. Polyakov's 1949 original design for Leningradskaya.

Right:
Rochegov at work on the design of Leningradskaya, 1949.

Maria Engelke working on the Leningradskaya interior, 1950. All three images on this page reproduced from: Elena Lisenkova, Anna Rochegova, Natalia Rochegova, *Maria Engelke* (Moscow: Bely Gorod, 2008), p. 13.

Pravda from 1985 onward are filled with speeches by party leaders on the success of the reform campaign and the importance of global economic stability and international peace. Gorbachev also traveled to the US and met with Ronald Reagan in a much-publicized event, which seemed to confirm Gorbachev's plans to "democratize" the USSR. Through Gorbachev's initiation, the relations between the USSR and capitalist countries had improved, easing decades of Cold War tensions, resulting in a decline of the geostrategic importance of Cuba.[7] Gorbachev carefully sought to remove ideology from the relationship between the USSR and Cuba, which were inconvenient to the domestic policies to liberalize the Soviet system. As a means of addressing the issues facing Cuba in the 1980s, Fidel Castro, in contrast, promoted an increasingly idealistic, 1960s-like revolutionary policy—the so-called "rectification of errors" campaign. Thus, in the mid-1980s, the Soviet Union was looking towards the liberal West, and Cuba was drawing on its revolutionary roots. Despite the economic interdependence and cultural exchange, the growing ideological differences between Castro and the Soviet leadership led to increasing tension, mistrust, and mutual critique. By the time of inauguration of the embassy in 1987, the 70th anniversary year of the October Revolution, the two countries' different understandings of the legacy of Marxism-Leninism came to the forefront of their relations. Their general ideological proximity notwithstanding, the Cuban-Soviet relationship fundamentally remained one between a superpower and an island that had only gained its independence in the late 1950s. As such, it was fraught with unstable notions of equality and domination built on the changing landscape of the Cold War, with these terms meaning different things to each side. According to Mervyn J. Bain, a scholar on Cuban-Soviet relations, "[t]he year 1987 was pivotal, as it was from this point that the number of critical articles about Cuba within the Soviet Union greatly increased. They appeared in a large variety of different publications including *Literaturnaya Gazeta, New Times, America Latina,* and even the party paper *Pravda,* with the lack of efficiency in the Cuban economy receiving the most attention."[8] This was also the moment when many Soviet publications were banned in Cuba.

The inauguration of the embassy in 1987 appears to have come at an inopportune time. While the embassy is covered in *Granma*, the official newspaper in Cuba, I have not found celebratory mention of its inauguration on the pages of *Pravda*, any discussion of it in the popular Soviet journal *Ogoniok*—one of the oldest weekly illustrated magazines in the USSR, or in *Arkhitektura SSSR*, the influential architecture journal; it is not present in the memoirs of Aleksandr S. Kapto, the Soviet consul to Cuba (1986-88)[9] and there is little available discussion of the embassy in interviews with Rochegov or Engelke.

7 A historian of Cuban-Soviet relations, Mervyn J. Bain discusses the geostrategic decline of Cuba for the USSR during the *perestroika* years, as Mikhail Gorbachev attempted to steer Soviet relations with its allies to become more pragmatic and financially beneficial to the USSR. Bain, "Cuba-Soviet Relations," 769-791.

8 "Cuba-Soviet Relations in the Gorbachev Era," 779.

9 Kapto, A. S. *Na Perekrestkakh Zhizni: Politicheskie Memuary*. Moscow: "Sotsial'no-polit. zhurnal," 1996.

10 http://www.st-gridasov.ru/

11 The Palace of the Soviets was to be an administrative center and congress hall in Moscow, to be built on the site of the demolished Cathedral of Christ the Savior. The project was to be realized from an open call (1931-33) in which Leonid Polyakov participated (it was awarded to Boris Iofan's neoclassical design). The project started to be built in 1937 but was abandoned due to the War. See also exhibition catalogue, Peter Noever and Boris Groys, *Tyrannei Des Schönen: Architektur Der Stalin-Zeit* (Munich: Prestel, 1994).

The inauguration was not mentioned during Gorbachev's April 1989 visit to the island, and Vladimir Putin, in his travels to Cuba had not been pictured there. In my research, I first found mention of the embassy on the webpage of Oleg P. Gridasov's architecture studio, alongside a history of Rochegov's work.[10] The architect Gridasov, married to Natalia Rochegova (an architecture professor at MArkhi) collaborated with Rochegov, as we have seen, on the design of the Moskovsky. The near absence of the embassy in the Soviet press at the time—and consequently in the Soviet imagination—when juxtaposed with its dominating physical presence on the Havana skyline, further speaks to the foundational inequalities in Cuban–Soviet relations and their dissonant revolutionary temporalities.

THE SOVIET EMBASSY AND HOTEL LENINGRADSKAYA: REVOLUTIONARY BELATEDNESS, ERASURES AND MANY FUTURE-ORIENTED RETURNS

The Soviet embassy connotes an architecture of revolutionary belatedness. Belatedness—as in, coming too late—in this case speaks to an architectural form that was meant for the utopic future of world socialism as it was imagined in the 1970s, and yet, the embassy being inaugurated in 1987, at the height of Soviet *perestroika* and following the Cuban rectification of errors campaign, it came too late for both the USSR and Cuba. The experimental design of the embassy can be seen as a testament of Engelke and Rochegov's mature collective vision of Soviet architecture, and read as a representation of the Soviet Union of the time—as one that it built on a series of deferred dreams. Through its monumental design and interior grandeur, Rochegov and Engelke needed to commemorate the importance of Cuban–Soviet relations, and in planning for the future of this alliance, they chose to look to the Soviet and Russian past.

L. M. Polyakov with a group of Leningrad architects who moved to Moscow in the 1930s to work on the proposal for the Palace of the Soviets. Note the Palace of the Soviets renderings in background.

Engelke and Rochegov, born in 1918 and 1917 respectively, belong to the first Soviet generation. In the post-Soviet time, one is struck by the deep historicity of their lives. Theirs is a biography that casts a positive light on the Soviet project, most particularly in terms of massive strides made for class and gender. The couple met in Samarkand, Uzbek SSR in 1944, where they were fortuitously relocated to escape the Leningrad Blockade. Engelke was in Samarkand with the evacuated Ilya Repin Leningrad Institute, while Rochegov was evacuated there while unconscious from a wound he received fighting in WWII. In 1949 they relocated to Moscow through an invitation by the then-renowned architect Leonid Polyakov, a distant family relation of Rochegov's. Polyakov had come to Moscow as part of a team of architects working on the design of the future Palace of the Soviets, a monumental project of Soviet utopian architecture of the Stalin era that was never realized.[11]

Hotel Leningradskaya (now Leningradskaya-Hilton).

In 1949, the architect Leonid Polyakov—working alongside architect Aleksandr Boretskij (1911-1982)—won the competition for the high-rise on Komsomolskaya Square, inviting Rochegov and Engelke to join the project. Leningradskaya is the smallest of the seven Stalinist "*vysotki*"—skyscrapers—in Moscow. The *vysotki* of the 1950s were designed to compete with the skyscrapers of New York; they give concrete form to the inception of Cold War rivalry. "Soviet architecture, having opened a new page in the history of world architecture, participates in the creation of the material base of communism and a great style of art," announced the official state architecture journal *Architektura SSSR*.[12] The construction of the skyscrapers in Moscow was initiated after a 1947 decree by Stalin titled "On the Construction of High-Rise Buildings in Moscow." In fact, the foundation stones for all the buildings were laid on the same day, September 7, 1947, commemorating the 800th anniversary of Moscow.[13]

For the competition of Leningradskaya, Polyakov submitted two proposals: one in the style of Neoclassicism, the other in Russian Naryshkin Baroque, also referred to as Moscow Baroque, an architectural style that was popularized in Moscow in the late 17th-early 18th centuries, which combined Western Baroque architecture with elements of Medieval Russian wooden architecture (*derevjannoe zodchestvo*), the latter being a style that is considered authentically Russian.[14] The Moscow Baroque version was selected for the project, making the Leningradskaya, the smallest of the seven realized buildings at 136m in height, the only one to mark such a dramatic turn towards so-called "authentic" Russianness.[15] The building is a

12 V. K. Oltarzhevskii, *Stroitelistvo Vysotnix zdanii v Moskve* (Moscow: Gosudarstvennoe izdatelstvo literatury po stroitelistvu i arkhitekture, 1953), p. 3.

13 The eighth building for the 800th anniversary, Zaryadye Administrative Building, was never realized due to lack of funds. It is noteworthy that Hotel Rossiya, in whose interior design Engelke participated, was built on the unfinished foundation of this building in 1964-67. In 1977 a massive fire destroyed much of the hotel. It was fully closed in 2006 and demolished in 2010.

14 A well-known example is the Kizhi Pogost XVII century architectural ensemble in Karelia, Russia, containing two churches and a bell tower. Defining of *derevjannoe zodchestvo* (wooden heritage style), the structures are made out of horizontal logs and topped with onion-shaped domes.

15 Liskenova et al., *Maria Engelke*, p. 12.

tower positioned on a rectangular shape, its base. A 24-meter spire—like the one on the Kremlin—rises from it, adorned with the insignia of the USSR—a golden star in a semi-circle of wheat. The Rochegov-designed façade of the building is rendered in red glazed tile, echoing the color of the Kremlin, and the main hotel entryway is shaped like that of a stylized *terem,* the traditional, medieval wooden house.[16] The references to traditional Russian and specifically Muscovite architectural heritage in Leningradskaya are part of the movement to privilege a Moscow-lineage of "Russianness" within the creation of the Soviet socialist imaginary.

The interiors of Leningradskaya's main halls were designed by Maria Engelke. Upon entry to the hotel lobby, one is struck by the grandeur and richness of decorative motifs in the design (Engelke participated in the Moscow Hilton's main lobby remodeling in 2009, and architectural tours are offered of the hotel main floors). The ever-present play on blue, red and gold reference the defining interior

16 A *terem* is a traditional wooden house with upper quarters that was used by the elite in Medieval Rus; not to be confused with *izba*, a log cabin that was made of similar materials.

The Russian embassy towering over the Miramar District in Havana. Photo: Fabien Bellat.

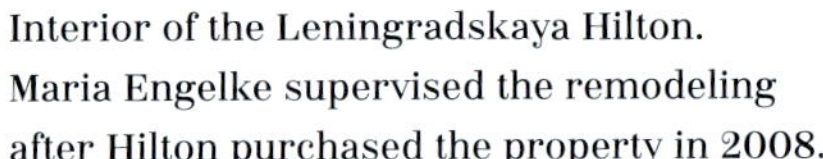

Interior of the Leningradskaya Hilton. Maria Engelke supervised the remodeling after Hilton purchased the property in 2008.

motifs of Orthodox churches, and some of the main hall entryways allude to an Orthodox church altar in form. Noteworthy are designs of the lamps and chandeliers, the bronze-covered ceilings, windows with stained glass inserts, the designed inserts on the marble floors; the massive golden door frame separating two halls is magnificent. The ubiquitous use of traditional Russian decorative floral motifs in wall reliefs and in murals—*russkoe uzoroch'e*—positioned Engelke as the master of Russian style of her time, a style she perfected in the myriad of commissions that followed.

The hotel was opened in 1954 as a 3-star hotel (it became Moscow's 5-star Hilton in 2008), awarding Polyakov's studio the Stalin Medal. However, in 1955 the State Committee published the "On Elimination of Excesses in Design and Construction" decree, a turning point for Soviet architecture in that it marked a radical departure from Stalin-era design (*Stalinskij ampir*) to more functional urban planning, defining of Nikita Khrushchev's tenure and of Soviet Modernism (1955-91), such as serial panel housing construction. Leningradskaya was swiftly critiqued for its interior excess: despite its relatively small

17 The original design included 352 hotel rooms and the cost per square meter would have been 32,000 rubles, an astronomical sum. N. O. Shashkova, "Istoriya, istoriko-kulturnoe ispolzovanie nasledia sovetskoi arkhitekturii: gostinica 'Leningradskaya.'" *Prostranstvo i bremya* 1 no. 15 (2014): 177.

18 Ibid.

size, its cost per sq. meter was disproportionately high and only 22 percent of the space was deemed "useful"—intended for use as hotel rooms.[17] Furthermore, much of the ground hall interior appeared to be done in gold (in fact, it was bronze) and the exquisite 15,5-m chandelier—that extended across several floors—was considered in bad taste (it was mentioned in the *Guinness Book of Records* for its height, adding to the infamy). The building was deemed an offence to proletarian class needs for its luxury and use of state funds, and Polyakov's medal was revoked: a devastating event, heavily impacting his career and health, and resulting in his near absence from the history of architecture to this day.[18] The sumptuously lit golden interiors of this "authentically Russian" palace, while in line with the Stalinist architectural vision, appeared in direct contradiction to the immediate needs of Soviet workers, who were experiencing desperate housing shortages. In effect, the hotel was something "for the few" and not for the masses, a type of elitism and empire-style within socialism that Engelke and Rochegov were complicit in, to a degree, reproducing it in Havana. Engelke and Rochegov, impacted but not

Russian embassy interior designed by Maria Engelke using local marble.
Note the embassy-shaped chandeliers.
Photo: Beatriz Colomina.

directly sanctioned by the shunning of Polyakov, felt this as a grave injustice to their mentor.

At first glance, the Leningradskaya Hotel in Moscow and the Soviet Embassy in Cuba, built more than thirty years apart, do not seem to share much other than their vertical drive. A closer look reveals a shared exploration of elements borrowed from the Russian wooden-heritage style (*derevjannoe zodchestvo),* where an onion-shaped cupola or another decorative, stylized form is set on a rectangular base: this influence can both speak to the idea behind the odd, rectangular structure on top of the embassy tower, and also, once more, show the consistent privileging of the "Russian" within the "Soviet." However, it is noteworthy how the two buildings complement each other in terms of their excess and extravagance vis-à-vis their respective historical moments, both marking the return of the past into the vision of the Soviet future. Theirs is a type of interior grandeur, rooted in the pre-revolutionary Russian aesthetic of the cathedral and the palace, that was appropriated in high Stalinism for the creation of interior utopias: the neoclassical style of the Moscow subway system, opened in 1935, is the quintessence of this transformation of public spaces into public palaces and of the sacralization of state power.[19] The Soviet embassy and Leningradskaya both manifest a notion of interior decor as an escapist fantasy from the sociopolitical reality outside, in that both indulge in an interior style that is dissonant to the style used for the exterior. At times, it seems that the relationship between the form (exterior) and the content (interior) frames a strategy of disguise. The embassy tower exterior, done in local porous limestone (*jaimanitas*), appears as *béton brut*—an important material for Soviet monumental architecture in the 1970s and 80s—creating a brutalist *trompe-l'oeil*; this subtle masking is evocative of the material conditions and labor needed to realize this Soviet vision on foreign soil, which are all but erased in the final presentation.

Behind this stark exterior is an interior that manifests a return to pre-revolutionary Russian aesthetics. Among the most striking elements of the interior are the chandeliers, miniature replicas of the embassy, hanging upside-down. (Conceptually, this creates an effect of being in a parallel reality—a double, which is the same but with an uncanny difference—evocative of the experience that Soviet citizens might have had when visiting Cuba.) The chandeliers light up a marble hall with walls adorned by framed paintings of snow-covered birch trees and frolicking bears in the style of the 19th-century Russian landscapes painted by Ivan Shishkin, a stark contrast to the lush palm trees and Caribbean sea beyond the windows. Whereas Engelke painted murals of laboring workers awkwardly framed by Baroque-style reliefs along with her signature floral motifs in the

19 Of note is the poem by Bertolt Brecht, 'The Moscow Workers Take Possession of the Great Metro on April 27th 1935,' which celebrates the opening of the "socialist metropolitan"; see also Katerina Clark, *Moscow, the Fourth Rome: Stalinism, Cosmopolitanism, and the Evolution of Soviet Culture, 1931-1941* (Cambridge, Mass.: Harvard University Press, 2011).

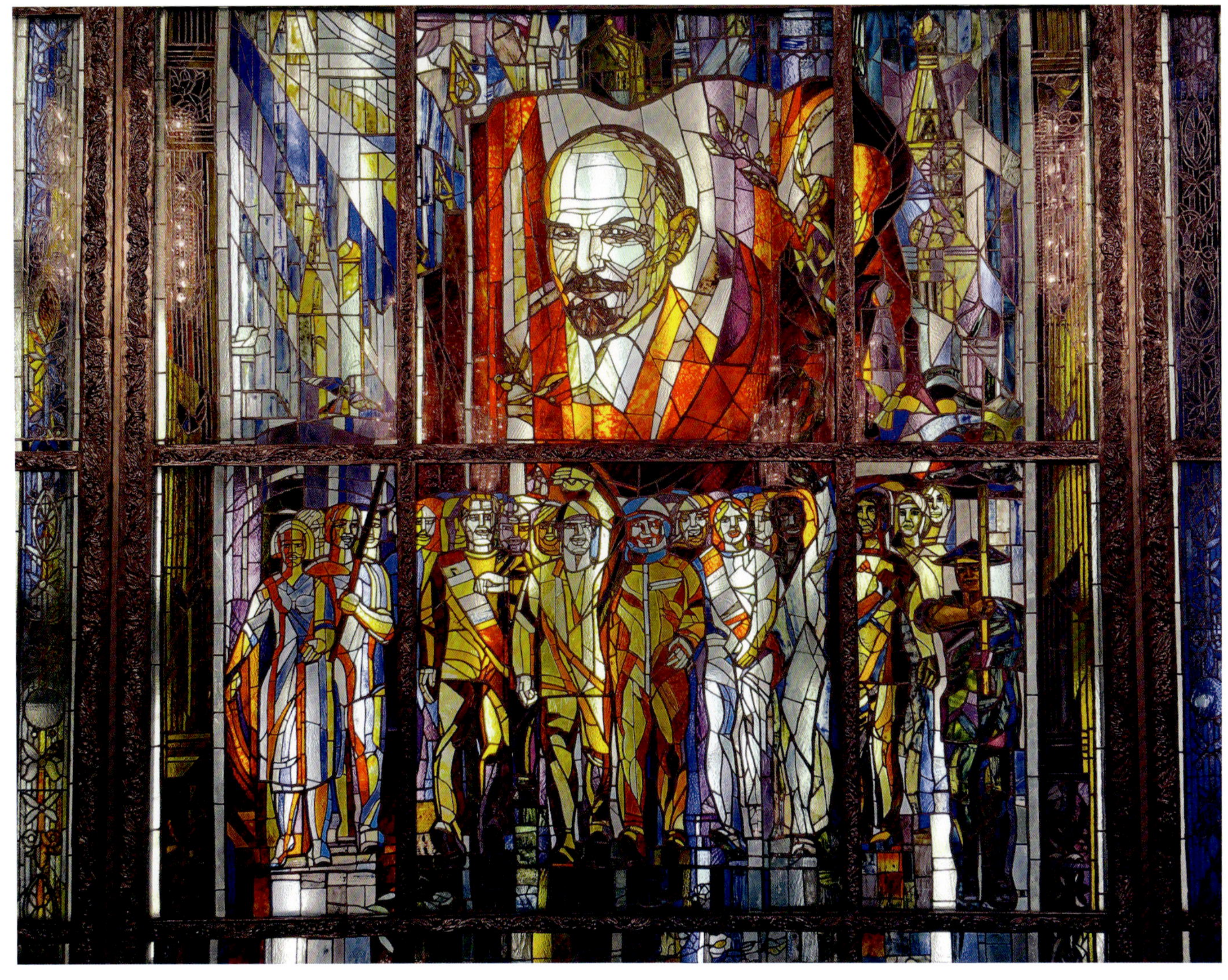

Embassy interior: stained glass window featuring Lenin. Photo: Beatriz Colomina.

Leningradskaya, the grand hall of the embassy displays floor-to-ceiling murals of the female personifications of the Soviet republics, painted on-site by the architect's daughter, Anna Rochegova, in the style of early 20th-century representational Russian painting. The women, dressed in each republic's traditional costume, appear floating in paradisiac, lilac-colored gardens, which they share with beautiful birds. In contradiction with the notion of the Soviet utopia as a collective ideal to come, the utopic grandeur of these interiors is quite restricted. The imaginative flights created by the interior luxury were designed to be guarded by rigid exteriors, enhanced by a controlled admission to the space: to enter the embassy, one must pass through a security checkpoint, and a stay at the Leningradskaya can be afforded only by high-class guests. Thus there is a dissonance between the projected image to the world and the reality that is to be enjoyed by the elite, perhaps marking the beginning of the socio-economic contradictions that led to the decline of the USSR over time.

Russian embassy (detail).
Similar geometric patterns appear in the Moskovsky supermarket, designed by Rochegov in the same years.
Photo: Beatriz Colomina.

Russian embassy (detail).
The surfaces look like raw concrete, But they are actually clad in *jaimanitas*, a local limestone. Photo: Fabien Bellat.

The embassy is supported by a series of piers, which give the impression that the tower is suspended above ground.
Photo: Fabien Bellat.

Leningradskaya and the embassy share a belatedness. They are both completed too late: one, just before the 1955 turn towards Modernism, the other just before the collapse of the USSR. It is noteworthy how their very extravagance stands on a series of erasures, a structuring loss for which they seem to compensate through their explicit luxury. These are the largely unrealized projects of Soviet Constructivism (a return to 1920s Constructivism was popular among the 1970s school of Soviet architects), of Stalinist style (*Stalinskij ampir*), and of Leonid Polyakov's legacy specifically. In relation to the revocation of Polyakov's Medal, Maria Engelke wrote at a later date: "L. M. Polyakov as if relived his nostalgia for all the destroyed Russian heritage—wrecked monasteries, torn-down churches. In his project he wanted to compensate, however little, this terrifying loss."[20] The notion of nostalgia and preservation creating a desire for excess factors in to the project of the monumental Moscow Pantheon—in which Rochegov participated while working for Polyakov in 1954—that was to house the sarcophagi of Lenin and Stalin, as well as of other future Soviet leaders. The Pantheon is most explicitly a symbol of loss, erected to preserve a memory. This grandiose project that drew on Neoclassical style, coming a year before the 1955 decree, was never built either—it was *belated*. Nonetheless, it reflects Rochegov's interest in the preservation of the past (Lenin's and Stalin's bodies) as relics, awaiting a potential resurrection in the future to come.

When addressing the loss associated with the unfulfilled promises of Soviet utopia, a myriad of roads lead to the unrealized project of the Palace of the Soviets, the competition that brought Polyakov—and subsequently Rochegov and Engelke—to Moscow. It appears that figuratively and sometimes quite literally, the realized projects of Soviet Modernism were often built on a pre-1955 foundation: for instance, it is upon the foundation of the eighth unrealized Stalinist *vysotka*—the administrative building in Zaryadye—that Hotel Rossiya was built (1964-67). With occupancy for 5300, it was the largest hotel of its time. Engelke was awarded the State Medal for her work in the design and decor of the interior concert hall.[21] For her last project, Engelke participated in the interior design of the Cathedral of Christ the Savior in Moscow, which was built in 2000 on the site of a former outdoor pool; the pool, in turn, was built on the foundation of the prior Cathedral of Christ the Savior, demolished in the 1930s to make space for the Palace of the Soviets (never built). Revolutionary belatedness appears as the constant deferral of these dreams, seeming to create a desire to encrypt an identity—which is itself made up of a series of erasures—and transport it elsewhere, to be preserved.

In the September–October 1987 edition of *Arkhitektura SSSR*, Aleksandr Rochegov gave an extensive four-page interview.[22] In it he spoke admiringly about the history of Russian architecture,

20 Stanislav Kuzmich, Iulia Marusina, *Tam gde nachinaetsja Moskva* (Moscow, 2014), p. 15.

21 The hotel was severely damaged in a fire in 1977, after which it was never adequately restored. It was closed in 2006 and demolished in 2010. It is unclear whether Engelke's work there has survived.

22 The interview took place on April 18, 1987.

Russian embassy, Havana.
Photo: Fabien Bellat.

narrating its roots in the wooden-heritage style—*zodchestvo*—and the architecture of defense, a medieval tradition upheld by master craftsmen from the people, with deep knowledge of local climate and tradition—not by architects. The Revolution, in the words of Rochegov, brought a radical vision of architecture and new principles of spatial organization, but few realized projects: "The 20s were not reflected in the realization [of projects], but they laid a deep theoretical groundwork, which continues to nurture us, and to a large extent, the whole world." This historical time also created the role of the architect as the initiator of new social formations, a socially privileged profession in Soviet society through the post-war years, one which Rochegov explicitly esteems. The deep professionalization and creative mastery of the post-war generation of largely Leningrad-based architects was epitomized in the design of the Palace of the Soviets, which Rochegov identifies as the defining project of Soviet architect-driven architecture up until the 1955 turn. However, according to him, the Khrushchev-era decree "On Elimination of Excesses in Design and Construction" initiated the top-down bureaucratic management of Soviet architecture, leading to decades of projects—the ubiquitous implementation of model-based (*tipovie*) panel construction without consideration of local, material, or historical conditions—that were lacking in the creative drive associated with authorship, and hence, in Rochegov's view, lacking in responsibility over the execution of the project. According to Rochegov, the result was that both the pre-revolutionary, architect-less history (with its consideration of local conditions) and the creativity of architect-driven projects, were lost. Speaking with a *perestroika* and *glasnost*-era frankness about the harms of centralized management of architecture in the USSR, Rochegov is explicit about a desire to turn to a more professionalized, architect's workshop-driven model of design, in order to unleash vital creative and humanist capacities. The Soviet Union, says Rochegov, "is a creative organization, not a bureaucratic one, as some hot young minds now say. This is a breaking point, and we need to use the language of architecture to show it. Not the language of a poet or a writer, or a cinematographer or a politician, but the language of our innovative contribution to architecture."[23] It is remarkable that Rochegov—an architect who has completed dozens of massive projects in his lifetime—articulates the failure to give appropriate form to the present. His interview takes place the same year that the embassy is finally completed. Read in this light, the statement is marked by architectural belatedness—born in 1917, Rochegov's life is thoroughly historical and Soviet, and, notwithstanding its seeming success, it is built on a series of deferred dreams, to which he is constantly returning. Cuba is where the desire for fortified citadel-like structures—akin to a medieval Russian

23 Interview with A. Rochegov," *Arkhitektura SSSR* 5, September-October 1987, p. 19.

monastery—and the architect-driven, revolutionary vision of Soviet architecture could be realized, and yet Cuba too was out of joint with time.

CONCLUSION: ARMOIRES, NON-RUINS AND CRYPTS

Four years after the embassy's inauguration, the Soviet Union, Cuba's closest ideological ally, collapsed, triggering an economic crisis on the island. The 1990s are remembered as a hard decade in Cuba—the *período especial*, one where the country was reduced to a state of chaos and bare subsistence. However, the structure of the embassy has not deteriorated. Renamed the Embassy of the Russian Federation, it shrank in staff but not in grandeur. The gray tower of the embassy compound still rises above the city, its solidity in stark juxtaposition to the ruinous state of the architecture of the Cuban capital. Other parts of the city, beloved for its pastel façades, bear the marks of time, climate, and economic neglect, with many buildings pierced by trees and on the verge of crumbling into the earth. The embassy is one of hundreds of Soviet-led projects built in Cuba, many of which, such as the nuclear power plant in Juraguá begun in 1979, were not fully completed before the sudden disappearance of the USSR, becoming ruins in a flash. And yet, the embassy does not become a ruin and its internal transformation—the reduction in staff, the rooms becoming filled with old cables—has not contaminated the external image it projects: for the locals, its non-ruinous status became the monument of a promise unfulfilled, the ever-present reminder of a future that will never arrive. As a result, the building is hated by most Cubans, making it the butt of many jokes: some call it a "syringe sucking the blood from the heart of Havana." Artists of the Cuban collective Los Carpinteros have repurposed the distinct shape of the embassy in a series of artworks (2003, 2015) that include an embassy-tower-shaped armoire, further highlighting the questionable utility of the building.

Los Carpinteros, *Embajada rusa* [Russian embassy, 2003].

To think of the embassy as an armoire—an enclosed structure with shelves that can neatly preserve the archive of one's disconnected, disembodied possessions—seems telling as to the role the embassy has come to play in Havana's imaginary. It is a kind of storage house, a crypt, preserving "personal" items from the past with the hope that one might need them, return to them in the future. Making Cuba, the "island of freedom," into the material site and fertile soil for the storage of this hope is problematic; other than the overt imperial tendencies of the Soviet Union, one can also, in a more generous reading, salute the faith placed in the longevity of the Cuban Revolution by many around the globe.

Is the embassy a stillborn remnant of a bygone era—a

dead form? Or is it better understood as a case of revolutionary belatedness, of the deferred dream of the socialist past haunting the present? It is the manifestation of disjointed temporalities: the difference in age and maturity of revolutionary rhetoric between the 1917 and 1959 revolutions, within the context of the geopolitical realities of the 1980s, as well as the dissonance between Rochegov and Engelke's architectural vision and the architectural landscape of Havana. Paraphrasing Hamlet in *Specters of Marx* to evoke history, Jacques Derrida writes: "The time is out of joint: time is disarticulated, dislocated, dislodged, time is run down, on the run and run down, both out of order and mad."[24] Since the collapse of the USSR and the death of Fidel Castro, Cuba seems to be living in a strange sense of the present, one that seems on the verge of collapse, of being absorbed by the incoming post-embargo future. Yet, socialism is always oriented toward the future. Perhaps, as opposed to post-socialism, we are communally entering into a *pre*-socialist time. In that sense, the embassy is a monument to that which is yet to come, under the slogan "*¡Hasta la victoria siempre!*"

24 Jacques Derrida, *Specters of Marx* (New York: Routledge, 1994), p. 20.

Opposite page:
Russian embassy, Havana.
Photo: Felix Lipov.

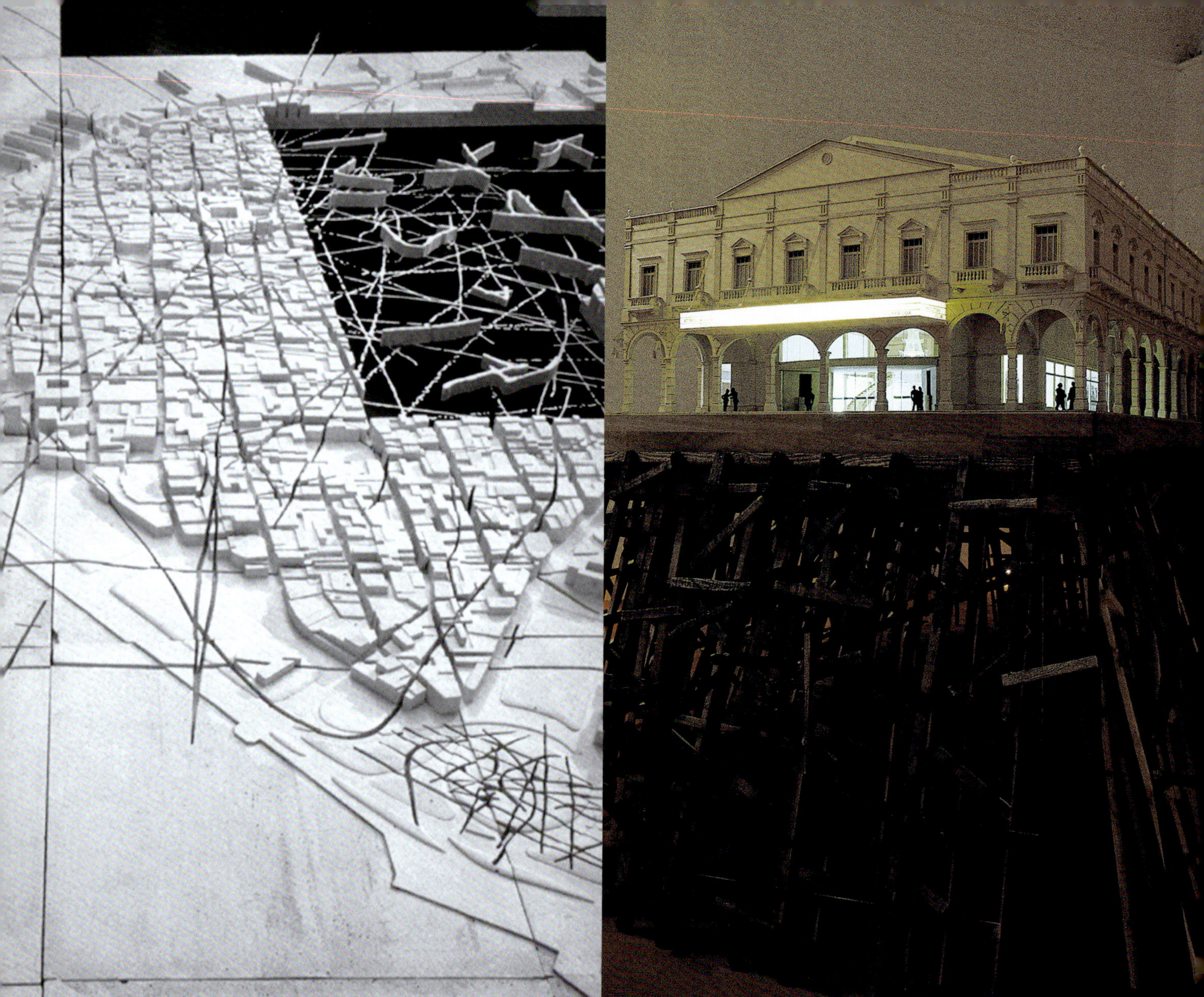

ART PROJECTS

THE HAVANA PROJECT *Coop Himmelb(l)au*

In 1994, Coop Himmelb(l)au and a number of other renowned architects were invited to a workshop aimed at developing new visions for the future of Havana. The state of the city was appalling, a sea of dilapidated houses. Yet the sun shone over the ruined city, and the people in the streets seemed cheerful and carefree. Once we became accustomed to the texture of its crumbling materials, we came to see Havana as the fulfilment of every urban planner's dream —the city as a public space—and dismiss its alleged "problem" as a mere projection of postcolonial Western European prejudices.

But in Havana, it is not only the houses that are crumbling, but also, though at a slower rate, the ground on which they stand. The state of the infrastructure is alarming. The underground water pipes are old and rusty, and half of the drinking water does not reach households, but seeps into the ground.

Given this situation, there was no place for conventional urban planning ideas. We had to start by recognizing our own helplessness in order to avoid the many mistakes that modern architecture had often committed in foreign cultures: One thinks of Le Corbusier's wooden built-in kitchens in Chandigarh, which were turned into firewood by tenants who had no use for them. We had the responsibility to acknowledge our own powerlessness (and deal with the feelings this provoked).

The question of what to do in Havana could only be addressed by working backwards: there would be no urban development and no architecture. We had to start by identifying the right level for a meaningful intervention, and thus we came to think of infrastructure, the fundamental layer on which the future of the city rests. Invisible, hidden under the body of the city, it had to be made visible in all its critical mass. Thus we covered the plaster model of Havana with a network of infrastructural lines: the resulting pattern does not follow actual plans, but rather a symbolic logic—we did not want to give the impression that we were proposing a concrete plan for action. The lines, carved out of the plaster model, appear like the wounds of the city's aging body. Conversely they also point to Havana's future potential: they can be read as subtractive spaces, but also as positive volumes. The lines cut in the L-shaped area in the model emerge as diagrammatic precursors for a potentially new form of architecture.

Not planning, but an intimation of a future Havana. No master plan, no dogmatic placement or design of buildings, but the visualization of a possible strategy for the future development of the city.

HABANA LIBRE

I would like to compare the architect's city planning methods with the cross punch delivered by the boxer Cassius Clay.

We believe we have complete freedom, but in fact, we do not have it. We are like boxers on the ring and must deal with physical constraints, just like the boxer has to take punches and deliver them too.

Cassius Clay's cross punch is a reactive move: he sees a punch coming and punches his opponent to block his attack.

We architects operate in a similar fashion.

The lack of vision in urban planning really upsets us.

There are two schools: the first, cloaked in progressive vocabulary, aims to fulfil reality. The second, more romantic and particularly visible in America, erects postmodern plazas, all while imagining they will actually work.

I just came back from Havana and find myself both fascinated and shocked by the city.

To me, Havana is at present the most interesting city because there, two contradictory systems are in constant tension: a socially-conscious system clashes against a capitalist model and this makes up "the substance of the city."

The substance of the city is built. But it is decaying, as Cuba has no money. The Cubans are now trying to avoid starvation by bringing in capitalism in the form of developers. The effects are terrible.

The political slogan "venceremos," written out in a 30-meter banner, is now used as a an advertisement.

My shock and fascination emerge from the following reasons:

Havana as built environment is a fascinating city, a small offspring of New York and Barcelona. It is a Spanish-American mixture, featuring fantastic urban spaces and extraordinary circumstances. When one walks through the old city, which is decaying and looks like Sarajevo, because there is no money, one is fascinated by the intimacy and then, suddenly, a building erected after the Revolution emerges out of this intimacy.

The system has been repeatedly denounced; it has many disadvantages, but also advantages. In other third-world cities I know—Mexico City, São Paulo, Guatemala City—children starve on the streets. In Havana, the children sit on the streets, but they have white teeth and go to school. I noticed this after two days of utter depression. Depression because one constantly walks through ruins—ruins which are inhabited by people.

After having visited Havana several times, I found out that this port city has neither prostitution nor drugs. One can walk around carefree after midnight. This is not a police state: it is a socialist country, similar and yet different from other Latin American cities.

But the city as a capitalist system must decay, because capital—the motor of the city—is missing.

Now Havana is becoming an urban laboratory for the third world, and it needs developers. Two contradictory systems are in opposition.

We were invited to design a project for the old city.

The inner city, with its high density, has many advantages. It is the most urban environment one can imagine—music everywhere.

Once it has been renovated to death, Havana will probably become America's whorehouse, as it was before the Revolution.

For these reasons, we refused to design a project and opted for writing a text.

In order to build, one needs water, Havana loses 50% of its drinking water every day.

It would be a much better urban project for Havana—instead of repeating forms and mouthing improbable theories—to repair the water pipes.

Our project is an interpretation of this refusal and at the same time the illustration of a statement.

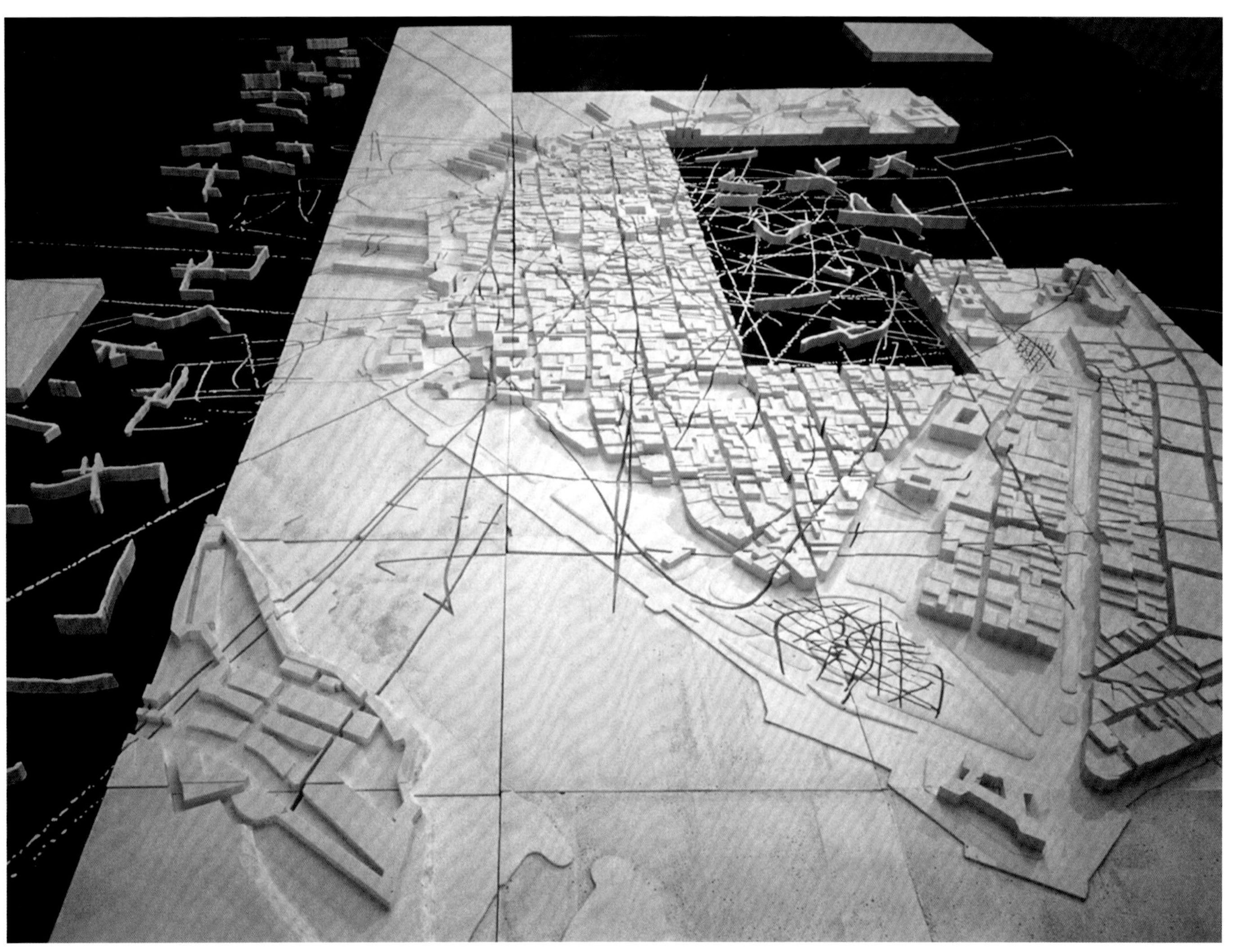

Coop Himmelb(l)au, model for *The Havana Project* (1994). Photo: Gerald Zugmann.

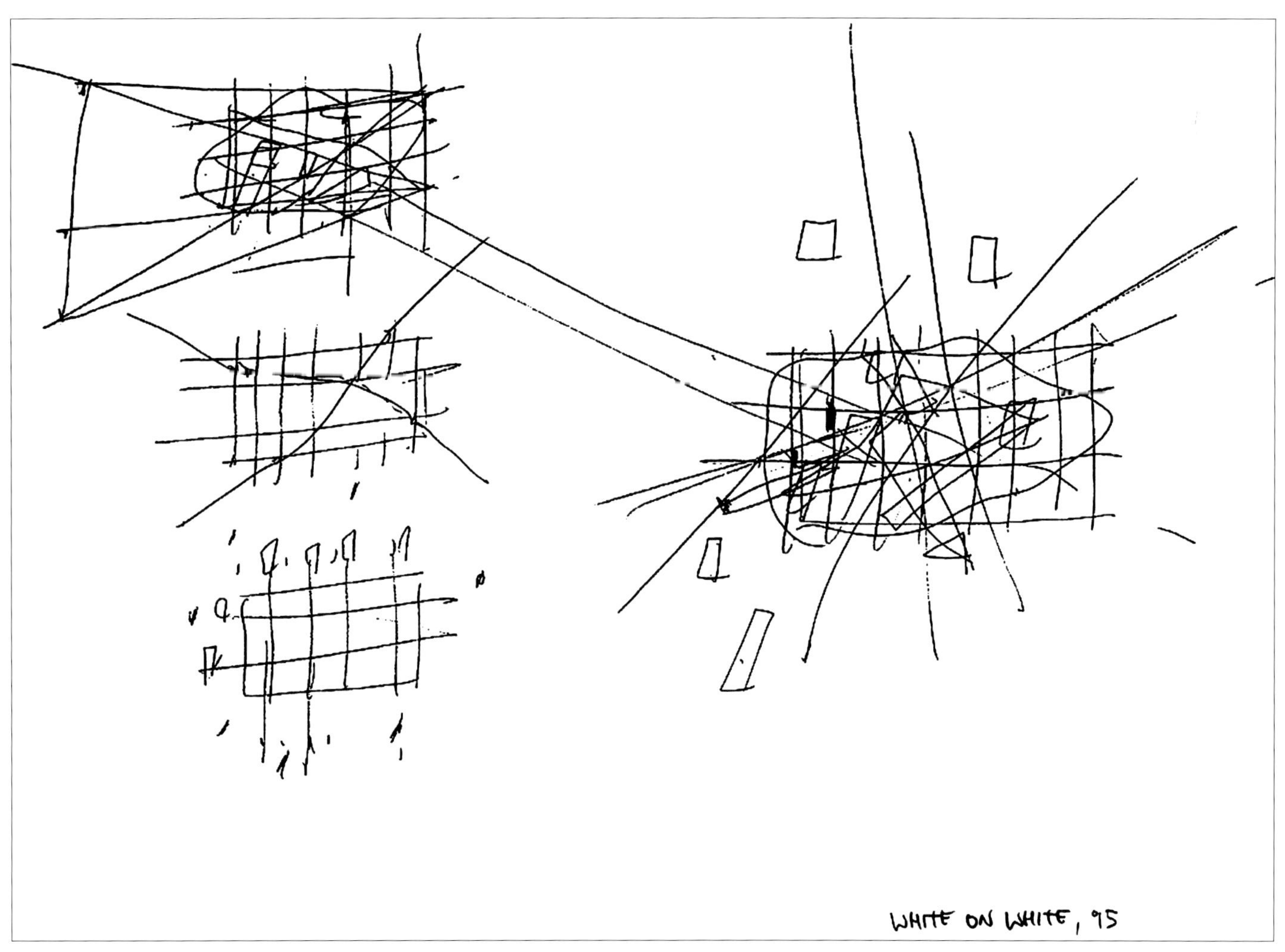

Coop Himmelb(l)au, *White on White* (1995).
Ink drawing on paper.

LIKE SUGAR. WHITE ON WHITE. 1994

The city offers no easy solution.

City planning strategies operate on the matrix of diverging choices.

The architect has to make a choice and be responsible for it.

HAVANA 1

Havana is about to be destroyed: money versus idealism, social progress, and liveliness.

Money will win, everything else will be lost.

Only the vivid shadows of liveliness, social thinking, and idealism will be left swimming and shimmering on the sea—like oil on water.

There is nothing we can plan for it. Today.

After all, we do not want to contribute to destruction.

But everything that once made us so happy in Havana should be preserved, invisibly.

The city builds itself invisibly, white on white.

None of the conventional rules of city planning seem to work here. Fixing all the water pipes in the city (leaks account for a loss of over than fifty percent of the drinking water) could produce the next architectural urban plan; perhaps recognition of the squatted palaces would be the next concept.

HAVANA 2

Superimposing drawings onto the city map records a possible strategy; it does not define future buildings.

Since the strategy could possibly acquire flesh and bones, one could call it a “body concept” for the city. But that would be later.

For now the concept is bodiless and therefore invisible. But it can be grasped. Like the music in the streets of Havana, which we can’t always see, but can always hear.

There is no more urban planning, the urban builds itself. If it doesn’t, it’s lost (just like Havana will be lost).

CINEMAS *Carlos Garaicoa*

Carlos Garaicoa, *Cine Maravillas* (2003). Black-and-white photograph.

All my life I've been a film buff, ever since I was small. My parents lived in Old Havana, between Sol and Muralla Streets. Whenever they went out they used to leave my siblings and me in the cinema watching a movie in the care of the usherette, who was like our babysitter. As they were real party animals, we spent a great deal of our childhood in cinemas; they'd leave us in one and come back two hours later to take us to another, so we got to see several movies a night. In that way we built up a pretty comprehensive cinematographic culture. I ended up knowing all the cinemas in Havana.

Later, when I finished pre-college and entered the Superior Art Institute, in the 1990s, cinema continued to be a very important area for me and other artists of my generation. We had been shaped by movie houses. When the crisis of the Special Period arrived, we went everywhere on bicycles because there was no gas and therefore no transport, and we rode our bikes to the film festival and the Cinemateca and other big festivals like those of theater or jazz. In those days there were two key cinemas for us, the Cinemateca, on La Rampa, and the theater on 23rd and Second. That's where I watched a lot of French, Italian, Russian movies. I remember going AWOL from the army, from military service, in order to catch a week of Tarkovsky films.

LETTER TO THE CENSORS

Years later, in 2003, I carried out a whole art project on Havana cinemas that I called *Letter to the Censors*. It all began with an invitation I got from Rome, from Volume!, which is a small but highly prestigious institution, and this got me thinking about two things: first, the long tradition of Italian movies made in that city after the war, in the Cinecittà studios; Rome is the city of cinema, and I wanted to pay homage to it.

The second idea was linked to censorship. I kept remembering "Letter to the Censors," the song by French group Mano Negra that talks about their hatred of bureaucracy and censorship. I, too, wanted to use this work to send a message to the censors, and I thought it would be great to somehow project a film about all the films that have been censored. That's how I arrived at the idea of building a huge maquette of a cinema, a model that would occupy an entire room and inside which a film would be screened like a vast text, a long archive.

As well as this huge model, the installation would show a series of photographs of the movie theaters where I spent so many hours as a child and that now lie derelict.

I had been taking photographs of Havana cinemas for a long time. It started in the early 2000s, when I was visiting my mother in a hospital that was very close to El Principal, one of the most beautiful cinemas I've ever seen: it was built in the 1940s and has a lot of decorative wrought iron, as well as a majestic façade covered in architectonic features. One day after leaving the hospital, I went to have a look and found it in ruins. This shook me deeply and I told myself that I should really do a project on the place, but I couldn't figure out what. Little by little I began to document all these gorgeous venues that fascinated me with their air of decadence, of wreckage—a theme on which I had already worked a lot.

Carlos Garaicoa, ***Cine La edad de oro*** (2003). Black-and-white photograph.

So, when I started to prepare the installation for Rome, I already had a set of photographs of Havana cinemas. I still had to build the maquette of the Cine Payret, it was a huge task, we spent more than 13 hours a day on making it. My idea was to screen a film inside the model, but I didn't want to use film clips because I am not a video artist. I therefore decided to use only the titles of censored films, those that had been banned in various countries on different continents. I was interested in exploring a notion of violence: the violence of images, of those destroyed spaces, of the cinematic tradition, of the history of art.

Among the cinemas I photographed in those years was the Cine Habana, in Plaza Vieja, next to the Fototeca, and the Cine Mayan on Calzada de Ayestarán. There was also the Universal, on the corner of Compostela and Jesús María, a little place in the Chinese quarter. And another one beside the Ursuline convent, on Compostela St. in the Jewish quarter. Another is the Cine Lamparilla, on Lamparilla St. Another on Reina, later converted to a carpentry shop. One called Cine Astral, like the one in New York. Others that were turned into stage theaters. I also photographed cinemas in other parts of the city: the Apolo, on Diez de octubre, the Record, on Playa...

There were so many picture houses—Guillermo Cabrera Infante claimed that before the Revolution there were more than 100 in Havana—and what I did was simply wander round different neighborhoods trying to capture what I could find. I was most interested in the ones that had already shut down, no longer active.

Page 248:
Above: Carlos Garaicoa, *Movie Theater in Ruins* (2003). Black-and-white photograph.

Below: Carlos Garaicoa, *Movie Theater in Ruins* (2003). Black-and-white photograph.

Page 249:
Above: Carlos Garaicoa, *Cine Cuba* (2003). Black-and-white photograph.

Below: Carlos Garaicoa, *Movie Theater in Ruins* (2003). Black-and-white photograph.

Page 250:
Above: Carlos Garaicoa, *Cine Bayamo* (2003). Black-and-white photograph.

Below: Carlos Garaicoa, *Cine Apolo* (2003). Black-and-white photograph.

Page 251:
Above: Carlos Garaicoa, *Cine Record* (2003). Black-and-white photograph.

Below: Carlos Garaicoa, *Cine Atlas* (2003). Black-and-white photograph.

THE MAQUETTE

When we started to build the model, I asked Jorgito, who was an architect, to help out. I wanted it to have the grandeur of a theater, one of those magnificent palaces that are so widespread in Cuba. I told my assistants that we were going to be doing high-level crafts, we were going to make something magnificent here, but slow and painstakingly. The final result should give the impression of a luxurious space, with plush seats. We put spectators in as well, miniature filmgoers: there's even a *tirador*, one of those characters who go to the movies to masturbate.

The maquette would reproduce the whole block of the Cine Payret, and of course it had to be open so the public could peek inside and see the film that was showing. We had to design a machine to do the projection, which was not easy in those days because video projectors were very big, and we also had to install a cooling system to stop it from overheating.

I wanted the public to first move through the photographs of the ruined picture houses and then arrive at this maquette of the great cine-theater in all its splendor, with a fabulous lobby, like the one at

Carlos Garaicoa, *Carta a los censores* [Letter to the Censors, 2003]. Model of Cine Payret with working projector.

the Opera, so they could admire all this luxury, all this production, and at the same time view a movie that was also a text narrating the history of cinema itself.

Back in the 1990s, I already made various works about the ruins of Havana. I had been drawing the ruins since the beginning of the decade. I was interested in a conceptual mechanism, the idea of representing space via the medium of photography. During those years, to photograph ruins was a politically very sensitive act, and it remains sensitive to this day. Although back then, before social media, the impact was far greater because there were so few images in circulation.

At the end of the day, this was a project about the utopia of cinema.

COLONIAL
CUBA

QUE VER

APOLO

Record

SOVIET EMBASSY: LOS CARPINTEROS *Marco Castillo*

Our work explores design and architecture: we wanted to research the intersection between art, politics and society. We became interested in the question of how architecture tells us about ways of thinking at certain moments in history, in a given generation. At the beginning there were three of us—Alexandre Arrechea, Dagoberto Rodríguez, and myself—but by the time we created these pieces only Dagoberto and I were working as Los Carpinteros.

In one of our installations [see pp. 6-7], we recreated a series of buildings from Havana and turned them into pieces of furniture. One of the buildings we selected was the Soviet—now Russian—embassy, completed in 1987. It made a very strong impact on the Havana cityscape, especially in the neighborhood where it is located, Miramar, mostly occupied by two-story luxury villas and several other embassies. For many years I lived nearby, and I saw this building whenever I left my house. This got me thinking and fantasizing about the site.

The installation also features replicas of other Havana landmarks, for example the Edificio FOCSA, another flat building which at one point served as a preparatory school for students planning to attend universities in Eastern Europe. There is also Retiro Radial—the thin, tall structure in the center—an apartment complex built in the 1950s for people who worked in radio. The smaller structure is a copy of an apartment building across the street from the American embassy: its shape—especially the sharp corner—reminds me of the Flatiron Building in New York.

Each one of these buildings has a specific function and a complex history, and we wanted to play on this by transforming them into furniture. They were designed to exist outdoors, but we turned them into objects to be used indoors, as decor. I liked the idea of using the architecture of Havana to furnish an interior.

As we built these models, we took some liberties, especially with the Embassy: our models are interpretations, not replicas, of the building. We were making furniture, not actual buildings. We had to simplify the design: we eliminated the vertical lines in the drawer area, but kept them in the sections where there are no drawers. We also designed some non-opening drawers to look like niches in a cemetery. These are only on one side of the sculpture, because we could not fit opening drawers on both sides. And each drawer also has an internal structure: they have to slide open and closed.

Just as buildings were transformed into furniture, so the individual apartments housed in those structures became drawers or compartments where one could store things or even hide small secrets. We wanted to think about secrecy: we live in a very closed country, where few things are transparent and much is veiled in mystery. While we were working on these pieces, certain events took place—Fidel Castro retired from power, his brother Raúl launched a series of reforms designed to open up the country—that seemed to herald major changes. In the end this never happened. But as we were working on the Russian embassy replica, I thought that one day the archives would be made public and we would then learn many things about our past. As if all the drawers in the cabinet were opened at once and suddenly all the secrets were brought out in the open: a kind of Pandora's box that could never be closed again.

I was also intrigued by a curious fact: everyone in Cuba hates the Russian embassy, as part of a wider rejection of everything that reminds them of the island's Soviet period. I actually love the embassy, because it represents an important chapter in the history of Havana. The Soviet presence in Cuba was crucial from the early 1960s to the early 1990s, and yet the embassy is the only building that remains from that era.

The embassy is important for other reasons: not much was built in Cuba after the 1959 Revolution. Even though there was much discussion of building socialism, Cuba did not launch a formal construction program like the Soviets did after 1917. Fidel Castro was very cheap. He didn't spend much on construction: all the funds went to promote the Revolution and to promote himself. You could say that instead of building he spent the money on advertising.

I often think the Revolution is more of an abstract concept than a reality.

Cubans have many fantasies about the Russian embassy: some say it looks like a sword, others see it as a robot. I like this image of a Russian robot in the middle of a city. And I also like the idea of a sword—a very thick sword—impaling the ground, on an island facing the United States. This is a very strong political gesture, a typically Soviet move, as if the Russians were telling the Americans: "Cuba belongs to us and not to you guys. If you want it you have to come here and steal the sword..."

We also made a model of the embassy covered with LEGO: it was part of a series of experiments with the texture of these building bricks. We made a drawing and later we built a sculpture. In Cuba, we never had LEGO as children: to us it represented the West, it was something only Western kids had. We did not grow up with LEGO,

Los Carpinteros, *Embajada rusa* [Russian embassy, 2003].
Wood. 300 x 110 x 110 cm
Courtesy of The Bronx Museum of the Arts.

Los Carpinteros, *Embajada rusa* [Russian Embassy, 2015].
Wood, and LEGO® bricks. 210 x 70 x 70 cm
Courtesy of Marco Castillo Studio.

Opposite page:
Los Carpinteros, *Embajada rusa de Legos* [LEGO Russian Embassy, 2015].
Watercolor on paper. 200 x 113 cm
Courtesy of Sean Kelly Gallery, New York.

or Coca-Cola, or many other things from the West. Whenever I meet artists from other parts of the world and we start to talk, at a certain point it becomes clear that our childhoods and backgrounds were very different—unless I'm talking to someone who grew up in Poland, or East Germany, or Yugoslavia, and then it turns out we have many of the same referents.

We also selected a number of monumental buildings from Eastern Europe, made large-scale models and clad them in LEGO. We did not actually build the structures using LEGO, we just used the LEGO bricks as a skin. This is a veiled reference to our childhood: Cuban children grow up immersed in politics and we became politicized at an early age. In elementary school we were taught to "fight for socialism" and we had to join the Pioneers, a sort of socialist boy-scout organization. All of this is present in the LEGO *Russian Embassy*, which looks like a monster, a Soviet robot.

I also imagine the Russian embassy housed plenty of secrets during Soviet times: it's a big building, with many offices, and I'm sure a lot happened there. Russians were very curious about Americans, and this building, though located in Cuba, is also related to the United States, because it was doubtless a base for espionage: the KGB station in Havana was probably housed there. The USSR used Cuba to spy on the US: there was, for instance, a listening base in Cuba called Base Lourdes, which apparently could listen in on communications between the United States and Cuba. But the operators were Soviets, not Cubans.

The Lourdes base is next to the University of Sciences, outside of Havana. It was full of strange equipment: radios, communication devices, sound recording machines. Apparently, it was one of the most sophisticated listening bases in the world, and many Soviets worked there, who might have also been connected to the embassy.

There was great secrecy in Soviet times. Cuba was involved in several wars, many of which had nothing to do with Cuban interests: Cuba fought in Angola, for instance, because it was committed to internationalism. Like the United States, it intervened in countries around the globe, moved by ideological concerns. But there was one important difference: the United States launched these interventions using its own funds, while Cuba paid for them using Russian money, since almost all funds came from Moscow. Russia sent us oil and Fidel sold it to finance guerrillas in South America. After the Revolution, the Soviet Union became Cuba's one and only sponsor. More than a politician, Fidel was a conceptual artist: he had great and beautiful ideas, grand ambitions, but most of these were unrealizable; they could never be executed, and remained as blueprints.

REVOLUTION AND ARCHITECTURE *Lisa Schmidt-Colinet, Alexander Schmoeger, and Florian Zeyfang.*

September 10 / October 31, 2021

The three of us are left over from a larger collective of artists which also included Susi Jirkuff and Siggi Hofer. We first met in Los Angeles in 2000: the five of us had fellowships at the Schindler House, an Austrian residency for artists and architects, where we stayed for six months, until March 2001.

There we met Eugenio Valdés Figueroa, a curator from Cuba. We spent several days together and even took a short trip to Las Vegas. We got very excited about the stories that Eugenio told us and we began to collaborate on a number of projects—exhibitions at the Schindler House, Houston, and Vienna. In 2003 we were invited as a group to curate a section of that year's Havana Biennial.

We decided to form a group, and Eugenio joined as a member: he did not want to assume the position of an individual curator above the group. In that way each of us could contribute our own expertise to the creation of what he always called "ephemeral projects."

Before then, in 1997, Florian had attended the Whitney Independent Study program in New York. He arrived there with many ideas about the fall of the Berlin Wall, revolution, and the history of socialism. Talking with the other fellows there he became even more interested in the Cuban Revolution: What was actually happening over there? What was the reality of the island?

One year before the Biennial, in 2002, we flew to Cuba, and selected the Pabellón Cuba on La Rampa as the location for our project. That scouting experience led us to think more about Havana, and the role of architecture, politics, and film in the city.

Looking back, what took us to Cuba was, first of all, an interest in the euphoric moment of the Revolution, and especially the art, architecture and films that emerged from it. We created films and installations about housing projects: we were interested in the building systems, in how such ambitious housing programs were constructed, in the people who made them, and in the prefabricated elements used in the construction.

PABELLÓN CUBA, 4D–4DIMENSIONS, 4DECADES, HAVANA 2003

The project we conceived for the 2003 Havana Biennial was called *4D–4Dimensions, 4Decades*. We were there 44 years after the Revolution, thinking about the euphoria of the first years, and wondering what was left. It took place as planned in the Pabellón Cuba, and consisted of an architectural intervention—we constructed a large scaffold inside the pavilion—that could host the 40 invited artists. We also curated an extensive film program about the city and architecture and in addition, asked the invited artists to bring videos from their countries; these were shown together with historical Cuban documentaries and films, as a kind of counterpoint. It was an effort to enlarge the audience and scope of the Biennial by incorporating voices from different countries. All the material came in totally uncensored.

Our exhibition at the Pabellón Cuba was open to the public, and for the duration of the Biennial it changed the neighborhood: everybody could come in for free. In the beginning we also invited musicians—the band Interactivo played our first concert. But it became so crowded that the authorities asked us to stop programming live music. We were not sure if it was for security reasons, or because it was so incredibly popular. Or possibly because the lyrics Interactivo sang on stage included the phrase: “What we need now is a Revolution!”

We used scaffolding to build a structure traversing the Pabellón, creating various entrances and opening it up to La Rampa. Since the Pabellón lacks interior walls, we wanted to create a space where the artists could present their work, and so we asked them to co-design this structure. Our intervention was also designed to highlight the Pabellón as an important architectural site on La Rampa, built in the 1960s. Walking through the different levels of our structure, visitors enjoyed different perspectives, and they could crisscross the Pabellón without ever touching the ground. This “not-touching-the-ground” is a concern that has remained with us, in all of our projects: most of the buildings we have filmed or worked with are elevated.

In 2008 we published a book about the Pabellón project, which included source material, texts, images of La Rampa and the development of Vedado in the 1960s, as well as documentation of the most important historical events held at Pabellón Cuba: “Historia y Arquitectura de Cuba” in 1963, “Primera Muestra de la Cultura Cubana” in 1966 and, perhaps the most significant, “Del Tercer Mundo,” from 1968.

THE CUBAN PAVILION FOR EXPO ’67

While preparing *4D*, we became interested in another pavilion: Cuba’s contribution to the World Expo 1967 in Montreal. One day in 2002 we spent an afternoon with Fernando Ayuso, the Cuban fashion designer, who told us lots of stories about the 1967 Pavilion, the Expo in Montreal, and the different artists who worked on the project. His way of talking about that moment, his enthusiasm about that era made a deep impression on all of us.

We became curious to know how the building materials for the pavilion traveled from Havana to Montreal and then disappeared. The building was supposed to be a revolutionary message from Cuba. Among other features it set out to be a projection machine, showing all the latest Cuban films. This was a creative solution to a practical shortcoming: because of the island's economic predicament, Cubans could not afford to send heavy industrial products to Canada. Film allowed them to bring the Revolution—plus rum and cigars, of course—to the Expo.

At first we found no good documentation about the Expo pavilion, until, by chance, we discovered some construction plans. In order to understand this building, we started to reconstruct it ourselves: first, using CAD, which also allowed us to generate our own images, renderings, and photographs of the Pavilion. That process was the first step towards an exhibition in Rio de Janeiro at the gallery A Gentil Carioca in 2008, where we constructed a model of the pavilion made of brazilwood. We sat it on aluminum caps to make it float and to evoke the sockets of the original Expo pavilion.

Here, as in all our projects, including the films, we began by collecting bits and pieces, finding information here and there, and then, when we felt ready, we pieced it all together.

INSTITUTE ABOVE-GROUND, 2015

As part of the programming for *4D*, we invited Roberto Gottardi to present a talk at the Pavilion. Gottardi was very important for the project: he knew La Rampa extremely well as he had designed a project across the street from the Pabellón Cuba in 1967, the transformation of the former Funeraria Caballero into a gallery. We invited Gottardi to talk about this work, which is no longer there, and to share his insights on La Rampa. We managed to find two or three images of the funeral home/gallery—there are hardly any in existence—and we included these in our *4D* book. Through Gottardi we learnt a lot about Cuba and its architecture. He is one of the three architects of the National Art Schools in Havana, along with Ricardo Porro and Vittorio Garatti. We met Garatti a year later: we contacted him after visiting one of his projects from 1964, the Instituto de Suelos y Fertilizantes André Voisin near Güines—an agricultural school displaying a unique architecture, prefabricated on site.

We tried to film there, which was a challenge, because filming was not allowed. The images we obtained—video shot "from the hip" and some 6x6 black-and-white images—were so poor that we decided to deliberately use the worst footage from our shoot. We "estranged" it even more, using filters, and constructed a story around the site, as if it were a hidden place, a forgotten utopia, or a UFO that had landed in the middle of the island... that way we could speak freely and let our imaginations run.

We found this site absolutely fascinating: it is raised above the ground, because the land floods regularly (it is a rice-growing area). Wanting to find out more, we contacted Garatti and traveled to Milan to interview him. He was very open, very friendly, and opened his archive for us: this material and the interview became an important part of our second film, *Institute Above-Ground*, which we made after the *Microbrigades* film.

MICROBRIGADES, 2013

What interested us about the microbrigades housing projects was the ambitious scope of the program and the process by which these blocks were built. How is a building conceived? And how is the knowledge of construction techniques disseminated so that unskilled people can effectively build large structures? This is how the buildings popularly known as "microbrigades" were introduced in Cuba in the 1970s as a solution to the island's housing shortage. Ten percent of the island's workforce was mobilized; workers would take leave from their regular jobs in order to build homes for themselves and their colleagues. It was a creative solution to the economic crisis that followed the failure of the 1970 Ten Million Ton sugar harvest. Those unskilled, or otherwise-skilled, workers would build structures six stories high, each containing 36 flats.

The archetypal microbrigade building was conceived to be erected with manual labor; in the course of its production it was adapted to accommodate available materials and elements left over from other building projects, such as pre-stressed concrete slabs.

We became curious about a system of prefabrication called "Sistema Girón," which had been developed for school buildings—the "schools in the countryside" or ESBECs—that are the subject of our 2021 film and installation, *La Nueva Escuela*. Our Microbrigade project led us to look closely at this system. We discovered prefab building elements in radically different contexts, recycled in very productive ways: in one case we found a prefab building panel serving as the roof of a bus station and, in another case, a similar panel used as a paving stone.

We immediately wanted to find out more about the residents' involvement in designing the houses they built. It turns out that their participation was minimal: the emphasis was on construction, not design. And of course, many Cubans are very critical of the microbrigades concept, which had many problems, including the poor quality of the ensuing constructions... But this simple method enabled the creation of tens of thousands of housing units, fulfilling one of the main promises of the Revolution: to build homes for all.

Our interest in microbrigades actually dates back to our first visits to Cuba. The *4D* book includes a contribution by our artist friend, Manuel Piña: a series of photographs about the microbrigades accompanied by a text, which highlight the technical aspect but also the human dimension. He recounts walking past a friend's house, a microbrigade building under construction, and as weeks and months and years go by, it remains unfinished. And for our film, another artist friend, Lázaro Saavedra, contributed a series of rather humorous paintings recalling how unpleasant it was for him to toil in a microbrigade.

POLITICAL CONTEXT

Our interest in Cuba focuses partly on architecture, partly on film, partly on art—but there is also a political dimension. Rubén Gallo once asked us whether our attraction to Cuba grew out of our experience as Germans and Austrians, Europeans who lived on the border of the Socialist Bloc during the Cold War: he discerned in our work a certain empathy towards Cuba that could only come from people familiar with the system. He pointed to the film *Institute Above-Ground*, which shows both the utopian potential of the original project and its downfall, and he liked the fact that it does not come out wholly for or against the Revolution: it lets the viewer draw her own conclusions.

There might be something to this observation about our geopolitical situation: we grew up with two German states, one Western, one Eastern, one capitalist, one socialist, and this defined our sense of self. Florian once said that our generation would always remember that there were two Germanies, and we had some sympathy for the GDR. This might now seem absurd, but it was, in part, a revolt against our parents who were so opposed to the GDR. East Germany represented an alternative to West Germany, which did not do enough to work through its Nazi past—although, as we found out later, neither did the GDR.

Now the Eastern bloc is gone, but Cuba is still there. After the fall of the Berlin Wall and the collapse of the Soviet Union, Cuba seems to be the last place on earth opting for a different political system. Obviously, there is an urgent need for reform, as we have seen with the uprisings and unjustified detentions of 2020 and 2021.

Cuba's architecture has echoes of the former East: some buildings remind us of projects we saw in Yugoslavia or Czechoslovakia. Prefabrication systems were used to build structures that are completely dislocated from their setting: they seem to have landed, again like UFOs, in the middle of the countryside, just like the "*escuelas en el campo*" (country schools) which are the subject of our most recent project.

WORKING METHOD

Our projects start out with questions, which then lead us to what we call "meandering research." When we piece the parts together, the result combines moving and still images, architectural drawing, and writing. All of our films include a written component—textual captions—because we have never wanted to include voice-off commentary. This method evokes the work of the long-neglected Cuban filmmaker, Nicolás Guillén Landrián, who used oversized captions on screen; we did the same in *Microbrigades*. In *Institute Above-Ground*, on the other hand, captions are hand-written, as in a letter. We used two different hands: Florian's writing appears in the part about the fictional elements, and Lisa's in the sections about construction and the site. *Pavilion-In-Parts* emphasizes the primacy of text in the Pavilion shown at Expo '67 in Montréal. The camera zooms into wall texts (one of them reads "Faim Hunger Mort Death," another, "Chantage Atomic," or numbers like "50, 54, 56, 58, 60, 61, 62, 63, 64") in an attempt to use film to "read" the pavilion.

We can describe our general working method as follows: we start from an idea, then continue with the production of very specific fragments or elements, a drawing, a text, moving images, models, or photographs. We sit together and discuss the different directions the project could take. Sometimes we decide to build a model. For instance, we once made a microbrigade-slab out of Styrofoam; another time we cast a model of the beams used in the Instituto André Voisin. We keep these models nearby while we continue to brainstorm until, at one point, we build larger versions, which can then be included in exhibitions, accompanied by our films. We did this at the Lumiar Cité in Lisbon, in Gdansk, or in the Haus der Kulturen der Welt in Berlin.

We often wonder if these large models should be considered architecture or sculpture. Their function is ambiguous: they are copies of building elements, but also works in themselves.

Most of our work aims to go beyond the documentary: we are interested in the history of these buildings, but we want to find ways to release the potential they held when they were first constructed. We want to make something new happen through our work.

4D—4Dimensions, 4Decades

As members of the artists' collective RAIN, we developed a project for the 8th Havana Biennial in 2003, exploring the Pabellón Cuba's architectural design and history. We created a new structure inside this landmark building: a scaffold that traversed the Pabellón, connecting the front and back entrances. The 40 invited artists presented their work on this modular structure, thus proposing a variety of functional and spatial interventions.

4D—4Dimensions, 4Decades, 2003. Installation and exhibition, curated for the 8th Havana Biennial by artists' collective RAIN (2001-06: Siggi Hofer, Susi Jirkuff, Lisa Schmidt-Colinet, Alexander Schmoeger, Eugenio Valdés Figueroa, Florian Zeyfang).

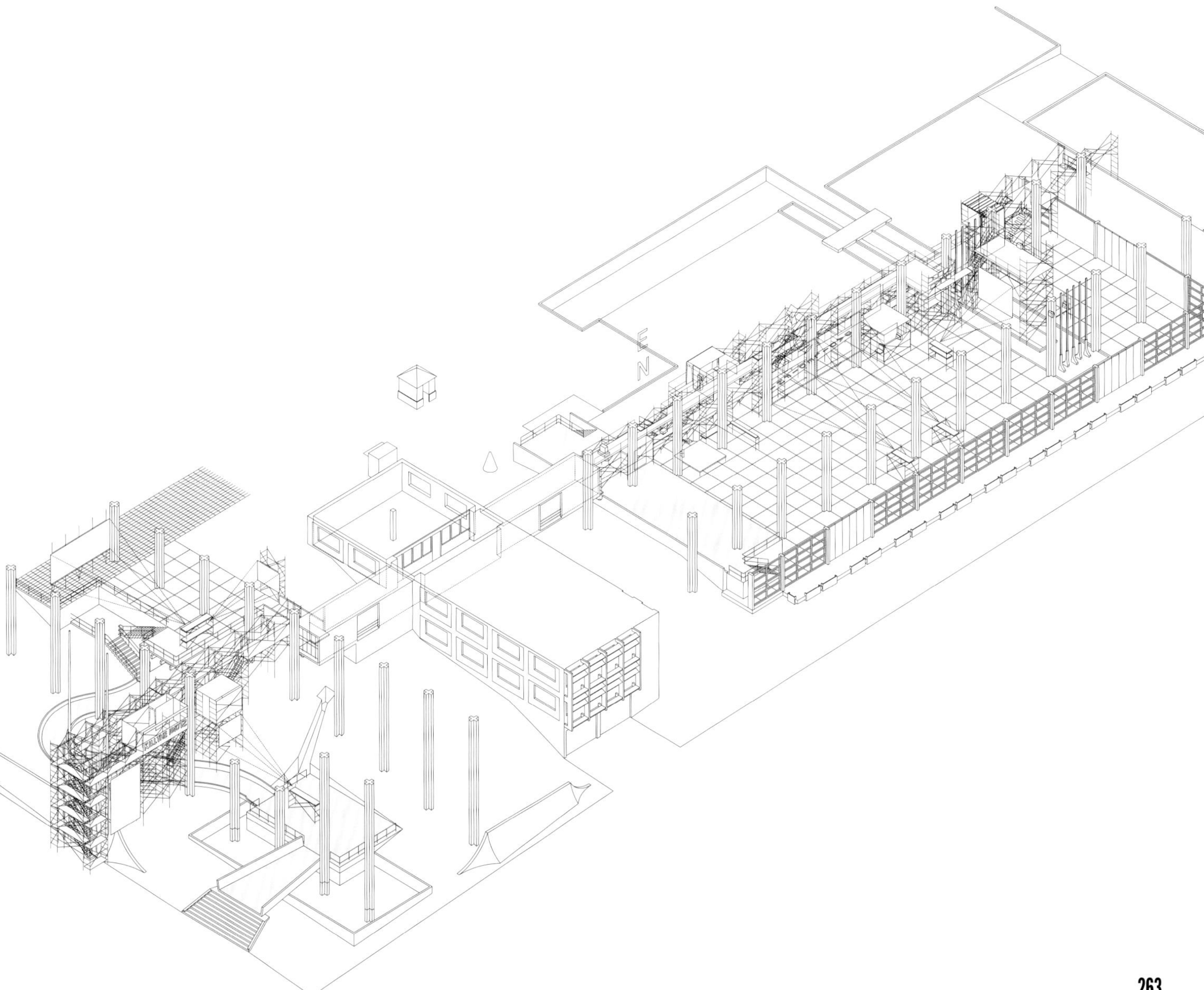

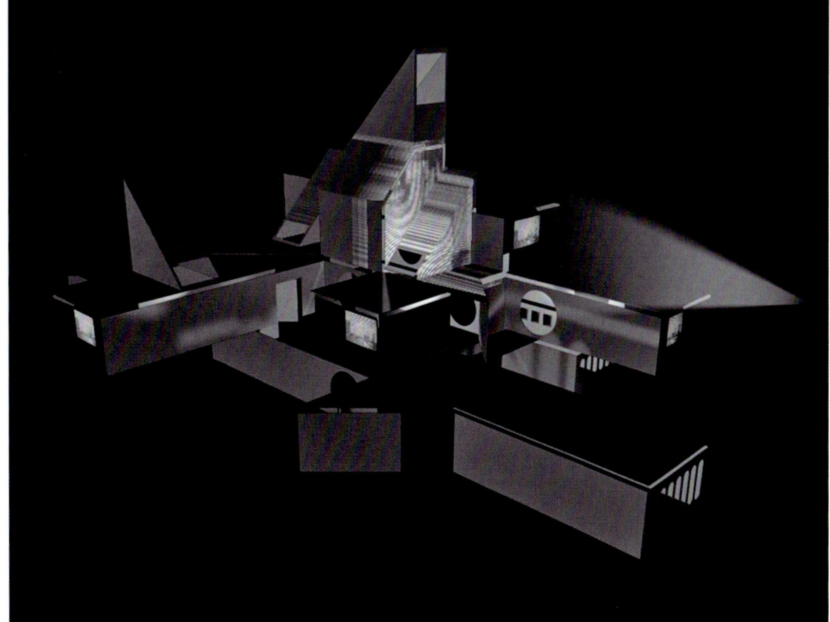

Pabellón Cuba. Wireframe model, digital prints, wall drawing. Exhibition view, A Gentil Carioca, Rio de Janeiro, 2008.

Opposite page and top:
Digital animation, still from *Pavilion-In-Parts*. HD Video, 25 min, 2018/2022.

Pabellón Cuba / Pavilion-In-Parts

The Cuban pavilion landed like a lunar module on the grounds of EXPO '67 in Montreal. This reusable construction, designed by Vittorio Garatti, Sergio Baroni, and Hugo D'Acosta, was intended to showcase revolutionary achievements. Faced with the scarcity of materials and technologies, the pavilion was conceived as a "projection machine" for Cuban film. We began by creating a wooden model of the Expo '67 pavilion in Rio de Janeiro, which then traveled to other parts of the world—a homage to the transportable architecture designed by Garatti and his collaborators. We used digital imaging to reproduce the convex windows of the original design. Several years later, we interviewed Vittorio Garatti and created the film *Pavilion-In-Parts*, which included archival images as well as our own animations and drawings.

Both pages:
Stills from *Institute Above-Ground.* HD Video, 22 min, 2015.

Institute Above-Ground

Institute Above-Ground is a documentary narrative about Cuba's visionary architecture. The Instituto Tecnológico de Suelos y Fertilizantes "André Voisin," conceived by Vittorio Garatti while he was working on the National Art Schools, is a symbol of the euphoric building experiments that blossomed immediately after the Revolution. The architecture has a futuristic look: the structures and walkways are raised above the ground, which was regularly flooded since the area was given to rice cultivation. Garatti used "in-situ prefabrication"—beams and other parts were made on-site by pouring concrete into molds—, a technique promoted in the early years of the Revolution as the perfect solution to the country's construction needs. The Institute was designed for about 2000 students who were to live, work, eat, and sleep on the premises. Later it served as an army prison and today it hovers on the landscape like a stranded spaceship: an ark for utopian ideas.

Both pages:
Stills from *Microbrigades*. HD Video, 30 min, 2013.

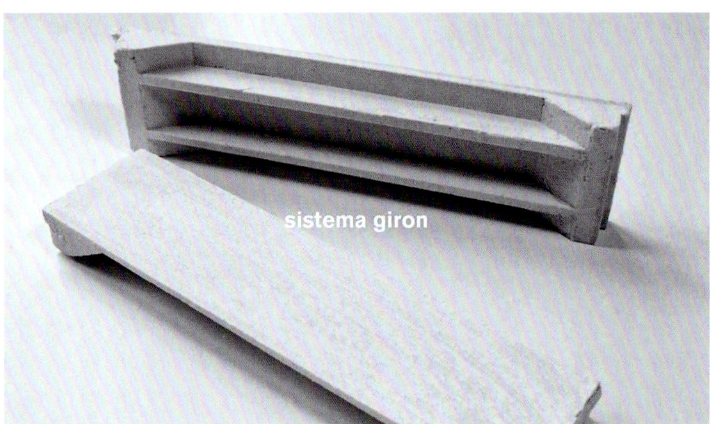

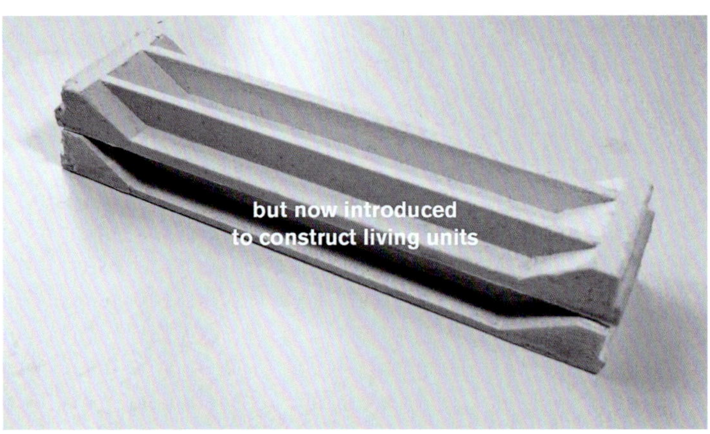

Microbrigades—Variations of a Story

These housing units are informally known as *microbrigadas*, after the small, unskilled construction crews (or "brigades") that built them. Following the economic downturn of the early 1970s, state-run companies were required to furlough up to 10 percent of their employees, who were then asked to work in construction. The microbrigades built multi-story apartment blocks as well as public buildings all over Cuba, and their labor continued until the late 1990s. Many of these housing units are raised above the ground—a detail present in many of the projects we observed. Our film—an inquiry into revolutionary pragmatism—creates an experimental collage by incorporating architectural images, archival material, and interviews.

Y—and half a year later, there was a lot of concrete. Sculptures, photographs, and HD videos. Exhibition view Lumiar Cité, Lisbon 2015/2016.

Y—and half a year later, there was a lot of concrete
In this exhibition at Lisbon's Lumiar Cité, we presented our films *Institute Above-Ground* and *Microbrigades—Variations of a Story*, next to two large elements built using two very different techniques of concrete prefabrication. The first element, "Sistema Girón," placed in the lower part of the space, was inspired by the slabs used in the eponymous prefab system. The other element, "Viga," is a 1:1 scale reproduction of a column designed by Vittorio Garatti for the Instituto Tecnológico de Suelos y Fertilizantes "André Voisin." Photographs from our research accompanied the films and sculptures.

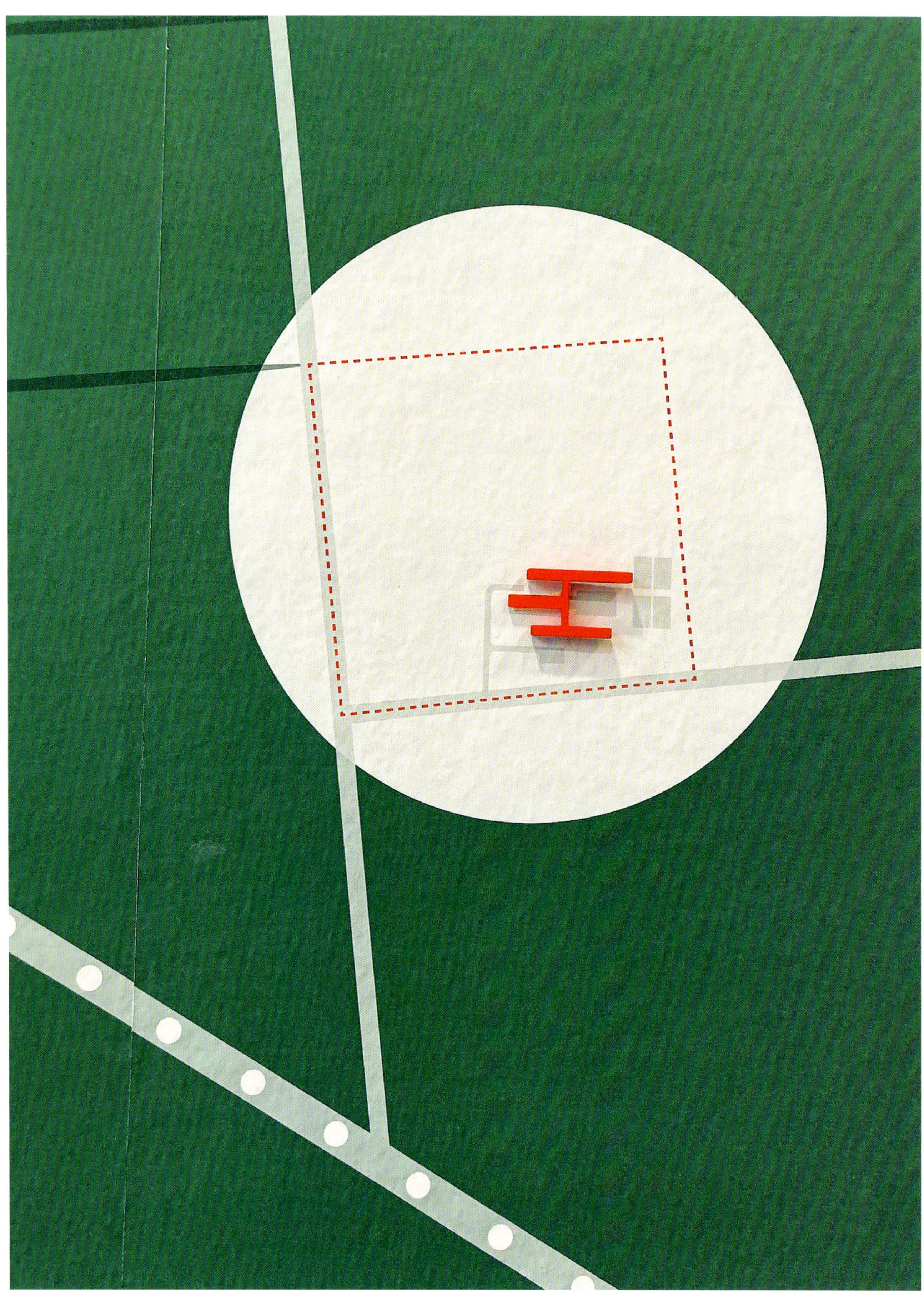

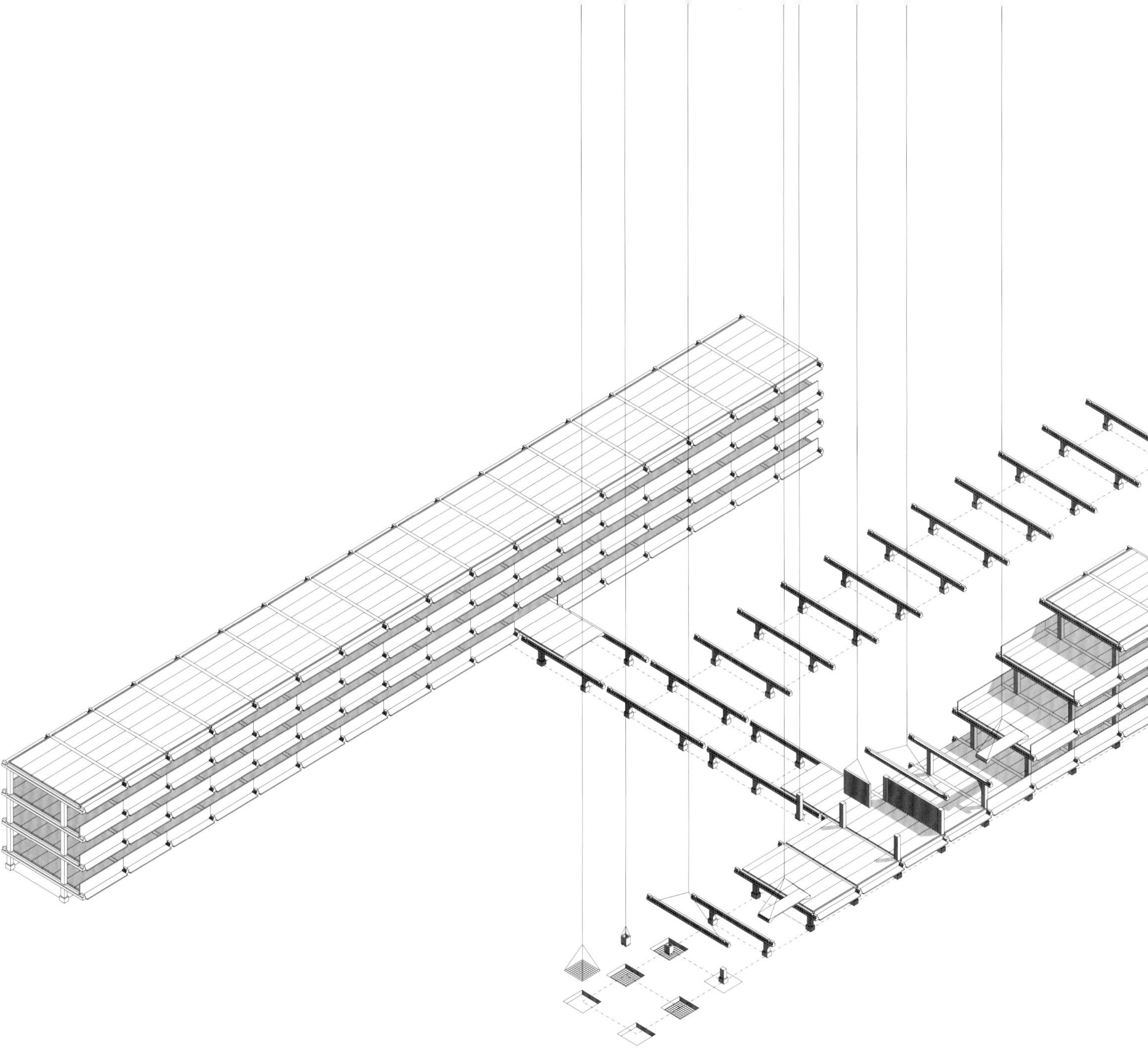

La Nueva Escuela

The national construction program "Schools in Rural Areas" was launched in the early 1970s. At a number of residential schools across the country, classroom instruction was to be combined with agricultural work—in this way, each student would contribute to achieving "education for all." Over the years, more than 350 standardized school buildings were constructed, using the prefab "Sistema Girón." The design was very simple and light, and the materials were transported and assembled on-site. The style of the schools is in frequent tension with the rural surroundings. Our film and installation *La Nueva Escuela* (The New School) sought to explore the relationship between architecture and education in post-revolutionary Cuba.

La Nueva Escuela. Installation with wall paper, 3D-printed models, and HD Video. Included in *Bildungsschock*, Haus der Kulturen der Welt, Berlin, 2021.

Casa Lamas (work in progress)

Over the years we often visited the Casa Lamas, designed by Humberto Alonso. It was started under Batista and completed in 1959 after the Revolution, thus establishing a bridge between pre- and post-revolutionary modernisms. This house—along with Humberto Alonso's and Fernando Salinas's CUJAE campus—is the focus of a forthcoming film and installation project, planned for release in 2023. We are especially interested in the house's structural openness and the seemingly endless angular perspectives created by the succession of walls and ceilings. Eduardo Luis Rodriguez describes it as "entirely composed of corners." It is not certain that Juan F. Lamas ever occupied this house: in 1959 the Lamas family, like so many others, probably left the country.

"Casa Lamas," project-in-progress (pin-hole photographs by A. Schmoeger).

BIBLIOGRAPHY

Alini, Luigi. *Vittorio Garatti: Opere e Progetti.* Naples: Clean Edizioni, 2020.

Arenas, Reinaldo. *Before Night Falls*, trans. Dolores Koch. New York: Viking, 1993.

Barber, Daniel A. *Modern Architecture and Climate: Design before Air Conditioning.* Princeton: Princeton University Press, 2020.

Barthes, Roland, et al. *Public Photographic Spaces: Exhibitions of Propaganda, from Pressa to The Family of Man, 1928-55.* Barcelona: Museu d'Art Contemporani de Barcelona, 2008.

Benjamin, Medea, et al. *No Free Lunch: Food & Revolution in Cuba Today.* San Francisco: Institute for Food and Development Policy, 1989.

Bergdoll, Barry, et al. (eds.). *Latin America in Construction: Architecture 1955-1980.* New York: Museum of Modern Art, 2015.

Betancourt, Enrique C. *Apuntes para la historia. Radio, televisión y farándula de la Cuba de ayer.* San Juan de Puerto Rico: Apuntes para la historia, 1986.

Boesinger, W. (ed.). *Richard Neutra, 1950-60, Buildings and Projects.* Zurich: Girsberger, 1959.

Bronfman, Alejandra. *Isles of Noise: Sonic Media in the Caribbean.* Chapel Hill: University of North Carolina Press, 2016.

Burdsall, Lorna. *More Than Just a Footnote: Dancing from Connecticut to Revolutionary Cuba.* Havana: Lorna Burdsall, 2001.

Cambre, María-Carolina. *The Semiotics of Che Guevara: Affective Gateways.* London: Bloomsbury Academic, 2014.

Cárdenas, Eliana (ed.). *Arquitectura y urbanismo: Cuba y América Latina desde el siglo XXI.* Havana: Editorial Arte y Cultura, 2013.

Carranza, Luis E., et al. *Modern Architecture in Latin America: Art, Technology, and Utopia.* Austin: University of Texas Press, 2014.

Casa de las Américas (ed.). *La sierra y el llano.* Havana: Casa de las Américas, 1969.

Castro, Fidel. *Palabras a los intelectuales.* Montevideo: Comité de Intelectuales y Artistas de Apoyo a la Revolución Cubana, 1961.

Centro de Información Técnica de la Construcción. *Construir la vida: Homenaje a los dignos hombres de los cascos blancos.* Havana: Centro de Información Técnica de la Construcción, 1977.

Clark, Katerina. *Moscow, the Fourth Rome: Stalinism, Cosmopolitanism, and the Evolution of Soviet Culture, 1931-1941.* Cambridge: Harvard University Press, 2011.

Cohen, Jean-Louis. *Building a New New World: Amerikanizm in Russian Architecture.* New Haven: Other Distribution, 2021.

Colomina, Beatriz. *Domesticity at War.* Cambridge: MIT Press, 2007.

Comité Estatal de la Construcción. *Arquitectura y Desarrollo Nacional, Cuba 1978.* Havana: Comité Estatal de la Construcción, 1978.

Cuadra, Manuel (ed.). *La arquitectura de la revolución cubana 1959-2018.* Kassel: Kassel University Press, 2018.

Cuadra, Manuel. *Aspiraciones y Espacios de una Revolución. Arquitectura y urbanismo en Cuba 1959-2018.* Kassel: Kassel University Press, 2019.

Cuadra, Manuel. *De Primera Mano.* Kassel: Kassel University Press, 2019.

Derrida, Jacques. *Specters of Marx.* New York: Routledge, 1994.

Deupí, Victor, and Lejeune, Jean-François. *Cuban Modernism: Mid-Century Architecture, 1940-1970.* Basel: Birkhäuser, 2021.

Díez-Pastor, Concha. *La arquitectura y la vida. Los artículos de Arniches y Domínguez en* El Sol *y otros escritos.* Self-published, Safe-Creative, 2016.

Ettinger, Catherine R. *Richard Neutra y América Latina: Una mirada desde el Sur.* Guadalajara: Arquitónica, 2018.

Expo (International Exhibitions Bureau). *Expo 67: Official Guide Officiel.* Toronto: Maclean-Hunter, 1967.

Goldhagen, Sarah Williams, and Legault, Réjean (eds.). *Anxious Modernisms: Experimentation in Postwar Architectural Culture.* Cambridge: MIT Press, 2000.

Gómez Díaz, Francisco. *De Forestier a Sert: Ciudad y Arquitectura en La Habana, 1925-1960.* Madrid: Abada Editores, 2008.

González, Reynaldo. *El más humano de los autores.* Havana: Ediciones Unión, 2009.

Graham, James (ed.). *Climates: Architecture and the Planetary Imaginary.* New York: Columbia Books on Architecture and the City, 2016.

Grigorievich Rochegov, Aleksandr. *Arkhitektura: Prospekt k vystavke rabot.* Moscow: TK, 1982.

Guerra, Lillian. *Visions of Power in Cuba: Revolution, Redemption, and Resistance, 1959-1971.* Chapel Hill: University of North Carolina Press, 2012.

Guevara, Ernesto. *El hombre nuevo.* Buenos Aires: Editorial del Noroeste, 1973.

Guillermoprieto, Alma. *Dancing with Cuba: A Memoir of the Revolution,* trans. Esther Allen. New York: Vintage, 2005.

Hall, Simon. *Ten Days in Harlem: Fidel Castro and the Making of the 1960s.* London: Faber and Faber, 2020.

Hines, Thomas S. *Richard Neutra and the Search for Modern Architecture.* New York: Oxford University Press, 1982.

Hobsbawm, Eric. *Viva La Revolución: Eric Hobsbawm on Latin America.* London: Little, Brown, 2016.

Hyde, Timothy. *Constitutional Modernism: Architecture and Civil Society in Cuba, 1933-1959.* Minneapolis: University of Minnesota Press, 2012.

James-Chakraborty, Kathleen. *Modernism as Memory.* Minneapolis: University of Minnesota Press, 2018.

Jaque, Andrés. *Superpowers of Scale.* New York: Columbia Books on Architecture and the City, 2020.

Kapto, A. S. *Na Perekrestkakh Zhizni: Politicheskie Memuary.* Moscow: Sotsial'no-polit. zhurnal, 1996.

Korda, Alberto. *Korda: A Revolutionary Lens.* Gottingen: Steild, 2008.

Krauss, Rosalind E. *The Originality of the Avant-Garde and Other Modernist Myths.* Cambridge: MIT Press, 1985.

Kuzmich, Stanislav, and Marusina, Iulia. *Tam gde nachinaetsja Moskva.* Moscow, 2014.

Lambert, Phyllis (ed.). *Mies in America.* New York: Harry N. Abrams, Inc., 2001.

Latour, Bruno. *Down to Earth: Politics in the New Climatic Regime.* Cambridge: Polity, 2019.

Lavin, Sylvia. *Architecture Itself and Other Postmodernization Effects.* Montreal: Canadian Centre for Architecture; Leipzig: Spector Books, 2020.

Lavin, Sylvia. *Form Follows Libido: Architecture and Richard Neutra in a Psychoanalytic Culture.* Cambridge: MIT Press, 2004.

LeoGrande, William, and Kornbluh, Peter. *Back Channel to Cuba.* Chapel Hill: University of North Carolina Press, 2014.

Lezama Lima, José. *Paradiso.* Havana: Editorial Letras Cubanas, 1991.

Lisenkova, E. A., et al. *Maria Engelke.* Moscow: Bely Gorod, 2008.

Loeffler, Jane C. *The Architecture of Diplomacy: Building America's Embassies.* New York: Princeton Architectural Press, 1998.

Loomis, John. *Revolution of Forms: Cuba's Forgotten Art Schools.* New York: Princeton Architectural Press, 1999.

López, Oscar Luis. *La radio en Cuba: Estudio de su desarrollo en la sociedad neocolonial.* Havana: Editorial Letras Cubanas, 1981.

Martín-Barbero, Jesús. *Oficio de cartógrafo. Travesías latinoamericanas de la comunicación en la cultura.* Mexico City: Fondo de Cultura Económica, 2002.

Martínez Víctores, Ricardo. *7RR. La historia de Radio Rebelde. Testimonio.* Havana: Editora Política, 2008.

McCoy, Esther. *Vienna to Los Angeles: Two Journeys.* Santa Monica: Arts & Architecture Press, 1979.

Mealy, Rosemari. *Fidel & Malcolm X: Memorias de un encuentro.* Havana: Letras Cubanas, 2018.

Menéndez-Conde, Ernesto. *Trazos en los márgenes: Arte abstracto e ideologías estéticas en Cuba.* Independently published, 2020.

Mesa-Lago, Carmelo (ed.). *Voices of change in Cuba from the Non-state Sector.* Pittsburgh: University of Pittsburgh Press, 2018.

Mesa-Lago, Carmelo, and Pérez-López, Jorge. *Cuba under Raúl Castro: Assessing the Reforms.* Boulder: Lynne Rienner Publishers, 2013.

Mosquera, Gerardo. *Contemporary Art from Cuba: Irony and Survival on the Utopian Island.* Arizona: Arizona State University, Delano Greenridge Editions, 2002.

National Academies of Sciences, Engineering, and Medicine. *An Assessment of Illness in U. S. Government Employees and Their Families at Overseas Embassies.* Washington DC: National Academies Press, 2020.

Neumeyer, Fritz. *Mies van der Rohe: The Artless Word.* Cambridge: MIT Press, 1991.

Neutra, Richard Joseph, and Neutra, Dione. *Wie Baut Amerika?* Stuttgart: J. Hoffmann, 1927.

Neutra, Richard Joseph. *Amerika: die Stilbildung des neuen Baues in den Vereinigten Staaten.* Vienna: A Schroll, 1930.

Neutra, Richard Joseph. *Architecture of Social Concern in Regions of Mild Climate.* São Paulo: G. Todtmann, 1948.

Neutra, Richard Joseph. *Life and Human Habitat.* Stuttgart: Alexander Koch, 1957.

Neutra, Richard Joseph. *Realismo biológico: Un nuevo renacimiento en la arquitectura.* Buenos Aires: Nueva Visión, 1958.

Neutra, Richard Joseph. *Richard Neutra: Complete Works.* Köln, New York: Taschen, 2000.

Neutra, Richard Joseph. *Survival Through Design.* New York: Oxford University Press, 1954.

Noever, Peter (ed.). *The Havana Project: Architecture Again.* Vienna: MAK, 1994.

Noever, Peter, and Groys, Boris. *Tyrannei Des Schönen: Architektur Der Stalin-Zeit.* Munich: Prestel, 1994.

Novikov, Felix. *Soviet Modernism 1955-1985.* Yekaterinburg: Tatlin Publishers, 2010.

Oltarzhevskii, V. K. *Stroitelistvo Vysotnix zdanii v Moskve.* Moscow: Gosudarstvennoe izdatelstvo literatury po stroitelistvu i arkhitekture, 1953.

Orovio, Helio. *Cuban Music from A to Z.* Durham: Duke University Press, 2004.

Pérez Jr., Louis A. *Cuba: Between Reform and Revolution.* New York: Oxford University Press, 2006.

Randall, Margaret. *Exporting Revolution: Cuba's Global Solidarity.* Durham: Duke University Press, 2017.

Roca, Miguel Ángel. *The Architecture of Latin America*. London: Academy Editions, 1995.
Rodríguez, Eduardo Luis, and Navarro, Pepe. *La Habana. Arquitectura del Siglo XX*. Barcelona: Blume, 1998.
Rodríguez, Eduardo Luis. *The Havana Guide, Modern Architecture, 1925-1965*. New York: Princeton Architectural Press, 2000.
Sartre, Jean Paul. *Sartre on Cuba*. New York: Ballantine Books, 1961.
Schmidt-Colinet, Lisa, and Schmoeger, Alex (eds.). *Pabellón Cuba: 4D—4Dimensions, 4Decades: Exhibition 4D—4Dimensions, 4Decades*. Berlin: b_books, 2008.
Schulze, Franz and Windhorst, Edward. *Mies van der Rohe*. Chicago: University of Chicago Press, 2012.
Schwall, Elizabeth B. *Dancing with the Revolution*. Chapel Hill: University of North Carolina Press, 2012.
Segre, Roberto. *Arquitectura y urbanismo de la revolución cubana*. Havana: Editorial Pueblo y Educación, 1989.
Segre, Roberto. *Cuba: l'architettura della rivoluzione*. Padova: Marsilio Editori, 1970.
Segre, Roberto. *Diez años de arquitectura revolucionaria*. Havana: Cuadernos de la Revista Unión, 1970.
Segre, Roberto. *Ensayos sobre Arquitectura e Ideología en Cuba Revolucionaria*. Havana: Centro de Información Científica y Técnica, Universidad de La Habana, 1970.
Segre, Roberto. *La arquitectura de la Revolución cubana*. Montevideo: Universidad de la República, Facultad de Arquitectura, 1968.
Segre, Roberto. *La vivienda en Cuba en el siglo XX: República y revolución*. Mexico City: Editorial Paz, 1980.
Segre, Roberto. *La vivienda en Cuba: república y revolución*. Havana: Universidad de La Habana, 1979.
Shulman, Allan T. *Building Bacardi: Architecture, Art & Identity*. New York: Rizzoli, 2016.
Soley, Lawrence C., and Nichols, John. *Clandestine Radio Broadcasting: A Study of Revolutionary and Counterrevolutionary Electronic Communication*. New York: Praeger, 1987.
Véjar Pérez-Rubio, Carlos (ed.). *Y el perro ladra y la luna enfría. Fernando Salinas: Diseño, ambiente y esperanza*. Mexico City: Universidad Autónoma Metropolitana, 1994.
Vidler, Anthony. *The Architectural Uncanny: Essays in the Modern Unhomely*. Cambridge: MIT Press, 1992.
War Department, United States. *War Department Annual Reports, 1908*. Washington DC: Government Printing Office, 1908.
Weiss, Joaquín E. *Arquitectura contemporánea: colección de fotografías de los más recientes y característicos edificios erigidos en Cuba*. Havana: Cultural, 1947.
Whitfield, Esther (ed.). *Un arte de hacer ruinas y otros cuentos*. Mexico City: Fondo de Cultura Económica, 2005.
Wigley, Mark. *Buckminster Fuller Inc.—Architecture in the Age of Radio*. Zurich: Lars Müller, 2015.
Wigley, Mark. *Konrad Wachsmann's Television: Post-Architectural Transmissions*. Berlin: Sternberg Press, 2020.

ACKNOWLEDGMENTS

Most of the chapters included in this volume began as research projects conducted for the graduate seminar on “Modern Havana” which I co-taught with Beatriz Colomina at Princeton’s School od Architecture in 2017.

We gratefully acknowledge the generous funding provided by Stephen Kotkin and Deborah Yashar, former and current directors of the Princeton Institute for International and Regional Studies; by the Cuban Research Network, and, especially, by the Bar-Ferree Publication Fund.

I thank Guillermo Arsuaga for his help in securing permissions for the images that accompany these essays.

Rubén Gallo
New York, October 12, 2022

CREDITS

Chapter 2: all images, unless otherwise noted, courtesy of the Neutra Family. Richard and Dion Neutra papers, UCLA Library Special Collections, Charles E. Young Research Library, University of California, Los Angeles.

Chapter 3: unless otherwise noted, images courtesy of Archivo Martín Dominguez, Museo Nacional Centro de Arte Reina Sofía, Madrid, Spain.

Chapter 4: unless otherwise noted, images courtesy of the Museum of Modern Art, Mies van der Rohe Archive © 2022 Artists Rights Society (ARS), New York / VG Bild-Kunst, Bonn.

Chapter 5: unless otherwise noted, images courtesy of Roberto Gottardi Papers, Special Collections, Princeton University Library.

Chapter 6: all images courtesy of Dolly Gómez. Mario Girona Archive, Havana, Cuba.

Chapter 7: unless otherwise noted, images courtesy of Vittorio Garatti archive, Archivio Progetti, Università IUAV di Venezia, Venice, Italy.